ACQUAINTANCE, KNOWLEDGE, AND LOGIC

CSLI Lecture Notes Number 214

ACQUAINTANCE, KNOWLEDGE, AND LOGIC

New Essays on Bertrand Russell's
The Problems of Philosophy

edited by
Donovan Wishon
Bernard Linsky

CSLI
PUBLICATIONS
Center for the Study of
Language and Information
Stanford, California

Library of Congress Cataloging-in-Publication Data

New essays on Bertrand Russell's The problems of philosophy / edited
by Donovan Wishon Bernard Linsky.
    pages cm. – (CSLI lecture notes ; 214)
Includes bibliographical references and index.
ISBN 978-1-57586-846-2 (pbk. : alk. paper)
1. Russell, Bertrand, 1872-1970. Problems of philosophy.
2. Philosophy–Introductions. 3. Metaphysics. 4. Knowledge,
Theory of. I. Wishon, Donovan, editor.

B1649.R93P6535 2015
110–dc23
                          CIP   2015016171

∞ The acid-free paper used in this book meets the minimum requirements
of the American National Standard for Information Sciences—Permanence
of Paper for Printed Library Materials, ANSI Z39.48-1984.

CSLI was founded in 1983 by researchers from Stanford University, SRI
International, and Xerox PARC to further the research and development of
integrated theories of language, information, and computation. CSLI headquarters
and CSLI Publications are located on the campus of Stanford University.

CSLI Publications reports new developments in the study of language,
information, and computation. Please visit our web site at
http://cslipublications.stanford.edu/
for comments on this and other titles, as well as for changes
and corrections by the author and publisher.

Contents

Contributors

ROBERT BARNARD: Department of Philosophy and Religion, University of Mississippi, Oxford MS 38677, USA.
rwbjr@olemiss.edu

ROSALIND CAREY: Department of Philosophy, City University of New York – Lehman College, Bronx, NY 10468, USA.
rosalind.carey@lehman.cuny.edu

PETER HYLTON: Department of Philosophy, University of Illinois at Chicago, Chicago IL 60607, USA.
hylton@uic.edu

KEVIN C. KLEMENT: Department of Philosophy, University of Massachusetts Amherst, Amherst, MA 01003, USA.
klement@philos.umass.edu

MICHAEL KREMER: Department of Philosophy, University of Chicago, Chicago IL 60637, USA.
kremer@uchicago.edu

GREGORY LANDINI: Department of Philosophy, University of Iowa, Iowa City IA 52242, USA.
gregory-landini@uiowa.edu

BERNARD LINSKY: Department of Philosophy, University of Alberta, Edmonton AB T6G 2E7, Canada.
bernard.linsky@ualberta.ca

KATARINA PEROVIC: Department of Philosophy, University of Iowa, Iowa City IA 52242, USA.
katarina-perovic@uiowa.edu

IAN PROOPS: Department of Philosophy, University of Texas at Austin, Austin TX 78712, USA.
iproops@austin.utexas.edu

RUSSELL WAHL: Department of English and Philosophy, Idaho State University, Pocatello ID 83209, USA.
wahlruss@isu.edu

DONOVAN WISHON: Department of Philosophy and Religion, University of Mississippi, University MS 38677, USA.
dwishon@olemiss.edu

Acknowledgements

The present volume brings together new essays on Bertrand Russell's remarkable introductory book *The Problems of Philosophy*. Most of these essays were presented at 'Bertrand Russell's *The Problems of Philosophy*: The Centenary Conference' which marked the 100th anniversary of the original publication of Russell's 1912 book and took place at the University of Mississippi on November 29th through December 1st in 2012. The conference would not have been possible without the sponsorship of the University of Mississippi, College of Liberal Arts, and the Department of Philosophy and Religion. We also warmly thank the Bertrand Russell Society, the Mississippi Humanities Council, and the National Endowment for the Humanities for financial support of the conference. In addition, we thank all of the participants of the conference, especially those who contributed to this volume or who provided helpful comments on the papers contained herein: Fatema Amijee, Robert Barnard, Rosalind Carey, Peter Hylton, Kevin Klement, Michael Kremer, Gregory Landini, Katarina Perovic, Christopher Pincock, Consuelo Preti, Ian Proops, John Shosky, and Russell Wahl. We also thank the faculty and graduate students at the University of Mississippi for valuable help during the conference.

Turning to the volume itself, we wish to acknowledge the support of the Bertrand Russell Archives at McMaster University, for access to Russell's library and correspondence. Kenneth Blackwell, as always, graciously shared his detailed knowledge of Russell's life and work, and most importantly, which boxes of papers and letters to examine. We also thank him, and Gregory Landini, for extensive feedback on the introductory chapter of this volume. We thank Dikran Karaguezian and the staff at CSLI Publications for their help during the process of publishing this volume. We thank Bryan Harper for invaluable assistance in preparing the manuscript. We give warm thanks to our teacher, John Perry, for his steady support and encouragement of this project. We also thank our families for their incredible patience with us. Lastly, we give our deepest thanks to Bertrand Russell for inspiring us in innumerable ways with his little 'Shilling Shocker'.

Donovan Wishon and Bernard Linsky

1

The Place of *The Problems of Philosophy* in Philosophy

DONOVAN WISHON AND BERNARD LINSKY

Russell's *The Problems of Philosophy*, which has passed its centenary of publication in 2012, has been used as a textbook in introduction to philosophy courses for years. It has consequently become a historical text in its own right. Of course, anyone who has encountered *Problems* in a course notices that some of the chapters are not quite introductory and contain doctrines which can seem obscure to those approaching the text from a contemporary perspective. Some instructors may feel that it is not worth the effort to explain sense data, when the beginning of prevailing wisdom in the philosophy of perception is the rejection of sense data.[1] Students will be stumped by the appearance of the Multiple Relation Theory of Judgment in Chapter XII.

Despite all of this, *The Problems of Philosophy* is enjoying a modest resurgence in interest, particularly among contemporary analytic philosophers. In recent years, Russell's doctrine of knowledge by acquaintance and knowledge by description has been recognized as the origin of many present-day issues in philosophy of mind and language. His structural realism about physics continues to be relevant to both philosophy of science and mind. In metaphysics, renewed attention has been paid to the theory of uni-

---

[1]Though notable recent defenses of sense data include Jackson 1977, Robinson 1994, 2005, Bermúdez 2000, Garcia-Carpintero 2001, and O'Shaughnessy 2003, among others.

Acquaintance, Knowledge, and Logic.
Donovan Wishon and Bernard Linsky (eds.).
Copyright © 2015, CSLI Publications.

versals in Chapter IX, and his arguments against Monistic Idealism in Chapter XIV remain relevant to ongoing discussions about the structure of reality. In epistemology, he gives us the first statement of cases which have since come to be called 'Gettier cases', a topic which has directed the field for years. Hence, *The Problems of Philosophy* has entered the canon of History of Philosophy that is relevant to current issues.

What's more, if we approach *The Problems of Philosophy* as an important text in the history of philosophy in its own right, then its 'obscure' doctrines and problems in fact come to the fore. In recent years there has been a great deal of new scholarship aimed at better understanding the origins of analytic philosophy and its relations to British Idealism, American Realism, Pragmatism, and even Phenomenology – as many of the papers in this volume demonstrate.

Approaching the book with the attitudes of a Russell scholar, it raises different questions. How did Russell come to write a book on general philosophy when his work since *The Principles of Mathematics* in 1903 largely focused on the philosophy of mathematics?[2] Why does Leibniz, the subject of one of his earlier books, make almost no appearance in *Problems*? Why does Russell leave out any discussion of William James and Pragmatism in the chapters on truth and knowledge? What did Russell know about the historical figures he does discuss more extensively, including Berkeley and Kant? What explains the content of the book? Why is there no ethics or philosophy of religion, and why nothing of the philosophy of mathematics? In what follows, we will attempt to answer some, but not all, of these questions, while also providing some sense of where Russell's book fits into the history and current state of philosophy.

Although there is no surviving manuscript of *The Problems of Philosophy*, a record of the writing of the book in 1910 through 1911, can be found in the papers and letters in the Bertrand Russell Archives at McMaster University in Canada. The material below including the history of Russell's work on *Problems* is presented as part of John Slater's scholarly apparatus in *The Collected Papers of Bertrand Russell, Volume 6*. Some of the letters, and much of the biographical information about those around Russell, can be found in Nicholas Griffin's edition of Russell's letters. Most of this knowledge is in print, consequently, but scattered in the scholarly literature. The two unpublished sources of information are correspondence with Gilbert Murray, an editor of the Home University Library, and unpublished

---

[2]In point of fact, Russell wrote a good deal on ethics, political philosophy, pragmatism, and truth, among other topics, during this period. For instance, see Russell 1910 and *CP* 4, 5, 6, and 12. We give our thanks to Ken Blackwell for helpful discussion of this point.

remarks in some of Russell's almost daily letters to Lady Ottoline Morrell during the period when he was working most intently on the book.

Gilbert Murray, a classicist, had been a friend of Russell's for years, and was married to a relative. He was Regius Professor of Greek at Oxford and worked for the publisher Williams and Norgate, who engaged Murray and four others to create a series of small books, sold for one Shilling each in a standard small size and length of 256 pages. There were fifty some titles in print when *Problems* appeared and almost as may listed as 'In Preparation'. Russell's collaborator on *Principia Mathematica*, Alfred North Whitehead had prepared number 18 in the 'Science' list, his *Introduction to Mathematics* published in 1911. G.E. Moore, Russell's philosophical collaborator since their time together as students at Cambridge in the 1890's was writing his contribution, *Ethics*, which appeared soon after Russell's in 1912. The Home University Library was aimed at a mass audience of working adults, and many other books in the series, including those of Whitehead and Moore, remained in print and widely available through many printings, at least into the 1960s.

Russell's joking correspondence with Murray shows that Russell himself shared the sense we have that *Problems* was an unusual book for him to write.

The first mention of the series is in a letter from Murray to Russell of September, 19, 1910:

My dear Bertie,

You have got a message to the shop assistants about philosophy, if you would only think it out. If you don't want to tell them what Mathematics is, can you not tell them what Philosophy is? You could do it with great detachment from the conventional schools, and you could put all the main problems in their very lowest terms.

It really is an important business. I cannot personally believe in the 75,000 but the publishers do; and if the circulation is even a third of that it is very important.

Tell me of another philosopher who is 1. completely alive and original; 2. democratic, so that he wants to communicate his thoughts to shop-assistants; 3. sharp-edged and not wobbly or sloppy in thought. And then I will cease to persecute you.

Both my big brothers have been here. So interesting, it has been.

Yours ever G.M.

Russell agreed to write a book on Philosophy, but set the assignment aside to the end of the academic year in 1911, as he had just been appointed as a lecturer at Trinity College for a five year term. In the Michaelmas, Lent, and Easter terms between mid-October 1910 and finishing at the end

of April 1911, Russell lectured on 'The Fundamental Concepts of Mathematics' for the Mathematics and Moral Sciences programs, and, for the first
term, to December, a course on 'Mathematical Logic' for Mathematics.
Henry Sheffer, then a new postdoctoral student from Harvard, attended both
series of lectures in 1910, and in his notes from the lectures we see no mention of the philosophical issues in *The Problems of Philosophy*. It was only
after the teaching year was finished that he determined to write his book.

Russell wrote the whole of the text of *The Problems of Philosophy* between June 1st and August 18th of 1911. In March of 1911 Russell had
started his love affair with Lady Ottoline Morrell, which was to continue for
several years. In the first flush of their relationship, Russell wrote letters to
Ottoline almost every day continuing through the summer when he was
writing *Problems*. The letters give a day by day report of Russell's progress
on the book, which he called his 'Shilling Shocker' from the first, and also
on his other work at the time. That other work was primarily reading the
proofs of the second volume of *Principia Mathematica*. Volume I had appeared in print in December of 1910, and work on the second volume proceeded throughout 1911 and 1912. The book would be set in sheets, proof
corrections made, and then printed in the 500 copies for which Russell and
Whitehead had to provide a subsidy. This work is regularly reported in the
letters over the summer. Then, towards the end of the summer, Russell began work on a book which dealt with ethics called 'Prisons', which does not
survive.[3] Russell had written some more florid personal philosophy at times
of personal crisis, going back to his 'A Free Man's Worship' in 1903. Portions of this 'Prisons' manuscript appear in the last chapter of Problems on
'The Value of Philosophy', and give an idea of what the rest of the text
must have comprised. Russell also published some of the material as 'The
Essence of Religion' in *The Hibbert Journal* in October of 1912.

Russell's new position as an academic was put to use with his wife
Alys' niece Karin Costelloe, who was studying for examinations in philosophy. In a letter to Ottoline, on 25 March, 1911, that 'I have undertaken to
coach her this Vacation in things I don't properly know myself, so that I
shall have to work hard to get them up. I have also undertaken to finish by
July a popular book on philosophy, which I have not yet begun. Heaven
knows how I shall manage, but I must do it as I have signed the contract'. In
a letter of April 11, 1911, Russell writes 'After giving Karin a lesson on
Locke and Hume and abstract ideas, I have escaped and gone off for a long
walk alone'.

---

[3]Fragments of *Prisons* and an account of its composition and fate are to be found in Volume
12 of *The Collected Papers of Bertrand Russell*.

Russell's familiarity with the historical figures he discusses is evident from his personal library, as well as references in the correspondence. Russell's copy of Berkeley's works is inscribed by the editor, Alexander Cambell Fraser to Russell's parents, 'Amberly and Kate' in April of 1871 when it was published. Although Russell did not write much in his treasured editions of classics, there are several notes in the margin of *Three Dialogues between Hylas and Philonus* which clearly date from his writing of *Problems*. One remark is an early formulation of Russell's summary of Berkeley's principal error: 'the confusion between idea as *act* (which is mental) and the idea as *object* (which may be non-mental) is absolutely necessary to B's argument'. Some of the comments don't end up so directly in *Problems*. Next to a line 'It is evident that things I perceive are my own ideas', Russell comments: 'My own ideas, therefore, do not exist in my mind. B's *arguments* tend to show that sense-data depend on *us*; his *conclusion* is that they depend on *God*'. By the argument that Berkeley can distinguish real experience from dreams by noticing the character of the 'visions of a dream, which are dim, irregular, and confused', Russell comments: 'Feeble. Dreams are no worse than buses in a fog'.[4] Next to a statement of the scholastic principle that 'Nothing can give to another that which it hath not itself' Russell simply writes 'Bosh'.

Russell thus re-read Berkeley specifically to prepare for *Problems* and was reading Plato's *Republic* with Ottoline to discuss Justice in the 'Prisons' book. They also read Spinoza together, and he published a review of a new translation of the *Ethics* in *The Nation* in 1910. Russell read through each of the books listed for 'Further Reading' at the end of *Problems*, Descartes' *Meditations*, Spinoza's *Ethics*, Hume's *Enquiry Concerning Human Understanding* and Kant's *Prolegomena*, either with Karin Costelloe, or on his own by early 1911.

Lectures having finished in May, on June 1st Russell says in a letter to Ottoline that he 'is bringing [his] thoughts round to the popular book'. He reports writing on 'my popular book' on June 5th. On the 9th he tells Ottoline that 'Whitehead's shilling shocker' is to appear in the same series. This is Whitehead's *Introduction to Mathematics*, also a successful element of the Home University series. Russell had turned down Murray's offer that he write on mathematics, and then later agreed to write his contribution. On the 23rd of June Russell reports a 'new start', apparently having given up on what would have been a sizable amount of text after three weeks. After this there is no report of any rejected material, and in fact, only reports that writ-

---

[4] See Carey's contribution to this volume for more on Russell's evolving views about dreams and their place in our knowledge of the world (107–27).

ing is going ever more smoothly. On the 24th Russell tells Ottoline that there is to be nothing on 'religion or morals' in the book, perhaps thinking that would be of more interest to her than the theory of knowledge and metaphysics that he discusses almost exclusively. As G. E. Moore was to write his book *Ethics* for the same series, the division of labor must have been known to Russell from when he was commissioned, in September of 1910. In any case, it was not Russell's idea from the beginning to exclude ethics and philosophy of religion from among the first problems of philosophy.

By the 27th of June Russell reports that he is writing 'easily' and that he is 'into the right vein' to complete the work. On July 8th Russell writes that he had spoken with Moore about their respective contributions to the Home University Library. Russell is pleased with his own ability to adapt his style to popular writing, something he suggests Moore cannot do:

> Moore and I compared notes on our respective S.S.'s yesterday. He is making his just as difficult as his *Principia Ethica*. He has only one style, and method, and can't alter for a different audience. He seems rather more behindhand with it than I am with mine. He is going to live in College next term, which I shall like. During the last few months I have read a good deal of the great philosophers: Descartes, Spinoza, Locke, Berkeley, Hume and Kant! (Also *some* Aristotle!) But I ought to read dull modern German books. I have tons more work in me, and I rather think Trinity in the long run will interfere with it - not at present, because the time for beginning another book is not come yet. But I can't attempt that while I have ordinary philosophy to write. I believe in my power of doing it, *some day* - I don't know when . . .[5]

Russell was indeed exhausted with the effort to finish *Principia Mathematica*, and, with the final breakup of his marriage which he had announced to friends in March.

By July 11th Russell is 'glad my MS pleases you'. He had sent the manuscript of the first four chapters to Ottoline, and later in the week asks her to return them so that he can send them to a typist. The first four chapters of *The Problems of Philosophy* consist of Russell's introduction of *sense data* as 'what is immediately known' through sensation and the 'problem of matter', which poses the question of whether there is matter in the world in addition to sense data – as well as the question of what we can know about its nature. These are Chapter I, 'Appearance and Reality', Chapter II, 'The

---

[5]The 'dull modern German books' may be an allusion to the second edition of Meinong's *Ueber Annahmen* (On Assumptions) in 1910, which contains extended responses to Russell's objections to Meinong in his reviews in *Mind* from 1904 and 1905. Russell left the *Mind* review of Meinong's second edition to C. D. Broad, who finally replied on Russell's behalf in 1913.

Existence of Matter', Chapter III, 'The Nature of Matter', and Chapter IV, 'Idealism'.

In Chapter I, Russell draws the distinction between sense data and matter largely on the basis of the problem of perspectival variation. To illustrate the issue, he presents his well-known description of the wooden table:

> To the eye it is oblong, brown and shiny, to the touch it is smooth cool and hard; when I tap it, it gives out a wooden sound. Any one else who sees and feels and hears the table will agree with this description, so that it might seem that no difficulty would arise... [But] although I believe that the table is 'really' of the same colour all over, the parts that reflect the light look much brighter than the other parts, and some parts look white because of reflected light. I know that, if I move, the parts that reflect light will be different, so that the apparent distribution of colours on the table will change. It follows that if several people are looking at the table at the same moment, no two of them will see exactly the same distribution of colours, because no two can see it from exactly the same point of view, and any change in the point of view makes some change in the way the light is reflected. (Russell 1912: 8–9)

Since we don't take the material table to change in its intrinsic features simply in virtue of changes in the perspective from which it is observed, Russell reasons, the shifting distributions of color we are presented with in sensation must not be 'inherent in the table, but something depending upon the table and the spectator and the way the light falls on the table'.[6] Generalizing from the visual case, he concludes that sensory experience 'cannot be supposed to reveal *directly* any definite property of the table, but at most to be *signs* of some property which perhaps *causes* all the sensations, but is not actually apparent in any of them'.

In the preface to *Problems* Russell acknowledges 'assistance from unpublished writings of Mr. G.E. Moore and Mr. J.M. Keynes: from the former, as regards the relations of sense-data to physical objects, and from the latter as regards probability and induction'. Moore writes in his preface to *Some Main Problems of Philosophy*, that those 'unpublished writings' were in fact the first ten chapters, which had been given as lectures in London in the fall of 1910. A comparison of the discussion of sense data and matter in Moore's lectures and in *Problems* reflects the difference of approach and style of Russell and Moore with which analytic philosophers have long been

---

[6]Recently, John Campbell (2009) has defended a Russell-inspired, 'relational' version of naïve realism according to which perceptual experience is a three-place relation between a subject, external objects and features, and the standpoint from which they are experienced. Typically, the problem of perspectival variation is taken to weigh in the favor of representational theories of perception.

familiar. Moore defines sense data in a way similar to Russell: 'And I propose to call these things, the colour and size and shape [that I see], *sense data*, things *given* or presented by the senses– given, in this case, by my sense of sight' (Moore 1953: 44). Whereas Russell immediately presents arguments that sense data are not material, Moore, characteristically, cautiously claims that we cannot be certain that sense data reveal the real properties of objects. (Though Russell soon changes his mind and insists that sense data are physical in his 1914 'The Relation of Sense-Data to Physics', a change which is explored by Peter Hylton, Ian Proops, and Russell Wahl in their respective contributions to this volume.)[7]

In Chapter II, Russell considers what reasons we have for supposing that there *is* a material world at all in addition to sense data. After considering and setting aside as unsatisfactory appeals to commonsense and the need for public objects to coordinate intersubjective thought and talk, Russell suggests that one strong reason for favoring the belief in a material world over its denial is that it is urged by 'every principle of simplicity' (Russell 1912: 24). In particular, the existence of a material world is the best explanation of 'the order and regularity of our sense-data', as Russell Wahl puts it (this volume: 94). Russell illustrates this point with his example of our episodic experience of a cat:

> If the cat appears at one moment in one part of the room, and at another in another part, it is natural to suppose that it has moved from the one to the other, passing over a series of intermediate positions. But if it is merely a set of sense-data, it cannot have ever been in any place where I did not see it; thus we shall have to suppose that it did not exist at all while I was not looking, but suddenly sprang into being in a new place. (Russell 1912: 23)

Russell finds it much more reasonable to suppose that this orderly pattern of experienced sense data is caused by the material body of a cat which is not directly revealed in sensation. He finds this supposition even more compelling when it comes to the complex patterns of sense data we experience regarding the verbal and nonverbal behavior of other persons. 'When human beings speak', he says, ' ... it is very difficult to suppose that what we hear is not the expression of a thought, as we know it would be if we emitted the same sounds'.

Chapter II also presents Russell's conception of the proper aims and methodology of philosophical inquiry. Though he begins the chapter with a discussion of the usefulness of Descartes' methodological skepticism for showing that 'subjective things are the most certain', he departs from it in maintaining that 'it is of course *possible* that all or any of our beliefs may be

---

[7]See Hylton this volume: 41–2, Proops this volume: 46, and Wahl this volume: 87–105.

mistaken, and therefore all ought to be held with at least some slight element of doubt'. As Peter Hylton (25–44), Bernard Linsky (65–85), Ian Proops (45–63), and Russell Wahl (87–105) note in their contributions, such remarks strongly suggest that Russell does not share the Cartesian aim of identifying knowledge which enjoys absolute certainty, contrary to many previous interpretations of *Problems*.

In fact, Russell goes on to say that the widespread view that philosophy can 'give us knowledge, not otherwise attainable, concerning the universe as a whole, and concerning the nature of ultimate reality' is a misguided one. Instead, Russell proposes the following alternative view of philosophy, one which deserves to be reconsidered alongside others in the recent contemporary debates concerning metaphilosophy:[8]

> Philosophy should show us the hierarchy of our instinctive beliefs [such as the belief in a material world], beginning with those held most strongly, and presenting each as much isolated and as free from irrelevant additions as possible. It should take care to show that, if the form in which they are finally set forth, our instinctive beliefs do not clash, but form a harmonious system... Hence, by organizing our instinctive beliefs and their consequences, by considering which among them is most possible, if necessary, to modify or abandon, we can arrive, on the basis of accepting as our sole data what we instinctively believe, at an orderly systematic organization of our knowledge, in which, though the *possibility* of error remains, its likelihood is diminished by the interrelation of the parts and by the critical scrutiny which has preceded acquiescence. (Russell 1912: 25–6)[9]

In Chapter III, Russell considers the scope and limits of our knowledge of the material world, focusing primarily on the knowledge provided by physical science. Here Russell gives an early statement of his belief in structuralism about physics:[10]

> The only properties which science assigns to [matter] are position in space, and the power of motion according to the laws of motion. Science does not deny that it *may* have other properties; but if so, such other properties are not useful to the man of science... (Russell 1912: 28)

One important consequence Russell draws from the structural character of physical science is that it leaves us deeply ignorant of the intrinsic nature

---

[8]A small sampling of recent work on metaphilosophy includes Cappelen 2012, Chalmers, Manley, and Wasserman 2009, Jackson 1998, Knobe and Nichols 2008, and Williamson 2007.

[9]Peter Hylton discusses Russell's burden-shifting use of the notion of instinctive beliefs in his contribution to this volume (33).

[10]Recent discussions of structuralism about physics include French 2006, Ladyman 1998, 2008, Lewis 2009, Psillos 2006, Saunders 2003, and Van Fraassen 2006, 2007, among others.

of the physical world, and perhaps inescapably so.[11] As he puts matters, 'thus we find that, although the *relations* of physical objects have all sorts of knowable properties, ...the physical objects themselves remain unknown in their intrinsic nature, so far at least as can be discovered by means of the senses' (Russell 1912: 34). What's more, Russell expresses the core intuition driving Frank Jackson's (1982) knowledge argument that no amount of knowledge from physics alone can fully capture the qualities presented to us in experience:[12]

> It is sometimes said that 'light *is* a form of wave-motion', but this is misleading, for the light which we immediately see, which we know directly by means of our senses, is *not* a form of wave-motion, but something quite different—something which we all know if we are not blind, though we cannot describe it so as to convey our knowledge to a man who is blind. A wave-motion, on the contrary, could quite well be described to a blind man... When it is said that light *is* waves, what is really meant is that waves are the physical cause of our sensation of light. But light itself, the thing which seeing people experience and blind people do not, is not supposed by science to form any part of the world that is independent of us and our senses. (Russell 1912: 28–9)

The Idealism in Chapter IV is a discussion of Berkeley. Russell there distinguishes between sense data and ideas by distinguishing sense data as the *object* of mental *acts* of perception. Russell here reveals his earlier allegiance to the intentional psychology of Brentano and his student Meinong, which Russell maintained long after giving up on the 'non-existent objects' such as 'the round square' and 'the present King of France' with his theory of descriptions.[13] The discussion here of the act-object distinction also highlights Russell's view that sense data are external to the subject's mind, a view that is not shared by most recent proponents of sense data.[14]

While Ottoline was reading the first four chapters, Russell had been proceeding with the next chapters, which take a turn into his technical theory of knowledge. Almost half of Chapter V, 'Knowledge by Acquaintance and Knowledge by Description' comes from the paper of the same name that Russell had presented to the Aristotelian Society earlier in the year, on

---

[11]Recent discussions of the thesis that we are ignorant of the intrinsic nature of the physical world include Alter and Nagasawa forthcoming, Chalmers 1996, 2010, Langton 1998, Lewis 2009, McGinn 1989, 1991, and Stoljar 2001, 2006, among others.

[12]For an excellent discussion of the similarities and differences between Russell and Jackson on this issue, see the introduction to Ludlow, Nagasawa, and Stoljar 2004.

[13]Linsky's contribution to this volume explores these issues in greater detail (65–85). Barnard's contribution compares Russell's views in Chapters IV and V to Husserl's phenomenology (153–70).

[14]Bermúdez 2000 is one notable exception.

March 6th of 1911. Indeed, eleven of the thirty two paragraphs in the chapter come directly from the paper.[15]

At the center of Russell's theory of knowledge are two key distinctions: the distinction between knowledge of things and knowledge of truths, on one hand, and between knowledge by acquaintance and knowledge by description, on the other. As many of the papers in this volume demonstrate, there are ongoing scholarly disagreements about how best to understand these key notions. Nevertheless, there is relatively broad agreement about the main outlines of Russell's distinctions.[16]

Knowledge of things is a matter of a subject simply being *aware* of particulars and universals such that the subject is in a position to think and talk about them. In contrast, knowledge of truths is a matter of the subject having a 'take' on the objects of his or her awareness, paradigmatically in the form of *judgments* about them. Whereas the latter can be evaluated in terms of truth or falsity, there is simply no sense to be made of the truth or falsity of the former—either the subject is aware of the relevant objects, or he or she isn't.

For Russell, there are two ways a subject can be aware of things. A subject can be *directly* aware of things, 'without the intermediary of any process of inference or any knowledge of truths', by being presented with them in experience (Russell 1912: 46). He calls this kind of knowledge of things 'knowledge by acquaintance'. At the time of *Problems*, Russell thinks the objects of a subject's direct awareness are restricted to present sense-data, present mental phenomena (including acquaintance itself), remembered sense-data and mental phenomena, universals, and (perhaps) the self. A subject can also be indirectly aware of things by description in cases where 'in virtue of some general principle, the existence of a thing answering to this description can be inferred from the existence of something with which [the subject is] acquainted' (Russell 1912: 45). Russell calls this kind of knowledge of things 'knowledge by description'. Unlike the case of knowledge by acquaintance, the possession of knowledge by description requires the antecedent possession of knowledge of truths about things known by acquaintance, including truths about general principles.

Both kinds of knowledge of things play crucial roles in Russell's theory of knowledge. Knowledge by acquaintance is the ultimate enabling condi-

---

[15]The chapter is fourteen pages, from 46 to 59, and seven of those, 52 to 58, come out of the paper. There are some slight changes in the borrowed material. The Unionist candidate 'Mr. A' in *Problems* is named as 'Sir Joseph Larmour' in the paper, and the variable 'B' in the paper is spelled out as 'the actual object which was the first Chancellor of the German Empire'.
[16]The following discussion of Chapter V draws on material from Wishon forthcoming.

tion for all thought and talk. Such direct conscious awareness of things puts a subject in a position to attend to them, to introduce proper names for them, and to acquire knowledge of truths about them. By exploiting this knowledge of truths about the objects of acquaintance, knowledge by description then enables the subject to extend thought and talk beyond the confines of his or her personal experience. Thus, knowledge by description is the crucial material that makes both ordinary and scientific knowledge of truths about the external world possible. But it all starts from knowledge by acquaintance (Russell 1912: 48). However, in his contribution to this volume, Michael Kremer expresses worries about whether Russell does full justice to our knowledge of other persons with his exhaustive distinction between our knowledge of things by acquaintance (in his technical sense) and our knowledge of them by description (129–52).

Chapter VI, 'On Induction', with its discussion of the standard epistemological problem of the justification of induction, seems to mark a break in direction, and in fact an almost inconsistent direction for those who look for a foundationalist epistemology based on certain knowledge of sense data in the first five chapters. Russell makes the familiar point that belief in 'the uniformity of nature' can itself only be a summary of the successes of induction in the past, rather than a justification for future inductive inferences and makes use of the familiar example of our belief that 'the sun will rise to-morrow'. Then there is Russell's famous chicken:

> Domestic animals expect food when they see the person who usually feeds them. We know that all these rather crude expectations of uniformity are liable to be misleading. The many who has fed the chicken every day throughout its life at last wrings its neck instead, showing that more refined views as to the uniformity of nature would have been useful to the chicken. (Russell 1912: 63)

The place of Russell's views on induction in the overall philosophy of *Problems*, and its juxtaposition next to the two succeeding chapters, VII, 'On Our Knowledge of General Principles' and VIII, 'How *A Priori* Knowledge is Possible', can be found by looking at the J.M. Keynes' *A Treatise of Probability*, published in 1921. This book had begun as Keynes' fellowship dissertation in 1908, when Keynes returned to King's College. There Keynes describes the theory of probability as part of *logic*: 'If logic investigates the general principles of valid thought, the study of arguments, to which it is rational to attach *some* weight, is as much a part of it as the study of those which are demonstrative' (Keynes 1921: 3).

Chapter VI is best read as an early statement of the *logical theory of probability*. Inductive and probabilistic reasoning is a branch of logic, dealing with arguments from certain premises to a conclusion, but, unlike deductive logic, we are not certain of the consequence, even given the truth of the premises. Inductive inference is consequently, always relative to a set of premises, and better arguments are based on better premises. The chicken who lacks in 'refined views of the uniformity of nature' is simply basing his inference on a smaller and inferior set of premises. The argument that there is no empirical evidence for our conclusion that 'the sun will rise tomorrow' shows that the principle of reasoning that we use are, like other logical principles, known *a priori*, that is, not based on empirical evidence. The study of inductive reasoning does not concern the habit of making an inference common to animals, as it did for Hume, but the study of what inference is *rational*, where that is an objective feature of the logic of probability. In *Human Knowledge: Its Scope and Limits*, Russell devotes a chapter to 'Keynes' Theory of Probability' registering differences only of detail with Keynes thirty six years later.

Inductive reasoning thus falls under Russell's general theory of *a priori* reasoning, along with the principles of deductive logic. Chapter VII, 'On our Knowledge of General Principles' presents a distinction between 'rationalists' and 'empiricists', and sides with rationalists to the extent that he agrees that we have *a priori* knowledge of truths, and that logic is the study of many of these truths. That logic is properly seen as a study of inference rather than of logical truths is defused with an explanation of the problematic statement of the rule of *modus ponens* from *Principia Mathematica* as rather the 'primitive proposition' that 'anything implied by a true proposition is true' (Russell 1912: 71).

Chapter VIII, 'How *A Priori* Knowledge is Possible' is a criticism of Kant's views on *a priori* knowledge, which, if we are to trust the list of recommended reading at the end as a description of some of Russell's own preparatory reading of 'some of the great philosophers', now should take its place alongside of his earlier book on Leibniz and later *History of Western Philosophy* as an opinionated but by no means uninformed treatment of the history of philosophy.

On July 11th, Russell also tells Ottoline that he has begun with 'two pages on Plato', and that almost half of the manuscript is done. The only discussion of Plato that might have taken two pages of manuscript is in the start of Chapter IX, 'The World of Universals'. This chapter contains Russell's famous 'infinite regress' argument for universals, which Katarina Perovic explores in her contribution to this volume (171–88);

> If we wish to avoid the universals *whiteness* and *triangularity*, we shall choose some particular patch of white or some particular triangle, and say that anything is white or a triangle if it has the right sort of resemblance to

our chosen particular. But then the resemblance required will have to be a universal. (Russell 1912: 96)

Infinite regress arguments are a familiar theme in Russell's philosophy. In *Principles of Mathematics* Russell had posed the problem of 'the unity of the proposition' as in part arising from a regress. The relation R in the proposition that aRb must be united with the a and b by yet another relation, so it would seem. That relation in turn must be related to the earlier R and so on. Years later Russell engaged in his famous dispute with F. H. Bradley, on whether there could be 'external relations' R between objects a and b rather than having 'being related by R to b' as an *intrinsic* property of a. The relation of a to R would be another relation R^1, which would be of the 'sort' that relates individuals to relations between individuals, and a further relation R^2 would relate a to R^1, etc. Russell allows for other infinite hierarchies of 'meaning' for symbols (Russell 1918–19: 233), and so however these hierarchies would be represented in the theory of types, he would allow them.[17] What is distinctive about the argument about Universals is that Russell insists that here the regress would be *vicious*, as unlike the infinite series of relations of ever higher types, that what we are concerned with is the *explanation* or *ground* of the relation. Russell in general avoids use of these notions of 'internal' properties or of 'grounding' of properties or relations in his metaphysics, just as he avoided use of notions of necessity different from simple generality. Russell describes his position without citing anyone who might actually have held the view, 'If we wish to wish to avoid the universal . . . we shall choose some particular . . . and say . . .' that it has the property if it bears the 'right sort' of resemblance to that particular. This is a good characterization of Berkeley's view of 'abstract ideas', but Russell does not cite Berkeley, nor does he give any reference to earlier uses of this regress argument. The view is exactly that presented in Hume's *A Treatise of Human Nature* (Hume 1739) in his account of 'Abstract Ideas':

> ...*some ideas are particular in their nature, but general in their representation.* A particular idea becomes general by being annexed to a general term; that is, to a term which from customary conjunction has a relation to many other particular ideas, and readily recalls them in the imagination. (Hume, I.I.VII)

For Hume the only possible basis for judgments of similarity will be the 'customary conjunction' of the idea of one thing with that of another, so Hume is here giving a theory of general ideas that exactly matches the proposal that Russell considers for a nominalist account of universals.

---

[17]Landini, in his contribution to this volume, affirms, as part of his account of *PM*, that all such relations, as well as all universals, will logically count as individuals.

One possible precedent for Russell's argument against this account can be found in a surprising place, namely Russell's reading notes on a paper by Alexius Meinong, that Russell made when preparing for his 1904 paper 'Meinong's Theory of Complexes and Assumptions'.[18] In some notes on a paper 'Abstrahieren und Vergleichen' (Abstraction and Comparison), we find a discussion of what Russell translates as 'comparison theory'. He talks of a 'Difficulty for comparison-theory in notion of two objects similar in one respect, not in another. Requires two further mutually totally dissimilar objects to compare them with'. This is definitely a theory by which similarity, in the sense of sharing a universal property, is abstracted from particular resemblances. Later in the notes we run into a striking passage:

> p.67. Comparison theory supposes similarity of a and b discovered by that of (a, b) and (c, d). Hence endless regress. p.68. This regress, unlike many, is objectionable, since its beginning, not its end, goes to infinity.

It is possible then, that when Russell tutored Karin Costelloe on 'Locke and Hume and abstract ideas' in April of 1911, memories of his study of 'comparison theory' from psychology came to mind.

Thus although it is easy to extrapolate from Hume and Berkeley's antipathy to abstract ideas to the alternative based on 'similarity' that Russell refutes, in fact it is not empiricist nominalists who are his opponent. Meinong in fact refers to a Gestalt psychologist, H. Cornelius for the similarity view that he refutes.[19] Cornelius holds that just as we judge the 'depth' of a tone by comparison with other tones (especially for those without absolute pitch), the perception of similarity of individuals is a 'Gestalt' feature of our experience of the two together. Thus, Cornelius argues, judgments of similarity and difference are not based on an 'abstract representation' ('abstracte Vorstellung') but instead on a number of distinct gestalt experiences of similarity.

Chapters X, 'On Our Knowledge of Universals' and XI, 'On Intuitive Knowledge' provide the basis of Russell's epistemology in the modern sense, of how certain beliefs can be justified, in the sense that it is objectively rational to believe them. Russell explains how knowledge of universals, which arises out of abstraction from experience of sensible qualities, and *a priori* knowledge of truths involving universals, can itself lead to justification which comes in various degrees of 'self evidence' ranging up to a limit with *certainty*. These considerations seem peculiar to the details of

---

[18]See Linsky 2014. Meinong had made a careful study of Hume's philosophy so he would likely have known of the source of this view in Hume.

[19]See Cornelius 1900: 118–19.

Russell's notions of knowledge by acquaintance of things, and knowledge of truths, which arises in various ways.

By the 12th of July Russell tells Ottoline that this work gives him a 'map of the theory of knowledge', and 'is a help to my own work'. Chapters VI through XI can be read as a group, giving the basis of his theory of knowledge. This is 'rationalist' in that it accepts *a priori* truths based on knowledge of the relations of universals and logical truths, but extended by inductive, probabilistic, inference, from knowledge of experience, starting with sense data and extending to matter and the physical world. In his contribution to this volume, Kevin Klement provides a detailed discussion of Russell's views about our a priori knowledge of logical truths and relations between universals as well as the nature of the objects this knowledge is about (189–229).

On July 12th, the day after his report to Ottoline, Russell wrote to Gilbert Murray, with this update:

> . . . I am writing my book for your series, and have written more than half of it. I find, however, that one or two things are happening to it which you may not desire. In the first place, I find it deals almost entirely with theory of knowledge, only occasionally arriving at metaphysics through theory of knowledge. This seems difficult to avoid owing to the exclusion of religion and ethics. In the second place, I find that, quite contrary to my intention, it is an exposition of my own views, not an impartial account of what is thought by various philosophers. I found it impossible to write interestingly or freely or with conviction, unless I was trying to persuade the reader to agree with me. In the third place, I find that after the first few chapters it grows rather difficult. It remains quite easily intelligible, without trouble, to any educated man, however little he may know about philosophy; but it would be difficult for a shop-assistant unless he were unusually intelligent. I hardly know myself whether it is too difficult or not. If it is, I must re-write it.
>
> Don't bother to answer if you think it will be all right. But if you really wish stupid shop-assistants to be able to read it in armchairs, I must do it again. My chapters are so far: [Here follows a list of Chapters I through XI with almost their final titles.] . . . The chapters grow naturally out of each other, and but for doubt about difficulty I should be satisfied with the stuff.
>
> . . .

If the 'more than half' of the book that Russell describes to Murray on the 12th of July includes everything through Chapter XI, then he must have gone back to write at least the two pages on Plato in IX (since he reported writing them on the 11th to Ottoline). This is the only hint in the letters that

Russell may not have composed *The Problems of Philosophy* straight through, chapter by chapter, after his fresh start in June.[20]

Later, on July 23rd, Russell reports to Ottoline that his mind is full of 'Prisons'. He now wants to finish the shilling shocker to make time for 'Prisons', and apparently is writing both at the same time (while all through the period of composition reading proofs of *Principia Mathematica*).

Chapter XII, 'Truth and Falsehood' was written over two days, started on July 30th and finished on the 31st. This chapter contains both very familiar and basic points about the distinction between the 'meaning' of truth and a criterion or test of truth, and a discussion of coherence versus correspondence theories of truth. It also presents Russell's distinctive 'multiple relation theory of judgment' the nature and development of which is currently much disputed by Russell scholars. First endorsed in *Principia Mathematica* and reaching its mature development in Russell's posthumously published 1913 manuscript *The Theory of Knowledge* (1984), the multiple relation theory of judgment was planned to be the centerpiece of his acquaintance based epistemology, and in particular his theory of our *a priori* knowledge of mathematical logic. The causes of Russell's abandoning the project have also remained controversial. Pointing to remarks in Russell's letters to Ottoline, many maintain that it was objections from Ludwig Wittgenstein, made in the summer of 1913, that finally led Russell to abandon the theory. Others point out that Russell continued to discuss the multiple relation theory of judgment until 1918 or so, suggesting that it was not Russell's stormy intellectual exchanges with Wittgenstein that were decisive. One plausible alternative (suggested by Gregory Landini in conversation) is that Russell gave up the multiple relation theory of judgment after ceasing to believe in the relational character of sensation and other mental occurrences and adopting neutral monism, an interpretation which is well-supported by Russell's own later account of matters in *My Philosophical Development* (Russell 1959: 134–6).[21] In any case, Landini's contribution to this volume (231–73) maintains that the multiple relation theory, modified by the addition of acquaintance with logical forms, is viable.

Chapter XIII, 'Knowledge, Error, and Probable Opinion' contains what in Russell's 'theory of knowledge' will feel familiar to contemporary philosophers as belonging to the subject of Epistemology. Russell shows what is wrong with defining knowledge as simply 'true belief', and shows that

---

[20]Ken Blackwell (in conversation) has raised the question of whether the two pages on Plato here concerned Atlantis instead. If so, then Russell very well could have completed *Problems* straight through.

[21]We give our thanks to Gregory Landini for helpful discussion of these issues.

we must add something about the justification we have for the belief. Here he proposes that example that many will see as familiar now as a 'Gettier example'. He says, of the man who believes truly that the last Prime Minister's name began with a 'B' on the basis of the false belief that it was Balfour rather than Campbell-Bannerman who held the position:

> The man who believes that Mr. Balfour was the late Prime Minister may proceed to draw valid deductions from the true premises that the late Prime Minister's name began with a B, but he cannot be said to *know* the conclusions based on the these deductions. . . (Russell 1912: 132)

Russell thus counts this as a counter-example to the proposal that 'nothing is knowledge except what is validly deduced from true premises'. But we can't say that the premises must be *known* without circularity . . .

On August 4th Russell tells Ottoline that 'Between lunch and tea today I wrote a whole chapter (11 pages) on the limits of philosophical knowledge'. This is Chapter XIV, 'The Limits of Philosophical Knowledge', in which Russell draws conclusions about the nature of philosophy from the epistemological theory advanced so far. It begins with the criticism of Hegel's philosophy on the basis of Russell's metaphysics just as he had rejected the Bradleyean version of monism, and epistemology based on acquaintance. The nature of an object does not involve all of its relations to all other objects and knowledge of an object, at least knowledge by acquaintance, does not 'theoretically' involve any knowledge of truths about the object at all. After giving his analysis of the error of idealist and other systematic metaphysical systems as arguing for the non-reality of various things on the basis of contradictions they engender, Russell proposes that we look to developments in science, as in response to the paradoxes of space and time, or to mathematics, resolving the paradoxes of infinity, as way of freeing ourselves from dogmatic metaphysics. Here Russell proposes a view of philosophy as continuous with science, but differing in its approach of criticism. That criticism may point to the impossibility of gaining knowledge of the 'universe as a whole' which distinguishes metaphysics, but this does not lead to a general skepticism, for, 'we have seen no reason to suppose man incapable of the kind of knowledge which he is generally believed to possess'.

On August 7th Russell sent the first twelve chapters to Murray, telling him that the XIII and XIV are written but still being typed, and that the last 'is not yet written'. That distinctive last chapter, XV, 'The Value of Philosophy' took another week to finish, a difficult effort given the pace at which the rest of the book was written. On August 12th he tells Murray that 'Chapter XV (the last) is written and should reach you in a day or two'. The letter

to Ottoline announcing that he has finished *Problems of Philosophy* is un-
dated, but is probably from August 18th. Russell had been reading Plato's
Republic with Ottoline and writing on justice, likely for the 'Prisons' manuscript at just the same time.

> . . . I finished my last chapter of the S.S. before tea, and sent it to be typed.
> It was not as good as it ought to be, but I didn't see how to improve it. I
> don't think it was bad, but it was rather too short. I took some sentences
> on contemplation out of the Prisons m.s., and the denunciation of those
> who make man the measure of all things.

> Today it occurred to me that the same impartiality of mind which, in
> thought, is love of truth, is justice in action and universal love in emotion.
> Plato, by the way, is quite hopeless on justice. His definition in Book IV
> seems to me to have no merit. . . .

This last chapter, with its soaring conclusion, is, as we have seen, one
of the few surviving pieces of the 'Prisons' manuscript, itself a move into
non-technical, inspirational, writing, which Russell had earlier engaged in at
another turning point in his personal life with 'A Free Man's Worship' in
1903. Its final paragraph seems so out of step with the rest of *Problems of
Philosophy*:

> Thus, to sum up our discussion of the value of philosophy; Philosophy is
> to be studied, not for the sake of any definite answers to its questions, sin-
> ce no definite answers can, as a rule, be known to be true, but rather for
> the sake of the questions themselves; because these questions enlarge our
> conception of what is possible, enrich our intellectual imagination and di-
> minish the dogmatic assurance which closes the mind against speculation;
> but above all because, through the greatness of the universe which philos-
> ophy contemplates, the mind also is rendered great, and becomes capable
> of that union with the universe which constitutes its highest good. (Russell
> 1912: 161)

This ending seems to present philosophy as a mystical practice, aimed
at producing a feeling of merging with the universe, and quite out of keeping with the keen attention to the importance of philosophical issues before.
But Russell in fact is arguing that there is a *value* to the study of philosophy, and that is the title of the chapter. But perhaps it is a non-utilitarian
value. It might seem that Russell is arguing that the value of the study of
philosophy is a distinctive, and absolute value, not a means for attaining
some further goal, and perhaps not even instrumental for advancing utility.

A small typesetter's error, introduced when the book was reset in 1946 and remaining to this day, adds to this sense.[22]

> ... the study of physical science is to be recommended, not only, or primarily, because of the effect on the student, but rather because of the effect on mankind in general. Thus utility does not belong to philosophy. If the study of philosophy has any value at all for others than students of philosophy, it must be only indirectly, through its effects upon the lives of those who study it. (Russell 1912: 153)

An examination of the first edition shows that the crucial sentence should be: '*This* utility does not belong to philosophy' (emphasis added). Philosophy does have a utility, through its effect on students of philosophy, and their effect on others. Russell is offering a utilitarian defense of the study of philosophy, but of the sort we associate with utilitarians of an older, more classically 'liberal' turn. It is the effect on the individual that is the basis of value, rather than the material benefits for humanity that result from an activity. It was these themes of classical liberalism, such as Russell would have inherited from his grandfather, Prime Minister John Russell, or his godfather, John Stuart Mill, rather than some irrationalist mysticism, that shines through in this last chapter. It was likely this attitude that was one of the reasons for Ludwig Wittgenstein's dislike of the book, rather than its attempt at reaching a public audience. Rather, as Russell reports in a letter to Ottoline on March 17th of 1912:

> ... What he disliked in my last chapter was saying philosophy had *value*; he says people who like philosophy will pursue it, and others won't, and there's an end to it.

On August 20th, 1911, Russell writes that he has sent the typescript to Williams and Norgate and tells Murray that he has made some changes to respond to 'the points you criticized'. He responds to a criticism that sometimes we assert propositions without having a clear grasp of the nature of the relation that is asserted by saying that his principle of acquaintance applies to a fully, and properly, analyzed proposition. He also ' ... extracted the island in the western ocean, reluctantly. I never said Plato said so, but it seemed to me any mystical reader might naturally regard the ideas as living in Atlantis until they were corrupted and I should have thought Plato intended this. What do you say[?]' As a classical scholar, Murray couldn't allow by even a joking reference to Atlantis as the home of the Forms. There is also a reference to the treatment of Hegel, that did result in an addi-

---

[22]Ken Blackwell has suggested in conversation (and previously at the 2012 annual meeting of the Bertrand Russell Society) that the 'typesetter's error' might have been an attempt to correct what the typesetter wrongly perceived as an error.

tion to the text: 'As for Hegel, I stick to my point, and have merely expanded the statement'.

Russell read proofs for the book in one week, between November 2 and 9th, and it appeared in print finally in the new year, at the end of January, with a print run of 15,000 copies, twenty times the 750 copies of the first volume of *Principia Mathematica* published a little more than a year before. This was certainly a best-seller for such academic books in the popular market. That first impression had sold out by 1913 as did twelve more impressions by 1927 and scores more, including new editions. *The Problems of Philosophy* was the basis for Russell's reputation as a popular philosopher, selling more copies than anything else he wrote until the *History of Western Philosophy* from 1945. Yet despite its popular character and success, *The Problems of Philosophy* remains a fruitful and rewarding work for philosophical and scholarly consideration, as the papers in this volume clearly demonstrate.

References

Alter, T. and Y. Nagasawa. Forthcoming. *Between Dualism and Materialism*. Oxford: Oxford University Press.

Barnard, R. 2015. *Problems* as Prolegomena: Russell's Analytic Phenomenology. In this volume: 153–70.

Berkeley, G. 1713. *Three Dialogues between Hylas and Philonous*. Reprinted in *The Works of George Berkeley, Bishop of Cloyne*, Volume 2, eds. A. A. Luce and T. E. Jessop, 163–263. London: Thomas Nelson and Sons 1949.

Bermúdez, J. L. 2000. Naturalized Sense Data. *Philosophy and Phenomenological Research* 61: 353–374.

Broad, C. D. 1913. Critical Notice of A. Meinong, *Über Annahmen. Mind* 22: 90–102.

Campbell, J. 2009. Consciousness and Reference. *Oxford Handbook to Philosophy of Mind*, eds. B. McLaughlin, A. Beckerman, and S. Walter, 648–62. Oxford: Oxford University Press.

Cappelen, H. 2012. *Philosophy Without Intuitions*. Oxford: Oxford University Press.

Carey, R. 2015. Seeing, Imagining, Believing: From *Problems* to *Theory of Knowledge*. In this volume: 107–127.

Chalmers, D. 1996. *The Conscious Mind: In Search of a Fundamental Theory*. Oxford: Oxford University Press.

Chalmers, D. 2010. *The Character of Consciousness*. Oxford: Oxford University Press.

Chalmers, D., D. Manley, and R. Wasserman. 2009. *Metametaphysics: New Essays on the Foundations of Ontology*. Oxford: Oxford University Press.

Cornelius, H. 1900. Ueber 'Gestaltqualitäten'. *Zeitschrift für Psychologie und Physiologie der Sinnesorgane* 22: 101–21. Available from The Virtual Laboratory – Max Planck-Institute, http://vlp.mpiwg-berlin.pmg.de/.

French, S. 2006. Structure as a Weapon of the Realist. *Proceedings of the Aristotelian Society* 106: 167–85.

García-Carpintero, M. 2001. Sense Data: The Sensible Approach. *Grazer Philosophische Studien* 62:17–63.

Hylton, P. 2015. *Problems of Philosophy* as a Stage in the Evolution of Russell's Views on Knowledge. In this volume: 25–44.

Hume, D. 1739. *A Treatise of Human Nature*. London.

Jackson, F. 1977. *Perception: A Representative Theory*. Cambridge: Cambridge University Press.

Jackson, F. 1982. Epiphenomenal Qualia. *Philosophical Quarterly* 32: 127–36.

Jackson, F. 1998. *From Metaphysics to Ethics*. Oxford: Oxford University Press.

Keynes, J. M. 1921. *A Treatise on Probability*. London: Macmillan.

Klement, K. 2015. The Constituents of the Propositions of Logic. In this volume: 189–229.

Knobe, J. and S. Nichols. 2008. *Experimental Philosophy*. Oxford: Oxford University Press.

Kremer, M. 2015. Russell on Acquaintance, Analysis, and Knowledge of Persons. In this volume: 129–52.

Ladyman, J. 1998. What is Structural Realism? *Studies in History and Philosophy of Science* 29: 409–24.

Landini, G. 2015. Types* and Russellian Facts. In this volume: 231–73.

Langton, R. 1998. *Kantian Humility: Our Ignorance of Things in Themselves*. Oxford: Oxford University Press.

Lewis, D. 2009. Ramseyan Humility. *The Canberra Programme*, eds. D. Braddon-Mitchell and R. Nola, 203–22. Oxford: Oxford University Press.

Linsky, B. 2014. Russell's Notes for 'Meinong's Theory of Complexes and Assumptions'. *Russell: The Journal of Bertrand Russell Studies* 33: 143–70.

Linsky, B. 2015. Acquaintance and Certainty in *The Problems of Philosophy*. In this volume: 65–85.

Ludlow, P., Y. Nagasawa, and D. Stoljar. 2004. *There's Something About Mary: Essays on Phenomenal Consciousness and Frank Jackson's Knowledge Argument*. Cambridge, MA: MIT Press.

McGinn, C. 1989. Can We Solve the Mind-Body Problem? *Mind* 98: 349–66.

McGinn, C. 1991. *The Problem of Consciousness: Essays Towards a Resolution*. Cambridge, MA: Blackwell.

Meinong, A. 1900. Abstrahieren und Vergleichen. *Zeitschrift für Psychologie und Physiologie der Sinnesorgane* 24: 38–82.

Meinong, A. 1910. *Über Annahmen*, 2nd ed. Leipzig: J. A. Barth.

Moore, G. E. 1912. *Ethics*. London: Williams and Norgate.

Moore, G. E. 1953. *Some Main Problems of Philosophy*. London: George Allen and Unwin.

O'Shaughnessy, B. 2003. Sense Data. *John Searle*, ed. B. Smith. Cambridge: Cambridge University Press.

Perovic, K. 2015. The Importance of Russell's Regress Argument for Universals. In this volume: 171–88.

Proops, I. 2015. Certainty, Error, and Acquaintance in *The Problems of Philosophy*. In this volume: 45–63.

Psillos, S. 2006. The Structure, the Whole Structure and Nothing But the Structure? *Philosophy of Science* 73: 560–70.

Robinson, H. 1994. *Perception*. New York: Routledge.

Robinson, H. 2005. Sense-Data, Intentionality, and Common Sense. *Intentionality: Past and Future*, eds. G. Forrai and G. Kampis, 79–90. New York: Rodopi.

Russell, B. 1900. *A Critical Exposition of the Philosophy of Leibniz*. Cambridge: Cambridge University Press.

Russell, B. 1903a. *The Principles of Mathematics*. Cambridge: Cambridge University Press.

Russell, B. 1903b. The Free Man's Worship. *The Independent Review* 1: 415–24. Reprinted in *CP* 12: 66–72.

Russell, B. 1904. Meinong's Theory of Complexes and Assumptions. *Mind* 13: 204–19. Reprinted in *CP* 4: 431–74.

Russell, B. 1910. *Philosophical Essays*. London: Longmans, Green and Co.

Russell, B. 1911. Knowledge by Acquaintance and Knowledge by Description. *Proceedings of the Aristotelian Society* 11: 108–28. Reprinted in *CP* 6: 147–61.

Russell, B. 1912a. *The Problems of Philosophy*. London: Williams and Norgate. Reprinted Oxford: Oxford University Press 1959.

Russell, B. 1912b. The Essence of Religion. *The Hibbert Journal* 11: 46–62. Reprinted in *CP* 12: 110–22.

Russell, B. 1914. The Relation of Sense-Data to Physics. *Scientia* 16: 1–27. Reprinted in *CP* 8: 3–26.

Russell, B. 1918-19. The Philosophy of Logical Atomism. *Monist* 28: 495–527, 29: 32–63, 190–222, 345–80. Reprinted in *CP* 8: 157–244.

Russell, B. 1945. *A History of Western Philosophy*. New York: Simon and Schuster.

Russell, B. 1948. *Human Knowledge: Its Scope and Limits*. London: George Allen and Unwin.

Russell, B. 1959. *My Philosophical Development*. London: George Allen and Unwin.

Russell, B. 1984. *The Collected Papers of Bertrand Russell, Volume 7: Theory of Knowledge: The 1913 Manuscript*, ed. E. R. Eames with K. Blackwell. London: George Allen and Unwin. [*CP* 7]

Russell, B. 1986. *The Collected Papers of Bertrand Russell, Volume 8: The Philosophy of Logical Atomism and Other Essays, 1914–19*, ed. J. Slater. London: George Allen and Unwin. [*CP* 8]

Russell, B. 1988. *The Collected Papers of Bertrand Russell, Volume 12: Contemplation and Action, 1902–14*, eds. R. Rempel, A. Brink, and M. Moran. London: George Allen and Unwin. [*CP* 12]

Russell, B. 1992. *The Collected Papers of Bertrand Russell, Volume 6: Logical and Philosophical Papers, 1909–13*, ed. J Slater with B. Frohmann. New York: Routledge. [*CP* 6]

Russell, B. 1994. *The Collected Papers of Bertrand Russell, Volume 4: Foundations of Logic, 1903–05*, ed. A. Urquhart with A. C. Lewis. London: Routledge. [*CP* 4]

Russell, B. 2014. *The Collected Papers of Bertrand Russell, Volume 5: Toward 'Principia Mathematica', 1905–08*, ed. G. H. Moore. London: Routledge. [*CP* 5]

Russell, B. and A. N. Whitehead. 1910-3. *Principia Mathematica*. Cambridge: Cambridge University Press

Saunders, S. 2003. Structural Realism Again. *Synthese* 136: 127–33.

Stoljar, D. 2001. Two Conceptions of the Physical. *Philosophy and Phenomenological Research* 62: 253–81.

Stoljar, D. 2006. *Ignorance and Imagination: The Epistemic Origin of the Problem of Consciousness*. Oxford: Oxford University Press.

Van Fraassen, B. C. 2006. Structure: Its Shadow and Substance. *The British Journal for the Philosophy of Science* 57: 275–307.

Van Fraassen, B. C. 2007. Structuralism(s) About Science: Some Common Problems. *Proceedings of the Aristotelian Society* 81: 45–61.

Wahl, R. 2015. Sense Data and the Inference to Material Objects: The Epistemological Project in *Problems* and Its Fate in Russell's Later Work. In this volume: 87–105.

Whitehead, A. N. 1911. *An Introduction to Mathematics*. London: Williams and Norgate.

Williamson, T. 2007. *The Philosophy of Philosophy*. Malden, MA: Blackwell.

Wishon, D. 2015. Russell on Russellian Monism. *Consciousness in the Physical World: Perspectives on Russellian Monism*, eds. T. Alter and Y. Nagasawa. Oxford: Oxford University Press.

2

Problems of Philosophy as a Stage in the Evolution of Russell's Views on Knowledge

PETER HYLTON

As my title implies, I'm going to consider *Problems of Philosophy*, and especially the views about knowledge which it presents, not in isolation but as a stage in the development of Russell's thought on the topic. (A stage in the dialectic, I might say, if I were out to annoy him.) A prelude was sounded in 'On Denoting', in which Russell makes some very brief remarks about knowledge more or less in passing, without elaborating on them at all. This was followed by a long period of almost complete silence on the topic.[1] He returned to the issue of knowledge in 1911 with two talks that he gave in March of that year, 'Analytic Realism', and 'Knowledge by Acquaintance and Knowledge by Description'.[2] Then in the summer of 1911

---

[1] *Almost* complete: in the essay 'On the Nature of Truth and Falsehood', first published in 1910, Russell mentions 'the relation between sense-data (i.e. the things we immediately perceive) and what we may call physical reality' (*CP* 6: 122) but he does so only in order to set the issues aside because '[i]t would take us too far from our subject to develop this theme' (ibid.). This passage seems to contain Russell's first published use of the term 'sense-data'. —I am grateful to Donovan Wishon for calling my attention to this passage.

[2] 'Analytic Realism' was given as a talk (in French) to La societé de philosophie française on March 23, 1911, and published the same year in the society's *Bulletin*. 'Knowledge by Acquaintance and Knowledge by Description' was read to the Aristotelian Society on March 6, 1911, and is published in the society's *Proceedings*.

Acquaintance, Knowledge, and Logic.
Donovan Wishon and Bernard Linsky (eds.).
Copyright © 2015, CSLI Publications.

he wrote *Problems of Philosophy*, which was published in 1912. The view he puts forward there is very much the same as that in the the two talks he gave in March, and I shall sometimes treat these 1911 works together. As so often with Russell, his working out the details of a view revealed to him both weaknesses and possible alternatives, thereby setting up the next stage of his thought. I shall briefly discuss the beginning of this stage, which can be seen in two works which he completed early in the Autumn of the following year: 'The Nature of Sense-Data' and 'On Matter'.[3]

I begin, then, with the brief remarks in 'On Denoting' and their connection with his earlier views. The penultimate paragraph of the essay includes this passage:

> ... [1] in every proposition that we can apprehend (i.e. not only in those whose truth or falsehood we can judge of, but in all those that we can think about), all the constituents are really entities with which we have immediate acquaintance. Now [2] such things as matter (in the sense in which matter occurs in physics) and the minds of other people are known to us only by denoting phrases, i.e. we are not *acquainted* with them, but we know them as what has such and such properties. (*CP* 4: 427; emphasis in the original; numbers in square brackets are my addition)

Here we have two theses, which I have numbered for convenience and will discuss in order.

The first, which is sometimes called the Principle of Acquaintance, is, I think, implicit in his earlier thought. In particular, it is implicit in the view that we understand a proposition by being acquainted with it, for being acquainted with a proposition requires—or so it seems plausible to suppose—being acquainted with its constituents. The principle is not, however, stated quite so generally and explicitly in Russell's earlier work.[4] This fact should

---

[3]'The Nature of Sense-Data: a Reply to Dr. Dawes Hicks' was completed on October 29th, 1912 and published in *Mind*. 'On Matter' was given as a talk at Cardiff on May 17th, 1912, and at Cambridge on October 25th, in different versions (see *CP* 6: 77–9). A version, which the editors of *CP* 6 assume to be the later one, is printed in *CP* 6: 80–95. See note 17, below. For further discussion of these two papers, see Russell Wahl's contribution to this volume.

[4]Although see the ms., 'Points about Denoting' (*CP* 4: 306–13), probably written in the second half of 1903 (see the note at *CP* 4: 305, and references given there). The context is, of course, a discussion of denoting. Russell says:

> It is necessary, for the understanding of a proposition, to have *acquaintance* with the *meaning* of every constituent of the meaning, and of the whole; it is not necessary to have acquaintance with such constituents of the denotation as are not constituents of the meaning. ... In the proposition 'there is one and / only one instance of *u*', the said instance is not a constituent of the meaning, hence the proposition may be known without our being acquainted with the instance. (307–8).

Russell states the principle in this form because he is here assuming a view according to which

not surprise us. First, issues of knowledge and understanding are not the focus of his attention during this period; it is only with the 1911 works that such issues occupy centre stage. Second, the importance of the thesis depends on the range of things with which we are acquainted. If one holds that we are acquainted with a very wide range of objects of all kinds then one may think that the thesis imposes no constraints at all on what propositions we can understand. In that case, the thesis may not seem to be worth articulating; indeed one may hardly be aware of holding it as a thesis. Something close to this, I think, is Russell's situation in the *Principles of Mathematics* (1903). In any case, it seems to me reasonable to attribute the first thesis to Russell from 1900 on, so that no special explanation is needed of why Russell holds it in 1905.[5]

Matters are different in the case of the second thesis.[6] The *Principles of Mathematics* suggests the contrary view, that we can be acquainted with any entity at all—including the Homeric gods and chimeras which he mentions in a well-known passage (Russell 1903: 449). Otherwise Russell would presumably have had something to say about how we can understand propositions about entities with which we are not acquainted. There is only one passage in *Principles* which discusses anything like this sort of issue, and it has to do specifically with propositions about the infinite. In section 141 Russell argues that there are no infinitely complex propositions, or at least none that we can know. It is thus only by means of denoting concepts that we are able to understand propositions about infinite totalities; he says, indeed, that enabling us to do so is 'the logical purpose which is served by the theory of denoting' (ibid.: 145). There are no similar passages about how we are able to understand propositions about physical objects; he

---

propositions and their constituents have both a meaning and a denotation.

[5]Ian Proops argues that Russell at the time of *Principles* does not have the notion of acquaintance that shortly thereafter became important for his thought, and thus does not at that time accept the Principle of Acquaintance (see Proops forthcoming). Proops does accept that at the time of *Principles* Russell employs a somewhat different notion which plays more or less the same role in his thought that acquaintance later played, and that Russell accepts a principle closely analogous to the Principle of Acquaintance. Proops also accepts that by the time of 'Points about Denoting' (see note 5, above) Russell has come to accept something very like the notion of acquaintance which figures in his subsequent work. These points are enough to allow the line of thought of the present paper to go through.

[6]I interpret the second thesis in the passage from the end of 'On Denoting', quoted above, as applying to physical objects in general, not only to the theoretical entities of physics, i.e. I do not interpret the parenthetical phrase '(in the sense in which matter occurs in physics)' as imposing any limitation. Donovan Wishon has made a contrary suggestion; see Proops' contribution to this volume for a response to that suggestion, a response which I endorse.

seems to accept that we can understand propositions about such objects simply by being acquainted with the relevant entities. The idea that Russell in 1903 thinks that we can be acquainted with material objects is further encouraged by the fact that Moore, with whom he was in very close contact at this period, holds this view at that time.[7]

So the second thesis is new in Russell's thought in 1905. In adopting it, he may again have been following Moore, who in 1905 claims that we do not 'directly perceive' or 'actually see' physical objects but rather 'colours, and the size and shape of colours, and spatial relations in three dimensions between these patches of colour ... [and] nothing else' (Moore 1905: 68).

The brief passage that I quoted above from the end of 'On Denoting' thus sets an agenda for Russell's thought about our knowledge of physical objects. The first thesis perhaps requires some argument (although one might think that it is obvious enough, given Russell's other commitments). The second thesis, since it contradicts Russell's earlier thought, certainly requires some argument. The second thesis also raises the question whether we in fact have reason to think that there are any physical objects at all. Finally, the two theses together might seem to imply that we cannot understand propositions about physical objects, a conclusion which might seem unacceptable on the face of it. So something must be done to defeat the implication (or to make the conclusion acceptable after all). —All of these are issues which Russell takes up in 1911, especially in *Problems of Philosophy*.

I begin with the first thesis, the Principle of Acquaintance. It, is explicitly stated at the end of Chapter V of *Problems* like this: 'Every proposition which we can understand must be composed wholly of constituents with which we are acquainted' (Russell 1912a: 58).[8] Russell goes on to argue for the thesis in the following paragraph. The heart of the argument is this sentence: 'We must attach *some* meaning to the words we use, if we are to speak significantly and not to utter mere noise; and the meaning we attach

---

[7]In spite of significant complexities in his view, Moore says unequivocally: 'I am as directly aware of the existence of material objects in space as of my own sensations' (Moore 1903: 30).

[8]There is overlapping discussion in Russell 1911: 154–5. Note that by 1911 Russell had adopted the multiple relation theory of judgment. According to that theory, there are no propositions. On Russell's previous view, our acts of judgment (and of propositional thought quite generally) were explained in terms of our acquaintance with propositions. On the multiple relation theory, they are explained in terms of our being acquainted with various entities (those which, on the old view, were the constituents of the proposition) and uniting them by our mental acts. In *Problems*, Russell writes as if he still held the old theory until he introduces that new theory in Chapter XII. What he says here could be translated into the idiom required by the new theory. I shall follow Russell in ignoring the multiple relation theory where it makes no difference.

to our words must be something with which we are acquainted' (ibid.). That sentence, however, might be accepted by someone who holds a wholly different kind of view of meaning—a Fregean, for example, might say that the meanings we attach to the words we use are *Sinne* and that we are acquainted with them. But Russell rejects any view of that kind, as is clear from the example that he gives in the next sentence:

> Thus when, for example, we make a statement about Julius Caesar, it is plain that Julius Caesar is not before our minds since we are not acquainted with him. We have in mind some *description* of Julius Caesar.... Thus our statement does not mean quite what it seems to mean.... (58–9)

Here, as in the *Principles of Mathematics*, Russell assumes that propositions are not made up of *Sinne*, or of ideas; rather they are, at least in paradigmatic cases, made up of the things that we are talking about: Julius Caesar is at least the right kind of thing to be a constituent of a proposition about him. Russell's argument for the Principle of Acquaintance depends on that assumption.

In 'Knowledge by Acquaintance and Knowledge by Description' Russell argues for the assumption, which he does not do in *Problems*. Specifically, he argues against the view that judgments about certain entities involve *ideas* of those entities, rather than those entities themselves. If they did involve ideas, Russell says, then 'ideas [would] become a veil between us and outside things' (*CP* 6: 155). In that case, Russell holds, 'we [would] never really, in knowledge, attain to those things we are supposed to be knowing about, but only to the ideas of those things' (ibid.). If our judgments were made up of ideas, we would need to explain how those judgments manage to be about what they are about: What makes a given idea the idea of a certain entity, distinct from the idea? How, in virtue of having the idea, do I succeed in thinking *about* that other entity? The answers are, at least, not obvious. As Russell says: 'The relation of mind, idea, and object, on this view, is utterly obscure...' (ibid.). This same general pattern of argument would work equally against the idea that judgments are made up of *Sinne*, or of any entities intermediate between us and those which the judgment is about.

The second thesis is that we are not acquainted with physical objects or, to put it the other way around, that sense-data, the things with which we are acquainted in sensation, are not physical objects. Given the notion of a sense-datum, this may seem quite obvious. And indeed in *KAKD* Russell offers no argument for it at all. He simply says, with no preparation: 'It will be seen that among the objects with which are acquainted are not included physical objects....' (*CP* 6: 151; the same clause occurs in Russell 1912a:

52, but there considerable ground work has been laid.) In 'Analytic Realism', he is almost as quick, saying:

> There is no *general* reason to reject naive realism, i.e. the realism that claims that sense-data are identical with physical objects and that they subsist unchanged when not perceived. There are, however, special reasons—the traditional reasons—for believing that sense-data do not depend (causally) only on the object, but also on the subject. In other words, one is forced to believe that sense-data are entities which exist only when there is a certain relation between the subject and the physical object.... (*CP* 6: 135f.)

He goes on to contrast 'the subjectivity of the sensible world' with 'the objectivity of the abstract world' (*CP* 6: 143); sense-data are subjective, universals are objective (see also *CP* 6: 136).

In *Problems*, perhaps because it is intended as an introductory work, he goes into more detail. In the first chapter he takes the table in his room as an example of a material object and argues (or perhaps merely points out) that the way it appears to us is not the same as the way we assume it really is. Again, there is overlap with Moore, who puts forward a very similar claim in the text of lectures he gave in 1910, a text which we know Russell read. [9] Moore emphasizes the fact that when a number of people look at the same physical object—an envelope, in his example—they may each see 'a slightly different shade of colour.... according to the way the light fell upon the paper', and takes this fact to show that what is 'directly apprehended' is not the physical object itself but rather sense-data (Moore 1953: 32).

In Russell's *Problems*, the argument has a distinctly sceptical, almost Cartesian, air to it, beginning with the first sentence of the chapter: 'Is there any knowledge in the world which is so certain that no reasonable man could doubt it?' (7). But scepticism is not Russell's real concern here, as becomes clear in Chapter II (which we shall discuss shortly). [10] The sceptical arguments of the first chapter are, I think, introduced primarily to make out the case for that we are not acquainted with physical objects. A difficulty is that precisely because we are not acquainted with physical objects we cannot put them side-by-side with sense-data and observe that the two kinds of

---

[9] The text of the lectures was later published as G. E. Moore, *Some Main Problems of Philosophy* (1953). In the Preface to *Problems*, Russell says he has 'derived invaluable assistance from unpublished writings of G. E. Moore and J. M. Keynes' (6); in the Preface to *SMPP*, Moore says that that the text of the first ten lectures constitute the writings that Russell is referring to. We shall discuss the writings of Keynes below.

[10] Here I am in agreement with the contributions to this volume by Ian Proops and Russell Wahl; in his contribution to this volume, by contrast, Robert Barnard attributes more Cartesian motivations to Russell.

things are different. Using the example of a table, Russell appeals to the reader's (and his own) pre-theoretical opinions about physical objects and argues that what is immediately given in experience does not conform to those opinions. We think, for example, that the 'real table' (he calls it) is the same colour all over, but, our experience is of a brown patch in which some parts are brighter than others. The perceived colour of the table, he says, 'is not something which is inherent in the table, but something depending upon the table and the spectator and the way the light falls on the table' (Russell 1912a: 9). He draws the conclusion that 'the immediate objects of our sensations', or sense-data, do not 'exist independently of us' (13), whereas the 'real table' does; later, he speaks of the sense-data we have when perceiving a tree as 'more or less subjective, in the sense that they depend upon us as much as upon the tree, and would not exist if the tree were not being perceived' (41). It is perhaps unclear precisely what this argument shows, and what Russell here takes it to show; this is a point to which we shall return.

It is notable that both in *Problems* and in 'Analytic Realism' Russell speaks of physical objects as 'things in themselves'. In *Problems* the term appears in Chapter VIII, much of which is a discussion of Kant: 'The physical object, which he [Kant] calls the 'thing in itself', he regards as essentially unknowable....' (86). In 'Analytic Realism' he says: 'The physical object is a "thing in itself" which cannot be known directly. Even its existence is doubtful, since it depends on a rather precarious induction' (*CP* 6: 136). Such remarks should remind us that Russell is still engaged with the work of Kant and of his Idealist successors, though less strenuously than he was when he and Moore initially rejected all forms of Idealism. Unlike the post-Kantian Idealists, Moore and Russell did not wholly reject the Kantian idea of things in themselves, things which are what they are wholly independent of us and our minds. In the first stages of their rejection of Idealism, they insisted, rather, in direct opposition to Kant, that we can know such things, and that our knowledge is not mediated by a cognitive apparatus which imposes form and structure upon them: we can have direct and immediate knowledge of things as they are in themselves. In the terminology which Russell adopted a few years later, we are *acquainted* with things in themselves.

Against this background, Russell's acceptance of the view that we are *not* acquainted with physical objects is a very significant concession to Kant (not the only one that he was forced to make around this time).[11] He tries to

---

[11] The other one I have in mind is his adoption of the multiple relation theory of judgment; see note 8, above. According to that theory, there are no propositions; the entities we judge about

mitigate the concession both in a footnote to page 86 of *Problems* and, more explicitly, in a passage in 'Analytic Realism' which immediately follows the two sentences just quoted:

> In saying that a physical object—i.e. that which subsists independently of the observer—is a 'thing in itself', I do not mean to say that the categories do not apply to the physical object, nor that it is unknowable in an absolute sense. It can be described; the nature of its relations with other things can be known—in a word one can know all that physics has to say on the subject. (*CP* 6: 136)

So Russell does not give up on the idea that there are physical objects, and indeed that we can have knowledge of them—it's just not *direct* knowledge.

So we are left with (at least) two questions: First, what reason do have to believe that there are physical objects? Second, how can we form judgments about physical objects, and thus at least hope to know truths about them? In *Problems* these questions are considered separately but there are important connections between them. (In particular, as we shall see, the answer to the second builds upon the answer to the first.)

The first question is most directly answered in Chapter II. Russell considers 'the supposition that the whole of life is a dream, in which we ourselves create all the objects that come before us' (22). This, he says, is not logically impossible, and cannot be ruled out absolutely, but it is 'a less simple hypothesis... than the common-sense hypothesis that there really are objects independent of us, whose actions on us cause our sensations' (ibid.). 'Simple' here seems to mean something like law-governed. Russell gives the example of our perceptions of a cat. We have various feline sense-data, as the cat comes and goes. If we focus solely on the sense-data we shall be unable to bring them under any laws, or find any regularities in them: 'The behaviour of the sense-data which represent the cat to me... becomes utterly inexplicable when regarded as mere movements and patches of colour' (23). When we accept 'the common-sense hypothesis' that there is a cat, an enduring physical object which is the cause of our sensations, things are quite different. We see the cat now in one place, later in another, because it has moved in the meantime, and its movements are subject to laws. The argument is all the stronger, Russell says, if we consider human beings. The noises they emit from time to time are wholly inexplicable if we take them merely as noises; if we take them as produced by an enduring object which

---

must be unified—synthesized, one might almost say—by the mind of the judging subject. Of course Russell is concerned to avoid any Kantian consequences of this step, first by denying that the act of judgment imposes constraints on what can be judged; and second by making the notion of a *fact*, rather than proposition or judgment, the fundamental idea of his metaphysics.

is capable of thought, and of expressing its thoughts, then we may hope to explain the noises in those terms.

Russell bolsters this argument by an appeal to the idea of 'instinctive belief'. In this context, this appeal seems to function primarily as a means of shifting the burden of proof onto those who deny that there are physical objects, and Russell thinks that it is a burden that they cannot bear. We have an 'instinctive belief that there *are* objects *corresponding* to our sense-data' (24); 'Since this belief does not lead to any difficulties, but on the contrary tends to simplify and systematize our account of our experiences, there seems to be no good reason for rejecting it' (ibid.). This is Russell's answer to our first question, why we should accept that there are physical objects which (at least typically) cause our sense-data.

Our second question was how, given the first thesis, we are able to think about physical objects, how it is possible for us to form judgments about them. How do I judge that the table in front of me is brown, even though I am not acquainted with the table? The answer relies on the theory of descriptions. In its most straightforward version: I can assert that there is one and only one object standing in a certain relation to certain tableish sense-data of mine and that it is brown. Even though I am not acquainted with physical objects I can still quantify over them—or so Russell assumes—and this is what enables me to talk or think about them. The same story, moreover, explains how communication between two people about physical objects is possible. You can also assert that there is one and only one object standing in a certain relation (not necessarily the same relation that I invoked) to certain sense-data of yours, and that that object is brown. It may happen, if all goes well, that there is in fact a single object which uniquely satisfies both the condition that I lay down and the different condition that you lay down. In such a case we are talking about the same thing; if we attribute the same property, we are in some sense saying the same thing, although we are not expressing the same proposition.

I speak of this as the most straightforward way in which the theory of descriptions enables us to form thoughts about physical objects. Russell himself describes, and seems to endorse, another view of the matter, according to which what is described is not the physical object but rather the proposition in which it figures. This occurs in the discussion of Bismark, in Chapter V of *Problems* (and also in 'Knowledge by Acquaintance and Knowledge by Description'). Bismark no doubt judged, from time to time, that he was an astute diplomat. In doing so, he would have taken advantage of the fact that he was acquainted with himself and formed a judgment of which he himself was a constituent. (Russell here assumes that each of us is acquainted with himself or herself, although he starts to have doubts about this around this time.) I can also, in some sense, judge that Bismark was an astute diplomat. When I form my judgment, Russell says, what I would like to be able to do is 'to make the judgement which Bismark alone can make, namely the judgement of which he himself is a constituent' (Russell 1912a: 57). But of course I cannot do so; the proposition which Bismark himself asserts contains a constituent with which I am not acquainted, namely Bismark, so I cannot understand it. But I do know that there is such a proposition and, Russell says, I can describe it as 'the proposition asserting, concerning the actual object which was the first Chancellor of the German Empire, that this object was an astute diplomatist' (57). Of course further analysis would be needed (most obviously of the term 'the German Empire') to get this into a form which accurately expresses a proposition with the constituents of which I am acquainted. Still the point is clear enough. I cannot assert the same proposition that Bismark asserts, but I can describe that proposition and assert that it is correct. More generally, communication is possible because you and I can describe the same proposition and say of it that it is true, or false, or dubious for this or that reason, and so on.

The problem with this view, and perhaps the reason that it plays no role in Russell's later work, is that it is incompatible with the multiple relation theory of judgement. According to that view, there are no propositions, so of course we cannot describe propositions. This point is somewhat obscured by Russell's choice of example. No doubt Bismark did, from time to time, form the belief or judgment that he was an astute diplomat, so it may look as if there is something, an act of judgment, that you and I could both describe in our discussion of Bismark's diplomatic skill. If you and I both happen to know that Bismark formed the belief that he was an astute diplomat at noon on March 18th, 1890, say, then each of us could describe that judgment and say that it was true. But this only works because the object of the judgment—Bismark—is one with which one person (also Bismark) was acquainted and formed judgments about. As an account of communication in general it is hopeless. Suppose we are talking about, say, a table, rather than a person. No one ever was or will be in a position to form a judgment of which that object is a constituent, since no one is or will be acquainted with it; there simply is no such judgment. Once we give up on the idea that there are propositions containing the table—once we adopt the multiple relation theory—we can no longer think that we communicate by describing the propositions or judgments which we should like to be able to assert or deny more directly.

It is worth stressing that even on the view that we communicate about physical objects by describing propositions about them, we still need descriptions of the physical objects themselves; a proposition will be described by means of a description of the physical object which it contains. So we can, without loss of generality, focus on description of physical objects, rather than of propositions.

One potential difficulty of the view that we form beliefs about physical objects by describing those objects is it requires that I understand propositions of the form '(∃x)Fx' although there is no proposition of the form 'Fa' which I can understand. So I must be able to understand propositions which quantify over entities with which I am not acquainted. This requirement is incompatible with the conception of quantification which Wittgenstein developed, in opposition to Russell, a few years after the publication of *Problems*.[12] There is, however, no sign that Russell was troubled by this requirement, or that it plays any role in his abandoning the view of empirical knowledge which he sets out in *Problems*, so I shall not discuss the issue further here.

A more obvious difficulty arises because I can only think about a physical object, on this account, by describing it in terms of its relations to entities with which I am acquainted. I might, for example, describe the table by thinking of it as *the* object which is causing certain tableish sense-data which I am currently having. My thought misses its mark unless there is in fact one and only one object which is causing the relevant sense-data. It is worth stressing that this is necessary if I am to form any judgments about the object; it is a requirement not only for *knowledge* of a physical object but for any thought about it, true or false. To *know* that the table is brown I must presumably know that it stands in such-and-such a relation to certain sense-data of mine, since that is part of what is asserted by the claim when we analyze it according to the theory of descriptions. If I am merely wondering whether the table is brown then a lower standard applies. I may not have knowledge of the relation between my sense-data and the physical object. On the other hand, the relation must hold, if my thought is to be about the table, and I must presumably have some reason to think that it holds or I would never form that thought in the first place.

So if I am to think about a physical object at all I must know, or at least have reason to believe, that it stands in some specific relation to some of my sense-data—by causing them, to take the most obvious candidate. As Russell says: 'In order to know anything at all about the table, we must know

---

[12]See Diamond 2000: 262–92.

truths connecting it with things with which we have acquaintance: we must know that "such-and-such sense-data are caused by a physical object"' (47). The difficulty, then, is how we can know that, or have reason to believe it. This is a quite general worry: the issue is not so much how I can be sure that this particular sense-datum is not uncaused, or in some other way anomalous, but rather how I can have any reason at all to think that any of my sense-data are caused by physical objects. In the nature of the case, I cannot know this by experience, by having observed past sense-data being caused by physical objects; that would require that I had knowledge of those physical objects, which is what is in question here. If I cannot know by experience that my sense-data are (in some cases) caused by physical objects, I must presumably know it *a priori*, if I can know it at all. But what exactly is it that is known? And what reason is there to accept that we really do have this alleged piece of knowledge?

Here we must draw on the reasons Russell offers for the existence of physical objects in Chapter II of *Problems*, briefly discussed above. As we saw, he puts forward a simplicity argument: we have reason to accept that there are physical objects, and that our sense-data are caused by them, because this hypothesis is simpler than the hypothesis that only the sense-data exist. To back this up, he needs some principle, knowable *a priori*, which justifies the claim that the simpler hypothesis is true, or at any rate more likely to be true, than the less simple. Or perhaps what is knowable *a priori* is some principle of causality, and the role of the simplicity argument is to give us reason to accept that principle. His discussion of *a priori* knowledge does not contain a formulation of the principle that would be needed. It does, however, show that he is willing to accept *a priori* principles other than those of deductive logic:

> In addition to the logical principles which enable us to prove from a given premiss that something is certainly true, there are other logical principles which enable us to prove, from a given premiss, that there is a greater or less probability that something is true. (Russell 1912a: 73)

As an example, he puts forward the principle of induction, which he discusses in Chapter VI. That principle would not be sufficient to show that our sense-data are related to physical objects, but would no doubt be necessary for such a demonstration. In any case, the relation between a sense-datum and the object which corresponds to it, and causes it, must be probabilistic; hallucinations and similar phenomena show that not every sense-datum stands in the relevant relation to a physical object.

A particularly striking feature of the passage just quoted is Russell's use of the word 'logical' for principles which are probabilistic rather than demonstrative. In this he is presumably influenced by the 'unpublished writings of... J. M. Keynes ...as regards probability and induction', which he acknowledges in the Preface to *Problems*.[13] Keynes's 1921 book, *A Treatise on Probablity*, partially based on those writings, insists that probability is a logical relation between two sets of propositions. The first chapter, he says, aims to emphasize 'the existence *of a logical relation between two sets of propositions* in cases where it is not possible to argue demonstratively from one to the other' (8; emphasis in the original). Like Russell on the fundamental concepts of logic, or Moore on goodness, Keynes claims that probability is simple and indefinable: 'We cannot analyse the probability-relation in terms of simpler ideas' (8). Again following Russell and Moore, he says that we 'cognise' that relation (5), and that when we make claims about probability we claim to be 'perceiving' an 'objective relation between sets of propositions' (6).

In order to account for even the simplest kind of knowledge of physical objects, Russell thus needs to postulate probabilistic *a priori* principles. So Russell is here making heavy demands on the idea of *a priori* knowledge and, in particular, of non-demonstrative *a priori* knowledge. It is perhaps for this reason that a significant proportion of *Problems* is taken up with *a priori* knowledge. All such knowledge, he argues, 'is concerned with entities which do not, properly speaking, exist, either in the mental or in the physical world' (90) although of course they are, or have Being. The criterion for existing, as opposed to being, is that existent entities are in time (98). So *a priori* knowledge concerns entities which are not in time—universals. Strikingly, such knowledge includes not only logic, both deductive and probabilistic, but also 'knowledge as to ethical value' (76).

In *Problems*, Russell seeks to explain our *a priori* knowledge in terms of our acquaintance with the relevant universals. Thus he says: 'the statement "two and two are four" deals exclusively with universals, and therefore may be known by anybody who is acquainted with the universals concerned and can perceive the relation between them' (105). Russell goes on to say 'It must be taken as a fact'—that is, presumably, not explained in other terms—'that we have the power of sometimes perceiving such relations between universals, and therefore of sometimes knowing general *a priori* propositions' (ibid.). One drawback of this idea is that it makes the

---

[13]Russell is almost certainly referring to the Fellowship Dissertation which Keynes submitted, unsuccessfully, to King's College Cambridge in December 1907. Keynes's *A Treatise on Probability* (1921) is the descendent of that dissertation, as Keynes says in the Preface to the book (page v).

idea of acquaintance with universals carry an explanatory burden, which might be thought to be more than it can bear. Fundamental disagreement over questions of ethical value, for example, would on this picture be cases in which one party insisted that she perceived the relevant universals standing in some relation while the other party insisted that he perceived them standing in some distinct and contrary relation. A more specific drawback to the idea is that while some propositions concerning only universals are knowable *a priori*, others are not. Russell himself gives the example of 'all men are mortal', which concerns only the relevant universals (since 'we can *understand* what the proposition means as soon as we understand the universals involved, namely *man* and *mortal*'; 106) but which cannot be known *a priori*. *Some* of the propositions which 'deal exclusively with universals' can be known *a priori* but some cannot; *sometimes* we can perceive relations among universals but sometimes we cannot, even though we are acquainted with all the universals concerned. But Russell offers nothing by way of a criterion to distinguish the two types of cases, much less an explanation of why some propositions are of one type and others of the other.

Russell's discussion of *a priori* knowledge in *Problems* also appeals to the idea of self-evidence: 'Our immediate knowledge of truths may be called *intuitive* knowledge, and the truths so known may be called *self-evident* truths. Among such truths are... certain abstract logical and arithmetical principles, and (though with less certainty), some ethical propositions' (109). In context it is perhaps unclear whether we should think of this as based upon the discussion of our perceiving relations among universals, perhaps as summing up the results of that discussion, or whether it is a separate attempt to account for the idea of *a priori* knowledge, this time in terms of self-evidence. Either way, it represents no advance.

As we saw, the account in *Problems* of our knowledge of physical objects relies heavily on our having *a priori* knowledge of principles beyond those of deductive logic. The suggestion of the last couple of paragraphs is that Russell has no account of such knowledge which can bear that weight. *Problems* thus plays a role in revealing the weaknesses in Russell's view of *a priori*, and thus perhaps in accounting for the readiness with which he accepts Wittgenstein's quite different view, even at a stage when he does not seem to understand it very well.[14] The most immediate reaction in Russell's work, however, is less general in its scope. In 'On Matter' he criti-

---

[14]Thus see *Introduction to Mathematical Philosophy* (1919: 203, 204f). In suggesting that Russell's account of empirical knowledge may have played a role in the development of his view of the *a priori*, I do not mean to deny or downplay the importance of other factors, especially logic (and, in particular, the status of the Axiom of Reducibility).

cizes the argument of Chapter II of *Problems*, which he calls 'the inductive argument'. He states the Chapter II argument like this:

> The appearance and disappearance of sense-data is *primâ facie* irregular and capricious, but by supposing them caused by the interaction of matter and the observer, they can be brought under general laws which are simple and render sense-data to some extent predictable. (*CP* 6: 85).

He then immediately says: 'This argument, though it has *some* weight, no longer appears to me to give any very overwhelming probability in favour of matter' (ibid.).

He makes two objections to it. The first is that even if the hypothesis of matter greatly simplifies our account of sense-data, this does not provide any reason to suppose the hypothesis it true: the universe may not be simple. Thus: 'The argument from simplicity, to begin with, is merely teleological, and has absolutely no weight whatever. ....there is no reason whatever to expect the true laws of nature to be simple' (*CP* 6: 85).

The second objection to the argument is essentially the possibility of what has become known as the underdetermination of theory by evidence:

> It is contended that, because a certain hypothesis fits all relevant known facts, therefore there is at least a probability that it is true. Such a contention is only valid if it is known that there are not likely to be other hypotheses which also fit the facts. In our case, this knowledge is lacking. (*CP* 6: 87)

Here the point is that there may be some other hypothesis, an alternative to the view that our sense-data are caused by matter with which we are not acquainted, which also 'fits the facts'. Since we do not know that there isn't, we have no reason to accept the hypothesis of matter, even though it does fit the facts.

Immediately after the passage just quoted, Russell elaborates on exactly what would be required of such an 'other hypothesis'. He phrases the point like this:

> Would it be possible, without assuming the existence of some non-sensible thing behind the sense-datum, to give to the symbols of dynamics a definition in terms of sense-data alone? If this is true, then the whole of dynamics remains symbolically true even if there is no such thing as matter. The question whether it is so is a straightforward one, obviously capable of a demonstrable answer either affirmative or negative. (*CP* 6: 87–8)

The approach that Russell is suggesting here is essentially that used in his reduction of mathematics to logic (where logic is taken sufficiently broadly). The goal is to reinterpret a body of theory so that it comes out true without presupposing the entities that it seems to be about, to make it, as

Russell says, 'symbolically true'. In this case, that would mean taking dynamics as a set of sentences and finding an interpretation of the symbols of those sentences on which they come out true. (Russell later credits Whitehead with the application of these ideas to physics).[15] In that way, a philosophical question is to be transformed into a technical question, one that can be given a 'demonstrable answer' and definitively settled.

The idea that physics might be true (at least 'symbolically') and yet that 'there is no such thing as matter' is a radical one. (Although in Russell's version it is perhaps less drastic than one might suppose, as we shall see.) The obvious problem with it is simply that it seems not to be feasible. Immediately after the passage from which I have drawn the quotations above, Russell asks the question again and answers it: 'Can Dynamics be interpreted in terms of sense-data alone? (Of course I mean the sense-data of one person.) The answer, I think, must be negative'. There must, he says, 'be some kind of law by which inference is possible from sense-data to other things' (*CP* 6: 88). What are these 'other things', if they are not matter? And why is inference to them more plausible than the inference to matter, which at least has the advantage of being in accord with our instinctive beliefs?

To see the context of Russell's answer these questions we shall have to return to a question left hanging from our discussion of the argument that we are not acquainted with physical objects: what exactly does that argument shows? In 1911 Russell seems to take it to show not merely that sense-data are not identical with physical objects but also that they are in a certain sense subjective: they are dependent upon the perceiving subject, and they exist only while they are data to the subject. At the same time, however, he denies that they are mental entities. This last point is crucial. The argument against Idealism which he puts forward in Chapter IV of *Problems* chiefly consists of an insistence on the distinction between the *act* of perception and the *object* of perception: the former is a mental occurrence but, Russell insists, that does not imply that the latter is a mental entity. '[O]ur whole power of acquiring knowledge', he says, 'is bound up with' this distinction (Russell 1912a: 42), since without it we should have to admit that we can know nothing outside of our own minds. With it, we can postulate, at least, that we have knowledge of things beyond our minds. Russell, indeed, goes so far as to claim that: 'Acquaintance with objects essentially consists in a relation between the mind and something other than

---

[15]See 'The Relation of Sense-Data to Physics' (1914) in *CP* 8: 5–12. The relevant passage is on page 12.

the mind; it is this that constitutes the mind's power of knowing things' (ibid.).

Russell's fundamental metaphysics is atomistic, with the atoms being externally related to one another (for a 1911 reiteration of this doctrine, see the opening paragraph of 'Analytic Realism', *CP* 6: 133). So the 'something other than the mind' with which we are acquainted in sense-perception—i.e. the sense-datum—must be an independent object; to adapt Moore's epigraph to *Principia Ethica*, it is what it is and no other. Perhaps it is consistent with this picture to claim that sense-data come into being only when a subject has sense-perception, but the matter seem far from clear—and it is still less clear how Russell could claim to *know* that sense-data only come into being in the act of sense-perception.

In view of this, it is not surprising that Russell retreats from the view that sense-data exist only when they are, as he says, 'sensated'. In his response to Dawes Hicks, written in the Fall of 1912, he seems to be agnostic about the matter, saying: 'there is no good reason to suppose that they [sense-data] exist when they are not sensated, or that a particular sense-datum is ever sensated by more than one subject' (*CP* 6: 187). In 'On Matter', he holds a position opposite to the one he started from: 'What is self-evident is, I think, what crude realism affirms, namely that qualities which are or resemble sense-data, or at least those of sight and touch, exist at times when they are not given in sense'.[16] He goes on to suggest that it may be correct to maintain a view according to which 'matter will be composed entirely of qualities of the nature of sense-data, but not only those which one observer perceives; it will be composed of all the sense-data which all possible observers would perceive in perceiving the same thing.' (*CP* 6: 94). (He goes on to say that such a view 'would preserve matter and avoid conflicting with any very strong instinctive belief' (ibid.). This is odd in part because it seems to deny a point (quoted above) made in a footnote on page 87 of the same work. In that passage, he implies that if a view does not

---

[16]'On Matter', *CP* 6: 93. There is puzzle here. It is natural to think that Russell gradually became more friendly towards the idea that entities exactly like sense-data can exist at times when they are not 'sensated' by anyone. By this criterion, one would expect 'On Matter' to be a later work than the reply to Dawes Hicks. But the latter seems to have been completed on October 29th, 1912 (see *CP* 6: 183), while 'On Matter' was read at Cardiff University in May of 1912 and, in a revised version, at Cambridge on October 25th, 1912. The editors of *CP* 6 assume that the paper reprinted in that volume is the revised version (see *CP* 6: 77). But, even so, it antedates the completion of the reply to Dawes Hicks. It may be that the reply to Dawes Hicks was begun significantly earlier and that the parts pertaining to the present issue were not revised. It is also possible, however, that Russell further revised 'On Matter', and that the version that survives is from later than October 25th 1912.

assume 'some non-sensible thing behind the sense-datum' then according to that view 'there is no such thing as matter'. The wavering here perhaps tells us something about the status of this work.)

The 'other things'—neither sense-data nor the things in themselves of *Problems*—which are needed for the interpretation of Dynamics thus turn out to be 'qualities of the nature of sense-data' which are not data to any subject—unsensed *sensibilia* as he later came to call them. We still need an *a priori* principle to assure us of the existence of such things, but Russell thinks that the principle 'seems less precarious and much more self-evident' than that required by other view of the matter (*CP* 6: 94). He also claims that the view—which he calls a modified form of naive realism—has two further advantages: '(1) that it avoids an unknowable noumenon, since matter will consist entirely of things of the kind with which we are acquainted; (2) that it avoids rejecting our instinctive belief in the independent reality of qualities...' (*CP* 6: 94).

This view, which Russell soon came to advocate in less tentative fashion, is a drastic change from the view in *Problems*: it rejects physical objects as entities wholly distinct from our sense data and entities of the same kind as sense data. The change may, however, be somewhat less drastic than first appears. To begin with, it may seem as if Russell is completely escaping from the idea that our ordinary knowledge depends upon, our making *a priori* inferences to things in themselves. But he still holds that our ordinary knowledge depends our knowledge of things with which we are not acquainted, and we still need an *a priori* principle to infer that they exist; the difference is that now those things are said to be *like* the things with which we are acquainted. (Unsensed *sensibilia* thus come to play one of the roles of things in themselves.)

A second point is that the new view may also look like an abandonment of the idea that our empirical knowledge is inter-subjective, an idea which *Problems* vindicated by claiming that different people, with different sense-data, might nevertheless be able to describe, and achieve some knowledge about, the same physical object. Here again, the change may appear greater than it really is. When I (apparently) talk about a physical object, what I say is to be understood not in terms of my own sense-data exclusively but also in terms relevant *sensibilia* which are not data for me but which I infer. My sense data are not data for you but you may nonetheless have access to them by inference. You may also have access to the other relevant *sensibilia* which are not data for me; some of them may be data for you, others you may be able to infer. So inter-subjectivity may be preserved, after all.

Third, and finally on this topic, it might seem as if the hypothesis of matter is explanatory in a way that is wholly lost if we give up on matter and interpret physics 'in terms of sense-data alone'. My having a given sense-datum at a given time can, presumably, be explained in terms of there being a desk in front of me, the light striking the desk and being reflected into my eyes, and so on; this explanation is of course impossible if we abandon the desk as an object distinct from *sensibilia*, sensed or unsensed. But upon reflection the contrast is not so clear. The explanation of sense-data in terms of matter presupposes—and does not explain—regularities in the way that matter behaves. In the idealized case, the regularities are the wholly exceptionless laws of physics. The re-interpretation of physics which Russell is contemplating would retain those regularities, no less general, but construe them as regularities among *sensibilia*; it is not clear, at least, why this should not be counted as equally explanatory. The sense-data of any one person, of course, do not exhibit the relevant regularity: this was the point Russell made in Chapter II of *Problems* about the feline sense-data. His new idea, however, is that when we consider all *sensibilia* we can give an interpretation of physics which preserves its exceptionless generalizations which are, presumably, no less explanatory in the new context than in the old. The idea that we can do this is an audacious assumption, or hope, and the next stage of his thought about knowledge is spent trying to work it out. But that is a story for another day.

References

Barnard, R. 2015. *Problems* as Prolegomena: Russell's Analytic Phenomenology. In this volume: 153–70.

Diamond, C. 2000. Does Bismark Have a Beetle in his Box?: The Private Language Argument in the *Tractatus*. New *Wittgenstein*, eds. A. Crary and R. J. Read, 262–92. London: Routledge.

Keynes, J. M. 1907. Fellowship Dissertation. Submitted to King's College London.

Keynes, J. M. 1921. *A Treatise on Probability*. London: Macmillan and Co., Limited.

Moore, G. E. 1903. Refutation of Idealism. *Mind* 12: 433–53. Reprinted in Moore 1922: 1–30.

Moore, G. E. 1905. The Nature and Reality of Objects of Perception. *Proceedings of the Aristotelian Society* 6: 68–127. Reprinted in Moore 1922: 31–96.

Moore, G. E. 1922. *Philosophical Studies*. London: Lund Humphries.

Moore, G. E. 1953. *Some Main Problems of Philosophy*. London: George Allen and Unwin.

Proops, I. Forthcoming. Russellian Acquaintance Revisited. *Journal of the History of Philosophy*.

Proops, I. 2015. Certainty, Error, and Acquaintance in *The Problems of Philosophy*. In this volume: 45–63.

Russell, B. 1903. *Principles of Mathematics*. Cambridge: Cambridge University Press.

Russell, B. 1903. Points about Denoting. In *CP* 4: 306–13.

Russell, B. 1905. On Denoting. *Mind*, 14: 479-93. Reprinted in *CP* 4: 414–27.

Russell, B. 1910. *Philosophical Essays*. London: Longmans, Green and Co.

Russell, B. 1911. Analytic Realism. *Bulletin la societé de philosophie française*, 11: 282–91. Reprinted in *CP* 6: 133–46.

Russell, B. 1911. Knowledge by Acquaintance and Knowledge by Description. *Proceedings of the Aristotelian Society*, 11: 209–32. Reprinted in *CP* 6: 148–61.

Russell, B. 1912a. *The Problems of Philosophy*. London: Williams and Norgate. Reprinted Oxford: Oxford University Press 1959.

Russell, B. 1912b. The Nature of Sense-Data: a Reply to Dr. Dawes Hicks. *Mind*, 22: 76–81. Reprinted in *CP* 6: 183–9.

Russell, B. 1912c. On Matter. In *CP* 6: 80–95.

Russell, B. 1914. The Relation of Sense-Data to Physics. *Scientia*, 16: 1-27. Reprinted in *CP* 8: 5–12.

Russell, B. 1918. *Mysticism and Logic*. London: Longmans, Green, and Co.

Russell, B. 1919. *Introduction to Mathematical Philosophy*. London: George Allen and Unwin.

Russell, B. 1937. *Principles of Mathematics, Second Edition*. London: George Allen & Unwin.

Russell, B. 1986. *The Collected Papers of Bertrand Russell, Vol. 8, The Philosophy of Logical Atomism and Other Essays, 1914-19*, ed. J. G. Slater. London: George Allen and Unwin. [*CP* 8]

Russell, B. 1992. *The Collected Papers of Bertrand Russell, Vol. 6: Logical and Philosophical Papers, 1909-13*, ed. J. G. Slater with B. Frohmann. London: George Allen & Unwin. [*CP* 6]

Russell, B. 1994. *The Collected Papers of Bertrand Russell, Volume 4: Foundations of Logic, 1903–05*, ed. A. Urquhart with A. C. Lewis. London: Routledge. [*CP* 4]

Wahl, R. 2015. Sense Data and the Inference to Material Objects: The Epistemological Project in *Problems* and Its Fate in Russell's Later Work. In this volume: 87–105.

3

Certainty, Error, and Acquaintance in
The Problems of Philosophy

Ian Proops

1 Introduction

If there is one trait that characterizes Russell's philosophical sensibility
more than any other, it is his surpassing intellectual honesty. Never one to
conceal from himself the problems with his own views, and never one to
ignore or shrug off the valid criticisms of others, Russell stands willing,
throughout his career, to re-think fundamental notions, arguments, and
commitments. In matters broadly logical, this intellectual flexibility manifests itself in frequent modifications to his ontology. In matters broadly
epistemological, it manifests itself in frequent changes of mind about the
range of the acquaintance relation—changes that are only in part related to
the modifications he makes in his ontology. A brief survey of this second
set of changes will serve to introduce my topic.

At various points prior to 'On Denoting' (hereafter *OD*) Russell takes
us to be acquainted with entities in each of the following categories: the
indefinables of mathematics and logic (1902: xv); denoting concepts (*CP* 4:
369), propositions (*CP* 4: 307), and material objects (Letter to Frege, December 12th, 1904). At various points during this same period he denies
that we are acquainted with spatial points, with temporal instants (*CP* 3:
323–4), or with other minds (*CP* 4: 369). In *OD* he comes to deny, in addition, that we are acquainted with 'matter in the sense in which [it] occurs in
physics' (Russell 1905: 56). In *The Problems of Philosophy* of 1912 (hereafter *POP*), in keeping with this last commitment, he comes to deny that we

Acquaintance, Knowledge, and Logic.
Donovan Wishon and Bernard Linsky (eds.).
Copyright © 2015, CSLI Publications.

have acquaintance with the intrinsic qualities of physical objects (34) or with physical space (34). He takes these positions while also continuing to deny that we have acquaintance with physical objects themselves (47) or with other minds (55). In the same work he maintains, on the positive side, that we have acquaintance with: past and present sense-data (48); universals (51–2); facts (135–6); distances in our private visual and tactile spaces (32), and (probably) ourselves (109). By the time of drafting the *Theory of Knowledge* manuscript of 1913, however, Russell comes to deny that we have acquaintance with the self (1913b: 36), and he now maintains that we have acquaintance with the 'forms' of complexes—entities that he sometimes calls 'logical forms' (1913: 99, 101) and which he conceives of as facts of a certain kind (1913b: 114). Finally, in 1914 Russell arrives at the view that we are acquainted with what he calls 'sensibilia'. These are physical entities that are existentially independent of minds and located in public space and in time. They can—or so he claims at one point in 1915—even possess velocities (*CP* 8: 82). Such sensibilia as we are acquainted with, he makes clear, count as 'sense-data' in virtue of our being acquainted with them, but this is not fundamental to their nature. Rather, sensed sensibilia count as sense-data only in virtue of being sensed. Thus he says:

> I shall give the name *sensibilia* to those objects which have the same metaphysical and physical status as sense-data, without necessarily being data to any mind. Thus the relation of a *sensibile* to a sense-datum is like that of a man to a husband: a man becomes a husband by entering into the relation of marriage, and similarly a *sensibile* becomes a sense-datum by entering into the relation of acquaintance. (*CP* 8: 7).

It would be unrealistic to attempt to describe the factors motivating each of these positions (and changes of position) in the space of a single essay; for to do so would be to tell much of the story of Russell's ontological and epistemological development during the first two decades of the twentieth century. My present goal is more modest: I propose to defend an account of Russell's motivations for just one of the changes mentioned, namely, his coming in 1905 to deny that we have acquaintance with what he calls 'matter as [it] occurs in physics' (Russell 1905: 56). Or rather, since I have offered a detailed account of those motivations elsewhere (Proops 2011), what I propose to do in the present essay is to defend that account by critically engaging with one of its competitors, namely, the account offered by Peter Geach in his book *Mental Acts*, 46.[1] This defense is necessary because, even though Geach offered his interpretation more than half a century ago,

---

[1] I argue that the change is motivated by the form taken by Russell's resolution of the George IV puzzle in *OD*.

it continues to find adherents today.[2] In fact, I think it would be fair to say that Geach's account tends to be the default interpretation among readers of Russell who have views on this matter but who would not necessarily describe themselves as Russell specialists.

Geach offers the following explanation of why Russell came to deny that we are acquainted with material objects:

> Russell's restricting our acquaintance to sense-data, rather than material objects and other people, is partly a matter of Cartesian doubt; I cannot doubt the existence of sense-data, whereas I can doubt the existence of material objects and other people, so it is only to the sense-data that I can stand in a 'direct cognitive relation' (Geach 1957: 46).

As far as I can tell, *OD* provides no evidence for this account of Russell's motivations. Instead, the account derives what plausibility it has from certain remarks in *POP* that can seem to suggest either that when one is acquainted with a sense-datum one knows (indubitably) that it exists or that when one is so situated one has exhaustive knowledge of the sense-datum's intrinsic qualities. A remark of the former kind runs: 'If I am acquainted with a thing that exists, then my acquaintance gives the knowledge that it exists' (1912: 45). Another in the same spirit runs: 'Some knowledge, such as knowledge of the existence of sense-data, appears quite indubitable, however calmly and thoroughly we reflect on it' (1912: 151).[3] Yet a third remark of this kind runs:

---

[2]Geach's line is taken by Pears (1981: 227), Miah (2006: 57), and Ludlow (2011). I am grateful to Fatema Amijee for alerting me to relevant passages in Pears and Miah.

[3]Superficially, the view can also seem to be supported by the following remark from *Principia*:

> Whenever the grammatical subject of a proposition can be supposed not to exist without rendering the proposition meaningless, it is plain that the grammatical subject is not a proper name, *i.e.*, not a name directly representing some object. (1914: 66)

This might suggest a picture according to which one first inquires whether '*NN* does not exist' might turn out to be true, and then, finding that it might do so, concludes that '*NN*' is not a genuine Russellian name. But in truth, one's view about whether a supposition of nonexistence would render the claim nonsensical will depend on one's antecedent opinion about whether the subject term is a genuine Russellian name—something itself dictated by one's views on what we can be acquainted with. In 1904, for example, Russell would have insisted that to suppose that Mont Blanc does not exist would be to suppose that the sentence 'Mont Blanc does not exist' was nonsense. And he would, accordingly, have concluded at this stage that we cannot imagine this sentence turning out to be true. Russell's judgment about this matter changed in 1905, but it did so only because his theory of meaning for such names had by that time also changed: they had now to be regarded as synonymous with definite descriptions simply because we are not—he now supposed—acquainted with material objects.

> In all cases where we know by acquaintance a complex fact consisting of certain terms in a certain relation, we say that the truth that these terms are so related has the first or absolute kind of self-evidence, and in these cases the judgment that the terms are so related must be true (1912: 137).

A remark that can seem—at least at first sight—to suggest that acquaintance with a sense-datum brings with it knowledge of its intrinsic properties is Russell's implication that acquaintance with sense-data yields knowledge that is 'perfect and complete' (cf. 1912: 47).

Geach's interpretation is further encouraged by Russell's having at one point described acquaintance as the 'foundation' of our knowledge: 'All our knowledge', he says, 'both knowledge of things and knowledge of truths, rests upon acquaintance as its foundation' (1912: 48). Given the remarks just quoted, it is natural to suppose that Russell takes acquaintance to constitute the foundation of our knowledge because he takes our beliefs about sense-data to be *indubitable*. And, accordingly, one naturally reads this remark as suggestive, specifically, of *Cartesian* foundationalism.

The *prima facie* evidence for Geach's account of these matters, then, is moderately abundant. Nonetheless, the texts are scarcely unequivocal, for *POP* also contains remarks that should give pause to any Cartesian interpretation of these remarks: 'All our knowledge of truths', says Russell, 'is infected with *some* degree of doubt, and a theory which ignored this fact would be plainly wrong' (1912: 135). This seems to suggest that even our knowledge that such-and-such a sense-datum exists must be infected with some small degree of doubt. Russell gives a reason for this view earlier in *POP*: 'It is of course *possible* that all or any of our beliefs may be mistaken, and therefore all ought to be held with at least some slight element of doubt' (1912: 25).

How are we to reconcile these two apparently opposed sets of claims? A follower of Geach might perhaps recommend that we understand the quantifier in the phrase 'all our knowledge of truths' as tacitly restricted in such a way as to make an exception for knowledge of the existence and intrinsic properties of sense-data. But this suggestion—as well as being on its face somewhat strained—is troubled by the fact that the ground Russell offers for his view suggests that no such restriction can be intended. In considering why we cannot be 'absolutely certain' of the truth of 'any given judgment', he says:

> Suppose we first perceive the sun shining, which is a complex fact, and thence proceed to make the judgment 'the sun is shining'. In passing from the perception to the judgment, it is necessary to analyse the given complex fact: we have to separate out 'the sun' and 'shining' as constituents of the fact. In this process it is possible to commit an error. (1912: 137)

On the assumption that this story is correct, it is hard to see why we should not be able to commit a similar error in 'separating out' the referents of 'this' and 'is F' as constituents of the fact which we perceive when we perceive a particular sense-datum as F (where F is an intrinsic property of the sense-datum). So, by the lights of *POP*, at least, even statements reporting the supposedly introspectable intrinsic qualities of sense-data ought to be infected with some small degree of doubt.

The current strategy for explaining away Russell's anti-Cartesian remarks therefore seems unpromising. There may be other strategies for doing so, of course, but to me it seems more promising to attempt to explain away those remarks that point the other way. At any rate, this will be my approach.

2 Does Acquaintance with Sense-Data Yield Indubitable Knowledge of Truths?

Those of Russell's remarks in *POP* that seem to indicate that acquaintance with sense-data yields, or is capable of yielding, indubitable knowledge of truths can, I think, be defused by a combination of strategies. As I argue in Proops forthcoming, the claim that when we know a sense-datum, we know it 'perfectly and completely' can be explained in one of two ways, depending on whether we assume that at this stage—that is, 1911—Russell already adheres to his 1914 view that knowledge by acquaintance fails to admit of degree.[4] If we assume that in 1911 he does not yet subscribe to such a view, the remark may be taken to mean merely that when we are acquainted with a sense-datum we are thereby *acquainted* with every intrinsic fact about it— something that does not of course require us to know any truths about it.[5] On the other hand, if we assume that the all-or-nothing conception of acquaintance is already in place in *POP*, we may take this remark to be allusive, and as meaning simply that our knowledge of sense-data must be so described by the lights of Russell's Monistic Idealist opponents, and in particular by the lights of F. H. Bradley. For Bradley maintains—or seems to anyway—that to possess a gradable quality—a quality that could take on various degrees—is *in itself* an imperfection, and that this is so *even if the*

---

[4]In a note to the seventeenth impression, written in 1943, Russell misleadingly claims that *POP* was written in the 'early part of 1912'. We know, however—both from his correspondence with Lady Ottoline and elsewhere—that it was composed and completed during the summer of 1911.

[5]By an 'intrinsic fact about a sense-datum' I mean the fact that a certain intrinsic property holds of it.

quality in question should happen to assume its maximum value. He states this view—or what sounds like this view—in a chapter of *Appearance and Reality* that would likely have been of special interest to Russell, namely, the chapter on degrees of truth and reality. 'The absolute, considered as such', says Bradley, 'has of course no degrees; for it is perfect, *and there can be no more or less in perfection*' (Bradley 1893: 359, emphasis added). In order to explain Russell's treating our knowledge of sense-data as perfect and complete (on the assumption that it does not admit of degrees) we need only suppose that he read Bradley as maintaining that failing to admit of degrees was not merely necessary for perfection—as his remark clearly suggests—but also that it was sufficient (further details and context are contained in Proops forthcoming).

The remarks suggesting that our acquaintance with a sense-datum yields indubitable knowledge that it exists may, I think, be explained using another strategy. We may merely regard them as incautious formulations of the idea that when one has acquaintance with a sense-datum one also *has acquaintance with* the fact of its existence. To maintain such a thesis—or indeed the thesis that when we have acquaintance with a sense-datum we have acquaintance with every intrinsic fact about it—would be perfectly compatible with also maintaining that all of our knowledge of *truths* is infected with some degree of doubt. For, on this interpretation, although acquaintance with a sense-datum would yield indubitable knowledge of the fact of its existence (as well as knowledge of the intrinsic facts about the sense-datum), the knowledge in question would be knowledge by acquaintance with facts rather than propositional knowledge. And such knowledge, since acquaintance is a dual relation, is not susceptible of error (1912: 136).

This interpretation has the merit of making Russell's claim about the knowledge-yielding capacity of acquaintance consistent with what I have elsewhere called his 'Independence Thesis'. This runs: 'Knowledge of things, when it is of the kind we call knowledge by *acquaintance*, is essentially simpler than any knowledge of truths, and logically independent of knowledge of truths' (1912: 46). According to the Independence Thesis, then, one may 'in principle' have acquaintance with a fact in perception without knowing *any* truth about it. Consequently, one may have acquaintance with the existence of a certain sense-datum (that is to say, acquaintance with a fact of a certain kind) without thereby knowing *that* the sense-datum in question exists.

So far, so good; but what are we to make of Russell's claims, first, that there are truths that are 'self-evident in a sense that ensures infallibility' (1912: 135), and, second, that this kind of self-evidence provides 'an absolute guarantee of truth' (1912: 136)? To understand these claims—and, indeed, to understand how they might be consistent with Russell's also maintaining in *POP* that all our knowledge of truths is infected with some degree of doubt, one needs to consider the discussion of kinds of self-evidence that occurs two chapters earlier. There Russell says:

> It seems, however, highly probable that two different notions are combined in 'self-evidence' ...[and] that one of them, which corresponds to the highest degree of self-evidence, is really an infallible guarantee of truth, while the other, which corresponds to all the other degrees, does not give an infallible guarantee, but only a greater or lesser presumption (1912: 117–8).

Russell explains the notion of *infallibility* that figures here in a passage we quoted earlier:

> In all cases where we know by acquaintance a complex fact consisting of certain terms in a certain relation, we say that the truth that these terms are so related has the first or absolute kind of self-evidence, and in these cases the judgment that the terms are so related *must* be true (1912: 137).

This may seem to suggest that Russell does after all countenance some genuinely indubitable judgments or beliefs. But that impression is immediately undermined by another remark:

> But although this sort of self-evidence is an absolute guarantee of truth, it does not enable us to be *absolutely* certain, in the case of any given judgment, that the judgment in question is true (1912: 137).

Russell's terminology is unfortunate, but his view is clear enough: a judgment's 'absolute self-evidence' does not, in spite of its status as an 'absolute guarantee of truth', enable the judger to be absolutely certain that it is true.

But what, then, is the significance of Russell's describing absolute self-evidence as an 'absolute guarantee of truth'? The answer begins to emerge only when he comes to explain how perceptually based judgments can be in erroneous. He says:

> Suppose we first perceive the sun shining, which is a complex fact, and then proceed to make the judgment 'the sun is shining'. In passing from the perception to the judgment, it is necessary to analyse the given complex *fact*: we have to separate out 'the sun' and 'shining' as constituents of the fact. In this process it is possible to commit an error; hence even where a fact has the first or absolute kind of self-evidence, a judgment believed to correspond to the fact is not absolutely infallible, because it may not really correspond to the fact. But if it does correspond ... then it *must* be true (1912: 137–8).

Russell's language here betrays his uncertainty in *POP* about exactly which item it is that is supposed to have the 'first' or 'absolute' kind of self-evidence. This passage suggests that the item in question is the *fact* that is perceived, but the first of the two remarks quoted from *POP* 137 suggests that it is rather a *truth* (that is, a true *judgment*) about the fact that is perceived. The same impression is created by a slightly earlier explanation: 'We may say that a truth is self-evident, in the first and most absolute sense, when we have acquaintance with the fact which corresponds to the truth' (1912: 136).

Nonetheless, Russell's picture is tolerably clear. The view he is struggling to articulate is that the *circumstance* of our perceiving some particular fact—our being acquainted with it—is an absolute guarantee of the truth of the judgment that corresponds to that particular fact. In other words, he means to convey the following idea:

> Given that a subject, S, perceives (that is, has acquaintance with) the complex a-R-b, the judgment, $J(S, a, R, b)$, if the subject manages to form it, must be true. And, more generally, given that S perceives a certain complex, the corresponding judgment, if S manages to form it, must be true.

On Russell's conception, to say that S's perceiving a complex is an absolute guarantee of the truth of the corresponding judgment is not to say (and neither does it entail) that when S perceives the complex in question S thereby knows with certainty that the corresponding judgment is true. For S might make a mistake in analyzing the complex and so (unwittingly) fail even to *form* the judgment that corresponds to the fact in question (Russell 1912: 138; Whitehead and Russell 1910: 43). In such a case, the judgment that S does form, and which S imagines herself to form on the basis of her perception of the fact in question, since it is not the judgment corresponding to that fact, will turn out to be false

3 Acquaintance as the 'Foundation' of our Knowledge

As we have noted, Russell at one point claims that all our knowledge, 'both knowledge of things and knowledge of truths, rests upon acquaintance as its foundation' (1912: 48). Insofar as it portrays our knowledge of truths as resting on some unitary foundation, this claim invites construal as an endorsement of a foundationalist picture of human knowledge, and insofar as it identifies that unitary foundation with acquaintance, it invites construal of an endorsement of a specifically *Cartesian* version of foundationalism. Nonetheless, there is another way of looking at this remark on which it carries no such implications. According to this interpretation, when Russell describes acquaintance as a 'foundation' of our knowledge he is merely alluding, in a concessionary spirit, to certain ideas in the writings of William James. The present section is devoted to defending this alternative interpretation.

In my article 'Russellian Acquaintance Revisited' (forthcoming) I argue that Russell, who had read James in the final decade of the nineteenth century, and who had likely returned to him in 1903, made yet another return shortly before composing *POP*—plausibly in order to prepare for writing his article 'Knowledge by Acquaintance and Knowledge by Description'. There I offer external evidence for such a return by describing the biographical factors that may have prompted it. Let me just mention the internal evidence. This comprises the occurrence in *POP* of certain remarks that echo things James says in the sections of *The Principles of Psychology* that deal with acquaintance. These remarks, which—so far as I know—occur for the first time in Russell's writings in *POP*, include Russell's use of James's example of knowledge of the causes of a toothache;[6] his drawing attention to the existence in foreign languages of pairs of verbs expressing two different senses of 'know',[7] and his inclusion within the range of the acquaintance relation of *distances*.[8]

If Russell had returned to James at this point, his claim that acquaintance forms the foundation of our knowledge would be readily explicable as an allusion to James's talk of 'sensation'—something that James does not distinguish from acquaintance—as 'the stable rock of thought'. James says:

> Conceptual systems which neither began nor left off in sensations would be like bridges without piers. Systems about fact must plunge themselves into sensation as bridges plunge their piers into rock. Sensations are the stable rock, the *terminus a quo and the terminus ad quem* of thought. (James 1890 Vol. 2: 7)

Insofar as he endorses the Principle of Acquaintance (hereafter *POA*), Russell agrees with James that thoughts must plunge themselves into acquaintance as bridges plunge their piers into rock. For, according to the *POA*, thoughts, speaking metaphorically, must, like bridges be supported along the whole length of their span by the stable rock—or foundation—of acquaintance. On the other hand, although Russell agrees with James that acquaintance is in this sense the *terminus a quo* of thought, he also departs from him insofar as he denies that it is thought's terminus *ad quem*. For, in Russell's view, denoting makes it possible for us to think about things with which we are not acquainted.

---

[6] James 1890 Vol. 2: 7; cf. Russell 1912: 144–5.

[7] James 1890 Vol. 1: 221; cf. Russell 1912: 44.

[8] James says: 'I know an inch when I move my finger through it' (James 1890 Vol. 1: 221); cf. Russell 1912: 32.

The hypothesis of an allusion to James, then, explains how Russell's 'foundations' claim can be compatible with his rejection of Cartesian epistemology. On Russell's conception, acquaintance is the foundation for our knowledge of truths merely in the sense that it functions as an enabling condition of the thoughts that are known. Such an interpretation must, of course, remain somewhat conjectural, but the point I wish to urge is just that its availability serves to diminish the appearance that Russell's claim about 'foundations' constitutes clear evidence for Geach's interpretation.

4   An Abrupt Change of View?

It speaks in favor of the present suggestion for resolving the apparent tension in Russell's view that its Geachean rival seems to raise as many questions as it answers. If Geach is right, Russell would seem to have fallen under the spell of Cartesian epistemology rather suddenly. After all, we know from Russell's correspondence with Frege that as late as December 1904 he took us to be acquainted with material objects. For there he insists that Mont Blanc is a propositional constituent and, since he subscribes to a version of the *POA* at this time (*CP* 4: 307), it follows that he must have regarded this mountain as an object of acquaintance.[9] Geach therefore owes us an explanation of why Russell should have changed his mind on this matter so suddenly in 1905; and yet he offers none. The question is especially pressing because in Russell's writings during 1905—and, indeed for several years afterwards—there is, so far as I can judge, not a single remark suggesting a commitment to Cartesian epistemology.

On the account I favor, by contrast, Russell's coming to deny that we are acquainted with material objects in 1905 is naturally explained not by a sudden, unmotivated endorsement of Cartesian epistemology, but by an independently verifiable development in his broader views, namely, his having arrived in *OD* at a solution to the George IV puzzle—a solution whose adequacy requires that we lack acquaintance with material objects. The pressure to arrive at such a solution is, in turn, explicable, I would argue, by Russell's need to defend the central notion of his 1905–1907 substitutional theory—namely, the 'substitution' of one entity for another (not

---

[9]Letter to Frege of December 12, 1904 [Frege 1980: 169]. In OF, which was composed in the summer of 1905, Russell says that we have acquaintance with a person's 'sensible manifestations' (*CP* 4: 369). This may also indicate a commitment to our being acquainted with physical objects, but since it is hard to rule out that the 'manifestations' might be sense-data, this is less definitive evidence.

necessarily distinct) entity within a proposition. For, from a naïve point of view, the example of George IV's curiosity seems to invite one to draw the absurd conclusion that the substitution of an entity for itself in a proposition can lead that proposition to change its truth value—or so I argue in my 2011.

Russell's solution to the puzzle involves treating at least one of the apparent names that figure in any true, informative identity statement as in truth a disguised definite description. Consequently, if there were any true and informative identities in which both names were genuine Russellian names, Russell's solution would be inadequate. Accordingly, he is committed to denying that multi-faceted (or, more generally, multi-*aspectual*) objects, such as material objects, can be given genuine names.[10] This demand is satisfied by supposing that we are not acquainted with such objects, for whatever we are not (at any time) acquainted with is, for Russell, something that we cannot, strictly speaking, name.

I should emphasize that I am not suggesting that mere acquaintance with an aspect-free object yields the knowledge *that* a certain identity fact holds. Such an idea would obviously offend against Russell's Independence Thesis. It is rather that, so long as the objects of acquaintance are aspect-free, there will simply *be* no informative genuine identities to contemplate. The view to which Russell is committed by his resolution of the George IV puzzle in 1905 might for this reason be stated more precisely in the form of the following Principle, which I will call the 'Transparency Principle':

> If I understand the sentence '$a = b$' and if $a = b$, then I will know (with a degree of certainty equal to that which attaches to my knowledge that $a = a$) that $a = b$ (Here I gloss over certain fine points concerning use and mention).[11]

Embracing this principle involves no transgression against the Independence Thesis because to understand '$a = b$' requires more than just having acquaintance with the object in question. For example, it requires grasping the concept of identity. Endorsing the principle therefore does not commit one to the claim that mere acquaintance with an object entails some knowledge *about* it. Nor does it commit one to holding that we are capable of being absolutely certain of anything; for it is compatible with the Transparency Principle to hold that even logical truths are known with something less than absolute certainty. I conclude that Geach's reading, but not my own, has the drawback of attributing to Russell an apparently unmotivated, ab-

---

[10] See Proops 2011: 175 especially.

[11] I am grateful to Fatema Amijee and Donovan Wishon for questions and criticisms that led me to see the need for this more precise formulation of Russell's commitment.

rupt change in his epistemology.   Nonetheless, there is a response that Geach might conceivably make to this charge. As Donovan Wishon has observed (in conversation), there is a possible reading of Russell's remarks in *OD* that might suggest that Russell came to deny that we have acquaintance with material objects at a somewhat later stage than I have suggested. For in *OD* Russell first denied that we are acquainted with matter 'in the sense in which [it] occurs in physics' (Russell 1905: 56). This qualification might seem to suggest an interpretation according to which Russell maintains in *OD* that although we do not have acquaintance with the minute pieces of matter that, according to our best physical theory, make up physical objects (that is, atoms, molecules, electrons, and so forth), we *do* have acquaintance with matter in the sense in which it occurs in common-sense talk (that is, furniture, heavenly bodies, mountains, and so forth). If this is correct, then Geach might claim that Russell's embrace of Cartesian epistemology occurred at some point after he wrote *OD*—in *POP*, say. And he could then explain the change in Russell's epistemology as arising from his endorsement in *POP* of an argument for the thesis that we are not acquainted with macroscopic physical objects.[12] He might thus avoid the need to posit an abrupt change of view that antedates by some years the texts from *POP* that might (albeit controversially) be taken to indicate a commitment to Cartesian epistemology. The issue is worth examining both for its relevance to the present question and also because it presents a challenge to my own account of the development of Russell's epistemology.

In response I would say the following. Although Wishon's interpretation of Russell's qualification, 'in the sense in which [it] occurs in physics', does have some initial plausibility, certain later texts provide some reason to doubt its correctness. Most importantly, in his unpublished article 'On Matter' of 1912 Russell draws a distinction between matter as it is discussed 'from the standpoint of philosophy' and matter as it is 'dealt with by physical science'. And, crucially for our purposes, he assigns to the latter category such macroscopic objects as the moon (*CP* 6: 82–3). If, as seems plausible, the 1912 phrase 'matter as it is dealt with by physical science' is meant to have the same significance as the 1905 phrase, 'matter in the sense in which [it] occurs in physics', Wishon's interpretation would oblige us to conclude that Russell's view of the subject matter of physics must have itself undergone an unexplained and fairly dramatic shift between 1905 and 1912. For, if Wishon is right, in 1905 that subject matter excludes, but in 1912 includes, the traditional objects of astronomy. On my reading, by con-

---

[12]See Russell 1912: ch. 1.

trast, there is no need to posit any such unexplained shift. A second point to note about the 1912 'two standpoints' view of matter is that Russell takes matter viewed 'from the standpoint of philosophy' to include *both* 'aether (if it exists)' and 'gross matter'. But since the phrase 'gross matter' is naturally taken to signal a contrast with the void-denying philosopher's space-filling *subtle* matter, and because the aether posited by certain physical theories as the medium of propagation of electromagnetic radiation would, if matter at all, presumably count as matter viewed from the standpoint of physics, it is natural to read Russell as treating 'aether' in this context as the matter conceived of *only by philosophy and not by physics*—that is, as the void-denying philosopher's 'subtle matter'. But if that is correct, then the point of Russell's qualification in *OD* could possibly be to indicate that while we have no acquaintance with the gross matter dealt with by physics, we may, for all he knows, be acquainted with the philosopher's subtle matter. That would make sense on the present reading, for there seems to be no reason to think that subtle matter would afford facets or aspects in the way that gross matter plainly does.

I conclude that when the context provided by these later remarks is taken into account, the qualification in *OD* is not happily read as leaving open the possibility that we may be acquainted with macroscopic material objects. In consequence, Geach's reading seems to be stuck with the problem of attributing to the Russell of 1905 an abrupt and wholly unexplained endorsement of Cartesian epistemology—a position, what is more, that Russell must (according to Geach) be supposed to have abandoned by 1911, when he came to claim that all our knowledge is infected with some degree of doubt.

5   Whence the Uncertainty?

I have emphasized that in *POP* Russell holds that *all* our knowledge of truths—even the knowledge expressed in our perceptually based judgments about sense-data—is subject to some degree of doubt. His reason for taking this line was already touched on in section 1. The present section examines that reason more closely.

Recall that when I form a perceptually based judgment to the effect that the sun is shining, I must, in Russell's view, pass from my acquaintance with the fact in question to the corresponding judgment, and in the process I must analyze the fact into the two components, *the sun*, and *shining*. Russell thinks that in performing this analysis I introduce the possibility of error. His idea is that since I may, for all I know, have analyzed the complex incorrectly, the judgment that I form on the basis of my perception may not, for all I know, correspond to any fact. And because I cannot be certain that no such error of analysis has crept in, I can be certain of the truth of no perceptually based judgment—not even a judgment about one or other of my present sense-data. Clearly, then, analyses—whatever they may be—must be capable of assessment as correct or incorrect. But beyond this minimal starting point we are told very little about their nature in *POP*. So what is an analysis, exactly?

One might be tempted to think that an analysis is just another judgment—the judgment, presumably, that the complex has such-and-such constituents. But the temptation is better resisted, for the suggestion threatens to generate a vicious regress. After all, the judgment that a perceived complex contains such-and-such constituents itself seems to be a perceptually based judgment. But if it is one, then it, too, will presuppose an analysis, hence another perceptually based judgment, and a vicious regress will ensue. But if an analysis is not a judgmental complex, what kind of entity is it?

Although Russell fails to address this question either in *POP* itself or in the related passage in *Principia* (43), he does provide the materials for an answer in his *Theory of Knowledge* manuscript—though whether that answer is one he would himself endorse is unclear. In that work he suggests that an analysis is a distinctive kind of 'propositional thought':

> There are various kinds of propositional thoughts, just as there are various kinds of dual relations to objects. Besides understanding a proposition, there are, for example, believing, disbelieving, doubting, analyzing, and synthesizing, to mention only purely cognitive relations—if we went outside what is cognitive, we should have to mention also such relations as desiring and willing. (Russell 1913: 110)[13]

Russell's inclusion of analyses within the class of 'propositional thoughts' makes it sound as though the complexes resulting from instantiating these 'multiple' relations ought to be truth assessable; for thoughts, as we ordinarily think of them, are so assessable. But his inclusion within this same class of non-cognitive relations, such as desiring and willing serves to cancel this implication. Nonetheless, I think we would proceed at least in a Russellian spirit if we were to think of analysis as a multiple relation (or class of such relations) whose instances—what we might call 'analytical complexes'—are assessable not for truth or falsehood but merely for correctness or incorrectness (Compare the practice of philosophers of perception of describing the state of an illuded subject as 'nonveridical' rather than false).[14] Since

---

[13]I am indebted to Fatema Amijee for bringing this passage to my attention.

[14]The parenthetical qualification, 'or class of such relations', is necessary because relations of analysis will vary in their n-adicity.

analyses will not be assessable for truth or falsity, they will not be judg-ments, and so will be capable of figuring in Russell's account of perceptual error without generating a regress.[15]

Which kinds of items would be related by this envisaged multiple rela-tion of analysis? One might be tempted by the following account. When a subject, S, stands in the relation of *analyzing* to the complex a-bearing-R-to-b, and when S *correctly* analyzes that complex, the resultant 'analytical complex' will be:

Analyzes (S, a-bearing-R-to-b, a, R, b).

But there are two reasons to be dissatisfied with this suggestion. First, this is an account, not of analysis *per se*, but of *correct* analysis. Second, although this might fit the picture of analysis sketched in *POP*, it does not fit the pic-ture developed in the *Theory of Knowledge* manuscript; for in that later work Russell makes clear that analysis has to reveal not merely the constit-uents of a complex but also their mode of combination—and this is not something that is supposed to be evident merely from the subject's being acquainted with the complex to be analysed.[16] Perhaps Russell's idea at this point is that the analytical complex would include as an additional element the form of the analysandum—in this case the form of dual complexes, xRy; but one cannot say for sure, especially as this proposal is so unpromising. The details of the picture, then, are far from clear, but what matters for our purposes is that it suggests the beginnings of an account of how judgment might presuppose a state that is, first, capable of correctness or incorrect-ness, and, second, not itself a judgment.

For Russell, when I form a false perceptual judgment on the basis of an incorrect analysis, the judgment I come up with will be false simply be-cause, owing to that incorrect analysis, it will fail to be constituted in such a way as to correspond to any fact in the world. To illustrate, suppose that on some evening there is a lot of dust in the atmosphere. Suppose that Max makes the perceptually based judgment that the moon is reddish. On Rus-sell's account, Max's judgment will contain a constituent—namely, red-dishness—that fails to occur as a constituent of the fact he is actually ac-quainted with, namely the fact of the (illuminated) moon's being white (or

---

[15]Cf. 'The fundamental characteristic which distinguishes propositions (whatever they may be) from objects of acquaintance is their truth or falsehood' (1913: 108). In this re-mark Russell is, of course, using 'proposition' loosely.

[16]'*Analysis* may be defined as the discovery of the constituents *and the manner of combination of a given complex*' (1913: 119 emphasis added).

non-uniform, greyish white).[17] According to the same account, the judgment comes to contain this extraneous element as the result of a flawed analysis of the fact perceived, and in virtue of containing this element it fails to correspond to any fact in the world.

In *Principia* (43) Russell suggests a further wrinkle, namely, the idea that (correct) analysis involves the subject's *attending* to the constituents of the fact to be analyzed.[18] When an analysis is incorrect, the subject will presumably have failed to attend to one or more of the complex's constituents (or will have failed to attend to their mode of combination—but we will set this complication aside).

When the faulty analysis leads to an incorrect perceptually based judgment, the situation will typically involve the subject's standing in the relation of analysis to elements that are not contained in the perceived fact. In these cases it seems natural to say that, owing to the flawed analysis, the complex fact will be *perceived as* containing elements that it does not in fact contain. It is plausible to suppose that Russell would regard such a state not as a *sui generis* multiple relation, but rather as constituted by the subject's being acquainted with a certain fact while at the same time engaging in a certain analysis of it. At any rate, this detail aside, we clearly have here the seeds of an account of how Russell might have been thinking in *POP* of the interrelations between non-veridical perception, analysis, and false perceptually based judgment.

6 Memory and Certainty

Before drawing this essay to a close I want to consider a final group of remarks that might seem to contain the last best hope for holdouts against the non-Cartesian interpretation I have been recommending. These remarks occur in the course of Russell's discussion of memory and self-evidence in the eleventh chapter of *POP* ('On Intuitive Knowledge'). In the course of arguing that memory judgments form a spectrum according to their degree of self-evidence, Russell remarks:

> Broadly speaking, memory is trustworthy in proportion to the vividness of the experience and to its nearness in time. If the house next door was struck by lightning half a minute ago, my memory of what I saw and heard will be so reliable that it would be preposterous to doubt whether there had been a flash at all. And the same applies to less vivid experiences, so long

---

[17]Here I follow Russell in treating material objects as objects of acquaintance purely for the sake of illustration.

[18]I am grateful to Fatema Amijee for drawing this point to my attention. See her 2013: 1186 for further discussion.

as they are recent. *I am absolutely certain that half a minute ago I was sitting in the same chair in which I am sitting now.* (1912: 115, emphasis added)

What are in question here are memory *judgments*: for example, my memory *that* I was stuck by lightning half a minute ago. In describing some of these judgments as 'absolutely certain' Russell certainly seems to be going against his claim that all our knowledge is infected with some degree of doubt. How can the discrepancy be explained?

I think we must infer that here Russell is using 'absolutely certain' in a non-technical way. He is describing cases in which we place extremely high confidence in our judgments but not the highest degree we might place in them. There are two considerations that support this conclusion. First, we know that Russell's official view in *POP* is that my knowledge that I am sitting in a chair—or more generally that my body is related in such-and-such a way to some other physical object—is something I can gain only by means of an abductive inference (1912: ch. 2). Accordingly, this knowledge must be infected with the usual doubts attending such inferences (cf. *CP* 8: 187). But if so, it seems that I cannot after all be certain that half a minute ago I was sitting in a chair—let alone that it was the same chair that I am sitting in now. Second, when Russell shifts to a more theoretical register, it becomes clear that memory-based judgments are not after all supposed to have the highest degree of self-evidence. Thus he says:

> Truths of perception and some of the principles of logic have the very highest degree of self-evidence; truths of immediate memory have an *almost* equally high degree. (1912: 117, emphasis added)

Arguably, then, when he steps back from the examples and theorizes about his hierarchy of 'self-evidence', Russell rejects any commitment to the idea that memory-based judgments possess the highest degree of certainty. We may, I think, take those of his remarks that appear to suggest otherwise to be nothing more than incautious formulations of his official view, which is simply that such judgments lie near one extreme of a spectrum running from beliefs held with some weak degree of confidence to those held with something akin to what is usually called 'moral certainty'.

7 Conclusion

I have argued that in *POP* Russell did not, contrary to Geach, endorse a Cartesian version of foundationalism. To be sure, he did embrace some species of foundationalism—for he sees our knowledge of truths as structured hierarchically and our reasons for our beliefs as tracing back to certain basic or 'intuitive' beliefs that receive no further justification (1912: 133). Nonetheless, the foundation does not comprise a body of beliefs that are known with certainty to be true in virtue of being beliefs about items—sense-data—upon which acquaintance affords us some privileged epistemic vantage point. Nor are these foundational beliefs at this stage yet conceived of as capable of resisting what Russell would come to call 'the solvent influence of critical reflection' (1914: 77–8)

Commentators can hardly be blamed for having missed these points. Russell's terminology in *POP* manifests the usual Russellian wobbliness, and the customary instability seems to have been exacerbated in this case by the pace at which his 'shilling shocker' was composed. Most importantly of all, his claim that acquaintance with a fact is an 'infallible guarantee' of the truth of the corresponding judgment is a highly misleading way of communicating his hedged—and far less interesting—thought that if a subject is acquainted with a fact, then, because that fact must exist for the subject to be acquainted with it, the corresponding judgment, if the subject can get so far as to form it, must be true. Nonetheless, the view Russell endorses, although roughly stated, is at least coherent, and the apparently conflicting texts can—or so I hope to have shown—be made to lie flat.

What motivates Russell's view in *OD* that we are not acquainted with material objects turns out to be no precipitous endorsement of Cartesian epistemology, but rather the need to defend the coherence of the basic notion of substitution that lies at the heart of the logical theory in which in 1905 Russell had planned to carry out his logicist reduction, namely, the so-called 'substitutional theory'.[19] As one might expect of a thinker as creative and independent-minded as Russell, it is not—or not only—the philosophical tradition that shapes his early epistemology: the commitments he incurs in the course of developing and refining his logical system also play an important role.[20]

References

Amijee, F. The Role of Attention in Russell's Theory of Knowledge. *British Journal for the History of Philosophy* 21: 1175–93.

Bradley F. H. 1893. *Appearance and Reality: A Metaphysical Essay*. Oxford: Clarendon, 1930.

---

[19]For details see Proops 2011.

[20]For their help with this essay I would like to thank Fatema Amijee, Sinan Dogramaci, Alex Grzankowski, Katherine Dunlop, Nicholas Griffin, Jeremy Heis, Peter Hylton, Mark Johnston, Bernard Linsky, Jim Levine, Mike Martin, Bryan Pickel, Michael Potter, Mark Sainsbury, Nicole Smith, Peter Sullivan, and Donovan Wishon.

Frege, G. 1980. *Philosophical and Mathematical Correspondence*, ed. G. Gabriel et al. Chicago: University of Chicago Press. Abridged from the German edition by B. McGuinness and H. Kaal.

Geach, P. 1957. *Mental Acts*. London: Routledge and Kegan Paul.

James, W. 1890. *The Principles of Psychology*. 2 vols. New York: Dover, 1950.

Levine, J. 2005. Aboutness and the Argument of 'On Denoting'. *On Denoting 1905–2005*, eds. B. Linsky and G. Imaguire, 1–69. Munich: Philosophia Verlag.

Ludlow, P. 2011. Descriptions. *The Stanford Encyclopedia of Philosophy*, Winter 2011 edition, eds. E. N. Zalta. Stanford, CA: Stanford University. http://plato.stanford.edu/archives/win2011/entries/descriptions/.

Miah, S. 2006. *Russell's Theory of Perception, 1905–1919*. London: Continuum.

Proops, I. 2011. Russell on Substitutivity and the Abandonment of Propositions. *Philosophical Review* 120: 151–205. ["Russell on Substitutivity"]

Proops, I. Forthcoming. Russellian Acquaintance Revisited. *Journal of the History of Philosophy*.

Russell, B. 1905 On Denoting. *Mind* 14: 479–93. Reprinted in *Logic and Knowledge: Essays, 1901–1950*, ed. R. Marsh, 41–56. [*OD*]

Russell, B. 1912. *Problems of Philosophy*. London: Williams and Norgate. Reprinted Oxford: Oxford University Press 1959. [*POP*]

Russell, B. 1913. *Theory of Knowledge: The 1913 Manuscript*, ed. E. R. Eames. London. Routledge 1992. [*TK*]

Russell, B. 1914. *Our Knowledge of the External World*. London: Routledge 1993. [*OKEW*]

Russell, B. 1956. *Logic and Knowledge: Essays, 1901–1950*, ed. R. Marsh. London: Unwin Hyman.

Russell, B. 1984. *The Collected Papers of Bertrand Russell, Volume 7: Theory of Knowledge: The 1913 Manuscript*, ed. E. R. Eames with K. Blackwell. London: George Allen and Unwin. [*CP 7*]

Russell, B. 1992. *The Collected Papers of Bertrand Russell, Volume 6: Logical and Philosophical Papers, 1909–13*, ed. J. G. Slater with B. Frohmann. London: Routledge. [*CP 6*]

Russell, B. 1994. *The Collected Papers of Bertrand Russell, Volume 4: Foundations of Logic, 1903–05*, ed. A. Urquhart with A. C. Lewis. London: Routledge. [*CP 4*]

Russell, B., and A. N. Whitehead. 1910. *Principia Mathematica to *56*. Cambridge: Cambridge University Press 1990. 2nd ed. 1927. [*PM*]

4

Acquaintance and Certainty in
The Problems of Philosophy

BERNARD LINSKY

1   Introduction

Bertrand Russell begins *The Problems of Philosophy* with this familiar question:

> Is there any knowledge in the world which is so certain that no reasonable man could doubt it? (1912: 7)[1]

Then, later, in Chapter V 'Knowledge by Acquaintance and Knowledge by Description', we are given the distinction between *knowledge of* things, including knowledge by acquaintance, and *knowledge of truths* about things. Russell says that when one is acquainted with the sense-data of the colour of the table in front of him we know the colour 'perfectly and completely' (1912: 47).

It would seem that acquaintance with sense data provides the answer to Russell's quest for what can be known with certainty. This is the view about sense data that came to be discussed more later in the Twentieth Century as the new analytic philosophy developed, that sense data are a source of certain knowledge which provides a foundation for the rest of our empirical

---

[1]An earlier version of this paper was read at the conference from which these papers arise. I am indebted to Ian Proops, Michael Kremer, Peter Hylton for discussion and especially to Fatema Amijee whose prepared commentary on my paper helped me considerably in preparing this essay.

Acquaintance, Knowledge, and Logic.
Donovan Wishon and Bernard Linsky (eds.).
Copyright © 2015, CSLI Publications.

knowledge. When philosophers of perception wanted to criticize the notion of sense data, one approach would be to argue that we are not certain of properties of sense data, for example, we do not know with certainty that two shades of color are the same, as they might differ slightly, below the thresh hold of discrimination.[2]

I want to argue against this view of how, at this time in Russell's thinking, sense-data provide 'certain' foundational judgments of perception, which are themselves 'certain'. In fact the only knowledge that we have of sense data with anything like certainty is at most knowledge that they exist, that is, all we know is that we are experiencing, or having the sense datum. Any judgments of experience that we may make based on experience rely on our analysis of the facts that are presented to us in experience, and in this analysis we may make an error. Judgments of the existence of sense data, and of certain basic logical and mathematical truths, are the only knowledge which we have which is certain in the sense of the opening line of the book.

My position on certain knowledge about sense data may not be news to scholars of *The Problems of Philosophy*, nor do philosophers talk as much about sense-data in this way outside of historical discussions.[3] I allude to these views in order to motivate a discussion of Russell's notion of sense data and certain knowledge, and also to fit this view in *Problems* into Russell's thinking and its changes. *Problems* was Russell's first book on philosophy after completing *Principia Mathematica* (hereafter *PM*), and was accompanied by papers and then books, on philosophy aimed at issues in epistemology and metaphysics, indeed, it has seemed, the end of Russell's interest in logic, and so a 'turn' in his philosophy. This turn away from logic was not as dramatic as some suggest. Russell continued to be interested in logical issues through his preparation of the second edition of *Principia Mathematica* in 1925, so it is not true that Russell had abandoned interest in logic in 1910. Indeed the *Philosophy of Logical Atomism* lectures maintained his interest in regions of philosophical logic that interact with his epistemology of acquaintance an analysis, and his metaphysics of facts and doubts about judgments and beliefs.

Sense data are now standardly introduced in this way, whether by their supporters or critics:

---

[2]See Sanford 1981, for example.
[3]See the entry on Sense Data in *The Stanford Encyclopedia of Philosophy*. Frank Jackson 1977 is a counter-example, and the very increase in interest in sense data is mentioned in the introduction to this volume.

> Sense data are the alleged mind-dependent objects that we are directly aware of in perception, and that have exactly the properties they appear to have. (Huemer 2011: 1)

The first feature is what is most important for Russell, that sense data are the direct objects of perception. Soon after writing *Problems*, in 1913, while he was preparing the lectures that became *Our Knowledge of the External World*, Russell began to think of sense data as existing even when not perceived, as *sensibilia*. Their existence was no longer dependent on a mind that was aware of them, merely their status as sense data, but they are initially discovered through the analysis of mental acts of perception, and not theoretical entities hypothesized by physical science. The second feature of sense-data, of having the properties that things appear to have, itself comes in two aspects, the second of which is crucial for this investigation. One aspect of having apparent properties is that sense data are supposed to literally possess the properties that perceived objects *appear* to have. Thus many have argued that there is a difference between the phenomenal property of 'red', and the physical properties of reflectance that is responsible for it. The sense data of an apple which appears red is actually *red*, and that whether or not the physical object has that property. But this notion of sense data having the properties that physical objects appear to is also meant to have epistemological force, the second aspect of having the properties things appear to, which is of most importance here. We can be certain that the sense data have those properties that the object may only appear to have. For some defenders of sense data, including, famously, A.J. Ayer 1940, the notion of sense data fits into a foundationalist (empiricist) epistemology. We can be certain of the properties of appearances, that is, of sense data, and our knowledge of matter and its properties is derived, with less certainty, from this foundation of certain knowledge of experience in the form of certain knowledge of our sense data. This view that we have certainty about our sense data was criticized by J.L. Austin (1962), *Sense and Sensibilia*, and is not part of fallibilist, yet foundationalist, epistemologies which have since become common, but it is a view that some incorrectly find in Russell. First, then, Russell's notion of acquaintance. Acquaintance is explained in *Problems* as follows:

> We shall say that we have *acquaintance* with anything of which we are directly aware, without the intermediary of any process of inference or any knowledge of truths. Thus in the presence of my table I am acquainted with the sense-data that make up the appearance of my table — its colour, shape, hardness, smoothness, etc.; all these are things of which I am immediately conscious when I am seeing and touching the table. The particular shade of colour that I am seeing may have many things said about it —

> I may say that it is brown, that it is rather dark, and so on. But such state-
> ments, though they make me know truths *about* the colour, do not make
> me know the colour itself any better than I did before: so far as concerns
> knowledge of the colour itself, as opposed to knowledge of truths about it,
> I know the colour perfectly and completely when I see it, and no further
> knowledge of it itself is even theoretically possible. Thus the sense-data
> which make up the appearance of my table are things with which I have
> acquaintance, things immediately known to me just as they are. (Russell
> 1912: 46–7)

To say that we have direct awareness of an object 'without the intermediary
of any process of inference' is not to say that the knowledge consists of
self-evident knowledge from perception, but rather that we know the object
without the intermediary of any 'knowledge of truths'. It is thus a species of
'knowledge of objects' which Russell contrasts with 'knowledge of truths',
what we might call 'knowledge of' rather than 'knowledge that'. This is a
logical distinction between a relation between a knower and an *object*, or
individual, and a relation between a knower and a *proposition* that gives us
what is known. That knowledge relates us to propositions is now embedded
in the notion of knowledge as a 'propositional attitude', and its representation as an operator in epistemic logic. But Russell also has the notion of a
direct sort of knowledge of objects, of the former sort, and this is the category into which acquaintance falls. It is in this sense, of knowledge of the
color of the table as object, that he has 'completely and perfectly, and no
further knowledge of it is even theoretically possible'. It is important to
notice that further knowledge is not even 'theoretically' possible. This is a
consequence of the logical form of 'acquaintance', and so the theory that
produces further knowledge is logic rather than some theory of knowledge
in a more contemporary sense of a theory that concerns itself with the justification of knowledge of propositions.

How little it is that we may know about an object with which we are
acquainted appears in the criticism of Hegel, who, according to Russell,
thought that to know an object we must know its nature, and that nature
includes its relations with other objects, and so on:

> There is a confusion, when this use of the word 'nature' is employed, be-
> tween knowledge of things and knowledge of truths. We have knowledge
> of a thing by acquaintance even if we know very few propositions about it
> —theoretically we need not know any propositions about it. Thus, ac-
> quaintance with a thing does not involve knowledge of its 'nature' in the
> above sense. (1912: 144)

This last sentence, 'acquaintance with a thing does not involve knowledge
of its "nature" in the above sense', was added to *Problems* after Russell had
circulated the first draft for comments. It makes even more definite a view

that he had in the book, but which could be misunderstood. In a letter to Russell's editor, Gilbert Murray, on 20 August 1911, we have a discussion of some corrections that Russell had made:

> As for Hegel, I stick to my point, and have merely expanded the statement Hegel turns (as do your objections, I think) on confusing knowledge of things with knowledge of truths. Acquaintance with a thing does not (theoretically) involve any knowledge of truths about the thing, and in practice involves often very little such knowledge. (Russell 1992: xliv)

Thus being acquainted with the color of the table may seem to have the very property of appearances that we know with certainty if we believe in sense data. When we perceive a table that appears brown, one would think, we have a sense datum that *is* brown, and so, it would seem that is something we know with certainty. But Russell says that we there are 'many things said about it', including, 'that it is brown', but those are *not* something that is part of knowing the object of acquaintance any more perfectly! If we do not know from acquaintance with it that a sense datum of a brown desk *is brown* then we do not need to know any truths at all, and, that, Russell says, is true 'theoretically' and mostly so 'in practice'.

To show what is known about an object of acquaintance, despite this knowledge being 'complete or perfect', let me turn to something which Ian Proops has argued to follow from the claim about acquaintance. In his contribution to this volume, Proops also correctly argues that Russell does not mean that acquaintance is at the highest level of a feature that comes in degrees. It must be all or nothing, one is acquainted with an object, or not. Proops argues against the view that Russell abandoned the view that we can be acquainted with matter and instead only with sense data on the grounds that we can be certain of the existence of sense data and not of the existence of matter, an argument based on 'Cartesian' certainty about sense data. He goes on, however, in Proops 2011, to draw further conclusions about the objects of acquaintance in Russell's philosophy, based on pushing the consequences of this anti-Cartesian account of acquaintance. The body of this paper will consist of an argument for the limitation of these insights for understanding of Russell's views about the objects of acquaintance in this period. In particular I will argue that the notion of acquaintance works well with perceptions of simple sensory qualities, such as a patch of 'brown color' in the visual field, but not in as direct a way with even complex sense data, such as the perception of the brown table in Russell's example, or some of the other categories of objects to which acquaintance is attributed at various times, in particular, remembered objects, universals, and propositions. I will conclude with a return to the comparison with Descartes' *Medi-*

tations and draw some conclusions about Russell's the notion of 'logical construction' of matter in his philosophy after *Problems*.

2   Acquaintance and Complexes

One reason that might be attributed for Russell to abandon the notion that we can be acquainted with material objects, Proops argues, comes from the possibility of what he calls 'George IV cases' involving singular terms. Russell famously argues, in 'On Denoting', that it is possible for George IV to wonder whether Scott is the author of *Waverly* without wondering whether Scott is Scott, on the grounds that while 'Scott' may be a 'logically proper name' for an object of acquaintance, but 'The author of *Waverly*' expresses a disguised description. Discussions of 'On Denoting' do not provide a proper analysis, Proops argues, for cases with two apparently proper names, such as 'Scott is Sir Walter'. These are Proops calls 'George IV cases'. Some might argue that there simply are no different beliefs attributed by 'Scott' and 'Sir Walter' on the grounds that both are disguised definite descriptions of material objects rather than sense data.[4] My interest here is in a principle that Proops attributes to Russell as leading to his alternative account of names and acquaintance in 'On Denoting'. Proops argues that there simply cannot be 'George IV cases' because in acquaintance we cannot be presented with the same object via distinct 'facets' or 'aspects' in such a way that there could be such cases, because Russell is committed to this principle:

> Full Disclosure: Whenever a subject, S, is acquainted (in Russell's technical sense of that term) with an object, x, S is acquainted with every part of x (Proops 2011: 152)

Proops argues that Russell adopts this in order to avoid the situation in which objects of acquaintance happen, as a matter of contingent fact, to be involved in genuinely informative, true, identities. The only way, it might seem, that something we are acquainted with *a*, might be identical with *b*, is if we could perhaps be acquainted with some part of the object when we name it '*a*', but some other parts when it is seen under the guise of '*b*'. Then, without having to make any judgments that these are parts of the

---

[4]Others, who wish to argue that in 'On Denoting' Russell believes that we can have acquaintance with material objects, such as Donovan Wishon forthcoming, will have other accounts of these cases.

same sense data, one would not be able to be informed by learning the identity '$a = b$'.[5]

I suggest, however, that this interpretation of 'aspects' or 'perspectives' as 'parts' of perceptual objects is not in keeping with Russell's thinking about complex objects in his 'logical atomist' philosophy.[6] Throughout a long period in Russell's thinking about complex objects, the relation of a whole to its parts is not the relation between objects that we see it to be in the generations after the discovery of mereology. For Russell the only complex objects, including objects with parts, are 'complexes'. This are, for Russell, facts, a's being F, or the fact that aRb, and the relation of a constituent object to such a fact is to be discovered by analysis.[7] That does not mean finding the objects which bear a relation of *part of* to a larger objects, but of finding a fact of which they are constituents.[8] We now see the notion of 'analysis' is ambiguous between the dissection of an object into its parts, and the analysis of a proposition. Russell, however had only one notion of analysis, and it was the analysis of the real complexes in the world, first propositions, and then, after he gave up on propositions, of facts in the world.

This way of thinking about the relation of part and whole is now difficult for us to comprehend, since the development of mereology as the first order theory of individuals related by the 'part of' relation. Since the arguments of Leonard and Goodman (1940) about the first order nature of the theory of part and whole, and identification of it as the theory of a genuinely nominalist metaphysics without the differences of category that exist between objects and propositions, or objects and facts. We naturally distinguish between the complexity of wholes made up of parts and the complexity of propositions or facts, and their constituents. But Russell does not.

One way of making clear this alien conception of part and whole is to consider the view that Wittgenstein rejects in §60 of the *Philosophical Investigations*.

> 60. When I say "My broom is in the corner", is this really a statement about the broomstick and the brush? Well, it could at any rate be replaced by a statement giving the position of the stick and the position of the brush. And this statement is surely a further analysed form of the first one.
> — But why do I call it "further analysed"? (2009)

---

[5] I am indebted to Ian Proops and Fatema Amijee for their explanations of the Full Disclosure principle.

[6] See Klement in this volume.

[7] See the discussion in the introduction to *Principia Mathematica* (1910-13: 43–4).

[8] I have argued this before in my proposed solution to the problem of why Russell abandoned propositions by 1910. See Linsky 1999.

Most contemporary philosophers would share Wittgenstein's view that a broom is not to be logically analyzed into the handle and the brush, which are the real objects in the world. A broom is a perfectly good object, which is made of several parts held together by nails and wire.

I claim that Proops' principle of 'Full Disclosure' cannot apply to acquaintance because any knowledge of the parts of an object must come from analysis, whether of a fact or of a proposition, and both sources only yield something knowledge of truths, including knowledge of truths about objects, but acquaintance with an object does not provide that.

Proops does not hold that his Full Disclosure principle requires that we have anything more than acquaintance with the parts of whatever we are acquainted with. As Fatema Amijee has argued, 'knowledge by acquaintance of the parts of an object (whether simple or complex) does not require knowledge of those parts *as parts*'.[9] But it seems rather that is still the case that we can make the judgment that a is F, and that b is G, and it still can be an issue for us whether $a = b$. Proops argues that if we know a through one 'part' and b through another, then the judgment that a is F is still just the same as the judgment that b is F, so there can be no 'George IV case' for a and b. My claim is that judging that a is F by means of a 'part' of a is to make a judgment that something with that part is F, hence this is different from the judgment that b is F, even though $a = b$. It is not, as he would claim, the same judgment about the same individual in each case, just *via* different parts. We do not resolve the question of whether it is the same judgment simply from our acquaintance with a and b. Instead we have to work back from our analysis of the propositions, to know whether they are about the same individual. This also follows if our acquaintance is by means of different 'parts' of an object. Being acquainted with a and b will not provide us with knowledge of truths of any sort, and not of knowledge of the parts of some object, for that must come from the analysis of 'knowledge that', of propositions. My argument is that a 'facet' or 'aspect' of an object of acquaintance is some property that is judged to be true of the object, not a part of the object. We cannot perceive 'Scott' and 'Sir Walter' through different perceptual 'facets' or 'aspects' simply by perceiving them as parts. 'Facets' and 'aspects' are properties that things have, like being the author of *Waverley* is for Scott.[10]

---

[9] In written comments on a presentation of an earlier version of this paper.

[10] Proops has a response to this argument in his contribution to this volume. He charges that this interpretation of aspects and facets of sense data as arising through judgment will lead to an infinite regress. As well, his claim is that Russell abandoned 'Full Disclosure' soon after 'On Denoting' on the basis that it would not work for acquaintance with propositions.

Now it is clear that Russell does seem to hold that sense data are not simple, in the sense that they may have parts.[11] In a passage in *Our Knowledge of the External World*, for example, he says:

> We have first of all to observe that there are no infinitesimal sense-data: any surface we can see, for example, must be of some finite extent. We assume that this applies, not to sense-data: any surface we can see, for example, must be of some finite extent. We assume that this applies, not only to sense data, but to the whole of the stuff composing the world: whatever is not an abstraction has some finite spatio-temporal size, though we cannot discover a lower limit to the sizes that are possible. But what appears as one undivided whole is often found, under the influence of attention, to split up into parts contained within the whole. Thus one spatial datum may be contained within another, and entirely enclosed by the other. This relation of enclosure, by the help of some very natural hypotheses, will enable us to define a "point" as a certain set of spatial objects; roughly speaking, the set will consist of all volumes which would naturally be said to contain the point. (1914: 120)

Thus sense-data with which we are acquainted may be complex, they can have one as a spatial part of another. But any inference which relies on changing attention from one part to another, or to the whole, which might be involved in the sort of identification judgment '$a=b$', will require a move from direct acquaintance with the sense datum as an object, to some judgment about it as a complex composed of parts, to the very sort of the *analysis* of an object into parts that Wittgenstein later came to reject.

3 Acquaintance and Memory

In the particular case of sense data I think there is yet another reason why there cannot be such problems of 're-identification' through different 'parts'.[12] Sense data are too fleeting and limited to one perspective for us ever to be in a situation where we might wonder whether 'two' sense data are really one. When we see a brown patch (say on the table), look away and then look again, perhaps after having moved, we have a new sense datum. When two people look at the table, or one person in two ways, say in a mirror and directly, we encounter distinct sense data. Russell might seem to say some things seemingly incompatible with this view, in particular in holding that memory is one way in which we are acquainted with particulars. Now it is true that a sense datum from the past no longer exists, and

---

[11]I am indebted to Fatema Amijee for this particular reference, although Peter Hylton and Rosalind Carey directed my attention to several others, in the same discussion.

[12]Not in the sense of the four-dimensionalist's *temporal parts*. See Evans 1982: 126. Evans gets the term and notion from Strawson 1959.

that in all the examples of acquaintance from sensation, we are only now acquainted with what now exists. Russell does say in *Problems* that an intuitive judgment of memory is one that involves, '... having immediately before the mind an object which is recognized as past' (1912: 115). But Russell precedes this by distinguishing the *image* involved in memory with the *object* of memory:

> There is some danger of confusion as to the nature of memory, owing to the fact that memory of an object is apt to be accompanied by an image of the object, and yet the image cannot be what constitutes memory. This is easily seen by merely noticing that the image is in the present, whereas what is remembered is known to be in the past. Moreover, we are certainly able to some extent to compare our image with the object remembered, so that we often know, within somewhat wide limits, how far our image is accurate; but this would be impossible unless the object, as opposed to the image, were in some way before the mind. Thus the essence of memory is not constituted by the image, but by having immediately before the mind an object which is recognized as past. (1912: 114–5)

If the way in which a sense datum is remembered, of 'having it immediately before the mind', or to be acquainted with it in memory, is to have before the mind an object which can be recognized as past, then it seems that we can be acquainted in memory with things that no longer exist.

To remember a sense datum would, it seems, be to come to be acquainted with the sense datum a second time, and so would, presumably, require us to know that it is the same sense datum, to re-identify it. In this way Russell has a rather novel theory of memory, at least for those of us who have knowledge of Martin and Deutscher's 'causal theory of memory' (1966). So perhaps Russell saw memory not as a case of a new relation of acquaintance with a sense datum with which we were once acquainted, mediated by acquaintance with a present image, but as a *resumption* of that same relationship of acquaintance. Maybe in the past we were acquainted with a brown sense datum, say when looking at a table, but now, when remembering it, we are able to extend that acquaintance back through time, to the original experience, and not re-identifying a single sense datum with which we are acquainted on two different occasions.[13]

---

[13]See Martin 2001 and Pears 1975 for a discussion of Russell's theory of memory in *Problems*. I am grateful for discussions of the relevance of 'episodic memory' to Russell's views to Rodrigo Jungmann de Castro, at the Third International Symposium on Philosophy of Language and Metaphysics at the Federal University at Fluminense, Brazil, April, 2013.

4   Acquaintance and Names

According to Proops, Russell identifies those things with which we can be acquainted with those for which we have (logically proper) names. Russell does conclude his discussions of descriptions by saying that the theory of descriptions explains the importance of identity (Russell 1905: 492). But, of course, the only occurrence of the identity symbol in the theory of descriptions is flanking bound variables. There is another possible use, namely, when the context of the description involves a name identified with a description, as in '$a = (\imath x)(\phi x)$', where a is a name, as in 'Scott is the Author of *Waverley*'.

Russell never discusses proper 'Frege cases' of the 'Hesperus is Phosphorus' sort, in which two names are identified.[14] Even in his notes on Frege's works, including 'On Sense and Reference', Russell does not comment on the examples involving the morning star and the evening star, and in other works, merely points out that in these cases both 'meaning' and 'denotation' are involved (his terms for *Sinn* and *Bedeutung*).[15] It does appear that Russell thought that the case of informative identities was to be explained solely with the notion of definite descriptions, thus denying that identities involving names could be informative.

It is no accident that in Russell's fully developed logic, *Principia Mathematica*, there are no individual constants, that is, no names at all. The only occurrence of identities will be flanked by individual variables, of the form '$x = y$', where both 'x' and 'y' are bound earlier in the formula. Russell viewed *PM* as a pure logic rather than an applied one. The project of *PM* is to reduce as much mathematics to pure logic as possible. In the later portions of Vol.III, for example, the theory of measurement is developed as the theory of certain abstract structures, and there is no discussion of the application to actual quantities (a feature which is quite striking in a theory of *measurement*).

Perhaps Russell's turn to the theory of knowledge and metaphysics, after the completion of *PM*, was in a move into areas in which logic could be applied. It is possible that his return to the issues of knowledge of truths and knowledge (by acquaintance) of objects was just such a step. But in that case one cannot say that the views about acquaintance with the constituents of propositions, such as acquaintance with sense data, are built into the no-

---

[14]Frege considers 'the Morning Star' and 'the Evening Star' to be *names*, not distinguishing a separate category of definite descriptions for the purposes of the theory of 'On Sense and Reference'.
[15]See Linsky 2004: 144.

tions of philosophical logic, such as individual, proposition, and propositional function, with which Russell was working.

5 Acquaintance and Universals

In addition to sense data, Russell says that we are acquainted with some universals. Can we have 'George IV cases' with universals? Consider the situation, which Russell himself raises in Chapter XIII of *Problems*, of an object slowly changing hue, so slowly that we are not able to discriminate or identify its colors? It certainly would seem that seeing a colored sense datum, and then seeing one of a different color, would be a case where we are faced with an '$a = b$' case. Again we run into the question of the application of logic. As Proops defines it, acquaintance is the mechanism for giving logically proper names their denotation. Yet there are no names in *PM*. What about universals? Again we have a problem in figuring out how *PM* is to be applied. As I have claimed before, I think there is no obvious way to apply *PM* to the theory of universals.[16] It is clear that propositional functions are not to be identified with universals. This is because propositional functions are not constituents of the propositions that are their values. The analysis of a proposition, such as Socrates is human, as the value of a function, x is human, for an argument, Socrates, is different from the analysis of the proposition into its constituents, Socrates, and the universal of humanity. Gregory Landini (in this volume and elsewhere) argues that a universal will be an individual in Russell's logic, the sort of thing that individual variables range over, and which names would name, if there were any. My alternative proposal is that they stand as the meaning of atomic predicates 'F' (opposed to the function 'x is F'). In the first case, but not in the second, it does seem that if one were acquainted with a universal, and then later, with the same universal, there would be propositions about the universal using distinct logically proper names, say 'humanity', and there would be a question of whether those are identical. In any case, this is a problem that presents itself when Russell moved to the consideration of the application of *Principia Mathematica* logic.

To see how poorly the notion of acquaintance as an epistemological notion fits with Russell's views on universals, consider the familiar argument for the existence of universals in Chapter IX of *Problems*.[17] Russell does not argue from any experience of acquaintance with universals, nor that

---

[16]See Linsky 1999.

[17]The history of regress arguments in Russell's thinking is traced by Katarina Perovic in this volume.

knowledge of universals requires direct acquaintance with them, as in the arguments for sense data in the first chapters. Instead we get the indirect argument against a theory of universals that is inspired by the nominalist empiricists, such as Berkeley or Hume, and more directly by Gestalt psychology.[18] The alternative is that in experience we are not acquainted with universal or 'abstract ideas', but instead only with particulars. We do have experiences of particulars as similar, and so may analyze a supposed universal such as 'whiteness or triangularity' in terms of the similarity of particular white or triangular things with each other. This is the project which was later carried further by Rudolf Carnap (1967) by comparison of 'total experiences', and then in the explicitly nominalist project of Nelson Goodman's *Structure of Appearance* (1951). Russell argues that if we think it is possible to avoid universals by instead talking of judgments of similarity then we still are committed to the presumably universal *relation* of similarity. As he says:

> It will be useless to say that there is a different resemblance for each pair, for then we shall have to say that these resemblances resemble each other, and thus at last we shall be forced to admit resemblance as a universal. The relation of resemblance, therefore, must be a true universal. And having been forced to admit this universal, we shall find that it is no longer worth while to invent difficult and unplausible theories to avoid the admission of such universals as whiteness and triangularity. (1912: 96–7)

This argument in no way invokes the notion of acquaintance with universals. In fact it seems to be an indirect argument for universals, namely that the judgments that we make about things being white or triangular must be analyzed in terms of some universals, whether a relation of similarity, or similarity between similarities, or, simply monadic universals of color or shape. This makes sense if universals are found to be ultimate constituents of propositions, after analysis, and that analysis is not given to us immediately in the act of judging. Acquaintance with universals then can fulfill its role of relating us to the ultimate constituents of propositions that we judge without playing a role in our recognizing what we are judging, or realizing that we are making the same judgment again. This is how some other empiricist philosophers might argue for the existence of universals, if not directly experienced, then inferred as the best explanation of what is experienced. Thus D. M. Armstrong (1989) argues that we must acknowledge the existence of universals as the only viable explanation, or at least best explanation, of our experience of objective similarities in the world.

---

[18]Russell got the argument from Meinong, who directed it against the Gestalt psychologist H. Cornelius. See the Introduction to this volume.

In Chapter X 'On our knowledge of universals', immediately after the indirect argument for universal relations, Russell says that we are acquainted with monadic universals, and uses the very example of *whiteness* from the previous chapter:

> Let us consider first the knowledge of universals by acquaintance. It is obvious, to begin with, that we are acquainted with such universals as white, red, black, sweet, sour, loud, hard, etc., i.e. with qualities which are exemplified in sense-data. When we see a white patch, we are acquainted, in the first instance, with the particular patch; but by seeing many white patches, we easily learn to abstract the whiteness which they all have in common, and in learning to do this we are learning to be acquainted with whiteness. A similar process will make us acquainted with any other universal of the same sort. Universals of this sort may be called 'sensible qualities'. They can be apprehended with less effort of abstraction than any others, and they seem less removed from particulars than other universals are. (1912: 101)

So we are acquainted with the monadic universals such as whiteness, which are called 'sensible qualities'. But this acquaintance is a result of the 'effort of abstraction'. In the process of abstraction we are 'learning to be acquainted with whiteness'. The first perception of white sense data does not immediately involve acquaintance with the whiteness, it requires a process of 'abstraction', which, while perhaps not the same as the analysis of facts, is a similar process, and which results in acquaintance with something other than the sense datum of which exemplifies it. Russell was of course, familiar with Berkeley's objections to the notion of abstraction, and wondered what the idea of universal such as whiteness could be other than the idea of a white thing from which it is 'abstracted', that idea used in some particular 'abstract' way. At the very least the 're-identification' of sensible qualities will not be simply the result of being directly acquainted with the same quality twice, and so an identification that cannot be informative. To identify the color F of this sense datum with the color G of a different sense datum, will presuppose having carried out the 'process' of abstraction and thus involve comparing the results of two acts of abstraction which we have learned to carry out. This is compatible with the interpretation give above of talk of the 'brown' of the table. Even though we can come to be acquainted with the shade of brown of the table, being acquainted with the color does not require that we have any such knowledge of a truth about the sense datum.

6   Acquaintance and Propositions

What Russell says explicitly about our acquaintance with propositions before he abandoned them by 1910, and thus before *Problems*, also does not support the view that acquaintance is epistemically rich. The contrary view that acquaintance does enable something like knowing the meaning of words or being able to re-identify referents is based on a certain view of the so-called 'Russell's Principle' presented in these words in *Problems*:

> Every proposition which we can understand must be composed wholly of constituents with which we are acquainted. (1912: 58)

The principle was stated earlier in 'On Denoting' in 1905:

> Thus in every proposition that we can apprehend (i.e. not only in those whose truth or falsehood we can judge of, but in all that we can think about), all the constituents are really entities with which we have immediate acquaintance. (*CP* 4: 427)

But what is it to 'apprehend' a proposition, or, simply 'think about' a proposition without judging of its truth or falsehood?[19]

Russell published 'On Denoting' in 1905, the year after his first three part paper 'Meinong's Theory of Complexes and Assumptions'.[20] In that review he goes to great lengths to refute Meinong's thesis that mental acts of 'assumption' have as their objects 'objectives' or propositions, and that this must be sharply distinguished from the 'presentations' by which objects are given to us in perception. For one thing, Meinong argues, we can only be presented with things that exist, or at least have being, whereas a judgment of a false proposition does not have any object at all. Our assumption is of something 'beyond being'.[21] What is the effect of Russell's insistence that we are in the same relation of 'presentation' to propositions that we think of or consider, that we have to objects in perception? Russell summarizes his difference with Meinong with these words:

> Two distinct attitudes occur towards objects, one that of presentation, the other of judgment. The latter is only possible towards complex objects, but

---

[19]It is interesting that Gareth Evans, who is the source of the title 'Russell's Principle' for this doctrine, speaks of 'understanding' a proposition, thus slipping his epistemological views about acquaintance into the very statement of the view. 'The Principle is that a subject cannot make a judgment about something unless he knows which object his judgment is about' (1982: 89). Michael Kremer, in his paper in this volume, agrees with this reading of the Principle as being about understanding as a competence, and citing examples where Russell uses such language to explain the principle.

[20]See Linsky 2014 for more on Meinong and Russell's notion of acquaintance with propositions.

[21]This is '*Aussersein*' in Meinong's obscure terminology.

the former is possible towards all objects. We may say that the first gives acquaintance, while the second gives knowledge, or at least belief. (*CP* 4: 463)

One should treat 'apprehending' a proposition in the statement of Russell's Principle, as not requiring that we know the meaning of a sentence, or that we know which proposition it expresses, but merely as the *presentation* of a proposition, of being acquainted with the complex object, in the way that we are presented with the simple objects which are its constituents. For Russell, in his dispute with Meinong, the most important feature of presentation of propositions is that the object of presentation exists, or rather has the being of abstract objects with some ordinary objects as constituents, and in that it is a form of acquaintance. Seen as coming directly out of Russell's dispute with Meinong over whether we are presented with propositions, or must have some other relation of assumption to only the true propositions, it is easy to see how is a direct, perception like relation to an object that has the being of abstract objects. There is no requirement that we know any at all about that with which we are acquainted.[22]

7 Conclusions About Acquaintance and Certainty

In chapter VII of *Problems*, 'On our knowledge of general principles', after talking of the principle of induction, which is itself not certain, and does not lead to certain knowledge, Russell describes 'other principles which cannot be proved or disproved by experience ...'

> Some of these principles have even greater evidence than the principle of induction, and the knowledge of them has the same degree of certainty as the knowledge of the existence of sense-data. They constitute the means of drawing inferences ... (1912: 70)

Finally, near the end of the book, in Chapter XIII, 'Knowledge, Error, and Probable Opinion', we get what seems to be an answer to the question with which the book began:

> In all cases where we know by acquaintance a complex fact consisting of certain terms in a certain relation, we say that the truth that these terms are so related has the first or absolute kind of self-evidence, and in these cases the judgement that the terms are so related *must* be true. Thus this sort of self-evidence is an absolute guarantee of truth.

---

[22]Of course, in *Problems* Russell denied that propositions are single entities to which we could be related by acquaintance. It seems however, that he has simply replace the earlier acquaintance with a proposition with acquaintance with its constituents, and is not talking about our understanding of how to use words, or our grasp of their meaning.

But although this sort of self-evidence is an absolute guarantee of truth, it does not enable us to be *absolutely* certain, in the case of any given judgement, that the judgement in question is true. Suppose we first perceive the sun shining, which is a complex fact, and thence proceed to make the judgement 'the sun is shining'. In passing from the perception to the judgment, it is necessary to analyse the given complex fact: we have to separate out 'the sun' and 'shining' as constituents of the fact. In this process it is possible to commit an error; hence even where a *fact* has the first or absolute kind of self-evidence, a judgement believed to correspond to the fact is not absolutely infallible, because it may not really correspond to the fact. (1912: 137–8)

So, although it looked as though judgments about sense data, of what one seems to perceive, are a source of certain knowledge, in fact it turns out that judgments of perception are self-evident in a way that admits of degrees, and none are the absolutely certain truths that Russell was looking for in the first sentence. Further evidence that Russell does not hold the common view of sense data as a source of certain knowledge of perception comes two paragraphs further on:

Or again: Suppose we are comparing two shades of colour, one blue and one green. We can be quite sure they are different shades of colour; but if the green colour is gradually altered to be more and more like the blue, becoming first a blue-green, then a greeny-blue, then blue, there will come a moment when we are doubtful whether we can see any difference, and then a moment when we know that we cannot see any difference. The same thing happens in tuning a musical instrument, or in any other case where there is a continuous gradation. Thus self-evidence of this sort is a matter of degree; and it seems plain that the higher degrees are more to be trusted than the lower degrees. (1912: 138–9)

It is ironic that the phenomenon of perceptual indiscriminability, as described in Donovan Wishon's forthcoming, which is sometimes taken as providing an argument *against* the existence of sense-data, is rather, for Russell, taken as providing an argument that certain judgments about perception are in fact not certain to the highest degree.[23]

The next paragraph sums up Russell's view, and so, it would seem, comes back to answer the opening question of *The Problems of Philosophy*:

From what has been said it is evident that, both as regards intuitive knowledge and as regards derivative knowledge, if we assume that intuitive knowledge is trustworthy in proportion to the degree of its self-evidence, there will be a gradation in trustworthiness, from the existence of noteworthy sense-data and the simpler truths of logic and arithmetic, which may

---

[23]See Sanford 1981 and Wishon forthcoming.

be taken as quite certain, down to judgments which seem only just more probably than their opposites. (1912: 139)

This may sound like a case of bait and switch. We are introduced to *Problems of Philosophy* by the hope for knowledge which is so 'certain that no reasonable man could doubt it'. In the end we find that certainty, in the form of self-evident truths, about the *existence* of sense data, (though not their sensory qualities), and the simpler truths of logic and arithmetic, on down to judgments that are only just more probable than their opposites.

In order to see what sort of certainty Russell thought that we are capable of attaining, let us turn briefly to another proposal for the certain knowledge for which Russell was looking. In the early chapters of *Problems* Russell responds to the idealism of Berkeley with the argument that, although we are not acquainted with matter in perception, we know do know it 'by description' as *the* source of our sense data. This position on matter is seems to have been Russell's only briefly, for soon after 1912, and certainly by the time of *Our Knowledge of the External World* matter has become a 'logical construction' for Russell, and remains so through the 1920s with *The Analysis of Matter*. It could be thought that Russell did not find the notion that matter is known by description to be an adequate response to skepticism about matter, and that the move to claiming that matter is really a logical construction of sense data, with the position known as 'neutral monism', was an attempt to argue that we do know some things about matter with the certainty with which we know the sense data out of which matter is constructed.[24] However, this is not a case where Russell was looking for certainty any more than in our knowledge about sense data. The issue that Russell faced in 'the problem of matter" was not of finding a way of showing that Berkeley was not only wrong about the existence of matter, but that we can be *certain* that matter exists. If that were his project, then the knowledge that we have of matter 'by description' would not be a very good solution, and might well be given up as a better solution came along. But a brief digression to Russell's earlier logical works, in this case *The Principles of Mathematics* from 1903:

> The nature of matter, even more than that of space, has always been regarded as a cardinal problem of philosophy. In the present work, however, we are not concerned with the question: What is the nature of the matter that actually exists? We are concerned merely with the analysis of rational Dynamics considered as a branch of pure mathematics, which intro-

---

[24]Michael Potter expresses this view. See Potter 2009: 37. This view is countered in Peter Hylton's article in this volume.

duces its subject matter by definition, not by observation of the actual world. (1903: §437)

In *Principles*, Russell's interest in matter had to do with proving certain theorems of rational dynamics. What might these include?

> The most fundamental characteristic of matter lies in the nature of its connection with space and time. Two pieces of matter cannot occupy the same place at the same moment, and the same piece cannot occupy two places at the same moment, though it may occupy two moments at the same place. (1903: §440)

When Russell turned to the method of 'logical construction' as a solution to 'the problem of matter', a problem for what he calls 'rational Dynamics'. This is the problem of proving, with certainty, that no two material objects can occupy the same place at the same time, for example. That is something that we, or at least Russell, think is certain knowledge, and the inference to matter as known by description would not solve that problem. My conclusion from this digression about the problem of matter is simply that in *Problems* Russell is not proposing to find any knowledge of matter that is certain, and so not looking for any inference from certain knowledge of sense data to knowledge of matter that will preserve certainty.[25]

We come back then to certainty about sense data. In this move from a search for certain knowledge to an understanding of the vast bulk of our empirical knowledge that is less than certain, Russell is not so different from René Descartes, who Russell is clearly echoing with his opening line. Descartes says, in his First Meditation, that to rid himself of false opinions, he must 'withhold assent no less carefully from opinions that are not completely certain and indubitable than I would from those that are patently false' (1993: 13). But then, by the Sixth Meditation, we have this:

> But now, having begun to have a better knowledge of myself and the author of my origin, I am of the opinion that I must not rashly admit everything that I seem to derive from the senses; but, neither, for that matter, should I call everything into doubt. (1993: 51)

So Russell follows Descartes in both raising the question of what knowledge is certain at the beginning of his work, but, by the end, showing that the knowledge we get from the senses is, for the most part, reliable, but not certain. Russell might put it by saying that 'no reasonable man' should

---

[25]Here I agree with Proops, Wahl and Hylton in this volume, that Russell's construction of matter is not a response to the discovery that we can only be certain of our sense data and not about matter. I disagree with them, however, about the role of matter in Russell's ontology after *Problems*.

call everything into doubt. Russell learned the bait and switch tactic from a master.

References

Armstrong, D. M. 1989. *Universals: An Opinionated Introduction.* Denver: Westview.

Austin, J. L. 1962. *Sense and Sensibilia.* Oxford: Clarendon.

Ayer, A. J. 1940. *The Foundations of Empirical Knowledge.* London: Macmillan. Reprinted in St. Martin's 1969.

Carnap, R. 1967. *The Logical Structure of the World.* tr. R. George. Berkeley: University of California.

Descartes, R. 1993. *Meditations on First Philosophy*, tr. D. A. Cress. Indianapolis: Hackett.

Evans, G. 1982. *The Varieties of Reference*, Oxford: Clarendon Press.

Goodman, N. 1951. *The Structure of Appearance.* Cambridge: Harvard University Press.

Huemer, M. 2011. Sense Data. *Stanford Encyclopedia of Philosophy*, ed. E. N. Zalta. Stanford, CA: Stanford University. http://plato.stanford.edu/entries/sense-data/

Jackson, F. 1977. *Perception: A Representative Theory.* Cambridge: Cambridge University Press.

Leonard H. S. and Goodman, N. 1940. The Calculus of Individuals and its Uses. *Journal of Symbolic Logic* 5: 45–55.

Linsky, B. 1993. Why Russell Abandoned Russellian Propositions. *Russell and Analytic Philosophy*, eds. A. D. Irvine and G. A. Wedeking, 193–209. Toronto: University of Toronto Press.

Linsky, B. 1999. *Russell's Metaphysical Logic.* Stanford: CSLI Press.

Linsky, B. 2004. Russell's Notes on Frege for Appendix A of *The Principles of Mathematics. Russell: the Journal of Bertrand Russell Studies* 24: 133–72.

Linsky, B. 2013. Russell's Notes for 'Meinong's Theory of Complexes and Assumptions'. *Russell: The Journal of Bertrand Russell Studies* 33: 143–170.

Martin, C. B. and M. Deutscher. 1966. Remembering. *The Philosophical Review* 75: 161–96.

Martin, M. G. F. 2001. Out of the Past: Episodic Recall as Retained Acquaintance. *Time and Memory: Issues in Philosophy and Psychology*, eds. C. Hoerl and T. McCormack, 257–284. Oxford: Oxford University Press.

Pears, D. F. 1975. Russell's Theories of Memory. *Questions in the Philosophy of Mind*, 224–250. London: Duckworth.

Potter, M. 2009. *Wittgenstein's Notes on Logic.* Oxford: Oxford University Press.

Proops, I. 2011. Russell on Substitutivity and the Abandonment of Propositions. *The Philosophical Review* 120: 151–205.

Russell, B. 1903. *The Principles of Mathematics*. Cambridge: University Press. (2nd printing, NY: Norton 1938).

Russell, B. 1904. Meinong's Theory of Complexes and Assumptions. *Mind* 13: 204–19, 336–54, 509–24. References to *CP* 4: 431–74.

Russell, B. 1905. On Denoting. *Mind* 14: 479–93. References to *CP* 4: 414–27.

Russell, B. 1912. *The Problems of Philosophy*. London: Williams and Norgate. Reprinted Oxford: Oxford University Press 1959.

Russell, B. 1914. *Our Knowledge of the External World*. London and Chicago: Open Court. (NY: New American Library, 1960).

Russell, B. 1927. *The Analysis of Matter*. London: Kegan Paul.

Russell, B. 1992. *Collected Papers of Bertrand Russell, Volume 6: Logical and Philosophical Papers, 1909-13*, ed. J. G. Slater with B. Frohmann. London: Routledge. [*CP* 6]

Russell, B., and A. N. Whitehead. 1925-27. *Principia Mathematica* 3 vols. Cambridge: Cambridge University Press. (1st ed., 1910-13)

Sanford, D. 1981. Illusions and Sense-data. *Midwest Studies in Philosophy* 6: 371–385.

Strawson, P. F. 1959. *Individuals: An Essay in Descriptive Metaphysics*. Methuen.

Wishon, D. Forthcoming. Russellian Acquaintance and Frege's Puzzle. *Mind*.

Wittgenstein, L. 2009. *Philosophical Investigations*, tr. G.E.M. Anscombe, revised fourth edition, P. M. S. Hacker and Joachim Schulte. New York: Wiley-Blackwell.

5

Sense-Data and the Inference to Material Objects:

The Epistemological Project in *Problems* and its Fate in Russell's Later Work

RUSSELL WAHL

1 Introduction

Russell published the *Problems of Philosophy* as an introductory book accessible to a wide audience, outlining key problems in epistemology. It includes a discussion of the problem of our knowledge of the external world, a criticism of idealism, the distinction between knowledge by acquaintance and knowledge by description, an argument in favor of realism with respect to universals, an account of *a priori* knowledge, a treatment of the problem of induction, Russell's multiple-relation theory of judgment, and a foundationalist treatment of knowledge of truths.[1] This is an enormous amount of material for such a small book. Because of the book's accessibility, it is probably the best known and most read of Russell's work today. A cursory look at contemporary anthologies of epistemology and even metaphysics

---

[1] See Linsky this volume and Proops this volume for further discussion of Russell's foundationalism with respect to truths.

Acquaintance, Knowledge, and Logic.
Donovan Wishon and Bernard Linsky (eds.).
Copyright © 2015, CSLI Publications.

reveals that when Russell's work is put in anthologies, it is generally from *Problems.*

Within ten years of the writings of *Problems*, Russell seems to have abandoned several of the central positions advocated in it. It is well known that he abandoned the multiple-relation theory of judgment. But he also modified many of the central points he had made concerning the issues of the opening chapters on what we know about the external world. Within months of the publication of *Problems*, Russell called into question the account of our knowledge of matter he had given there.[2] Russell had held that our knowledge of matter is indirect, a species of knowledge by description of causes of our sense-data. In his draft paper of 1912, 'On Matter', Russell suggested that this view was no longer tenable. Then, starting in 1914 he embraced another position, proposed, but not fully endorsed, in his unpublished 'On Matter'. This was the radical position that physical objects should be viewed as logical constructions from sense-data. Russell's rejection of the account in *Problems* and its replacement with the logical constructions of 1914 is the focus of this paper. Russell's rejection of the account of our knowledge of matter in *Problems* has often been thought a consequence of his realization that the foundational project of *Problems* was compromised, as the belief in physical objects as explained in *Problems* was not justified on the evidence we have. On this view, Russell therefore adopted the more secure position that matter should be thought of as a logical construction out of sense-data, as this position will answer the skeptical challenge.

In this paper I will examine Russell's position on our knowledge of matter as it is set out in *Problems*, look at Russell's second thoughts on this topic as they were developed in 1912–1914, and try to determine what led Russell to the new position. To accomplish this I need to examine Russell's attitude toward skepticism and determine what role it played in the development of his logical constructions. The issue is more complicated than simply a quest for greater epistemological certainty.[3]

---

[2]For a discussion of Russell's views on matter prior to *Problems* see Hylton this volume.

[3]Again, see Proops this volume and Linsky this volume for further arguments that *Problems* itself should not be viewed as endorsing a Cartesian foundationalism. Given that, it would be odd to suppose that the account of our knowledge of matter given there was abandoned for that concern.

2   Acquaintance, Sense-Data, and Inference to Material Objects in *Problems*

In the first chapter of *Problems*, Russell argued that we do not have immediate knowledge of matter, because what we immediately experience has features we do not attribute to enduring physical objects, and he defined matter simply as the collection of physical objects. He then labeled what we are immediately acquainted with 'sense-data'. While he presented the argument as showing that we are not acquainted with physical objects, it is important to realize that the argument assumes certain background assumptions about these objects, e.g. that they do not change shape or color when we move about them and that they continue to exist when we are not perceiving them. These are features he thinks we attribute to 'ordinary' physical objects such as the table in his example.

Russell took the relativity argument to show that we are not acquainted with such ordinary objects, but the argument in no way establishes that we are not acquainted with anything physical. When George Dawes Hicks suggested that Russell had argued that we are not acquainted with physical objects on principle, Russell responded by saying that he did not hold a general *a priori* reason that prohibited minds from being acquainted with physical objects, but rather that for 'various empirical reasons of detail, it is not certain that the quality which is the sense-datum ever exists at times when it is not a sense-datum' (*CP* 6: 186). The 'empirical reasons of detail' that Russell had in mind are that the qualities we perceive change with changes in us, and so seem to be dependent on our state. It is important to distinguish this concern from Berkeley's claim that being perceived by a mind is what is required for the existence of what is perceived. Russell's concerns are about physiological conditions, not the requirement that those things perceived could only exist in a mind (*CP* 6: 188). As he says in his reply to Dawes Hicks: 'I hold that the sense-datum is certainly something other than the subject, something to which the subject's relation is just as "external" as to the physical object' (*CP* 6: 186). This point is extremely important in understanding Russell's position. It is easy to see him as thinking that to be certain of things we must retreat to an inner world of mental entities of which we can be absolutely certain. But this is a position which he had rejected earlier in his 1911 'Knowledge by Acquaintance, Knowledge by Description', where he argued that such a position leads to a view that 'ideas become a veil between us and outside things – we never really, in knowledge, attain to the things we are supposed to be knowing about, but only to the ideas of those things' (*CP* 6: 155). Russell's sense-data were not ideas; they were already external to the mind.

Russell emphasized that the relation we had with things presented to us, such as sense-data, was a dual relation, rather than a multiple relation, as he held any sort of judgment or even understanding to be. He called the relation 'acquaintance' and held it to be a species of knowledge of things. Russell held that knowledge of things was primary and that it was 'simpler' and 'logically independent' of knowledge of truths. He divided knowledge of things into two varieties, knowledge by acquaintance and knowledge by description. Insofar as we are used to thinking of knowledge as propositional, we may find it misleading to call knowledge of things 'knowledge' at all. Knowledge of things simply involves having something before one's mind. Knowledge by acquaintance is prior to any conceptualization and is perhaps better understood simply as awareness. Knowledge by description does involve some conceptualization, for it involves having a description before one's mind, a description which picks out an object which can then be something we can know truths about. But what knowledge by description enables us to do is to think about and talk about objects with which we are not acquainted, and in that sense should also be seen as a species of awareness, although an indirect awareness. Knowledge by description plays an important role in Russell's account of our knowledge of matter in *Problems*, because there he held that matter was known by description as the cause of sense-data and of their order and regularity. A key claim made in *Problems* is that we can know truths about things with which we are not acquainted. Despite changes in his view of our knowledge of an external world, Russell continued to hold this view.

With respect to knowledge by acquaintance, Russell made the following claims:

> ...in the presence of my table I am acquainted with the sense-data that make up the appearance of my table – its colour, shape, hardness, smoothness, etc.; all these are things of which I am immediately conscious when I am seeing and touching my table. The particular shade of colour that I am seeing may have many things said about it – I may say that it is brown, that it is rather dark, and so on. But such statements, though they make me know truths about the colour, do not make me know the colour itself any better than I did before: so far as concerns knowledge of the colour itself, as opposed to knowledge of truths about it, I know the colour perfectly and completely when I see it, and no further knowledge of it itself is even theoretically possible. Thus the sense-data which make up the appearance of my table are things with which I have acquaintance, things immediately known to me just as they are (Russell 1912: 46–7).

This passage has been taken, not surprisingly, to hold that we have perfect knowledge about those things with which we are acquainted: that, given that they are immediately known 'just as they are', we cannot be mistaken about them, and so they can serve as a foundation for knowledge.

If Russell is seen as attempting to answer the skeptic by showing that our knowledge rests on certain foundations this would naturally be the way to understand what he is doing here, and many commentators have just assumed this. But those who think this will be puzzled by several remarks Russell made concerning the movement from knowledge of things to knowledge of truths. In particular, he did not hold that our sense-data have all and only the qualities they appear to have, a feature often attributed to sense-data theories, since he held we could be mistaken about whether two sense-data we are presented with at a given time are a different color, or the same color (1912: 138). Thus we need to understand the above passage on knowing the color perfectly and completely as being a statement about knowledge of things. This kind of knowledge does not come in degrees, but is either there or not. It in no way should be read as a claim about knowledge of truths.[4] The passage was in fact to illustrate this claim about knowledge of things by acquaintance, which he said was 'logically independent of knowledge of truths, though it would be rash to assume that human beings ever, in fact, have acquaintance with things without at the same time knowing some truths about them' (1912: 46). In a letter to Gilbert Murray on this point Russell was a bit more forceful, saying: 'Acquaintance with a thing does not (theoretically) involve *any* knowledge of truths about the thing, & in practice involves often very little such knowledge'.[5]

Knowledge by acquaintance is a required foundation for judgment in the sense that it gives the raw materials which the mind organizes in forming judgments. It is not a foundation in the sense of a foundationalist theory of propositional knowledge, as it is not propositional at all. Now in *Prob-*

---

[4]Recent work has suggested that one motivation for Russell's statement of this involves an attack on holistic idealism which held that knowledge of a particular is always partial (Proops forthcoming). What I am saying is independent of that thesis unless this claim is taken to be about knowledge of truths. Russell makes it clear that the 'complete' knowledge he is talking about here is not knowledge of truths.

5Letter to Gilbert Murray, Aug. 20, 1911 Copy in the Russell Archives, RA3 71d. In his 'Knowledge by Acquaintance, Knowledge by Causation', Thomas Baldwin claims that knowledge by acquaintance requires an object being presented in such a way that 'the subject acquires some knowledge about it, that it exists and has the properties it is presented as having' (Baldwin 2003: 422). Russell does think that given that we are presented with a sense-datum we are in a position to know that it exists, but as these remarks make clear, he sharply distinguished knowledge of things from knowledge of truths in a way Baldwin refuses to see.

lems Russell does present a foundationalist theory of knowledge with what he calls intuitive knowledge as the foundation, and all other knowledge being derivative. But importantly he characterizes intuitive knowledge as knowledge 'not...capable of being deduced from anything more evident' (1912: 111–2). He does not think most intuitive knowledge is infallible, although he does say that that with the 'highest degree' of self-evidence is (1912: 118).[6] In *Problems* Russell also held we are acquainted with facts such as that one sense-datum is next to another, and he did hold that if we were in fact acquainted with a fact, then the fact must exist, and the proposition corresponding to that fact must be true (1912: 136). However, he still thought that even if this were the case, we would never be absolutely certain that we had made the correct judgment, so that even in this case we do not have the foundational propositions that would satisfy a skeptic (1912: 137). A good way to see Russell's position on acquaintance is that knowledge by acquaintance of an object puts someone in the position of being able to know the object exists, and knowledge by acquaintance of a fact such as a-R-b puts someone in the position of being able to know that a-R-b.

Clearly on the position in *Problems* most knowledge is not going to be traceable back by absolutely self-evident principles to absolutely self-evident pieces of intuitive knowledge. Russell makes this clear in *Problems*. Russell holds that ordinary physical objects, and so matter, are inferred from the existence of sense-data as the cause of the order and regularity of this data. Russell saw this in part as an argument from simplicity and it fits what is often called the argument to the best explanation or an abductive argument, though Russell tended to call all non-deductive arguments 'inductive' (1912: 24). This argument for matter as something postulated in order to explain the order and regularity of our sense-data was the first to go in Russell's move away from the epistemology in *Problems*.[7] Coupled with his claim about the reason for the existence of matter was the further claim that we could know features of this matter only to the extent that they would help explain the observed order and regularity. Russell confined those features to the spatial and temporal order. As the existence of the objects were postulated to explain the order and regularity of sense-data, so were these spatial and temporal features.

---

[6]This issue is addressed in greater detail in Proops this volume.

[7]Another position dropped fairly early was acquaintance with the self. This is clear from the opening chapters of *Theory of Knowledge*, which were written in May of 1913.

3 Skepticism and 'On Matter'

Russell opened *Problems* with the question, 'Is there any knowledge in the world which is so certain that no reasonable man could doubt it?' This is a remark that is naturally interpreted as fitting in with classic epistemological concerns with skepticism and the quest for certainty. Russell's presentation here, and many of his remarks in other works which I will discuss, suggest that his positions on a variety of epistemological issues are driven by the need to answer the skeptic. Many of the positions Russell takes on these issues are positions it may seem no one would take unless he or she was concerned with skeptical problems and wished to retreat to a world of certainty or at least more relative certainty even at the expense of other philosophical goals. Russell's doctrine of acquaintance, with its lack of a possibility of error, the maxim of the preference of logical constructions over inferred entities, which played an important role in Russell's 1914-1915 writings, and the rejection of alleged *a priori* principles are all examples of positions which seem to be held for reasons concerned with a response to skepticism.

Russell in *Problems* and in his 1914 works was very much interested in what exactly we are licensed to affirm on the basis of our evidence, and did at times endorse Descartes's method of doubt as a proper method of inquiry. But Russell's skepticism was tempered in *Problems*. In Chapter 2 of *Problems* Russell argued that our beliefs in enduring matter were 'instinctive', and that they therefore shouldn't be given up unless confronted with another instinctive belief (Russell 1912: 25). He did not think instinctive beliefs were certain, but rather he was rejecting the position that we should accept only those beliefs which were certain. This is hardly the position of someone determined to answer the skeptic. In fact, when it came to judgments, Russell seems to have been ambivalent as to whether any could pass the skeptic's test. While he suggested in Chapter 11 (1912: 118) that there may be judgments which possess the highest degree of self-evidence and are therefore infallible, he also asserted that 'all our knowledge of truths is infected with *some* degree of doubt' (1912: 135).[8]

However, it is true that Russell appeared to have a burst of skepticism shortly after completing *Problems,* and many have seen this new-found skepticism as leading to the dissatisfaction with some of the results of *Problems* and so accounting for the changes. Much of the evidence for this new-found skepticism comes from letters Russell wrote to Lady Ottoline Morrell

---

[8]Linsky (this volume) also argues that Russell does not hold judgments about sense-data to be certain.

during 1912, and from 'On Matter'. Several of the letters suggest that it was Wittgenstein who aroused this new skepticism.[9] Commentators have seen Russell's abandonment of matter as an inferred entity and his replacement of the inferred material objects by logical constructions as driven by skeptical concerns.[10]

As we have seen, Russell held in *Problems* that even sense-data statements were liable to error, although he also held that judgments about the existence of sense-data were certain. There was no change in his views on these points in 'On Matter', nor is it skepticism about truths about sense-data which interest him. The skepticism manifest in the period immediately after the completion of *Problems* concerns doubt about the *a priori* principles required for the inference from any given existent to any other. In *Problems* Russell did not distinguish logical principles from other *a priori* principles, and sought to ground our knowledge of these principles on our awareness of relations among universals. Russell had argued there that we had knowledge of a principle of induction, but his argument did not make use of any inspection of relations among universals. Given that Russell was calling into question whether a given principle was true *a priori*, one would hope for a discussion of what should count as an *a priori* principle and perhaps a further discussion and perhaps criticism of the account given in *Problems*. Unfortunately, neither discussion is found in 'On Matter', although there are some musings on *a priori* principles in some of the parts which were deleted.

'On Matter' is a messy paper where several streams of argument are developed together. Russell revised the paper heavily after he decided that one line of thought, namely the idea of exhibiting physics in terms of his own sense-data alone, would not work. The paper states at the outset that all knowledge rests on two foundations: immediate acquaintance, 'which assures us of the existence of our thoughts and feelings and sense-data' and general principles, 'according to which the existence of one thing can be

---

[9] In a letter to Ottoline Morrell of 23 April 1912, Russell talked of discussing matter with Wittgenstein who had said that 'if there is no matter then no one exists but himself, but he says that doesn't hurt, since physics and astronomy, and all the other sciences could still be interpreted so as to be true' (letter 422). On the 24th he said, 'I haven't had enough courage hitherto about matter, I haven't been sceptical enough' (letter 423); on 29 April he said of his paper on matter, 'It will shock people, especially those who would like to agree with me – it is altogether too sceptical' (letter 427); and finally, on 21 May Russell said that he 'discovered that I have so little belief in philosophy ... but I found I really couldn't think it very valuable. This is partly due to Wittgenstein, who made me more of a sceptic...' (459).
[10] See for example Sainsbury 1979: 200–1, Soames 2003: 174, and Miah 2006: 106–8, 173–82. Landini.is a noticeable exception to this general view. See Landini 2011: 273–9.

inferred from that of another' (*CP* 6: 80). The focus is simply on the knowledge of the existence of things, and the skepticism of the paper focuses on the second foundation, namely the general principle from which one thing is inferred from another. In passages deleted from the final version of the paper Russell did suggest that the only general principles acceptable would be 'logical principles' which he characterized as 'purely formal' and would perhaps include the principle of induction but not 'causality or the uniformity of nature of any of the other general laws which are supposed to distinguish our actual world from other logically possible worlds' (*CP* 6: 514). Despite these musings there is little discussion of what constitutes a logical principle in the final version.[11] Russell's reasons for not finding principles of causality or statements about the uniformity of nature acceptable did not stem from a positive account of the *a priori*, but rather from observations that any principle which might be true would not be useful.[12]

In the revised portion of 'On Matter' Russell recognized that in his discussion of reasons to accept the existence of matter he was actually dealing with two distinct questions: first, what he called the 'metaphysical question', 'Have we any ground for assuming the existence of anything except sense-data?' and second, the question, 'Does physics in fact essentially require the existence of anything other than sense-data if it is to be true?' (*CP* 6: 89). These two questions are also important in trying to understand the role of skepticism in his argument.

On the one hand, Russell often presented skepticism in the guise of solipsism, understood as the view that only his mind and his actual sense-data exist. Skepticism about the external world is then related to solipsism, since if solipsism were true, there would be no external world.[13] In this way he thought of the problem of matter as directly related to refuting solipsism, and said in the opening paragraph of 'On Matter' that solipsism 'has never been treated with the respect which logically it deserves' (*CP* 6: 80). Russell retained these words in the later draft, but it is clear from the revisions he made that his enthusiasm for solipsism becomes muted in the course of his investigation.

---

[11]Perhaps Russell was putting off the discussion for 'What is Logic?', which he began in September of 1912 and in which he sought to explain logic as the study of the forms of complexes. The paper did not get developed. See *CP* 6, 54–6 and Griffin, 'Russell on the Nature of Logic'. In his 1914 'On Scientific Method in Philosophy' Russell contrasts 'synthetic' with 'deducible from logic alone', (Russell 1986: 70) reserving the *a priori* to the logical.

[12]See the discussion on pp. 90–1 of 'On Matter' (*CP* 6).

[13]As this is ordinarily taken. As I mentioned earlier, the experienced sense-data are already external to the mind.

On the other hand the solipsist position can be seen as attempting to answer the skeptic, not with respect to the existence of traditional matter, but with respect to the truth of physics. In fact this seems to be what Russell was suggesting by talking of the respect which solipsism logically deserves. For there is here the suggestion that if physics could be interpreted solipsistically, i.e. as a function of just one person's sense-data, then it would be on firm epistemological foundations and the skeptic would be answered. This was Wittgenstein's position as reported by Russell,[14] and it is the focus of the second question Russell formulated, 'Does physics in fact essentially require the existence of anything other than sense-data if it is to be true?' Answering this question in the negative secures the truths of physics, but removes any argument for the existence of matter of the kind present in *Problems*. As he revised 'On Matter', Russell argued against the solipsistic solution by answering this question in the affirmative, interestingly enough using a skeptical argument against the solipsistic solution. His argument is essentially an argument for the underdetermination of the physical laws on the basis of the positions and movements of observables alone.[15]

What is important in terms of the question of skepticism is that 'On Matter' concluded that while the solution of *Problems* did not appear to be justified, neither was the plan to construct matter from one's own sense-data. 'On Matter' ends with a tentative proposal to develop his constructions out of both sense-data and sensibilia, a plan later developed in 'The Relation of Sense Data to Physics' and *Our Knowledge of the External World*. This plan, which will be discussed in the next section, is not driven by the need to answer the skeptic, for it included sensibilia as well as sense-data and also included the sense-data of others. In terms of the skeptic's project the sense-data of others are as problematic as the existence of matter, since these are presumably inferred from other people's bodies. These inclusions have bothered commentators who see them as a flawed plan for securing knowledge from the skeptic. Russell was well aware of these diffi-

---

[14]See Russell's letter to Ottoline Morrell of 23 April 1912.

[15]Russell's argument involves first the observation that the planetary system can be modeled as 'mere bright patches moving on the celestial sphere'. The actual distance of the planets from the earth, Russell argued, introduces an unobservable distinction in cases where the sense-data would be the same. It is difficult to follow his argument in part because he seems to use the argument against his own argument for matter in *Problems*, which he calls the inductive argument (but is better understood as abductive): 'It is contended that, because a certain hypothesis fits all relevant known facts, therefore there is at least a probability that it is true. Such a contention is only valid if it is known that there are not likely to be other hypotheses which also fit the facts' (*CP* 6: 87). But he then used the same point to argue against the solipsist who wishes to interpret physics in terms of his own sense-data (*CP* 6: 88).

culties. That he developed the logical constructions despite them is evidence that responding to skepticism was not the main driving force of his philosophy of matter, nor of the modifications made to it after 1912. The view that skepticism is driving the changes in Russell's philosophy is rebutted in *Our Knowledge of the External World*:

> While admitting that doubt is possible with regard to our common knowledge, we must nevertheless accept that knowledge in the main if philosophy is to be possible at all. There is not any superfine brand of knowledge, obtainable by the philosopher, which can give us a standpoint from which to criticize the whole of the knowledge of daily life. …Philosophy cannot boast of having achieved such a degree of certainty that it can have authority to condemn the facts of experience and the laws of science….it is not that common knowledge must be true, but that we possess no radically different kind of knowledge derived from some other source. Universal skepticism, though logically irrefutable, is practically barren… (Russell 1914: 73–4).

4 Construction versus Inference

In 'On Matter' Russell first laid out the issue of construction versus inference with respect to matter, where he tentatively defined matter as those objects, which are inferable from sense-data and satisfy the hypotheses of physics (*CP* 6: 83). This may seem as though the position given in *Problems*, taking matter as inferred entities, is the only one which doesn't deny the existence of matter, but Russell himself didn't quite see it that way. He presented the following two choices as keeping matter in the sense of his definition, one of which involves construction from sense-data:

> …there are only two alternatives in regard to matter, if we are to have any reason to believe in matter. (1) It may happen that a piece of matter is a mere logical construction from certain sense-data, for example a combination of visual, tactile and other sense-data associated together by some experienced relation. (2) It may happen that we know some à priori principle by which, from sense-data, we can infer the existence of entities of a sort with which we are not acquainted, but which possess the kind of properties that physics assigns to matter, such as impenetrability and indestructibility and motion in a physical space… (*CP* 6: 84–5).

The second alternative here, which is clearly the one from *Problems*, is being rejected. The first alternative involves thinking of matter as a logical construction. Russell had first thought of these constructions entirely in terms of his own sense-data, and found that task impossible. It was this conclusion which most likely made him revise the paper so heavily and delete those passages which held out this possibility. In the concluding pages of 'On Matter', Russell tentatively proposed that logical constructions of

physical objects include other people's sense-data and 'qualities of the nature of sense-data' (*CP* 6: 94). He recognized that this move would not answer the skeptic, because *a priori* principles would still be needed, but he
thought a principle which infers the existence of things of the same kind as
the data of sense is 'less precarious' and 'more self-evident' (*CP* 6).

This was the first suggestion Russell gave that what A. J. Ayer would
later call 'horizontal inferences' are to be preferred over 'vertical inferences'.[16] The firmer ground of these horizontal inferences has been called
into question by Sainsbury (1979: 202–3). Sainsbury's criticism presupposes that the overall purpose of the constructions is to answer the skeptic and
so to minimalize what is known only inferentially. Sainsbury then pointed
out first that claims about unsensed sensibilia are always inferentially
known, so that in that sense horizontal inferences are on a par with vertical
ones, and second that 'a preference for vertical over horizontal inferences is
deeply built into our conception of rational belief' (1979: 203). Russell's
preference for the horizontal inferences is important for understanding his
constructions, and it is a preference which remained into his later philosophy.[17] It is important, then, to examine his position and see how he might
address Sainsbury's complaints.

There is not much in 'On Matter' to help us here, but there is more in
the published works which developed the constructions, 'The Relation of
Sense-Data to Physics', *Our Knowledge of the External World*, and 'The
Ultimate Constituents of Matter'. The preference for constructions is given
by what Russell called 'the supreme maxim in scientific philosophizing',
namely the principle that 'Whenever possible, logical constructions are to
be substituted for inferred entities' (*CP* 8: 11). Russell had used such a
principle of construction before, in his construction of mathematical concepts from logical ones, and he now applied the principle to the problem of
matter. Russell's way of phrasing the problem in these works is important
for understanding his solution. He was not engaged in a purely epistemological inquiry into what we know. He was instead trying to preserve both the
physics, which sees sense-data as a causal result of physical objects and
makes general claims about such objects, and an empiricism which sees our
knowledge as based on what we experience and what we can validly infer
from those experiences. A reconciliation of these two positions is what he
was seeking, and it is essentially unchanged in *The Analysis of Matter*.[18]

---

[16]Ayer 1972: 34 and 77.
[17]Some hold that he abandoned this preference in the *Analysis of Matter*. This issue is addressed below.
[18]Russell 1927: 7.

Before continuing, it is important to dispel a common misunderstanding. It is often thought that the move from inference to construction is an application of the principle of acquaintance, articulated in Chapter 5 of *Problems*, that 'every proposition which we can understand must be composed wholly of constituents with which we are acquainted' (Russell 1912: 58). This view is that the principle of acquaintance requires that all our propositions that appear to be about matter must really be about objects of acquaintance, such as our sense-data.[19] While Russell sometimes expressed himself in a way that may lend itself to this interpretation, this was not his position. Russell's principle of acquaintance required that the elements of the proposition which we had before our minds were always items with which we were acquainted. This was a principle of understanding propositions, which presumably applied to propositions anyone entertained, whether true or false, justified or unjustified, the result of analysis or not. The definite descriptions in these propositions picked out objects with which no one needed to be acquainted. The principle of acquaintance, coupled with the concept of knowledge by description, allowed that people were able to think about objects even though they were not acquainted with them. Thus the inferred matter of *Problems* was something people could think about, despite not being acquainted with it, and so too on the theory of 1914–15 could people think about the logical constructions. While some sense-data were taken to be objects of acquaintance, the *series* of sense-data and sensibilia of the constructions were not themselves taken to be objects of acquaintance. The examples Russell gave in 'The Relation of Sense-Data to Physics' of a successful construction were the construction of irrational numbers as classes of ratios, and the construction of classes from propositional functions. The examples are not ones which take the elements to be objects of acquaintance.

What is motivating the construction, then, is not a demand that the constituents of our judgments, or of the world be objects of acquaintance. Russell recognized that the constructions involve 'inferred entities', but he held that the inferred entities should 'be similar to those whose existence is given, rather than, like the Kantian *Ding an sich*, something wholly remote from the data which nominally support the inference' (*CP* 8: 12). Sainsbury criticized this restriction on epistemological grounds. Russell's reasons for maintaining the preference for the horizontal over the vertical inferences

---

[19]See for example Pears 1987 where he says the 'doctrine of forced acquaintance is the foundation of Russell's logical atomism' (63). Peter Hylton also suggested that the elements of constructions have to be objects of acquaintance (see Hylton 1990: 385). This way of putting it is not repeated in Hylton's recent paper (this volume).

seem to be a blend of epistemological and ontological concerns. Ockham's razor is taken by Russell to be involved with different kinds of entities, in particular the permanent things of traditional physics (Russell 1914: 112). The razor is motivated by ontological considerations, in that different kinds of hypothetical entities would involve metaphysical postulates and it is also motivated by epistemological considerations in that Russell takes it that we know that entities of the *kind* sense-data, qualities, aspects exist, but not of the *kind* enduring physical objects (*CP* 8: 11). Sainsbury's criticism is that we do not know that the kind 'unsensed sensibilia' exist any more than we know that enduring physical objects exist. But this is why Russell insisted that the postulated sensibilia are in fact of the same kind as sense-data, and their differences have to do with their relations to other entities. This is why it was important for him to insist that whatever subjectivity there is to sense-data is physiological, not psychological (*CP* 8: 9). In 'The Ultimate Constituents of Matter' Russell held with respect to a seen flash of lightning, 'if my body could remain in exactly the same state in which it is, although my mind had ceased to exist, precisely that object which I now see when I see the flash would exist, although of course I should not see it, since my seeing is mental' (*CP* 8: 78). The flash would then not be a sense-datum, but a sensibile, but it would be 'precisely the same object'. Sensibilia must be of the same ontological kind as sense-data.

So while there are epistemological reasons for the preference of constructions over inferred matter, they have to do with an ontological parsimony rather than with an attempt to answer skeptical concerns about our knowledge of truths about the world.[20] The preference for constructions and the ontological parsimony is further revealed by the analogy Russell used when expounding his supreme maxim. The analogy was with his mathematical construction. In treating numbers as classes of classes, rational numbers as classes of these and irrational numbers as series of these, Russell was able to derive rather than simply postulate the various truths about these and to reveal their relations. Russell's way of putting this somewhat later (in 'Logical Atomism' 1924) was, 'When some set of supposed entities has neat logical properties, it turns out, in a great many instances, that the supposed entities can be replaced by purely logical structures composed of entities which have not such neat properties' (*CP* 9: 164). The neat properties

---

[20]This ontological parsimony is related to questions about the knowledge of such truths about the world as whether a given kind of thing exists. Russell also did not think of Ockham's razor as some sort of *a priori* principle which ruled out entities of different kinds. So he did not dogmatically assert that enduring objects, irrational numbers, etc. did not exist, but rather that there was no need to postulate them.

which had to be postulated as necessary of the inferred entities can be revealed to be a matter of logic with the constructions. Further on in this essay Russell tied this remark to the question of matter: 'Matter, traditionally, has two of those "neat" properties which are the mark of a logical construction; first, that two pieces of matter cannot be at the same place at the same time; secondly, that one piece of matter cannot be in two places at the same time. Experience in the substitution of constructions for inferences makes one suspicious of anything so tidy and exact. One cannot help feeling that impenetrability is not an empirical fact, derived from observation of billiard-balls, but is something logically necessary' (*CP* 9: 166–7). That Russell had earlier explicitly tied his use of constructions in physics to his use of constructions in his earlier mathematical work strongly suggests that the considerations articulated in 'Logical Atomism' were of concern to him even in 1914.

While 'On Matter' is probably the closest Russell came to trying to construct our knowledge of things from a solipsistic starting point, it ended with a move away from that point. Russell did not publish 'On Matter', and in fact seems to have laid it aside while he worked on his book *Theory of Knowledge*, which was supposed to incorporate our knowledge of matter in its later chapters.[21] Russell reported being inspired by Whitehead in his return to the problem late in 1913 while writing the Lowell lectures. The inspiration led to a breakthrough and the rapid composing of 'The Relation of Sense-Data to Physics' in the beginning of 1914. The breakthrough appears to be the solution to the problem that the different sense data cannot all be where they are taken to be. This was a problem which Percy Nunn had thought he had solved in his 'Are Secondary Qualities Independent of Perception?' where he boldly held that contradictory qualities can exist at the same place at the same time, and it is also mentioned by G. E. Moore in his paper on Sense-Data of 1913.[22]

---

[21]There are nine short manuscripts on matter written between 'On Matter' and 'The Relation of Sense-Data to Physics' which suggest that Russell did continue thinking about the issue. It is unclear when some of the papers were written, although one very brief outline is dated 1912 and another is dated 1913. The editors of *CP* 6 suggest that the papers were all written in 1912 or in the early part of 1913 before Russell began working on *Theory of Knowledge*. If this is true, then one important part of Russell's self-reported 'breakthrough' was present earlier, as the papers 11a, 11b and 11i include Russell's distinction that a sense-datum is in a place from another place (110, earlier characterized as here and there in sensation, 98, 99–103).

[22]See Nunn, 'Are Secondary Qualities Independent of Perception?' and G. E. Moore, 'The Status of Sense-data' (184). Neither Russell nor Moore mentions the other in their discussions of sense-data. Russell mentions Nunn's article in both 'The Relation of Sense-Data to Physics' and 'The Ultimate Constituents of Matter'.

Russell's sympathetic remarks about Nunn and Alexander in 'The Ultimate Constituents of Matter' show that his constructions should not be
thought of as phenomenalist. But using a technique he said he got from
Whitehead, he solved the problem of contradictory properties being at the
same place and same time by thinking that the constructed space, as he put
it, has six dimensions. The constructed space is a three-dimensional series
of perspectives, and an object is in the three-dimensional space of the perspective. Russell had already distinguished private space from public space
in *Problems*, but there he had seen the public space as simply inferred as the
space of the causes of what was experienced. In 'The Relation of Sense-
Data to Physics', Russell sought to define the public space in terms of series
of perspective spaces. This was the breakthrough to which Russell referred.

What is important with respect to the issue of Russell's replacement of
the inference of *Problems* with the constructions of 'The Relation of Sense-
Data to Physics' is that the breakthrough involved a detail in the construction of space from the private spaces and a solution to the problem of
whether incompatible qualities could be in the same space. The breakthrough in no way involved a study of *a priori* principles and finding one
which satisfactorily led to the inference of other people's sense-data or to
sensibilia from our own sense-data.

We are now in a position to assess Russell's transition from inference
to material objects of a traditional sort to logical constructions of objects
from sense-data and sensibilia. One concern involves ontological parsimony. Russell often expressed this concern by referring to entities which
would be conjectured by a vertical inference as 'doubtful entities'. This
concern is related to, but nevertheless distinct from, a general skeptical concern. Russell clearly thought that ocurrent sense-data were not 'doubtful
entities' in that our direct awareness of them puts us in the position to know
that they exist. But sensibilia and other people's sense data could also be
thought of as 'doubtful entities', in the sense that we are not in the same
position with respect to them as we are to our own sense-data. Yet at the
level of what kind of entity we have in our ontology, there is a difference.
Starting with 'On Matter' and continuing through to *The Analysis of Matter*,
what Russell was seeking was an account of the physical world which ena-
bled our physics to be true, revealed a logical structure of physics so that the
necessary truths of physics, particularly of space and time, would be shown
to be logical truths, and allowed for an account of our knowledge of this

external world. All these points Russell believed were handled better by the constructions than by the inference to traditional pieces of matter.[23]

It has been thought that Russell changed his mind about constructions as opposed to inferred matter in *Analysis of Matter* and that there was a return to the method of inferred entities there.[24] One reason for holding this is his statement that 'It is impossible to lay down a hard-and-fast rule that we can never validly infer something radically different from what we observe' (Russell 1927: 16) and a more striking one is his advocating a causal theory of perception which to many appear to be a return to the theory of *Problems* and a turn away from the constructions of 1914–15. But an examination of Russell's remarks in *The Analysis of Matter* reveal that he has not at all abandoned the constructions for the inferences of *Problems*.

In the *Analysis of Matter*, Russell takes as his building blocks, at least initially, what he calls percepts. Percepts are what we immediately perceive, and he characterizes them as 'patches of colour, noises, smells, hardness, etc.'(1927: 257). In this sense the percepts as building blocks are close to the sense-data of the earlier constructions. They play both the epistemological role that sense-data played, and they also serve as the building blocks for the constructions of the external world in Russell's old sense. In his chapter on the causal theory of perception, Russell argued that we have essentially what he called instinctive beliefs in the existence of things we are not perceiving, a position one might think close to that of Chapter II of *Problems*. He gave a fairly long argument for the existence of other people's percepts which attempted to bypass the standard criticism. The standard criticism, well-articulated by Soames, is that the inference to other people's percepts (or sense-data) requires the inference first to their bodies as material objects (Soames 2003: 178). Russell argues that we can form a tentative conception of a physical body based on simply the order of our own percepts, and from there infer the corresponding percepts that would be associated with that body (Russell 1927: 201–5). Once we have the percepts of others, we can then refine our constructions of bodies. He also allowed

---

[23]Russell doesn't directly say in these works that the traditional inferred matter was something that the new physics called in to question, but even in *Problems* he said that 'sober science' tells us that a table 'is a vast collection of electric charges in violent motion' (Russell 1912: 16) and he later reported to Lady Ottoline Morrel that the scientists who heard 'The Ultimate Constituents of Matter', when it was delivered in Manchester, including Ernest Rutherford, were in agreement with the paper.

[24]See e.g. Sainsbury 1979: 203–4. Bostock also sees a change in Russell here, but recognizes that Russell still has logical constructions in *Analysis of Matter*. He sees this work as quite different from Russell's earlier work because he supposes the earlier work to be far more phenomenalic than I do. See Bostock 2012: 192–6.

for events just like percepts, but which do not actually enter into a relation with a nervous system so as to be an actual percept. After rejecting the supposition that these are only 'ideal' events, in the sense that they are simply possibilities of percepts, Russell wished to admit these elements to his ontology, as they serve in his explanation of our own percepts being caused by the physical world. It is likely this move that has been taken to signal a shift back to the theory of *Problems*. But this is a mistake. The hypothesized entities are, as were sensibilia, of the same kind as the percepts. This is especially clear from Russell's intermediate argument for the 'ideal' percepts. When Russell stated at the end of this chapter that 'I shall assume henceforth not only that there are percepts which I do not perceive, connected with other people's bodies, but also that there are events causally connected with percepts, as to which we do not know whether they are perceived or not' (1927: 215–6), these two assumptions correspond exactly to the assumption of other people's sense data and also the sensibilia of 'The Relation of Sense-Data to Physics'. What we end up with are constructions that look very close to the constructions of this era. Russell saw the series of percepts and events like them as constituting a causal series, but this position was anticipated in 'The Relation of Sense-data to Physics'.[25] What we do not end up with are inferred tables of the sort conjectured in *Problems*.

References

Ayer, A. J. 1972. *Russell*. London: Fontana-Collins.

Baldwin, T. 2003. From Knowledge by Acquaintance to Knowledge by Causation. *The Cambridge Companion to Bertrand Russell*, ed. N. Griffin. Cambridge: Cambridge University Press.

Bostock, D. 2012. *Russell's Logical Atomism*. Oxford: Oxford University Press.

Dawes Hicks, G. 1912. The Nature of Sense-Data. *Mind* 21: 399–409. Reprinted in *CP* 6: 433–43.

Griffin, N. 1980. Russell on the Nature of Logic (1903-1913). *Synthese* 45: 117–188.

Hylton, P. 1990. *Russell, Idealism and the Emergence of Analytic Philosophy*. Oxford: Clarendon.

---

[25]See Russell (*CP* 8: 16–17) where Russell said 'We want to be able to express the fact that the appearance of a thing in a given perspective is causally affected by the matter between the thing and the perspective'. Russell defines the matter of a thing as 'the limit of its appearances as their distance from the thing diminishes'. These 'appearances' are of course sensibilia rather than actual sense-data. The causal theory of perception can therefore be stated in the 1914 theory as well as the 1927 *Analysis of Matter*.

Hylton, P. 2015. *Problems of Philosophy* as a stage in the evolution of Russell's views on knowledge. In this volume: 25–44.

Landini, G. 2011. *Russell*. London: Routledge.

Linsky, B. 2015. Acquaintance and Certainty in *The Problems of Philosophy*. In this volume: 65–85.

Miah, S. 2006. *Russell's Theory of Perception, 1905–1919*. London: Continuum.

Moore, G. E. 1913-14. The Status of Sense-Data. *Proceedings of the Aristotelian Society* 14: 355–406. Reprinted in Moore 1922.

Moore, G. E. 1922. *Philosophical Studies*. London: Routledge.

Nasim, O. 2008. *Bertrand Russell and the Edwardian Philosophers*. Basingstoke: Palgrave Macmillan.

Nunn, P. 1909-10. Are Secondary Qualities Independent of Perception? *Proceedings of the Aristotelian Society* 10: 191–218

Pears, D. F. 1987. *The False Prison* I. Oxford: Clarendon Press.

Proops, I. 2015. Certainty, Error and Acquaintance in *The Problems of Philosophy*. In this volume: 45–63.

Russell, B. 1912. *The Problems of Philosophy*. London: Williams and Norgate. Reprinted Oxford: Oxford University Press 1959.

Russell, B. 1914. *Our Knowledge of the External World.* London: Allen and Unwin. References to the 1926 edition.

Russell, B. 1927. *The Analysis of Matter*. London: Kegan Paul.

Russell, B. 1984. *The Collected Papers of Bertrand Russell, Volume 7: Theory of Knowledge*, ed. E. A. Eames. London: George Allen & Unwin. [*CP* 7]

Russell, B. 1986. *The Collected Papers of Bertrand Russell, Volume 8: The Philosophy of Logical Atomism and Other Essays, 1914–1919*, ed. J. Slater. London: George Allen and Unwin. [*CP* 8]

Russell, B. 1988. *The Collected Papers of Bertrand Russell, Volume 9: Essays on Language, Mind and Matter, 1919–26*, ed. J. Slater. London: Unwin Hyman. [*CP* 9]

Russell, B. 1992. *The Collected Papers of Bertrand Russell, Volume 6: Logical and Philosophical Papers, 1909–1913*, ed. J. Slater with B. Frohmann. London: Routledge. [*CP* 6]

Sainsbury, R. M. 1979. *Russell*. London: Routledge.

Soames, S. 2003. *Philosophical Analysis in the Twentieth Century, Vol. I: The Dawn of Analysis*. Princeton: Princeton University Press.

6

Seeing, Imagining, Believing: From *Problems* to *Theory of Knowledge*

ROSALIND CAREY

1 Introduction

The *Problems of Philosophy* is a brief but systematic study of knowledge, which focuses, in the opening chapters, on data given in sensation. Introspection is crucial to its project. Were we unconscious of our sensations (e.g. if we could not know that we felt warmth or pleasure or saw a color), there would be no data with which to begin the study. The book therefore assumes that we have experiences *and* can be aware of having them. Despite attributing great importance to apprehending and correctly reporting present sensations, in some respects the book is dismissive of the evidence given in *sight*. Russell recognizes that sight leads many to think that what we see *is* the external world. Nevertheless, he does not regard that conviction as unassailable and proceeds to argue that we do not experience objects in the external world, but only data associated with those objects. In this respect, the book sometimes falls short of its goal of attending to what is given in sensation. The aim in this paper is to show how this aspect of *Problems*, when Russell recognizes and repudiates it, paves the way for the work immediately following in 1912 and 1913. When he begins to take seriously the convictions based on sensation and sight, his work begins to reshape itself two directions, towards a new doctrine of space and matter as well as towards new views about images and the nature of imagination. To the extent that it is the background to this branching development, *Problems of Philosophy* is an important stage in Russell's emerging theory of our

Acquaintance, Knowledge, and Logic.
Donovan Wishon and Bernard Linsky (eds.).
Copyright © 2015, CSLI Publications.

knowledge of the external world *and* an important stage in his emerging theory of what is known from within.

On the account given here, the key issue in this period is the 'epistemological problem of the physical knowledge to be derived from sight' (*CP* 7: 51). In notes in 1912a and early 1913 that reexamine what occurs in seeing colors and shapes, Russell reverses his position in *Problems* and decides that a color or shape seen *is* the 'external' reality. He provides an essential piece to a construction of objects from qualities when he gives a novel theory of how the colors and shapes that an object presents to different people can coexist. Yet we see colors and shapes in dreams and hallucinations as well as in ordinary sensation; if sight gives us 'external things', why are these not relevant to physics? In order to answer questions like these, he turns in 1913 to the theory of knowledge, separating normal sensation from what is seen in dreams and hallucinations.

The attempt to distinguish *seeing* into the physically relevant and irrelevant forms is complicated by another consideration. Even though the imagined colors seen in dreams and hallucinations are not relevant to objects constructed from sense data, that is, to what physical knowledge is about, images are often relevant to beliefs, the medium of knowledge. In particular, many memories comprise images, and without such memories of the past, knowledge would be extremely limited. For this reason, the 1913 analysis of sensing and imagining extends to memory. In both ways, by dismissing the relevance of images to constructions and by investigating their importance to memory and meaning, the 1913 work moves several steps closer to the analysis of matter and mind in the 1920s. Despite many differences between his views in the two periods, the trajectory Russell's thought takes towards that later work can already be detected.

2   *Problems*: Reporting the Data of Sensation

Early in the first chapter of *Problems* Russell asks whether there is knowledge 'so certain that no reasonable man could doubt it' (Russell 1912a: 7). The word 'doubt' is used as shorthand for 'suspend belief'. The question is not whether there is absolutely certain knowledge. Rather, granting that there is knowledge (i.e. statements expressing knowledge), the question is whether any of it resists suspension of belief. It is implied that something might be *knowledge* and yet not be resistant to suspension of belief. An example is 'I am sitting in a chair'. A person who reports this present experience knows the statement to be true but can be given reasons to suspend belief in its complete accuracy. As shortly becomes clear, by referring to a chair, the statement 'I am sitting in a chair' incorrectly reports what the experience made the person know, which is more carefully described as awareness of sensing colors and of having feelings of solidity. Hence his opening remarks alert the reader to the necessity of phrasing reports of present experience with great care. Indeed, without care, 'any statement as to what it is that our immediate experiences make us know is very likely to be wrong' (Russell 1912a: 8) and it is probable that we can suspend belief in some aspect of what it reports.

This method of suspending belief is broadly Cartesian, but Russell is under no delusion that it prevents error, and his interest in it has to do with maneuvering the reader into a certain way of speaking and thinking that at least avoids prejudging the question at issue. The question is what objects, if any, are known besides the data of sensation. The principle difficulty confronting that inquiry is overcoming the naïve point of view that reports a present experience ('I am seeing a table') as if observing something (a table) that exists independently of the perceiver. Although, at least in the case of sight, we seem to naturally assume that what is seen is the object (1912a: 24), Russell believes this is an error. To show why it is, he imagines moving around a table and noticing different colors and shapes from different points of view.[1] On the assumption that different colors and shapes cannot exist in the same place at the same time, he concludes that none of the colors or shapes can be the real object (the table) or even one of its properties. For which color or shape could be given preeminence? These reflections suggest that the real table, if there is one, 'is not the same as what we immediately experience' (1912a: 11). If there is an enduring real table, it must be impartial to appearances and distinct from all of them.

Intertwined with this argument are supporting arguments about the dependence of appearances on conditions in the perceiver. Circumnavigating the table corresponds to seeing changes in color and shape, and it is difficult to avoid concluding that these are brought about by changes in the subject, especially as they cannot belong to the object. Russell anticipates the theories of physicists when he says that a patch of color is not 'inherent in the table, but something depending upon the table and the spectator and the way the light falls on the table' (1912a: 9), but this analysis is not essential to his present argument. Whether or not physical hypotheses are invoked to explain the fact, his point is that changes in appearances are cued to changes in the perceiver. Thus, however such changes are ultimately explained, it

---

[1] See Robert Barnard's contribution to this volume for an analysis of how Russell uses the table example to serve the methodological purpose of suspending belief in the external world.

seems likely that the colors and shapes depend for their existence on being perceived and do not exist independently of the perceiver.[2]

Thus, against the natural tendency to think that we see the enduring or real table, Russell concludes that the senses do not give us 'the truth about the table itself, but only about the appearance of the table' (1912a: 11). In saying that the senses tell us truths about appearances, he is condensing a more complicated account of how we arrive at truths about immediate experience. The terms *sensation* and *sense data* are part of this story.

Sensation refers to 'the experience of being immediately aware' of 'such things as colours, sounds, smells, hardnesses, roughnesses, and so on' (1912a: 12). The colors, sounds, smells, and so forth are *sense data*.[3] Sensation presents sense data but does not provide knowledge *about* them. We know *of* a color in sensation and therefore sensation is a kind of knowledge, but it does not make us know *truths* about a datum, such as that it is a color.[4] Indeed, on Russell's view a person may have knowledge in sensation of a sense datum without being aware of having the sensation. Introspective awareness of having a sensation, feeling, or thought is therefore a prerequisite of forming a statement about any such present experience.[5] When, in the second chapter, Russell says that in seeing a ghost, we 'certainly do ha-

---

[2]This does not imply that they are mental entities or in the mind. On Russell's view (1914: 9) sense data would have to be mental or in the mind if it were logically impossible to conceive of them as existing apart from mind. This is not impossible since the belief that sense data exist apart from the mind is a naïve belief. Thus, he concludes that there is no *a priori* reason why sense data must be mental or in the mind.

[3]Except in cases of nose-to-the-table scrutiny, what appears from any single perspective is usually not a single patch of color. Yet the notion of a sense datum helps to formulate precise and accurate statements of what appears.

[4]Several contributors to this volume – Bernard Linsky, Ian Proops, and Russell Wahl – have drawn attention to the problematic relation between knowledge of sense data and knowledge of truths. In different ways, they argue against the tendency to regard Russell's theory of sensation as a source of knowledge of truths and, further, to attribute infallibility to his theory of knowledge of truths. They are correct in both assessments, I think, and also in the suggestion that this way of reading of *Problems* misrepresents the kind of foundationalism that Russell is interested in.

[5]Russell thinks there is no *a priori* reason why sense data *are* mental or in the mind. In discussion, Peter Hylton has raised the difficult question whether Russell assumes from the outset of *Problems* that sense data are not mental or in the mind. I think Russell does not assume this but comes close to doing so. In chapter one, he says that sensation is distinct from sense data. If he had also said that sensation is a relation (as he does in chapter four), then it would imply that sense data are 'before the mind', and '*may* ...*be* not mental' (1912a: 43, emphasis added). Together with the arguments in chapter three about the dependence of sense data on the body, this suggests that most sense data *are not* mental or in the mind. But none of these points are assumed in his first chapter.

ve the sensations *we think we have*' (1912a: 19, emphasis added) he is alluding to the role of introspection in arriving at statements of present experience.[6]

Even introspection does not make a person know a *truth* about that experience (1912a: 144): it merely presents its data, which are mental facts of having feelings or thoughts. It also does not necessitate forming a belief about what is introspected.[7] I *may* form a belief or statement, such as 'a brown color is being seen', about my present experience. Analogous statements can be formed about the sensations involved in seeing a ghost, such as, perhaps, 'a whitish patch is being seen'. If so, the statement may 'make me know truths about [it]' (1912a: 47). Yet it is the *statements* that make a person know the truth, not the experiences, which are inarticulate knowledge *of* data. Since statements about present experiences are attempts to articulate what is apprehended inarticulately, there is inevitable obscurity in judging the success of such a report. The reports will probably seem true and feel certain initially no matter how they are phrased, but the opening chapters of *Problems* move the reader towards careful introspective reports such as 'a sensation of brown is occurring',[8] and to the extent that such reports succeed in unveiling experiences so well that no reason can be given for a person to suspend belief in any part of what they assert, the 'knowledge of our own experiences' provides, 'for what it is worth, a solid basis from which to begin our pursuit of knowledge' (1912a: 19).

3 *Problems*: **The Products of Imagination**

On that basis, we can begin to inquire whether there is anything other than 'ourselves and our private experiences' (Russell 1912a: 22). Russell compares a 'no' answer to this question to 'the supposition that the whole of life is a dream, in which we ourselves create all the objects that come before us' (1912a: 22). The same idea underlies his question, 'Is there a table which

---

[6]Introspection is important, as Russell explains in chapter five of *Problems*, because it 'is the source of all our knowledge of mental things' (Russell 1912a: 49). Awareness of our own mental life makes it possible to understand that other bodies like our own have minds like our own.

[7]Russell says that when we have introspective acquaintance with the fact of seeing a sense datum, we 'know the truth "I am acquainted with this sense datum"' (Russell 1912a: 51). This does not mean that introspection *must* be followed by a judgment about it. It means that if we made the judgment then, we would be acquainted with what causes us to think that the judgment is true.

[8]The second chapter continues that refrain by warning the reader that even more careful statements like 'I am sensing a brown color' may convey a misinterpretation of the experience underlying 'I'.

has a certain intrinsic nature, and continues to exist when I am not looking, or is the table merely a product of my imagination, a dream table in a very prolonged dream?' (1912a: 17).

Russell has argued that sensation does not tell us anything about an enduring, real table but only about sense data whose fleeting existence depends on being sensed. If there is no enduring table, if 'a table' is a collection of fleeting colors and shapes inseparable from the perceiver's perception, then the table is on a par with a dream object – assuming the commonplace view that dream objects have no existence apart from dreaming.[9] In that sense, we *author* tables as much as we author dreams: as he later says about dreams, they are 'our own invention' (*CP* 7: 61). The quality of being produced or invented is shared in another sense, too. Though we experience only fleeting sense data and never the real table, our table experiences never seem to contain gaps: What we observe seems to be whole and complete and real. This is largely due to the fact that we learn to correlate sense data and come to expect or fill in missing data. What we observe and call a table is a fiction of the imagination, in Hume's sense. If so, if sense data collections in waking life are augmented by imagination and expectation, then they are doubly like a dream object: They depend on the perceiver's perception and are a put together affair. On the basis of either or both of these reasons, Russell's question is not *whether* the observed table is a product of imagination, but whether it is *merely* this.

Against this possibility, he proposes the existence of objects corresponding to sensations. Though they correspond only in some cases (not to dreams and illusions), he is not particularly anxious to show how, within experience, we are able to know *which* sensations correspond to objects. The hypothesis of objects does not provide a criterion for determining this and so far none have been mentioned, yet various places in *Problems* suggest that he has the makings of an account. The text alludes to how people learn to correlate the data of one sense with that of another (e.g. sight and touch) and come to expect particular correlations. It is the absence of the usual correlations that is responsible for the horror of ghosts, he says, for unlike usual visual appearances, they yield no sensation to touch (Russell 1912a: 62). Probably, he assumes that imagination and sensation are distinguished by their correlations. If so, it becomes possible to say that, in some dreams, sensation intrudes on imagination at certain points, as when a dreamer hears a banging and dreams of a naval battle, and that *parts* of the dream are sensation and other parts, not. And Russell seems to assume

---

[9]Russell does not explain what aspect of a dream is relevant to the comparison. The interpretation given above is based on remarks in *Theory of Knowledge* (*CP* 7: 49).

some way of drawing this kind of distinction because he does say that, if an external world is assumed, a dream event can be shown to have physical causes (banging doors) but to correspond to no physical objects (1912a: 22).

But if we distinguish sensation from imagination by correlating experiences, why bother with the hypothesis of objects? The reason is that sense data do not exist apart from perception and cannot constitute objects or be their qualities. If, as he argues, appearances do not continue independently of sensation, then, if no other objects are assumed to exist independently of them, ordinary experiences will have to be explained by properties of appearances, that is, by the properties of patches of color and other sense data. This is difficult for obvious reasons. Sets of color patches appear and reappear without obeying physical laws. More accurately, a set of sense data does not reappear; it is replaced. Supposing a cat to be 'merely a set of sense data' is allowing that it 'cannot have ever been in any place where I did not see it; thus we shall have to suppose that it did not exist at all while I was not looking, but suddenly sprang into being in a new place' (Russell 1912a: 23). Russell concludes that this theory, 'as a means of accounting for the facts of our own life', is 'less simple' than the 'hypothesis that there really are objects independent of us, whose action on us causes our sensations' (1912a: 23).

This is an argument from the simplicity of the theory of objects, but *Problems* does not elaborate on the nature of the simplicity gained, though it is plainly not attributable to a reduction in number or kinds of entities. In his contribution to this volume, Peter Hylton explains that the hypothesis of objects is simpler because it makes it possible to find regularities in experiences and bring them under laws. This interpretation is supported by the text and also fits with Russell's notes in 1912 and 1913, following 'On Matter'. Russell's work in these notes suggest that a theory is simpler if it takes less work to construct and makes experience easier to imagine and describe.[10] This kind of simplicity is taken as illustrating Occam's razor. For example, after considering whether to deny absolute time and persistence, the labor involved in working out such a theory leads him to conclude that it is 'simpler to admit persistence' and that 'Occam's razor is *better* satisfied by admitting absolute space and time than by rejecting them' (*CP* 6: 102).

It is this sense of simplicity that is involved in *Problems*, in arguing for the persisting cat, and probably also this interpretation of Occam's razor. But by 1914, the notion of simplicity has changed and Occam's razor is

---

[10]In these notes Russell is working out the details of the construction of matter but in the analysis of space and time he has not decided whether to admit or deny points and instants.

interpreted differently.[11] In *Our Knowledge of the External World* Occam's principle is satisfied by stating everything about a subject matter in terms of entities that are 'undeniably involved' in it, even though this may result in a more 'complicated and difficult statement' of the subject (Russell 1914a: 107). It is *not* satisfied by theories that admit unwarranted hypothetical entities because they look for what is 'easy and natural in thought' (1914a: 107). The metaphysical cat in *Problems* has become metaphysical wallpaper, with the suggestion that it is easier but not better to 'imagine a wallpaper with changing colors than to think merely of the series of colors' (1914a: 107).

In *Problems*, the argument from simplicity leads to the conclusion that sense data are signs of objects existing apart from them. This belief is instinctive, or, at least, it is instinctive upon reflection. But we would never come to reflect on whether there is an external world corresponding to our sensations except that 'in the case of sight, it seems as if the sense datum itself were instinctively believed to be the independent object, whereas argument shows that the object cannot be identical with the sense datum' (Russell 1912a: 24). The object cannot be identified with the sense datum because, as noted above, competing appearances (colors or shapes) cannot coexist in the same place. To be sure, the instinctive belief in objects is frequently wrong: the whole population of dreamers may be 'mistaken as to the existence of other people' (1912a: 24). Nevertheless, because the naïve belief has been shown to be fruitless, the doubt cast by dreams on the belief that sense data are signs of objects is judged to be 'slight' (1912a: 25).

4 'On Matter': Seeing Colors from a Place

By May of 1912, in the unpublished paper 'On Matter', the 'slight doubt' has taken on new seriousness. The primitive belief that sense data indicate objects cannot be reliable if it is 'as strongly present during the sensations of dreams as during those of what we are pleased to regard as waking life' (*CP* 6: 93). This consideration did not cause Russell much concern before, and it is therefore not likely to be why 'On Matter' goes on to question the hypothesis of objects. Rather, something has caused the construction of objects from sense data to seem superior to the hypothesis of objects; and as a result the doubt introduced by dreams about that hypothesis has gained seriousness. In his contribution to this volume, Russell Wahl has argued that

---

[11]Russell rejects the argument from simplicity in 'On Matter', but the 1912–13 notes on matter and sensation suggest that he retains his earlier interpretation of Occam's razor for a little longer.

Russell's shift from inferred objects to constructions depends on his solving the problem of whether incompatible sense data can occur in the same place in space. This is surely correct, but there is still the question of why he sought that solution and what prevented his doing so before.

The suggestion here is that Russell seeks out that solution after realizing (perhaps helped by reading A. N. Whitehead's critique of *Problems*) that he had been making certain dubious assumptions about sensation and place. These mistaken assumptions could well have prevented him from arriving at this solution earlier. Recognizing these apparently leads him to reconsider whether colors and shapes can occur in the same space and whether they depend for existence on the body of the perceiver. As noted above, in *Problems* Russell argues against naively believing that a color or shape is where it appears to be. The different colors or shapes that appear on observing a table from different angles cannot be qualities occurring at one and the same place but must be sense data that exist in being perceived. Moreover, they can be explained as the result of perceptual causal chains (object, light, retina, brain, etc.) unique to each observer. The existence of bodies needs defense for this view to work, but once the physical world is assumed, it is possible to explain each person's experience of an object as having a distinct causal history with nothing in common but the object, which has no color.[12]

Our Knowledge of the External World (Russell 1914a) indicates one mistake in the above reasoning. In accounting for the changing aspects of a table, we are prone, it writes, to assume that 'there can be something more real than objects of sense' (Russell 1914a: 86). Ironically, despite being keen to record present experience, *Problems* is eager to stamp out by argument the evidence given in sight. While noticing that the naïve belief that what appears to the eye *is* the object is particularly strong concerning visual data, he does not pause to consider what this implies but attempts instead to dissolve the naïvely realist belief by argument. Rather than investigating further, the procedure, to borrow a line from the 1913 *Theory of Knowledge*, is as if he had 'already solved the epistemological problem of the physical knowledge derived from sight' (*CP* 7: 51). In particular, his assumption that

---

[12]*Problems* concedes that an intermediate color, a blend of colors visible from different perspectives, might be a property of the object, but argues that this is unlikely considering the fact that alterations in colors and shapes can be attributed to changes in the perceiver. If these changes can be explained by supposing that eye sees a certain color when light rays hit the retina in a certain way, that is, by supposing an intervening physical medium, then it is 'gratuitous to suppose that physical objects have colours' (Russell 1912a: 35) since the eye will see as it sees regardless of the putative color of the object.

different colors and shapes cannot occur in the *same place* presupposes 'that all our difficulties [i.e. about what can be derived by sight] have been solved' (Russell 1914a: 86). If it is true that colors and other visual data cannot share the same place, this is not because there is a place in a super real space from which they are excluded. It is because, in moving around the table and observing it (to use the usual way of speaking about objects), 'no place remains the same as it was' (1914a: 86–7).

In *Problems*, Russell already believes that the colors and shapes seen in it define the space of sight, but he has contrasted this 'sensible space' with physical space and not taken it seriously. Once the mistake has been noticed, he can be relatively confident that the solution to the color problem lies in an analysis of sensation and what is known in sight. He can also see, in outline, another way of explaining the different colors observed of the same object than by explaining them as the result of a causal chain. 'On Matter' therefore moves sharply away from the earlier view. What is objectionable in naïve realism is not the idea that qualities exist apart from sensation, but insufficient boldness in carrying that very point: It identifies an object with what appears in a place but is unwilling to allow that other appearances occur in the same place. In sketching the need for 'sufficient boldness' (*CP* 6: 93) on this point, Russell cites the work of T. P. Nunn on secondary qualities.[13] Nunn argues, for example, that talk about the 'real' temperature of water is 'a symbol for the totality of the experiences of hotness or coldness obtainable from the water at the moment in question, each under its proper conditions of perception' (Nunn 1909–10: 208).[14] Analogously, Russell states that: 'many colors may coexist in a place, each being only visible to observers in certain directions from the place in question' (*CP* 6: 93–4).

Without elaborating on what it means to say that colors are visible from a place, 'On Matter' proceeds as though nothing remains to stand in the way of the principle that qualities exist 'at times when they are not given in sense' (*CP* 6: 93). This is not to say that qualities exist for a long time.[15] At any moment, a great many observed or unobserved qualities exist, and many others may exist at the following moment. But, if qualities can exist apart from sense, there will be none of the gaps and insufficiencies that ma-

---

[13]A. N. Whitehead's definition of points and instants in terms of classes of sense data is also an influence on the paper.

[14]About the properties of warmth and coldness, T. P. Nunn argues, 'under the appropriate conditions, both *are there to be experienced*' (Nunn 1909–10: 208).

[15]Gregory Landini has noted in conversation that qualities cannot endure long if they resemble fleeting sense data.

de the metaphysical cat in *Problems* so necessary. An object will consist of qualities, and 'not only of those which are actually given, but of many others besides' (*CP* 6: 94). It is irrelevant that qualities existing apart from sense are not known: Their resemblance to sense data ensures that they are not unknowable in theory. The principle that qualities exist that are not sensed is 'less precarious' as a premise than the previous hypothesis of objects because it does not require induction to something without precedent in experience (*CP* 6: 94). This fact lends plausibility to the emerging construction.[16]

5 *Here* and *There*: A Novelty as to the Nature of Sensation

'On Matter' assumes that there is a solution to the color problem and hints at its nature, but goes no further on that subject. The issue is taken up in a series of notes, written between 1912 and early 1913, which analyze sensation and the physical knowledge to be derived from sight.[17] The notes help to explain what Russell means, in February 1913, when he says that to 'get on with Matter' what is most wanted is a 'fundamental novelty as to the nature of sensation' (*CP* 8: xiii). In a reversal of *Problems*, the guiding idea is that 'sensation gives true knowledge of external things' (*CP* 6: 98). Russell has always admitted that in sight colors and shapes seem to be external things, but in *Problems* he judged the naïve belief in their externality to be misguided. Now, he takes seriously that sight gives colors and shapes as external to the self. Sight is awareness of a color shape as at a place *there*, from a place *here*; it is awareness of a quality that is associated with two places.

This doctrine of two places is a response to the difficulties of the place of qualities. *Problems* argued that a table appears to be different colors when viewed from different perspectives because the colors seen from each perspective are the result of the unique causal chains involved in sensing the table from different points. By locating the color at the end of a causal chain, it was possible to avoid crowding colors into the place of the object. And this avoided the problem posed by naively assuming that a color is simply in the place it appears to be in. He now sees that it is possible to synthesize the physical causal account and the naïve belief into a third. There must be nothing more real than the objects of sense, but the function served

---

[16]The implausibility of the earlier hypothesis is not the motivation for the move towards construction. That hypothesis did not seem implausible earlier, given his assumptions about the implausibility of naïve realism, based on the place of sense data.

[17]See Russell *CP* 7: 96–7 for the editor's discussion of these notes.

by assuming a causal chain can be satisfied if a color or shape *itself* involves not just the place it is *at* but the place it is *from*. The notes therefore stress that the double placement that makes a color or shape external to the self and constitutes its relation to the perceiver is part of the *datum* (the color or shape) and is not a result of sensation. Of course, when sensation occurs, the *place from* which the color occurs is the place from which the subject experiences the sensation. But the particular color or shape that is at a place *x*, from a place *y* would be recorded by a camera (*CP* 6: 99) and has nothing to do with psychology. In short, the *place at* and *place from* are involved in the quality (*CP* 6: 100). Similarly, 'a spatial relation to the percipient' is a 'part of the *datum* in sight' (*CP* 6: 98).

The theory anticipates the 1914 doctrine that sense data are associated with two places (that of the object and that of a perspective on it) in a constructed space of perspectives.[18] In 1914, however, the role of sensation is muted, making it harder to grasp how 'a fundamental novelty as to the nature of sensation', especially sight, has any bearing on it. Since the analysis of sensation is part of the theory of knowledge, it is difficult to see why Russell turns to the theory of knowledge before the construction of matter. There is, of course, the fact that he plans to explain objects in terms of sensation and sense data and therefore has to say something about them. Yet these notes and letters suggest that the necessity of starting with theory of knowledge is very specific: He plans to elaborate a novel theory of how, in sight, colors and shapes are experienced as external to the self (as there, from here) as the basis of a construction of space and matter.

Yet this plan runs into a snag. In order to use sensation to construct space, it seems necessary to decide between an absolute or relative theory of space.[19] On a relative theory there are no absolute positions or points, and what defines two places, here and there, is a relation. Yet if 'the *here-and-there* is to be in the qualities, not in sensation only' (*CP* 6: 101), the relation that defines these terms cannot be sensation, nor can the perceiver be part of the definition of what is meant by 'here'. On a theory of absolute space, 'here' and 'there' would be defined by unique properties, so that there

---

[18]See, for example, *Our Knowledge of the External World* (Russell 1914a: 92): 'The two places associated with a single aspect correspond to the two ways of classifying it [as an element of the thing and as an element of the perspective on the thing]. We may distinguish the two places as that at which, and that from which, the aspect appears'.

[19]*Our Knowledge* is agnostic as to whether there are points and instants; in practice it adopts a relational theory (Ibid: 145–6). *The Theory of Knowledge* adopts a relational theory of time, or at least it denies the need to assume instants. A similar approach to space seems intended (*CP* 7: 122), but the book is abandoned before it is developed and it is quite possible that Russell began the book undecided as to what theory of space he would ultimately defend.

would be an absolute here and an absolute there. This is the theory Russell prefers, in part because for reasons of simplicity he prefers a theory of absolute time. Yet an absolute theory of space would have to apply to sensations in dreams and hallucinations, and it is awkward to say that when we see colors and shapes in a dream, they occur at a point there, from a point here, which is *not* relative to sensation. This gives the places of dream sensations too much objectivity. 'Dreams are a difficulty in the above theory, and indeed in any theory which brings absolute space into sense data', he notes (*CP* 6: 103).

Obviously, many questions about sensation require resolution before work on construction can begin. How, in general, is *sensation* to be understood? As in *Problems*, in the 1912–13 notes Russell embraces a dualist theory of sensation. On that theory, sensation is a mental act of apprehending and has the form of a relation holding between a subject of consciousness and typically non-mental entities (sense data). Against this view, a neutral monist might argue that there is no difference between acts of sensation and what is sensed because both can be constructed from relations among fundamentally neutral objects. In these notes, when Russell says that the externality of objects (colors, etc.) from each other cannot explain the experience of space as external (*CP* 6: 111), he is alluding to the inadequacy of such a theory. Despite being willing to reject the hypothesis of objects, he thinks that the externality of space can only be explained by retaining a hypothesis of mental subjects and a theory of mental relations between subjects and objects.[20]

6   *Theory of Knowledge*: Sensations and Imagination

In a letter from April of 1913, Russell declares that the 'theory of knowledge must come first', before the construction of matter, 'chiefly because of dreams'.[21] In May, he begins to work on a large book on this subject. Although dreams are problematic to the analysis of space, in referring to them in the April letter he likely has in mind the general issue of distinguishing dreams and other cases of imagination from ordinary sensation. If we have 'true knowledge of external things' (*CP* 6: 98) in seeing colors and shapes, why is the sight of colors and shapes in dreams and hallucinations regarded as irrelevant to physics? Why are the terms 'sensation' and 'imagination'

---

[20]Russell does not identify the subject(s) of consciousness with a mind. By 1913, minds are regarded as constructions. His mind/matter dualism rests on commitment to a mental subject and mental acts like sensation.

[21]Russell to Ottoline Morrell, 22 April 1913, #750, cited in Russell *CP* 6: xlvii.

distinguished, as though one but not the other has greater purchase on reality? If this can be explained without resorting to hypotheses about objects, causal stimuli, and so on, it will amount to 'a great simplification' in 'the problem of our knowledge of the external world' (*CP* 7: 62). It will be possible to argue that colors and other sense data are 'the actual substance of the physical world' (Russell 1914b: 26).

Russell already has in hand a means of distinguishing between what is seen in normal sensation and in hallucinations and dreams. *Problems of Philosophy* suggests that we distinguish these cases by the presence or absence of correlations with other data. When 'On Matter' turns to the construction of objects, it appropriates this idea. On the assumption that colors and other qualities are constituents of the physical world (and not merely 'non-mental' as in *Problems*), the paper argues that some of these constituents are 'erratic' and that 'it is these erratic constituents which are perceived in dreams and hallucinations' (*CP* 6: 95). A dream object is erratic because it has none of the usual links with other sensations, nor any continuity with experience. A dreamer can see a table in a dream, but apart from the dream no one can sit at it, and it does not usually reappear to the dreamer night after night, dream after dream. Thus, the colors and shapes seen in a dream are constituents of the physical world but they are not related with other constituents in the way that constitutes a physical object. In *Theory of Knowledge*, this idea underlies the comment that a world constructed assuming that dreams and waking life have '*immediate* reality' is one in which 'dream objects are less intimately related to *other* entities than are the objects of our waking sensations' (*CP* 7: 49).[22] Later, he explains the point more clearly: A physical object is a system of particulars (i.e. colors, sounds, etc.) and a particular is 'wild' when it cannot be 'linked up with other particulars in respectable, conventional ways' (1918: 239), that is, when it cannot be part of the system of entities that is an object.

Despite having this means of drawing the relevant distinctions, Russell is not content to explain the difference between what is seen in sensation and in imagination by correlations and behavior alone. He seeks an introspectively observable intrinsic difference. One reason is that differences in the way images and sensible objects behave does not help us understand why people sometimes confuse the products of imagination with sensible objects. Additionally, his dualist analysis of sensation, described earlier, is likely to make an account based on correlations alone seem inadequate. One

---

[22]Russell also writes: 'what is *called* the unreality of an immediate object must always be really the unreality of some other object inferred from the immediate object and described by reference to it' (1912b: 49).

feature of his dualism is that a subject *can* introspectively experience the relation of experiencing. For example, awareness *of* a sensation can detect in sensation a special mental quality that a sense datum need not possess; this is why neutral monism is wrong and sensation differs from what is sensed.[23] Similarly, if the objects known by seeing in sensation and in dreams and hallucinations are the same in point of 'reality', introspection of the relations may yet reveal a difference.[24] He therefore aims to find an intrinsic difference between the acquaintance *relations* sufficient to explain why we call images 'unreal' and do not believe them to be relevant to physics. When Russell later abandons dualism, one consequence is that sense data (then, called *sensations*) can be distinguished from images *only* by different correlations with an external world (Russell 1922: 129).

Wherein lies the difference between sensation and imagination? In May, on the verge of starting *Theory of Knowledge*, Russell tells Lady Ottoline that he has 'a bright idea as to the difference between sensation and imagination' that helps explain dreams, his old 'bugbears', as well as memories.[25] He links the issue to matter, as 'really still the same problem' (*CP* 8: xiv). The bright idea is to distinguish seeing in sensation from seeing in imagination by the presence or absence of a time relation to a subject. This notion has grown out of the 1912–13 analysis of how externality or *space* is given in sight. Just as externality to the self was part of the datum of sight in the notes, so, in *Theory of Knowledge*, is temporal *presence* (*simultaneity*).[26] On this hypothesis, in contrast, an imaginary color or shape is not experienced as *present*. If this hypothesis is supportable, it suggests that images are like universals: They are in a relation to a thinker at some moment, but are not experienced as occurring at that moment.[27]

Russell is undecided about this theory, since it is introspectively just as likely that imagined qualities are experienced as simultaneous with the sub-

---

[23]Russell disagrees with Idealism over whether the distinctively mental aspect extends to what is known in having a sensation, but both parties are in agreement that mental facts have a distinctive quality.

[24]They cannot be called equally real, since 'real' and 'unreal' apply to descriptions, not to immediate objects.

[25]Russell to Ottline Morrell, 16 May 1913, cited in Russell (*CP* 8: xiv).

[26]The 1912–13 notes probably already anticipated a theory of the knowledge of time derived from sight to parallel or partner the theory of the knowledge space derived from sight. The notes discussed even briefly entertain the notion that a memory relation gives what is 'in a time from a time (*CP* 6: 102).

[27]This theory seems to imply that the sensation of a brown color results in a belief 'a (present) brown color is being seen', while imagining the same color results in 'a brown color is being seen'.

ject, as they are in sensation. If the latter view is adopted, the difference between sensation and imagination can still be explained in terms of correlations. Yet the theory of imagination as missing a temporal aspect is useful because it explains why the difference between sensation and imagination might be overlooked. Any explanation of the difference between sensation and imagination has to avoid injury to the fact that dream experiences are confusingly felt to be sensations and often call up the emotions that sensations do. It also has to allow for the fact that images are sometimes judged to be memories. Dreams are a kind of test case of the theory in question because on any of the usual grounds (sense of willed effort, vividness, etc.) it is difficult to determine whether they are sensation or imagination.

If an external world is assumed, certain parts of certain dreams can be explained in terms of a response to stimuli. Using the example in *Problems* of dreaming of cannon fire because of a banging door, 'the noise in the dream may be considered sensation, while the rest of the dream is taken as imagination together with false interpretation' (*CP* 7: 60). However, a complicated theory of causal relations to stimuli is closed to him. What about the sensation of willing or differences in vividness or in our belief about their reality? None of these are helpful in the case of dreams, particularly the last. Some images occur like sensations, without our willing them, and if it is doubtful whether the will distinguishes sensation from imagination, dreams cannot be confidently classed with sensation by that measure. Nor is the relative vividness of sensation as opposed to imagination enough to classify dreams, given the exceptions on either side (faint sensations, convincing illusions). Lastly, nothing is gained by considering our beliefs about reality. Belief is peculiar with respect to dreams. That is, 'while they last', dreams appear not to be 'our own invention', but on waking, 'they are dismissed from belief' (*CP* 7: 61). This is not to say that a dreamer actually judges the dream appearances to be sensed and then stops believing this on waking. A dreamer does not explicitly judge: Judging is suppressed. Rather, a dreamer's feelings and reactions are those that on waking would be held toward sensible objects. While sleeping, we have feelings towards dream objects that we 'usually have only towards objects of sense ... ' (*CP* 7: 61).

The inappropriateness of the reaction in the dream goes undetected because the dreamer has an experience without full awareness of what the experience is. This fact is understandable if imagination provides data without any indication of time. Ordinarily, other markers (faintness, unusual correlations, etc.) suffice to notify a subject that an appearance is not a case of sensation. A person in doubt can decide whether an appearance is actually present. However, in sleep, appearances are strong at a moment when critical faculties are weak. Under such conditions, imagination passes as sensation. Russell's conclusion is that what is seen in dreams is mainly a product of imagination, but is treated as normal sensation 'even in their imagined parts' (*CP* 7: 61).

7 *Theory of Knowledge*: Imagination and Memory

Russell's analysis of imagination and sensation explains why we normally assume that the colors and shapes seen in dreams and hallucinations are not relevant to physics and why this belief is suspended in dreams. It allows him an introspective account of how imagined data are not constituents of objects even though they are constituents of the physical world. However, images are often relevant to beliefs, or at least to memories, and the idea that imagination lacks a temporal relation to the subject is also useful in accounting for memory, or rather, for separating it from pseudo-memory.

A discussion of pseudo-memory arises in the context of discussing propositional memories, beliefs *about* the past. (It is separate from discussion of direct awareness of something past.) What forms of memory beliefs are there? The answer depends on whether the relation to the past is perceived or judged, and on whether the object is known by acquaintance or known by description, by means of an image. The forms of memory beliefs relevant to the present discussion are those in which the object is described by an image.[28] Even so, a person may judge an image to be of something in the past or perceive that it is of something existing in the past: Pseudo-memories are cases of *judging* that some imagined scene actually occurred. Imagined objects occur when sense data become new objects of acquaintance but without a temporal relation, present or past, to the subject. But by itself, the existence of an image does not result in a pseudo-memory: If the image were perceived to have a relation to a past object, the resulting belief would be a genuine memory. However, the nature of images does explain why pseudo-memories occur. If the absence of a time relation is overlooked and the person experiencing the image *judges* that there is a relation to the past, then the image becomes a source of error. Pseudo-memories of this kind therefore originate in *judging* an image to have a relation to the past. As in dreams, where the dreamer reacts to a datum as though it were present and given in sensation, such cases are really instances of imagination.

---

[28]See Peter Hylton's contribution to the present volume for a discussion of Russell's arguments against the view that judgments consist of ideas. See also Russell Wahl in this volume for a related discussion.

One reason to address this phenomenon is to show why such instances do not count as premises to knowledge even if they happen to be correct. As in *Problems*, when Russell turns to propositional knowledge, he describes the starting point in an inquiry into what we know as consisting of beliefs whose truth is supplied by experience. The truth of most beliefs is derived from the support they receive from other beliefs, but this cannot always be the case, and a person must possess at least some beliefs whose truth is supplied by confrontation with experience. The kind of belief whose truth is know this way include those about the present moment, such as 'a patch of brown is being seen', and those about the recent past, such as 'a patch of brown was seen'. Whatever else we know about the world, that knowledge can, in theory, be derived from such premises, but it is necessary to clarify what kinds of beliefs about the past actually count as premises. Pseudo-memories obviously do not, nor does any memory that relies on judging that there is a temporal relation.

Once pseudo-memories are accounted for, it is still necessary to explain why and how memory beliefs involving images are acceptable as premises. The acceptable ones are those in which relation to the past is perceived, not judged. But there is a complication. In remembering with images, we are not directly aware of an object as past. Rather, we perceive an image to *be* an image, something that resembles and means something else in the past. That is, we 'immediately perceive the sort of connection of our present image with the past which is involved in calling it an image "of" the past' (*CP* 7: 172-73).

It is not easy to see how we can know that an image is an image and had an original if we cannot compare it to its original and cannot appeal to memory. Russell's account here is not fully developed. It seems to be like his later theory in assuming images to be the decay of their sense datum originals, so that we are conscious of the connection and resemblance because conscious of the image coming to pass from the sense datum as the latter exits the specious present.[29] This doctrine, if assumed now, as it more or less seems to be, would explain why a person imagining a man seen shortly before perceives that the image had an original. He or she grasps the complex: *O' resembles an object O that is recently past*. Without suggesting that we actually scan across from the image in the mind's eye to the sensible object, the point is that we do notice when, for example, a person's actual height differs or resembles the image we have of it. No experience like this could take place if there were no relation between image and the

---

[29]See e.g. Russell 1921: 174.

sense datum to enable the one to represent the other. 'This relation', therefore, '... is part of what makes the image "representative"' (*CP* 7: 175). Descriptive memories are certain because the resemblance is immediately known.

However, that representing ('meaning') relation serves a double purpose. Besides explaining why descriptive memories can be counted among a person's basic premises, it explains why they are usually also felt to be uncertain. The uncertainty is due to their vagueness. Knowledge of the object is vague, 'due to the vagueness of the relation of "representing" which connects the image with the past fact' (*CP* 7: 174). Suppose, for example, that a person's image of a man represents him as being of a height anywhere between 5'11 and 6'1. This latitude is to be expected and it would be more remarkable to imagine a man's height as, say, *exactly* 5'11. As Russell puts it, 'the relation of "representing", which holds between images and sense data, is not one-one; a whole stretch of objects may be represented by a given image, and a whole stretch of images may represent a given object' (*CP* 7: 176). In recalling a man's height ('he had *this* height'), the truth of the memory may be indisputable even though there is no exactness in the memory. Someone might not be able to answer a question based on the memory ('Was he 5'10 or 6'0?'), but still be convinced that the image was correct.

What is the conclusion? Except for pseudo-memories, image containing memories are a source of certainty, since the source of the uncertainty attributed to them is the vagueness of the images. The belief itself is not uncertain. Just as dreams are wrongly attributed the unreality that describes what is inferred from them, so beliefs are wrongly attributed the uncertainty due to the vagueness of images used as symbols.

8 Conclusion

In *Problems*, Russell's unwillingness to accept the testimony of sight that colors and shapes are 'external things' leads him to endorse a physical theory of the causes of sense data. Shortly thereafter, he reconsiders the assumptions about sensation and sight that led him to adopt the hypothesis of objects, and this change in perspective leads to a novel theory of sensation and a radical revision of his theory of the physical world. This shift in thought makes it necessary to explain the difference between seeing colors and shapes in normal sensation and in dreams and hallucinations. At the same time, images have to be defended as a source of certain beliefs about the past.

In presenting these doctrines, Russell is moving in two directions, towards a new analysis of the external world and towards a deeper analysis of the internal, mental world. Both of these strands continue in later work. The first is worked out in *Our Knowledge of the External World* (Russell 1914a) and again in *Analysis of Matter* (Russell 1927). The second is brought to fruition in *Analysis of Mind* (Russell 1921), when Russell moves away from metaphysical dualism towards a critical adaptation of neutral monism and behaviorism. Then, seeing a color is not a mental occurrence distinct from the color seen. Rather, the seeing and the color are a single event occurring in different causal chains, with different connections.[30] In this context, the theory of images takes on new importance.

References

Barnard, R. 2015. Problems as Prolegomena: Russell's Analytic Phenomenology. In this volume: 153–70.

Hylton, P. 2015. *Problems of Philosophy* as a Stage in the Evolution of Russell's Views on Knowledge. In this volume: 25–44.

Linsky, B. 2015. Acquaintance and Certainty in *The Problems of Philosophy*. In this volume: 65–85.

Nunn, P. 1909-10. Are Secondary Qualities Independent of Perception? *Proceedings of the Aristotelian Society* 10: 191–218

Proops, I. 2015. Certainty, Error, and Acquaintance in *The Problems of Philosophy*. In this volume: 45–63.

Russell, B. 1912a. *The Problems of Philosophy*. London: Williams and Norgate. Reprinted Oxford: Oxford University Press 1959.

Russell, B. 1912b. On Matter. In *CP* 6: 80–95.

Russell, B. 1912-1913? Nine Short Manuscripts on Matter. In *CP* 6: 98–111.

Russell, B. 1914a. *Our Knowledge of the External World as a Field for Scientific Method in Philosophy*. Chicago: Open Court.

Russell, B. 1914b. The relation of sense data to physics. In *CP* 8: 3–26.

Russell, B. 1918. *The philosophy of logical atomism*. In *CP* 8: 160–244.

Russell, B. 1921. *The Analysis of Mind*. London: Routledge 1997.

Russell, B. 1922. Physics and Perception. In *CP* 9: 125–133.

Russell, B. 1984. *The Collected Papers of Bertrand Russell, Volume 7: Theory of Knowledge: The 1913 Manuscript*, ed. E. R. Eames with K. Blackwell. London: George Allen and Unwin. [*CP* 7]

---

[30]See Donovan Wishon in 'Russell on Russellian Monism' (2015) for an analysis of Russell's neutral monism as moving through distinct stages and exhibiting distinct types.

Russell, B. 1986. *The Collected Papers of Bertrand Russell, Volume 8: The Philosophy of Logical Atomism and Other Essays, 1914–19*, ed. J. Slater. London: George Allen and Unwin. [*CP* 8]

Russell, B. 1988. *The Collected Papers of Bertrand Russell, Volume 9: Essays on Language, Mind and Matter, 1919–26*, ed. J. Slater. London: Unwin Hyman. [*CP* 9]

Russell, B. 1992. *The Collected Papers of Bertrand Russell, Volume 6: Logical and Philosophical Papers, 1909–13*, ed. J Slater with B. Frohmann. New York: Routledge. [*CP* 6]

Wahl, R. 2015. Sense Data and the Inference to Material Objects: The Epistemological Project in *Problems* and Its Fate in Russell's Later Work. In this volume: 87–105.

Wishon, D. 2015. Russell on Russellian Monism. *Consciousness in the Physical World: Perspectives on Russellian Monism*, eds. T. Alter and Y. Nagasawa. Oxford: Oxford University Press.

7

Russell on Acquaintance, Analysis, and Knowledge of Persons

MICHAEL KREMER

One of the distinctive features of the *Problems of Philosophy* is the role played in Russell's epistemology by the relation that he calls 'acquaintance'. Acquaintance is a direct and immediate cognitive relation, a converse of 'presentation'. It yields a special form of knowledge of things which is foundational for both the understanding of propositions (via the famous 'principle of acquaintance'), and for the knowledge of truths expressed by such propositions. The conception of such a direct cognitive relation is present in G.E. Moore's early philosophy, though he does not use the term. In 'The Refutation of Idealism', he writes of a form of 'awareness', which is 'included in sensation', that it 'is the very same unique fact which constitutes every kind of knowledge' (Moore 1903a: 452). Russell similarly claims in *Problems* that 'acquaintance with objects essentially consists in a relation between the mind and something other than the mind; it is this that constitutes the mind's power of knowing things' (Russell 1912: 42). Moore appeals to awareness in this sense to block skeptical and idealist arguments (Moore 1903a: 451):

> 'blue' is as much an object, and as little a mere content, of my experience, when I experience it, as the most exalted and independent real thing of which I am ever aware. There is, therefore, no question of how we are to 'get outside the circle of our own ideas and sensations'. Merely to have a sensation is already to *be* outside that circle. It is to know something which is as truly and really *not* a part of *my* experience, as anything which I can ever know.

Acquaintance, Knowledge, and Logic.
Donovan Wishon and Bernard Linsky (eds.).
Copyright © 2015, CSLI Publications.

In the same year in which Moore published the 'Refutation', Russell first used the term acquaintance, in the Preface to the *Principles of Mathematics*, writing that:

> The discussion of indefinables which forms the chief part of philosophical Logic is the endeavour to see clearly, and to make others see clearly, the entities concerned, in order that the mind may have that kind of acquaintance with them which it has with redness or the taste of a pineapple. (Russell 1903a: v)

As is well known, Russell derived the term 'acquaintance' from John Grote (1865) via William James, who used the term in roughly Russell's sense as early as 1885 (31–2); the term and the concept it stood for came to play a prominent role in Russell's thinking in the period leading from *Principles* (1903a) to 'On Denoting' (1905b) and remained central for his epistemology until the very idea of a subject of experience came into question with his tentative embrace of neutral monism.

As did Moore with 'awareness', Russell deploys the notion of 'acquaintance' to evade skeptical and idealist arguments. This is evident in Chapter IV of *Problems*, 'Idealism', where Russell accuses the idealists of relying on the seeming truism 'that we cannot know that anything exists which we do not know' (1912: 43). Russell responds that the appeal of this principle depends on eliding a crucial distinction:

> The word 'know' is here used in two different senses. (1) In its first use it is applicable to the sort of knowledge which is opposed to error, the sense in which what we know is true ... This sort of knowledge may be described as knowledge of truths. (2) In the second use ... the word applies to our knowledge of things, which we may call acquaintance. This is the sense in which we know sense-data. ...Thus the statement which seemed like a truism becomes, when re-stated, the following: 'We can never truly judge that something with which we are not acquainted exists.' This is by no means a truism, but on the contrary a palpable falsehood. (1912: 44)

To show the falsehood of the truism, so understood, Russell appeals to an intuitive example: 'I have not the honour to be acquainted with the Emperor of China, but I truly judge that he exists' (44). Here acquaintance is used in a fairly ordinary sense, one in which it is possible to be acquainted with another person. When Russell goes on to consider the possible objection that '...I judge this because of other people's acquaintance with him', he doesn't reject this because other people cannot be acquainted with the emperor; rather he replies that this 'would be an irrelevant retort, since, if the principle were true, I could not know that anyone else is acquainted with him' (1912: 45). In the 'Refutation', Moore similarly used 'awareness' in a broad and intuitive way, so that 'the existence of a table in space' can be as much an object of awareness as a 'sensation of blue' (Moore 1903a: 453). When the term 'acquaintance' first gets an extended introduction by Russell in the 1903 manuscript 'Points about Denoting', he uses it to illustrate the claim that 'sometimes we know that something is denoted, without knowing what'. His example concerns the denoting phrase 'Smith's wife' – if we know that Smith is married but do not know to whom, we may say that we know that this phrase denotes someone but do not know what it denotes. Russell explains:

> We may distinguish the terms with which we are *acquainted* from others which are merely denoted. E.g. in the above case, I am supposed to be acquainted with the term *Smith* and the relation *marriage*, and thence to be able to conceive a term having this relation to Smith, although I am not acquainted with any such term. (Russell 1903b: 360)

Here again, *Smith*, another person, appears as a possible object of acquaintance.

However, by the time of *Problems of Philosophy* (and much earlier as we shall see), Russell's position had shifted so that neither a material object like the table discussed at length in chapter 1, nor a person like Smith, could be an object of acquaintance. The range of possible objects of acquaintance had become much narrower, encompassing sense-data, remembered sensibilia, universals, one's own mind, and (perhaps) the self. Thus Russell's use of the term 'acquaintance' had come to depart widely from that ordinary usage in which one can be said to be acquainted with Smith or the Emperor of China. This fact has long constituted a minor obstacle in my attempts, in teaching the history of analytic philosophy to undergraduates, to explain Russell's contrast between knowledge by acquaintance and knowledge by description.

From time to time, my students remark on the strangeness of Russell's use of the term 'acquaintance'. This is, after all, a word in common usage, and this usage does not fit very well with the sorts of philosophical work to which Russell puts it. Russell uses the term 'acquaintance' to designate a privileged source of knowledge – a direct cognitive relation to objects which yields non-propositional knowledge of those objects. He emphasizes that knowledge by acquaintance is independent of knowledge of truths about the objects known; in contrast all knowledge of truths depends on acquaintance, since, among other things, to grasp a true proposition one must be acquainted with its constituents. Acquaintance, for Russell is never a matter of degree; it is perfect and complete as soon as an object is presented to a subject, and acquiring knowledge of truths about the object in no way increases or improves upon one's knowledge of the object, which is already entirely provided by one's acquaintance with it. Thus in *Problems* he writes that:

> ...knowledge of things, when it is of the kind we call knowledge by *acquaintance*, is essentially simpler than any knowledge of truths, and logically independent of knowledge of truths (1912: 46)

since

> we have *acquaintance* with anything of which we are directly aware, without the intermediary of any process of inference or any knowledge of truths. (1912: 46)

What we know through acquaintance, we know 'perfectly and completely', and 'no further knowledge of it itself is even theoretically possible'. 'Things with which I have acquaintance' are 'immediately known to me just as they are' (1912: 47). The independence of acquaintance from knowledge of truths is so strong that not only may we 'have knowledge of a thing by acquaintance even if we know very few propositions about it; theoretically we need not know any propositions about it' (1912: 144; see also, 1915: 151).

As we have seen, this strong notion of acquaintance first becomes prominent in Russell's thinking in the period leading up to the publication of 'On Denoting' in 1905. As early as 'On Fundamentals', an unpublished manuscript written just before 'On Denoting', Russell denies that it is possible to have acquaintance with other people. In *Problems*, other people are entities which we infer on the basis of the sense data with which we are acquainted, just as we infer the existence of physical bodies on this basis. Each of us has acquaintance with only one person, his or her self. In fact, even this much acquaintance with selves is already taken as somewhat doubtful in *Problems*. Later, even this is denied, and people in general are taken not as inferred entities but as logical constructions out of sense-data, in accordance with the logical atomist maxim 'Wherever possible, logical constructions are to be substituted for inferred entities' (1914: 115). Here, persons are logical fictions, and every proposition that seems to refer to persons is analyzed into a form in which this apparent reference disappears.

Now Russell's use of 'acquaintance' here departs widely from the ordinary use of this term – a fact which is noticed by my students and at least sometimes puzzles them. In ordinary usage, the paradigm example of acquaintance is surely with other people, as is made clear even by dictionary entries. Moreover, in the ordinary sense of acquaintance, acquaintance comes in degrees – it can be casual, for example, or deep. In fact, according to the Oxford English Dictionary, the original meaning of 'acquaintance' was 'the state of being closely acquainted with a person; friendship, companionship', but it later came to mean 'the state of knowing someone slightly, without the depth or intimacy of a friendship' – but as this explanation itself demonstrates, even in this later usage 'acquaintance' can be qualified as more or less 'close'. But for Russell, in contrast, 'acquaintance' names a relation I cannot have to other people (and eventually not even to myself); moreover, it names a relation that does not admit of degrees.

My students' recurring puzzlement about Russell's use of the term 'acquaintance' has led me to concur with Wilfrid Sellars's suggestion in 'Empiricism and the Philosophy of Mind' that Russell has here created something like a philosophical metaphor, a metaphor which 'like other useful metaphors, has congealed into a technical term' (Sellars 1956: 130). Sellars sees this metaphor as philosophically dangerous, however, since it offers a prop to the Myth of the Given. His thought is that the idea of a privileged form of knowledge, logically independent of knowledge of truths yet somehow able to provide a foundation for such knowledge, arises through a several stage process. In the first stage, a conception of knowledge of sense-data is introduced stipulatively as an abbreviation: 'To say of a *sense content* — a color patch, for example — that it was "known" would be to say that *some fact about it* was non-inferentially known'. This guarantees the foundational inference from knowledge of things to knowledge of truths, but only at the price of making the knowledge of things logically dependent on knowledge of truths. In the second stage, 'this *stipulated* sense of *know*' receives 'aid and comfort from the fact that there is, in ordinary usage, a sense of *know* in which it is followed by a noun or descriptive phrase which refers to a particular, thus "Do you know John?"'. At this stage, because this question can be rephrased as 'Are you acquainted with John?', 'the phrase "knowledge by acquaintance" suggests itself as a useful metaphor for this stipulated sense of *know*'. In the final stage, when the metaphor has congealed into a technical term, we are left with the appearance of an unanalyzable simple relation of acquaintance; the inference from knowledge by acquaintance to knowledge of truths is held onto, but its origin in the stipulated definition of knowledge of things in terms of knowledge of truths is forgotten, and the Myth of the Given has slipped through the crack (1956: 130–1).

It is not my purpose to defend Sellars's particular story concerning the philosophical dangers of the metaphor of acquaintance. But I do want to develop another way to ask whether this kind of philosophical use of metaphor might be in some way philosophically dangerous or troubling. The worry I have in mind is more directly tied to the point my students noticed, which plays a subsidiary role in Sellars's account – that in ordinary usage a paradigm of acquaintance is knowledge of another person, yet on Russell's use of the term acquaintance with another person is precisely one of the things that is ruled out. This question was revived in my mind by a passage that I came across in re-reading Russell's 1905 manuscript 'On Fundamentals'. This manuscript is now widely recognized to be a crucial document for understanding Russell's reasons for rejecting the theory of denoting concepts of his *Principles of Mathematics* in favor of the theory of incomplete symbols of 'On Denoting'. More commonly known as the 'theory of descriptions', the latter is itself closely associated with the distinction between knowledge by acquaintance and knowledge by description which plays such an important role in Russell's thought in *Problems*.

Early in 'On Fundamentals', Russell makes some brief remarks about acquaintance and its relation to the topic of denoting. He writes:

> This topic is very interesting in regard to theory of knowledge, because most things are only known to us by denoting concepts. Thus Jones = the person who inhabits Jones's body. We don't have acquaintance with Jones himself, but only with his sensible manifestations. Thus if we think we know propositions about Jones, this is not quite right; we only know propositional functions which he satisfies, unless indeed we are Jones. *Thus there can be no such thing as affection for persons other than ourselves*; it must be either their sensible manifestations, or the concepts denoting them that we like. It cannot be the latter, for it would be absurd to say we loved some of these and hated others. Denoted objects only known to us as denoted may be identified, without such great error as in other cases, with the sum of their predicates; for it is only their predicates that we know, and these (all or some of those we know) must be meant by us whenever we speak of such objects. But we can only know an object as denoted if we are acquainted with the denoting concept; thus immediate acquaintance with the constituents of the denoting concept is presupposed in what we may call denotative knowledge. (1905a: 369, my emphasis)

In his recent *The Russellian Origins of Analytical Philosophy*, Graham Stevens cites this passage as containing an 'observation concerning the relation of denoting to knowledge'. For Stevens the passage is significant because it marks Russell's early adoption of a distinction between acquaintance and 'denotative knowledge' – the later 'knowledge by description' – and illustrates Russell's use of the distinction to serve 'metaphysical and epistemological ends' (Stevens 2005: 109–10). But in this otherwise little-remarked passage, Russell draws not only the conclusion, familiar to readers of *Problems*, that it is impossible to have acquaintance with other people – 'we don't have acquaintance with Jones, but only with his sensible manifestations' – but also the striking consequence that 'there can no such thing as *affection* for persons other than ourselves', concluding, in effect, that when we say we have affection for another person, it is really 'their sensible manifestations ... that we like'. It is this remark – an aside within an aside, quoted by Stevens but not otherwise taken notice of by him – which took me aback when I first read it, and which is the proximate cause for the writing of this paper.

For the picture of human affection presented here seemed to me so bizarre, not to say disturbing, that I wanted to think about what kind of philosophical reasoning and assumptions could lead one to it. And it was here that I wondered whether there was hidden philosophical danger in the way in which Russell had taken the notion of 'acquaintance' from ordinary usage – a term originally applied to close and intimate friendships – and turned it into a technical term for a kind of knowledge of objects that excluded the knowledge of other people and to which all other knowledge, including the knowledge of other people (and indeed ultimately the knowledge of one's own self), was to be reduced.

Now it must be said that the thought that struck me as disturbing in this unpublished manuscript of Russell's is not one that I know to have appeared in any of his published work. Indeed, when I presented an earlier version of this paper at a conference on the origins of early analytic philosophy, some in the audience suggested that the remark was just a bad joke on Russell's part. Nonetheless it seems to me that the sentence that I was seized by was written by Russell to record what he at least took at one point to be a logical consequence of his epistemological position. And in fact, I will suggest, this seemingly bizarre view *is* the consequence of Russell's account of knowledge in general, and of knowledge of other people in particular.

I propose to reconstruct Russell's reasoning as follows:

> If I have affection for, like, or love, someone *x*, I must *know who it is* that I have affection for, like, or love. But then I must *know x*, that is, I must be acquainted with *x*. But if *x* is *another* person, I do not have acquaintance with *x*. Therefore I do not know them. And for this reason I cannot have affection for them, either.

It may be objected that I have here foisted a patently bad argument on Russell: surely it is sufficient for me to know *who it is* that I have affection for, that I know that person *by description*. However, the argument I have given here bears a strong structural similarity to Russell's *own* argument in *Problems* for the 'Principle of Acquaintance', that 'every proposition that we can understand must be composed wholly of objects with which we are acquainted' (Russell 1912: 58).

> ...it is scarcely conceivable that we can make a judgment or entertain a supposition without knowing what it is that we are judging or supposing about. We must attach *some* meaning to the words we use, if we are to

> speak significantly and not utter mere noise; and the meaning we attach to
> our words must be something with which we are acquainted. (1912: 58)

Here he seems to argue, in strict parallel to the first part of my reconstruction above:

> If I attach x to a word w as its meaning, I must I must *know what it is* that I
> mean by x, what it is that I judge or make a supposition about. But then I
> must *know x*, that is, I must be acquainted with x.

So here he assumes that to know the meaning of a word is to be acquainted with the term that it means. Similarly, in 'On Fundamentals', he assumes that to have affection for anything I must know it the same strong sense, as an object of acquaintance.

What do we know in this sense, according to Russell's epistemology at the point of writing this passage, just before the onset of the theory of descriptions? We know those things with which we are directly acquainted – this includes, if we can follow the later position of *The Problems of Philosophy*, sense-data, universals, our own minds, and (perhaps) the self. Presumably it also includes the 'denoting concepts' which at the point of writing our passage, Russell takes to be the meanings of 'denoting phrases' like 'the present queen of England' and 'all human beings'.

So, consider my affection for my friend Jones. I am not acquainted with Jones; literally speaking I do not *know* Jones, in the sense that he is not *presented* to me. What I am acquainted with, what is presented to me, are certain sense-data that are Jones's 'manifestations'. As the term 'manifestation' suggests, I know of Jones's existence only by an *inference*. As Russell puts it in *Problems*, 'other people are represented to me by certain sense-data, such as the sight of them or the sound of their voices' (1912: 21). Russell illustrates this point through various examples. Concerning 'a person who knew Bismarck' he explains that:

> What this person was acquainted with were certain sense-data which he
> connected (rightly, we will suppose) with Bismarck's body. His body, as a
> physical object, and still more his mind, were only known as the body and
> the mind connected with these sense-data. That is, they were known by
> description. (1912: 54–5)

Similarly, I know my friend Jones 'by description' as 'the human being who is the cause of these sense-data'. But, as *Problems* makes clear, knowledge of things by description is not really knowledge of the *things*. It is, rather, knowledge of certain *truths* which depend on the *existence* of the described things (1912: 52ff). This is the 'only sense in which one can be acquainted with someone else', as Russell puts it (1912: 53).

Now return to my affection for Jones. In the terms of the theory of denoting concepts, I know truths involving the denoting concept *the human being who is the cause of these sense-data*; but I am only acquainted with this denoting concept, and with the sense-data it involves. I do not *know* Jones; he is not a *datum* for me. Therefore I cannot like *him*. Supposed affection for him must reduce to my liking some or other of the items with which I *am* acquainted. Russell eliminates the possibility that I like something like the concept *human being who is the cause of these sense-data*, and so is left with the alternative that what I like is some of the sense-data themselves.

Now it seems clear that something has gone wrong here. To understand what has gone wrong, I would like to return to the ordinary notion of acquaintance, and the contrast I have already suggested between this ordinary notion of acquaintance and Russell's technical notion, referred to by the same term.

I noted above that in the ordinary sense of the term, 'acquaintance', other people are the paradigm objects of acquaintance. Certainly, one can be said to be acquainted with things other than people. Many of the things commonly treated as objects of acquaintance are, however, in some broader sense human things. We speak of being acquainted with cuisines, cities, rituals, pieces of music, games... It would be fairly strange to say of, for example, a rock, that I am acquainted with it. If one were to say such a thing, that would usually call upon some broader context in which the rock would acquire some significance.

Nonetheless, there are many uses of the term 'acquaintance', and the objects of acquaintance in ordinary speech can be quite varied. Robert Frost speaks of being acquainted with the night; Isaiah's suffering servant is said to be acquainted with grief; Audubon was desirous of being acquainted with nature; God is said by the Psalmist (at least in the words of the translators who produced the Authorized Version) to be acquainted with 'all my ways'. A search of Shakespeare's writings online turns up many cases of acquaintance with other people, but also cases of acquaintance with change, with the waves, with 'my own weakness', with desires, with intentions, with pieces of information, and even – in one case – with something like a sense-datum, a smell (this last in Two Gentlemen of Verona, Act IV, Scene 4). In some of these cases, it is possible to see personification (as in Frost's acquaintance with the night, and Shakespeare's 'I saw him hold acquaintance with the waves'); but not in all. But in almost all of these cases, whether personification is involved or not, it seems clear that acquaintance can come in degrees – it can be casual, for example, or deep.

In very many cases of the ordinary use of 'acquaintance', therefore, there is a direct contrast with Russell's use of the term – for as we saw, for Russell, acquaintance never comes in degrees. Russell is not unaware of this fact about our ordinary use of 'acquaintance'. In *Our Knowledge of the External World*, he explains that 'it is a mistake to speak as if acquaintance had degrees; there is merely acquaintance and non-acquaintance. When we speak of becoming "better acquainted," as for instance with a person, what we *must mean* is becoming acquainted with more parts of a certain whole; but the acquaintance with each part is either complete or non-existent' (Russell 1914: 151, my emphasis). Here, in his 'logical atomist' period, Russell reduces the objects of ordinary acquaintance to complexes of simples with which we can have acquaintance in his favored sense, complexes which are themselves, in the end, nothing but *logical fictions*. This analysis applies to other people (and eventually even to one's own self).

I want to argue, however, that in thus treating other people as analyzable complexes, Russell misrepresents both the objects of ordinary acquaintance and the form of knowledge that this acquaintance makes possible. I start from the idea that people, the paradigm objects of ordinary acquaintance, and more generally many of the 'human' objects of ordinary acquaintance in a more general sense, have something of the character of what the British Idealists called 'organic unities'. They resist analysis into interrelated simpler parts; the parts of the whole have being and identity only in virtue of being parts of that whole. Because of this, knowledge of other people cannot be reduced to knowledge of the metaphysically independent parts of a complex whole and their external relations to one another.

Now Russell, following Moore, rejects the idealist conception of organic unities to which I am appealing here. Both Russell and Moore do, however, accept a weaker notion of 'organic unity', which is central to Moore's 'principle of organic unities' in *Principia Ethica*, according to which 'the intrinsic value of a whole is neither identical with nor proportional to the sum of its parts' (Moore 1903b: 184). Russell summarizes this conception in his essay 'The Elements of Ethics'. He considers cases in which:

> ...some things which in isolation are bad or indifferent are essential ingredients in what is good as a whole, and some things which in isolation are good or indifferent are essential ingredients in what is bad as a whole. (Russell 1910: 55)

To judge whether something is good or bad *in isolation* we have to consider it as if it were *not* part of the whole. But it can happen that 'the value of a complex whole cannot be measured by adding together the values of its parts'. 'Thus many goods must be estimated as wholes, not piecemeal; and exactly the same applies to evils. In such cases the wholes may be called *organic unities*' (1910: 56). Moore's 'principle of organic unities' simply recognizes the existence of organic unities in this sense. But the parts of such organic unities nonetheless have value independently of, and consequently have a nature and identity independently of, the whole of which they are parts. Metaphysically this whole is a complex of interrelated constituents, and the conception of such unities as complexes of interrelated simple parts underlies Russell's program of logical analysis.

I would certainly agree that people are organic unities in this sense. And recognizing this might seem to be sufficient to avoid the conclusion that Russell draws in the passage from 'On Fundamentals', that it is impossible to have affection for other people, because we cannot have acquaintance with them. At the very least, we have with Moore's idea of organic unities the possibility of ascribing a value to other people that is distinct from the sum of the values of their 'sensible manifestations', even when other people are analyzed as 'logical constructions' out of these (actual and possible) sensible manifestations, as Russell began to do shortly after *Problems*. I would like to argue, however, that conceiving of persons as organic unities in this weak sense only is insufficient for accounting for both knowledge of, and love for, other people. A proper account of both of these requires that we recognize other people to be akin to organic unities in a stronger sense than is here allowed for.

However, both Russell and Moore present *arguments* against such more demanding conceptions of organic unities. Their arguments tend to come in two sorts. On the one hand, they argue that their idealist opponents presuppose the 'denial of external relations' – they suppose that all relations are 'internal' and somehow affect the nature of their relata. In consequence, on the idealists' view, given any complex made up out of interrelated constituents, to treat its constituents as metaphysically independent of the whole is to in some way falsify their natures. This first form of argument doesn't seem to me at all dangerous to the idea that *there are* organic unities, among them persons; the target here can only be the claim that *every* whole made up out of parts (and so ultimately the whole of everything there is), is such an organic unity.

A more dangerous argument, which appears in various forms in both Moore and Russell, holds that the *very idea* of an organic unity is self-contradictory and trades on some form of equivocation, for example, concerning the relation of part and whole. Arguments of this type can be found in Moore's 'Refutation of Idealism' (1903a: 442–3) and *Principia Ethica* (1903b: 33ff), and in Russell's *Principles of Mathematics* (466) and his

1905 paper 'On the Nature of Truth' (561). To take perhaps the clearest instance, consider Moore's argument in *Principia Ethica*.

According to this argument, the idea of an organic unity 'asserts the parts of such a whole to have a property which the parts of no whole can possibly have'. This is the property that 'the part is no distinct object of thought – that the whole, of which it is a part, is in its turn a part of it' (1903b: 33). This doctrine Moore judges to be self-contradictory: it amounts to asserting both that the part is, and that it is not, distinct from the whole. He claims that it arises from confusing two distinct ways in which a whole can be related to its parts (or the parts to one another). First, the parts of the whole may *causally depend* on the other parts and their organization into the whole, while the whole in turn may causally depend on the parts and their mutual relations. Second, the *value* of the whole may be greater than yet dependent on the values of the parts, and the parts *qua* parts of the whole may be conceived as having a greater value than they would if separated from the whole. Both these facts may be expressed by saying that parts and whole stand in mutual means-end relations; but the two senses of 'means-end' need to be kept distinct. Conflating them, Moore thinks, leads to the position he describes as self-contradictory.

There isn't really time to assess this argument in detail here, and Moore may well be right about the position of his Idealist opponents. But for myself I do not find it a convincing argument if it is meant to establish that there can *never* be internal relations between the parts of a whole, or between the parts of a whole and the whole itself. I cannot see how this position requires that we identify the whole with the parts. It does, of course, require that we distinguish between the parts of a whole and certain related objects which are composed of the same elements – as for example the dead arm and the living arm – and it requires some account of the relations between the 'parts' of an organic whole and the 'constituents' which might be seen as forming its matter. While I am not in any position to develop such an account here; I do not see Moore has demonstrated its impossibility. Moreover, I think that some such account is required for a satisfactory understanding of what we should say about knowledge of other people. And so to this I now briefly turn.

Suppose, then, we do not accept Moore's argument that the very concept of an organic unity is self-contradictory and confused, then. What happens to our conception of the knowledge of, and love for, other people? I do not have even the beginnings of a dispositive argument here; but I would like to begin to sketch an answer.[1]

In a recent book on the problem of suffering, *Wandering in Darkness*, Eleonore Stump distinguishes between what she calls 'Dominican' knowledge and 'Franciscan' knowledge. Dominican knowledge (so-called after the great medieval preacher St. Dominic) is knowledge-that, knowledge of truths. Franciscan knowledge (after St. Francis of Assisi) is knowledge that cannot be reduced to knowledge-that. Stump motivates this distinction by introducing Russell's conception of acquaintance as knowledge of things, not truths; for her Russellian acquaintance is a kind of 'Franciscan knowledge'. But there is also, for her, *knowledge of persons*. According to her, this too is not reducible to propositional knowledge, Dominican knowledge *that*. But it is intrinsically second-personal, and therefore contrasts also with knowledge of *things* that is the model of Russellian acquaintance. She motivates both of these claims with a variation on Frank Jackson's well-known 'black and white Mary' example:

> Imagine... that Mary in her imprisonment has had access to any and all information about the world as long as that information is *only* in the form of third-person accounts giving her knowledge *that*. ... In short, Mary has been kept from anything that could count as a second-person experience, in which one can say 'you' to another person. And then suppose that Mary is finally rescued from her imprisonment and united for the first time with her mother, who loves her deeply. ... Mary will know things she did not know before.... What is new for her, what she learns, has to do with her personal interaction with another person. What is new for Mary is a second-person experience. ... This thought experiment thus shows that there are things we come to know from our experience of other persons and that these things are difficult or impossible to formulate in terms of knowing *that*. (Stump 2010: 50)

Stump elaborates the example to argue that the kind of knowledge Mary acquires in meeting her mother cannot be treated as anything like Russellian acquaintance: 'it is not necessary for Franciscan knowledge of this sort that there be any direct causal contact between the knower and the person known' (Stump 2010: 53). Thus, she considers the possibility that, when

---

[1] The following suggestions are highly speculative. They also raise issues on which much ink has been spilled: the relations between the first and second-person, between knowledge of self and of other people, and between love and knowledge; also the appeal to narrativity in accounting for the unity of the self. There is no space to address the enormous literature on these topics here, nor would this be suitable for a paper on themes in Russell's philosophy. In any case I have only begun to dip my toes into this ocean. I hope to return to some of these issues in later work. I make a few suggestive remarks in several of the notes below.

Mary meets her mother, 'unbeknownst to Mary, she had a brother who has since died.' In spite of his absence, Stump, argues, Mary can come to *know* her brother 'to one degree or another.' This is because such knowledge can be conveyed through *narrative*, in which we 're-present the experience itself in such a way that we can share the second-person experience' (2010: 78). Thus, suppose that 'when Mary is reunited with her mother, her mother gives Mary pictures of her brother and tells her stories about him'. Stump argues that 'Through the pictures and stories, Mary may come to know her brother, with Franciscan knowledge, to one degree or another. But she will do so without having "special causal contact" with her brother. At the time Mary comes to know him, he is dead' (2010: 53). So for Stump, second-personal knowledge of persons is distinct from both propositional knowledge *that*, and knowledge of things. And, importantly for my argument, knowledge of persons comes in degrees.[2]

Stump's appeal to narrative as a source of second-personal knowledge of others is reminiscent of Alasdair MacIntyre's famous claim in *After Virtue* that the unity of a human life is 'the unity of a narrative which links

---

[2]One might wonder in what sense Mary achieves 'second-personal' knowledge of her brother, since she cannot come to know him as another self, a 'thou' to her 'I' – he is, after all, dead. It may help here to imagine Mary speaking to her brother in thought, lamenting the fact that they did not meet in life, addressing him in the second person. Similar remarks could be made concerning Murdoch's story of M and D below: paradoxically, M only comes to be in a position to enter into a truly reciprocal I-you relationship with D after D's death, which we may imagine as causing her re-evaluation of D's life and character, with its attendant focused attention on the individual person, D. Again, it may help to engage one's imagination: picture M writing a letter to D, perhaps apologizing for the ways in which she misunderstood and mistreated her during her life.

One might also wonder whether Stump's example really shows that second-personal knowledge comes in degrees. After all, Mary was in possession of all the *facts* of the case prior to meeting her mother. So wouldn't she already have had all the knowledge her mother's stories could provide to her, albeit in third-personal, non-narrative terms? A response to this is suggested by the realization that Stump posits it as *news* to Mary 'that she had a brother who has since died'. This, then, cannot be among the *facts* to which Mary has had unlimited access in her imprisonment. She may have known the biological facts of human reproduction, and of human death, and have known that there a male human was an offspring of the same parents as her, but is no longer alive; but this would not be to know that she had a *brother* who is now *dead*, in the sense of a person in relationship to her, with a completed life structured as a 'narrative running from birth to death' (see the discussion of MacIntyre below). Only by coming to know *stories* about her brother, rather than mere catalogs of facts about his career, does she begin to place those facts in the narrative of his life, and through them come to *know her brother*; and this process is a gradual one in which knowledge can only be achieved 'to one degree or another'. (In this paragraph I am responding to a query of Donovan Wishon.)

birth to life to death as narrative beginning to middle to end' (MacIntyre 1984: 205). MacIntyre argues that it is only in taking human lives to have a narrative unity that we can see them, and the actions and events that make them up, as intelligible. This is an essentially holistic view of human life and action, in which an act 'becomes intelligible by finding its place in a narrative' (1984: 210). On this view we can even so much as 'identify a particular action only by invoking two kinds of contexts' – placing 'the agent's intentions in causal and temporal order with reference to their role in his or her history' while also placing them 'with reference to their role in the history of the setting or settings to which they belong' (1984: 208). MacIntyre directly contrasts this conception with the atomistic account which he finds in 'those analytic philosophers who have constructed accounts of human action which make central the notion of "a" human action'. On such accounts, 'a course of human events is ... seen as a complex sequence of individual actions'. But, MacIntyre argues, 'the concept of an intelligible action is a more fundamental concept than the concept of an action as such. Unintelligible actions are failed candidates for the status of intelligible actions ...' and it is a mistake to just 'lump intelligible and unintelligible actions together into a single class of actions' characterized 'in terms of what items of both sets have in common' (1984: 209).

All this suggests that, for MacIntyre, the narrative unity that he sees as constitutive of the self is something like a form of organic unity, in the idealists' sense. MacIntyre's claim, then, can be seen as a way of spelling out my thought that persons are akin to organic unities, above.[3] Stump's suggestion, however, shifts the focus from narrative conceptions of the self to narrative as a way of arriving at knowledge of *other* people. This move brings together the perhaps more familiar (to me, at least) ideas of the second-person standpoint, and the first-personal conception of the self as having a narrative form into an account of knowledge of others.[4] I will not pursue this line further in the main body of the paper, however. I make some very tentative baby-step remarks in some of the footnotes. For our present purposes what is most important about Stump's argument is the way it em-

---

[3] MacIntyre's claim, also commonly associated with Charles Taylor, has been controverted by a number of philosophers, beginning with Galen Strawson in 'Against Narrativity', and a large literature is now devoted to narrative conceptions of the self and their problems. For a strong reply to such skeptical attacks see Anthony Rudd, 'In Defense of Narrative'.

[4] Donovan Wishon pointed out to me that this topic has been explored by contemporary phenomenologists. For an introduction, see Gallagher and Zahavi, 208–17. Also see note 12 below.

phasizes the distinction *within* her 'Franciscan knowledge' between knowledge of *things* and knowledge of *persons*. What I want to suggest here is that *this* distinction is as fundamental as, indeed perhaps even more fundamental than, the Russellian distinction between knowledge of truths and knowledge of things. It is *this* crucial distinction that is elided in Russell's use of the originally *personal* term 'acquaintance' for the knowledge of *objects* that is the foundation of his philosophy.[5]

In 'The Idea of Perfection', Iris Murdoch[6] argues that 'love is knowledge of the individual', and that the 'central concept of morality is

---

[5]'Second-personal' cannot be understood here simply to mean that we can use the word 'you' to address the other. It is entirely possible to address non-human animals and even inanimate objects as 'you' and thereby to treat them as if they were other persons. Ian Proops suggested to me in this context the example of the volleyball in the movie *Cast Away* – the protagonist in the movie, Chuck Noland, alone on a deserted island, paints a face on the ball, dubs it 'Wilson', and adopts it as his companion. Chuck has conversations with Wilson, in the course of which he addresses it as 'you', yet Wilson is not another person, and is no real sense an organic unity. It is easy to answer that anthropomorphism or personification is involved here. But more can be said: in treating Wilson as if it were a 'you', Chuck is responding to Wilson as if it were something with its own life and own life-story, someone he can *know as a person*. In an early version of the movie script, Chuck even asks Wilson 'What's your story?' (see Broyles 1998); and in the movie itself Chuck at one point tells Wilson 'I *know* you', as if he had intimate knowledge of Wilson's character and ways of thinking. Thus Chuck engages in an analogical or perhaps metaphorical extension of the normal use of 'you', to communicate with a person having the unity of a narrative from birth death, to enable the fiction of having a companion in Wilson. Indeed a psychological study inspired in part by *Cast Away* found that this form of projection is common among lonely people. (See Epley *et al.*; participants in the study were at one point made to view a clip from the film representing a state of loneliness, and New York Times blogger John Tierney reported that 'Science Explains Wilson the Volleyball'.) But of course, Wilson has no life, character, or thoughts, other than what Chuck attributes to him. Any narrative Chuck might construct for Wilson would be in no way constrained by the hard reality of a person confronting him.

[6]I first grasped the relevance of Murdoch's work for my argument – and especially of the case of M and D below – while observing the teaching of our doctoral student, Mark Hopwood. In his dissertation Mark develops a much deeper reading of Murdoch's claim that love is knowledge of the individual than I have been able to offer here.

"the individual" thought of as knowable by love' (321, 323).[7] Here it is love that is given the primary role; whereas I traced Russell's thinking in 'On Fundamentals' to the idea that we cannot have affection for other people unless we know them, and we cannot know them unless we are acquainted with them in Russell's technical sense of the term, for Murdoch, we cannot *begin* to know another person except by loving them. Why should this be the case, however? Stump suggests that knowledge of other persons is second-personal – it is knowledge of the other as 'you'. Murdoch's famous example of the mother-in-law M and the daughter-in-law D can be seen as developing this point. M begins by thinking of D as 'quite a good-hearted girl, but while not exactly common yet certainly unpolished and lacking in dignity and refinement' (312). But as time passes, M, who is 'an intelligent and well-intentioned person, capable of self-criticism, capable of giving careful and just *attention* to an object which confronts her', finds that 'gradually her vision of D alters'. 'D is discovered to be not vulgar but refreshingly simple, not undignified but spontaneous, not noisy but gay, not tiresomely juvenile but delightfully youthful, and so on' (313).

---

[7]It may seem wrong-headed to bring Murdoch's work to the defense of a view according to which persons are in some sense 'organic unities'. For Murdoch, both as philosopher and as novelist, was fully aware of the ways in which 'the self is a divided thing and the whole of it cannot be redeemed any more than it can be known' – how in our 'human frailty' we are 'blinded by self', 'largely mechanical creatures, the slaves of relentlessly strong selfish forces ... as decent persons ... usually very specialized' ('The Sovereignty of the Good Over Other Concepts', 381-2). (I was reminded of this passage in reading a paper by one of our doctoral students, Pascal Brixel; the general worry I am addressing here was raised in comments from Ian Proops, independently of Murdoch.) I think, though, that in recognizing the unity of the person as that of a narrative which is never completely achieved at any point during a lifetime we can come to see the idea of this unity as something like a 'regulative ideal' governing any attempt to achieve the human good. In this light, the disunity which Murdoch emphasizes in passages such as the above is a defect, a falling away from what human life should be. This would comport with Catriona MacKenzie and Jacqui Poltera's defense of narrative unity as a condition of a good human life, in their 'Narrative Integration, Fragmented Selves and Autonomy'. They use the memoir of the schizophrenic Elyn Saks to argue that 'the capacity to integrate one's experience into a self-narrative is necessary for a flourishing life'. Schizophrenia, a recognizable disorder and defect, here images the less dramatic failures to achieve integration that mar all our lives. This may not suffice to answer the worry, but it is the best I can now offer. In the end, if forced to choose, I would prefer to give up any attempt to *explain* the unity of the person, and stick to the essential points I draw from Murdoch: that the other person is a given for me and cannot be seen as any kind of construction out of other, more primitive data; and that knowledge of the other person demands a form of attention which can be called love.

Murdoch emphasizes that this change in M's vision of D is a growth in *knowledge*, and is brought about by M's attention: 'M *looks* at D, she attends to D, she focuses her attention'. Moreover, this attention is *loving*: 'What M is *ex hypothesi* attempting to do is not just to see D accurately, but to see her justly and lovingly' (317). But this means that knowledge of the individual is inherently 'something progressive': 'M is engaged in an endless task. As soon as we begin to use words such as "love" and "justice" in characterizing M, we introduce into our whole conceptual picture of her situation the idea of progress' (318). Knowledge of persons requires 'a just and loving gaze directed upon an individual reality' (327). But this means that to attempt to know another is 'an endless task' (321).

So here, as in Stump, the idea present in the ordinary concept of acquaintance, that knowledge of other people comes in degrees, is reflected. But Russell could only understand this as meaning that individuals are endlessly complex, so that knowing them has to be understood as directing our attention to their infinitely many parts and their interrelations, a process that can never be completed. On Murdoch's view in contrast the task is endless 'because as we move and look our concepts themselves are changing' (321). M is not merely discovering new bits and pieces of D, and new ways in which the bits are interrelated. Nor is D changing; the change is in M, it is a transformation of vision. Murdoch makes this point clear by considering the possibility that M's change of heart towards D might take place while D is absent or even entirely after D is dead.[8] M is attending to what has been there all along, but in her act of attending she is coming to new ways of thinking about D, and thereby coming to know D better. If Stump is right, she is entering more and more into a second-personal relationship with D, a relationship between an 'I' and a 'thou'; and it is only in entering into this relationship that M comes to know D, in the second-personal way in which one person can know another.[9]

---

[8]Murdoch, like Stump, uses an example in which one person comes to real knowledge of another person only after the death of the other. MacIntyre too refers to death in his conception of the unity of human life as that of 'a narrative which links birth to life to death'. As Anthony Rudd emphasizes, the narrative of a life is never complete while the subject of the narrative is living; if the form of unity of human life is narrative form, then this unity is never finally and completely achieved in life: 'Our narratives grow and change as we live. There is no sense in supposing that we could say—well, I've attained narrative unity, now what shall I do? The struggle to unify the elements of one's personality, and to incorporate the contingencies that life throws at one into one's narrative is a continual process' (Rudd 2007: 67).

[9]On the suggestion that M comes to have 'second-person' knowledge of D, see note 3. Here I would like to add the thought that M's paying loving attention to D can be understood as M

This conception of our knowledge of and love for other people is at odds not only with the logical atomist view of other people as logical constructions out of immediate data; it opposes also, I claim, the view of *Problems* that other people are known 'by description' through an inference from such data. For on the conception that I am here sketching, it is other people themselves that are *given* to me, *presented* to me in my experience, as unities that confront me with the task of deepening my knowledge of them, a task which demands that I in the first instance recognize them as persons and devote 'loving attention' to them. Contrast this conception of the 'endless task' of coming to know another person with the vision of knowledge of (and friendship with) others expressed by Russell in the following passage from the *Philosophy of Logical Atomism*:

> Take a person. What is it that makes you say when you meet your friend Jones, "Why, this is Jones"? It is clearly not the persistence of a metaphysical entity inside Jones somewhere, because even if there be such an entity, it certainly is not what you see when you see Jones coming along the street; it certainly is something that you are not acquainted with, not an empirical datum. Therefore plainly there is something in the empirical appearances which he presents to you, something in their relations one to another, which enables you to collect all these together and say, "These are what I call the appearances of one person", and that something that makes you collect them together is not the persistence of a metaphysical subject, because that, whether there be such a persistent subject or not, is certainly not a datum, and that which makes you say "Why, it is Jones" is a datum. Therefore Jones is not constituted as he is known by a sort of pin-

---

trying to construct a true narrative of D's life. However, Samantha Vice has argued that the idea that the unity of human life is narrative is incompatible with Murdoch's emphasis on 'the real impenetrable human person' (Vice 2003: 105–7, citing Murdoch, 'Against Dryness', 294). She presupposes that in speaking of the unity of narrative, we are considering the unity of a 'good story', where this is contrasted with 'trying to tell things as they were', and her argument turns on the tensions between form and contingency in the writing of fiction. However, not all narrative is fictional. As I understand the case of M and D, M is rewriting her narrative of D's life, attempting to bring her narrative into more accurate relationship with the true story of D, and is at the same time revising her ongoing narrative of her own life. In 'The Sublime and the Good' Murdoch writes of 'the tragic freedom implied by love' which is 'that we all have an indefinitely extended capacity to imagine the being of others' (216). I see this imaginative work as the construction of narrative. But, in spite of Murdoch's talk of 'freedom', this is imaginative work is *not* unconstrained by the reality of the other's being. As Murdoch puts it, this freedom is 'tragic, because there is no prefabricated harmony, and others are, to an extend we never cease discovering, different from ourselves. ... Freedom is exercised in the confrontation with the other, in the context of an infinitely extensible work of imaginative understanding, of two irreducibly dissimilar individuals. Love is the imaginative recognition of, that is respect for, this otherness' (216). See also note 11.

point ego that is underlying his appearances, and you have got to find some correlations among the appearances which are of the sort that make you put all those appearances together and say, they are the appearances of one person. ... you can collect a whole set of experiences into one string as all belonging to you, and similarly other people's experiences can be collected together as all belonging to them by relations that actually are observable and without assuming the existence of the persistent ego. ... Therefore we shall say that a person is a certain series of experiences. We shall not deny that there may be a metaphysical ego. We shall merely say that it is a question that does not concern us in any way, because it is a matter about which we know nothing and can know nothing, and therefore it obviously cannot be a thing that comes into science in any way. What we know is this string of experiences that makes up a person, and that is put together by means of certain empirically given relations such, e.g., as memory. (Russell 1918: 276–7)

While this passage is from the 'logical atomism' period, apart from the explicit identification of people with strings of experiences much of the same could be said by Russell in *Problems*. But the obvious response to all of this is that when I see my friend Jones on the street, what I see is neither a 'pinpoint ego' nor a 'metaphysical subject', but neither is it merely a collection of 'empirical appearances'. What I see is *my friend*, Jones, and my heart is gladdened at the sight. I do this without collecting together those appearances which I have somehow noticed to belong together as belonging to one person. It is my friend that is presented to me in my experience, as a whole person whom I am called to know and love ever more deeply. To take any other view is to be profoundly alienated from those around us, and ultimately from ourselves.[10]

---

[10]It might be thought that the narrative view of the unity of the person I have gestured at above is itself a 'constructivist' view of the sort I am criticizing in Russell, and undercuts my thought that what I meet on the street is a 'whole person'. This criticism is apt if the narrative view is one in which we in some sense "construct" ourselves, endowing our lives with narrative unity by making up stories to fit them. But this is not what I take to be the point of the claim that the *form* of unity of a human life is narrative. As mentioned in footnote 6, not all narratives are fictional. But human lives are essentially *tellable* and for this they must share narrative *form* with the true stories that can be told about them. (Compare Wittgenstein's claim in the *Tractatus* that the form of a fact is shared by the fact and the picture that represents it; this does not entail the semi-idealist view that we impose form on the world in making pictures of it.) This is not to say that the self whose life is to be told is the 'author' of that story in some sense that would give her liberty to make up the story as she pleases. Rudd points out that 'MacIntyrean narrative theory ... has never suggested that our narratives are totally under our control. As MacIntyre states "we are never more (and sometimes much less) than the co-authors of our own narratives. Only in fantasy do we live what story we please"' (Rudd 2007: 66, quoting MacIntyre 1984: 199). Rudd goes on to remark that 'Our narratives are intertwined with those

It is true that in *Our Knowledge of the External World*, Russell admits a sense in which other people count among our 'data', the items that are given to us. They are among the 'soft data' or 'data in the wide sense' which philosophical analysis must take into account. That is to say that 'when we first begin to reflect, we find ourselves already believing in them, not because of any argument, but because the belief is natural to us' (Russell 1914: 72, 102). But they are not 'hard data', (1914: 79, 102) because they do not 'resist the solvent effect of critical reflection' – they lack the luminous certainty, increased rather than decreased on reflection, of the 'hardest of hard data… the particular facts of sense and the general truths of logic' (1914: 78).

This is an instance of a more general maneuver which Russell employs over and over again in this area: when we say that acquaintance comes in degrees, we '*must mean*' that we can be acquainted with more and more parts of a complex whole; the '*only sense*' in which we can be said to be acquainted with another person is to have made an inference from appearances with which we are really acquainted; if we speak of other people as given to us, as data, we are really referring to a natural and instinctive belief which needs to be given a grounding in something more certain.

But on my view, we cannot begin to work towards knowledge of other people unless we *from the start* accept them as the hardest of hard data.[11] Murdoch famously identifies this acceptance with a form of love: 'Love is the perception of individuals. Love is the extremely difficult realization that something else is real. … and most particular and individual of all natural things is the mind of man' (1951: 215). None of this is to deny that in knowing another person, my sense organs and the processing capacities of

---

of many others' – I am not the only character in the narrative of my life. This means that my narrative depends essentially on the narratives that constitute the unities of those other lives that figure in the story of my life. I cannot tell my own story well unless I can know and integrate into that story as much as possible of those other stories.

[11]Gallagher and Zahavi similarly speak of 'acquaintance' with others from a phenomenological perspective (2012: 206), and suggest following Merleau-Ponty that the 'bridge' between 'my self-acquaintance and acquaintance with others' is 'embodied being in the world'. They sketch a developmental story moving from a 'primary intersubjectivity', and interpersonal immediacy available to infants, through a 'secondary intersubjectivity' of shared situations and activities in which we negotiate multiple intentions and desires, to 'narrative competency' in which we 'shape our own self-understandings' as we come to narrative understanding of the others we encounter in the social contexts in which we 'acquire the capacity for understanding' (2012: 208-17). I take this story to fit well with Murdoch's vision of the other as given to me as presenting an unending task, although Murdoch's sense of this task as a moral demand on me does not seem to be present in Zahavi and Gallagher's account.

my brain are involved. Nor is it to deny that we can sometimes be mistaken in thinking we recognize someone, or even in thinking that someone is present when no one is there (as when a bereaved person has a vision of their dead spouse). But from none of this does it follow that when I am genuinely in the presence of another person and recognize them as such, my knowledge of them is therefore to be seen as epistemically dependent on some sort of process of inference or construction from harder 'data of sense'. Indeed, if I am right, to take this position seriously would lead to an inability to genuinely come to know anyone else. Therefore, it would undercut that laudable aspiration of philosophy itself, which Russell expresses at the close of *Problems*, to foster an impartiality which 'in contemplation, is the unalloyed desire for truth, …in action, is justice, and in emotion is that universal love which can be given to all, and not only to those who are judged useful or admirable' (Russell 1912: 161).

Fortunately perhaps, Russell's own attitude towards his philosophical arguments and principles in some ways resembles Hume's famous remark concerning the arguments of the skeptics:

> …as soon as they leave the shade, and by the presence of the real objects, which actuate our passions and sentiments, are put in opposition to the more powerful principles of our nature, they vanish like smoke, and leave the most determined skeptic in the same condition as other mortals. (Hume 1748: 206)

So says Russell, in *Our Knowledge of the External World*: 'In actual fact, whatever we may try to think as philosophers, we cannot help believing in the minds of other people, so that the question whether our belief is justified has a merely speculative interest' (Russell 1914: 104). Once again, I am reminded of Hume, who wrote of Berkeley's arguments, intended to answer the skeptics, that they actually 'form the best lessons of skepticism'. 'That all his arguments, though otherwise intended, are, in reality, merely sceptical, appears from this, *that they admit of no answer and produce no conviction*. Their only effect is to cause that momentary amazement and irresolution and confusion, which is the result of scepticism' (Hume 1748: 203). If I may be so bold, I think too that Russell's arguments concerning our knowledge of other persons, though intended as part of an answer to both skepticism and idealism, end up being the 'the best lessons of scepticism', a scepticism which, most fortunately cannot be sustained outside of the seminar room.[12]

---

[12]I read previous versions of this paper at Mind, Language and Cognition: Historical Perspectives, McMaster University, May 24, 2012; Bertrand Russell's The Problems of Philosophy: The Centenary Conference, University of Mississippi, December 1, 2012; and at the University

References

Broyles, W. 1998. *Cast Away*. http://www.dailyscript.com/scripts/CastAway.txt. Accessed 2/7/2014.

Epley, N. *et al*. 2008. Creating Social Connection Through Inferential Reproduction: Loneliness and Perceived Agency in Gadgets, Gods, and Greyhounds. *Psychological Science* 19: 114–120.

Gallagher, S. and D. Zahavi. 2012. *The Phenomenological Mind*, 2nd ed. London and New York: Routledge.

Hume, D. 1748. *An Enquiry concerning the Human Understanding*. Ed. T. L. Beauchamp. New York: Oxford University Press 1999.

James, W. 1885. On the Function of Cognition. *Mind* 10: 27–44.

MacIntyre, A. 1984. *After Virtue*. 2nd ed. Notre Dame, IN: University of Notre Dame Press.

Moore, G. E. 1903a. The Refutation of Idealism. *Mind* 12: 433–53.

Moore, G. E. 1903b. *Principia Ethica*. Cambridge: Cambridge University Press.

Moore, G. E. 1912. *Ethics*. London: Williams and Norgate.

Murdoch, I. 1951. The Sublime and the Good. In Murdoch 1997: 205–20.

Murdoch, I. 1961. Against Dryness. In Murdoch 1997: 287–96.

Murdoch, I. 1964. The Idea of Perfection. In Murdoch 1997: 299–336.

Murdoch, I. 1967. The Sovereignty of Good Over Other Concepts. In Murdoch 1997: 363–85.

Murdoch, I. 1997. *Existentialists and Mystics: Writings on Philosophy and Literature*, ed. P. Conradi. New York: Penguin Books.

Rudd, A. 2007. In Defense of Narrative. *European Journal of Philosophy* 17: 60–75.

Russell, B. 1903a. *Principles of Mathematics*. Cambridge: Cambridge University Press.

Russell, B. 1903b. Points about Denoting. In *CP* 4: 306–13.

Russell, B. 1905a. On Fundamentals. In *CP* 4: 359–413.

Russell, B. 1905b. On Denoting. In *CP* 4: 414–27.

Russell, B. 1905c. The Nature of Truth. In *CP* 4: 490–506.

Russell, B. 1910a. The Elements of Ethics. Reprinted in Russell 1910b: 1–58.

Russell, B. 1910b. *Philosophical Essays*. London: Longmans, Green and Co.

Russell, B. 1910-11. Knowledge by Acquaintance and Knowledge by Description. *Proceedings of the Aristotelian Society* 11: 108–28. Reprinted in Russell 1957: 209–32.

---

of Arkansas, Nov. 15, 2013. Thanks are due to the audience members at all three conferences, especially Ian Proops and Donovan Wishon, for valuable comments and challenging questions.

Russell, B. 1912. *The Problems of Philosophy*. London: Williams and Norgate. Reprinted Oxford: Oxford University Press 1959.

Russell, B. 1913. *Theory of Knowledge: The 1913 Manuscript*, ed. E. R. Eames. London. Routledge 1992.

Russell, B. 1914. The Relation of Sense-Data to Physics. *Scientia* 16: 1–27. Reprinted in Russell 1957: 145–79.

Russell, B. 1914. *Our Knowledge of the External World*. Chicago and London: Open Court Publishing.

Russell, B. 1918. *The Philosophy of Logical Atomism*. In Russell 1956: 175–282.

Russell, B. 1924. Logical Atomism. In Russell 1956: 321–44.

Russell, B. 1956. *Logic and Knowledge: Essays, 1901–1950*, ed. R. Marsh. London: Unwin Hyman.

Russell, B. 1957. *Mysticism and Logic*. New York: Anchor Books.

Russell, B. 1994. *The Collected Papers of Bertrand Russell, Volume 4: Foundations of Logic, 1903-05*, ed. A. Urquhart with A. C. Lewis. London: Routledge. [*CP* 4]

Sellars, W. 1956. Empiricism and the Philosophy of Mind. In Sellars 1963: 127–96.

Sellars, W. 1963. *Science, Perception and Reality*. London: Routledge and Kegan Paul.

Stevens, G. 2005. *The Russellian Origins of Analytical Philosophy: Bertrand Russell and the Unity of the Proposition*. New York: Routledge.

Strawson, G. 2004. Against Narrativity. *Ratio* 17: 428-452.

Stump, E. 2010. *Wandering in Darkness: Narrative and the Problem of Suffering*. Oxford: Clarendon Press.

Tierney, J. 2008. Science Explains Wilson the Volleyball. http://tierneylab.blogs.nytimes.com/2008/01/22/science-explains-wilson-the-volleyball/. Accessed 2/7/2014.

Vice, S. 2003. Literature and the Narrative Self. *Philosophy* 78: 93-108.

Zemeckis, R. and W. Broyles, Jr. 2000. *Cast away* [Motion picture]. United States: DreamWorks SKG.

8

Problems as Prolegomena: Russell's Analytic Phenomenology

ROBERT BARNARD

1 Introduction

The Problems of Philosophy (hereafter *POP*) appeared in 1912. It was the product of a period of philosophical reflection that represented an 'escape from the rigors of symbolic-deductive reasoning' that had marked Russell's work on *Principia Mathematica* (hereafter *PM*). The difference from *PM* style philosophy is further seen in the fact that rather than rushing headlong into the virtues and uses of plainly logical methods, as he would later do in Chapter II ('Logic as the Essence of Philosophy') of *Our Knowledge of the External World* (1914), in *POP* Russell chose to begin and motivate his 'general outline' of philosophy with the Cartesian question 'Is there any knowledge in the world which is so certain that no reasonable man could doubt it?' This epistemological program was further developed in what is now called the 1913 *Theory of Knowledge* (hereafter *TK*) manuscript.

At almost the same time, Edmund Husserl was laying the foundations for the philosophical movement he called 'Phenomenology'. Like Russell, Husserl had spent many years working on problems in the philosophy of mathematics and, also like Russell, his work was influenced by interaction with Frege. Again like Russell, Husserl was motivated by something akin to the Cartesian problem. My focus in this paper is to consider how deep the roots of these surface similarities go. To that end, I will offer an opinionated comparison of Husserlian Phenomenology and Russell's epistemological

Acquaintance, Knowledge, and Logic.
Donovan Wishon and Bernard Linsky (eds.).
Copyright © 2015, CSLI Publications.

philosophy in the period after *PM* and before *Our Knowledge of the External World.*

To be clear: The specific aim of this paper is to highlight the deep similarities between the position developed in Russell's *POP* and the posthumously published 1913 *Theory of Knowledge* manuscript and the early versions of phenomenology outlined by Husserl in works written at about the same time.[1] I am not advancing any claims about the influence of Husserl on Russell, nor am I advancing any claims about the deep influence of Frege on both or either.[2] Instead, I intend only to argue that a compelling case can be made that Russell's views in this period—growing out of *POP* and as more fully developed in *TK* may be profitably understood as a form of analytic phenomenology.[3] In §1 I will motivate my comparison by considering a well-known example from *POP*. §2 will develop a set of criteria for a minimal phenomenology. §§ 3–5 will argue that Russell's view, especially in *TK*, meets these criteria. §6 considers the significance of reading Russell as a phenomenologist.

2 Preliminary Motivation

The epistemological problems behind the Cartesian demand for certainty are made manifest for Russell's readers by the famous passage describing a wooden table:

> To make our difficulties plain, let us concentrate attention on the table. To the eye it is oblong, brown and shiny, to the touch it is smooth and cool and hard; when I tap it, it gives out a wooden sound. Anyone else who sees and feels and hears the table will agree with this description, so that it might seem as if no difficulty would arise; but as soon as we try to be more precise our troubles begin. Although I believe that the table is 'really' of the same colour all over, the parts that reflect the light look much brighter than the other parts, and some parts look white because of reflected light. I know that, if I move, the parts that reflect the light will be dif-

---

[1] The second volume of Husserl 1970 originally published 1913 and also Husserl 1962 originally published in 1913, and his 1964 which corresponds to a series of lectures in 1907.

[2] Recent work by Nikolay Milkov (2004a, 2004b) also notes the parallelism between Russell and Husserl during the 1911–13 period, but goes much further in suggesting that Husserl exerts an indirect influence on Russell by way of Moore's 1910 review in *Mind* of August Messer's, *Empfindung und Denken* (1908), which Milkov regards as a summary and explication of Husserl's *Logical Investigations*. (See also, Milkov 2004b for support of the claim that Messer influenced Moore).

[3] I will adopt the convention of using 'Phenomenology' to refer to Husserl's view and lowercase 'phenomenology' to refer any view that meets the standards articulated in §2. Thus, Husserl's Phenomenology will count as a kind of phenomenology, while not all instances of phenomenology need be Phenomenology.

ferent, so that the apparent distribution of colours on the table will change. It follows that if several people are looking at the table at the same moment, no two of them will see exactly the same distribution of colours, because no two can see it from exactly the same point of view, and any change in the point of view makes some change in the way the light is reflected.

For most practical purposes these differences are unimportant, but to the painter they are all important: the painter has to unlearn the habit of thinking that things seem to have the colour which common sense says they 'really' have, and to learn the habit of seeing things as they appear. Here we have already the beginning of one of the distinctions that cause most trouble in philosophy—the distinction between 'appearance' and 'reality', between what things seem to be and what they are. (Russell 1912: 8)[4]

What is not often noticed is that a very similar strategy is also employed to make plain the problematic towards which Husserl's early phenomenology is directed. Consider the following passage from *Ideas*:

Keeping this table steadily in view as I go around it, changing my position in space all the time, I have continually the consciousness of the bodily presence out there of this one and self-same table, which itself remains unchanged throughout. But the perception of the table is one that changes continuously, it is a continuum of changing perceptions. I close my eyes.

My other senses have no relation to the table. Now I have no perception of it. I open my eyes; and I have the perception again. The perception? Let us be more precise. Returning, it is not, under any circumstances, individually the same. Only the table is the same, intended to as the same in the synthetical consciousness which connects the new perception with the memory. The perceived physical thing can exist without being perceived, without even being potentially intended to (in the already described mode of nonactionality); and it can exist without changing. The perception itself, however, is what it is in the continuous flux of consciousness and is itself a continuous flux: ...The same colour appears 'in' continuously varying patterns of perspective colour *variations*. Similarly for every sensory quality and likewise for every spatial shape! One and the same shape (given *as* bodily the same) appears continuously ever again "in another way," in ever differing perspective variations of shape. (Husserl 1962: 117–8)

---

[4]The precise purpose of the description of the table is uncertain. Clearly it functions to illuminate the nature of the distinction between appearance and reality. I am suggesting that it is also being employed as a kind of methodological example. A different take on the table example can be found in Peter Hylton's '*Problems of Philosophy* as a stage in the evolution of Russell's views on knowledge' in this volume.

This is a striking juxtaposition. No doubt, the simple of availability of tables to philosophers in search of an example must not be discounted, but the nature of the descriptions is sufficiently close to suggest that they are attempting similar projects.

To evaluate the degree of similarity, we need to make nature of phenomenology clear.

3   A Minimal Phenomenology: Criteria

Let me now turn to the heart of the matter. I propose to argue that Russell actually develops a form of minimal phenomenology starting in *POP* and coming to fruition in *TK*.

Now, insofar as I understand Husserl, I take it that the following three conditions are necessary and sufficient (or nearly so) to distinguish phenomenological philosophy: (1) There must be a methodological suspension of presuppositions. This captures the distinction which Husserl made between descriptive psychology and phenomenology; I shall call this the *suspension requirement*; (2) the project must be primarily descriptive; it must seek to account for conscious experience as *experienced* in all its (nonpathological) varieties, I shall call this the *description requirement*; and (3) consciousness must be structured by intentionality.[5] This, I take it, is the *sine qua non* condition for phenomenology, since it undergirds the constitution of experienced objects, (and later the world which is central to later developments in the direction of intersubjectivity).[6] This is the *intentionality requirement*.

Further, the intentionality requirement itself is composed of two parts. The first I will call the *target* of the intention. This is what a mental state is about or directed toward. Following the development of Brentano's work in Meinong,[7] Husserl,[8] and Twardowski[9] further distinctions can also be made within the target. These thinkers are usually understood to distinguish between what are called the *content* (the object as presented, Meinong's Inhalt) and the object itself of an intentional state (Meinong's *Gegenstande*).[10]

---

[5]This, as Husserl (1964) points out, is one mark which distinguished phenomenology from descriptive psychology. The analysis must describe the experience after our preconceptions about its meaning have been suspended.

[6]See, e.g. Husserl 1995, especially the discussion of intersubjectivity in the fifth meditation.

[7]See Meinong 1899 and also his 1972 especially Chapter 6.

[8]See Husserl 1970: 533–659.

[9]Twardowski 1977.

[10]If I look at a house my content will only include presentations of one side, but the object of the intentional state, the house-itself, is not one sided, but rather will have 4 or more sides. The

However, it is possible to conflate the two and still have an account which meets the target requirement. In fact, such a conflation is often attributed to Brentano himself, and to certain interpretations of Husserl.[11] The second part of the intentionality requirement involves the ability to distinguish between kinds of intentional states. This amounts to making a distinction between, e.g., making a judgment that P and imagining that P. I shall call this the *mode* of the intentional state.[12] One additional feature may be invoked; it is usually supposed that the intentional state is somehow a qualitative property of the subject,[13] but this seems a trivial requirement for even if the intentional event is described relationally, the property of being in the relation still seems to be a coincident quality of the subject in question, the subject is 'in an intentional state'.[14] Thus we shall say that imagining that P and believing that P have the same target, but differ in mode, while believing that P and believing that Q differ in target but share a mode. Having established a clear set of tests, let us now consider whether Russell did in fact independently develop an analytic version of phenomenological philosophy.[15]

4 The Suspension Requirement

The suspension requirement is explained by Husserl in his 1907 lecture series collected in The *Idea of Phenomenology* (see 1964: 3–4, 35). There he notes that the proper method in theory of knowledge is to exclude everything presupposed 'transcendent', outside of the subject's mere (immanent) experience. This requires that one confront her experiences as phenomena and not as experiences of, e.g., trees or people. Of this precaution, Husserl explicitly notes that, if 'the critique of cognition is a science, ... a science

---

distinction is often compared to Frege's sense (mode of presentation) and reference (denoted object). See 'On Sense and Reference' in Frege 1960: 56–78.

[11] See Smith 1995: 23–4. Specifically, Husserl's view develops and changes over time. I am dealing, for the most part, with a particular early version of his phenomenology.

[12] The recognition of the target and mode as conditions for an intentional account of conscious are ubiquitous, see Addis 1989: Chapter 3. They are the 'intentional property' and the 'mode property' respectively in his terms.

[13] This is the avowed view of Addis 1989 and implicit in Meinong 1899.

[14] While it is sometimes claimed that Russell holds that there is nothing mental, 'no state of mind' involved in, e.g. acquaintance relations, one aim of this paper is to suggest that Russell, in fact had a less desolate picture of mental subjectivity.

[15] I shall not pursue the task of tracing the historical development of Russell's views from those in his comments on Meinong up to the *Theory of Knowledge*; such a genealogy has already been attempted, see Griffin 1985: especially 213–26.

which is to clarify all species and forms of cognition, *it can make no use of any science of the natural sort*. It cannot tie itself to the conclusions that any natural science has reached about what is. For [theory of knowledge] they remain in question' (Husserl 1964: 4). Further, he notes that the aim of this 'reduction' is to facilitate the isolation of 'a pure phenomenon, which exhibits its intrinsic essence (taken individually) as an absolute datum', which is immediately grasped in a 'pure seeing' (1964: 35).

Russell's method is almost identical to Husserl's. This is not surprising given Russell's larger goal (at least in the *POP* and *TK* period) of devising a logically sophisticated foundationalist epistemology.[16] Thus the isolation of certain self-evident epistemological data would be expected. Regarding suspension, in *TK* Chapter IV, Russell makes the following remarks:

> a certain naïveté is required in beginning epistemology: we must avoid assuming many things which we firmly believe to be true, but which only can be reached by a process of inference. (Russell 1984: 50)
>
> A knowledge of physics and physiology must not be assumed in theory of knowledge. This maxim follows from the preceding account of epistemological order. Physics and physiology belong to our knowledge of what is called the external world; our knowledge of them is obviously dependent upon sensation, and is obtained by methods which the theory of knowledge must investigate. (1984: 50-1)
>
> In Epistemology it is important to reduce our problems to what is actually experienced. (1984: 51)

These passages certainly indicate that some sort of methodological suspension is in play for Russell (as it was for Descartes). But the distinctively phenomenological aspect of Husserl's reduction is found in the isolation of pure data. Can Russell be said to have isolated something like pure phenomenological data? I think so.

According to Russell, the most basic cognitive relation is the relation of *acquaintance* between a subject and an object. Acquaintance is a dual relation where the domain contains subjects and the converse domain contains objects. Thus, if there is a subject in an acquaintance relation, then there must be an object. But little yet is said about either subject or object.

The primary data of epistemology then are the objects (particulars and universals) with which a subject is acquainted (Russell 1984: 45–7). That these objects are given as pure phenomena, as absolute data, can be inferred from two related points. First, Russell explicitly identifies the subject-object relation in acquaintance with what Meinong refers to as 'presentation' which means that acquaintance involves an experience's being before the

---

[16]Husserl's aim was similar, to produce a presuppositionless theory of knowledge.

mind in a way which implicitly points to a transcendent object. [17] The second comes from a related discussion in *TK* Chapter IV. Russell claims there that the objects of acquaintance cannot be 'unreal', but at the same time that the acquaintance relation is incorrigible. He notes several consequences of this view.[18] (1) Only objects known by description can be 'unreal' and only then because the way the world is fails to satisfy a description. (2) Given that we can be acquainted with objects in dreams and hallucinations, we are forced into a 'certain attitude of respect' toward such experiences. Russell will ultimately distinguish between sensation, imagination, and the like, but his admission that as regards acquaintance they are alike is significant. Likewise (3), the supposition that an object of acquaintance is unreal, as in hallucination, ought always be interpreted as really meaning that there is an object inferable from the immediate object of experience which is unreal in the sense of its not actually existing. Meanwhile, the incorrigibility of the acquaintance demands 'respect' for what Russell calls the 'immediate object' (ibid: 48–9). Where the immediate object is something akin to, or experienced at the same level as, sense-data.

If the passages I have pointed out can be taken at their word, then it seems certain that Russell did have a methodological procedure whereby presuppositions about the 'external world' of macrophysical objects were suspended, and where epistemological certainty was grounded in incorrigible data of consciousness. Let us now consider the extent to which Russell attempted to describe conscious experience as experienced.

---

[17]See Russell 1984: 41 fn. 3.

[18]The matter of how much epistemic license Russell intends to give to acquaintance is a matter of some dispute. In *POP*, there are strong suggestions that acquaintance is an error free epistemic connection, e.g. 'we may draw wrong inferences from our acquaintance, but the acquaintance itself cannot be deceptive' (Russell 1959: Chapter XII). Linsky (this volume) suggests this reading may be too strong, even if acquaintance is still understood as a high-grade epistemic relation. However, the stronger reading is also supported by *TK* Ch IV where the second epistemic maxim offered by Russell insists that 'The possibility of error in any cognitive occurrence shows that the occurrence is not an instance of a dual relation', where acquaintance is one kind of dual relation (Russell 1984: 84). I argue in this paper under the assumption that acquaintance is incorrigible full stop, with the burden of proof on those who would argue otherwise. By comparison, Proops (this volume) argues for a stronger account of infallibility through acquaintance, but rejects the Cartesian foundationalist framework to which I appeal.

5   The Descriptive Requirement

The description of conscious experience is a curious thing. It would be hard to know whether any given description was ultimately correct. It seems that, at best, we shall only be able to assess whether Russell's approach to description comports well with Husserl's and leave the question of their collective or individual correctness for another time. Returning to the relatively simple presentation in his *Idea of Phenomenology*, we find Husserl makes the following points. First, we confront cognition as a 'manifold sphere of being which can be given to us absolutely, and which can be given absolutely each time in the particular case' (Husserl 1964: 23). Second, one's cognitive states can themselves become objects of presentation. Husserl claims that every form of thinking and cognition can be put on the same level as reflective seeing and reflective imagination, or, more directly, that 'Every intellectual process and indeed every mental process whatever, while being enacted, can be made the object of a pure "seeing" and understanding, and is something absolutely given in this "seeing". It is something that is, that is here and now, and whose being cannot be doubted' (1964: 23–4). And this, he claims will serve as the 'foundation' of what is to come.

Husserl describes the manifold of conscious in more abstract terms as 'the field of pure phenomena', and asks what he can say about this field: 'What assertions can I make about it? Now, while "seeing," I can say: *this here:* No doubt it is. Perhaps I can say further that this phenomenon includes that one as a part, or is connected to that one; this spreads over that one, etc.' (1964: 37, my italics). Husserl then describes how this field of pure data and the ability to isolate the 'this here' leads us to discover in our phenomenal experience other kinds of givenness, absolute data which transcend the present instant. This is because the ability to make judgments which compare, or assert other facts about the structure or content of the manifold, depend upon the possibility of logical 'something more' 'which does not at all consist of a mere agglomeration of new *cogitationes*' (1964: 19). This something more is said to constitute the 'predicational facts' underlying these assertions. These Husserl calls 'logical forms' (1964: 40).

Further, we are also able to isolate essences or universals of various kinds. These we isolate by means of 'eidetic abstraction', which yields 'inspectable universals, species and essences'. And these essences combined with the logical forms make it possible for us to conceive of what exists transcendently, for these universals exist because they are given, but exceed our experience of them. They transcend our awareness of them. Finally one should also note the early discussion of the experience of time. Husserl here uses the example of an enduring sound with its own 'now-phase and past-phases'. This too points to the transcendent for Husserl, for momentary experiences may be said to exceed themselves in time.[19]

Interestingly enough, Russell's account of the same phenomena deviates only minutely with respect to the descriptions of what is given in consciousness, or in Russell's terms: what we are acquainted with in consciousness. The difficulty in recognizing the similarity comes from having to overcome the difference in vocabulary but only for certain points.[20] Within Husserl's descriptive account I focused upon eight distinct elements: the manifold of consciousness, the ability to reflect upon cognitive states, the limited claims we can make about the manifold, that we can designate it by means of a 'this here', and that we can make claims about its structure; logical forms and universals were uncovered, and their ability to signify transcendent objects was considered; finally, our consciousness of time was briefly described as including now-phases and past-phases. I want to suggest that Russell has clear analogues for each.

Russell clearly accepts the account of consciousness as a sort of manifold. He writes that the contents of a person's experience:

> are the things given in sensation, his own thoughts and feelings (at any rate so far as he is aware of them), and perhaps ... the facts which he comes to know by thinking. At any given moment, there are certain things of which a man is "aware", certain things which are "before his mind". (Russell 1984: 7)

There is said to be a 'unity' in 'my present experience' where everything is 'being experienced together' (1984: 8). Later, and more specifically, Russell devotes *TK* Chapter V to 'Sensation and Imagination'; there he remarks on the fact that it is possible for sensation and imagination to have the same object, and that dreams and hallucinations are included with imagination. Thus, at certain level Russell seems to accept the unity of all particular cognitive data, instances of color, sounds, and tactile sensations. Further he collects them, moment to moment, under the designation 'the present experience', or 'the present time'. The differences between objects and sensation are said to be of two possible kinds, either objects given in sensation are experienced as being given in a determinate relation with the present time and objects of imagination are not, or objects of imagination will fail upon testing to correlate with other expected sensory experiences which objects of sensation will satisfy (see 1984: 59–60).

Russell also clearly believes that it is possible to have a kind of acquaintance with the contents of consciousness. However, whereas sensation

---

[19]See summary of discussion in Husserl 1964: 8–9.
[20]The relevant sections in Russell come primarily from TK Chapters V–IX of Part I.

gives particular data in acquaintance, the relation of 'perception' is said to give the existence of simple facts in acquaintance.[21] Reflection upon consciousness is always given as perception of mental facts. Thus we are never given particular data of consciousness, as such, in distinction to data of sensation, we only have perceptions of mental facts, where a fact means that 'so and so is the case'. This helps confirm that Russell viewed immediate consciousness as a manifold, but also shows that Russell appreciated the fact that *self-awareness* is more complex than simple experience. This is probably because directing one's awareness back upon consciousness requires a different kind of *attention*. ('Attention' is Russell's technical term for isolating discrete parts of the experiential manifold.) Russell calls all facts which involve or presuppose acquaintance, 'mental facts'.[22] An example of a mental fact would be that subject S is acquainted with green. In such a case S would merely have green given in acquaintance, thus S would only have a particular experience and not be immediately aware of the fact which describes the situation.[23] When a subject is aware of mental facts then we should say that S *perceives* that a subject is acquainted with green.[24] Thus the fact that I have a sensation, imagine a color, remember a sound, or perceive that a subject desires apples would all be instances of mental facts.

It is worth noting in this context the degree to which Russell's 'mental realm' was a complicated place, for some have dismissed Russell for dismissing the mental.[25] The mental, according to Russell, is the realm of experiencing (another name for acquaintance), judging, feeling, desiring, willing, etc., where the latter all presuppose acquaintance. And a large number of the things that are experienced are experienced by only one subject (Russell 1984: 34–5). Mental facts are certainly among these.

---

[21] Russell 1984: 37. On the distinction between acquaintance and sensation and perception, see discussion page 100. Sensation, imagination, and perception are said to be 'subordinate' to acquaintance. Perception would also count as a dual relation since there could not be perception with perceiver and fact.

[22] There are resonances here with Brentano (1995: 77) who claims that all consciousness is divided into physical phenomena and mental phenomena.

[23] The exact nature of this fact is unclear.

[24] Russell (1984: 36–44ff) symbolizes this situation as follows on p. 38: S'-P- (S-A-O), A subject S' perceives that a subject S is acquainted with an object O. In a footnote he revises this to S'-P- (∃S. S-A-O), a subject S' perceives that there is some subject S such that S is acquainted with an object O. This later formulation invites speculation as to whether S and S' are identical.

[25] Addis 1989 and Grossmann's introduction to Twardowski 1977 may be examples.

After establishing the field of pure data, Husserl considered the kinds of immediate claims one could make about what is given in the manifold of phenomena. Russell does not explicitly ask this question, but rather proceeds immediately to describe the other kinds of experiences given in experience, perhaps due to his desire to treat all cognition relationally. And Russell's project at this point is to identify all the different kinds of objects given in acquaintance. The first is the manifold itself, the present time. And this instant, or parts of the instant, isolated by the attention are all alike in being designated by the Russellian proper name 'this' (1984: 40). And among the candidates for isolation by attention, are facts given in perception, which are all facts of acquaintance. Thus Russell too, may single out cases where sense-data A is similar to sense-data B, or where A is a part of a more complex sensation C. But if this is the case then there must be something over and above the particular sense-data given in acquaintance, universals. Russell recognizes three species of universals and devotes a chapter to each type: Relations, Predicates, and Logical Forms (See 1984: Chapters VII, VIII, and IX respectively). Russell's explication of each is detailed and sometimes convoluted, and a full examination would be beyond the scope of this paper.

For present purposes we note that Russell concludes that we probably do have direct acquaintance with some *relations* and that these relations are abstract logical entities. Other relations are known only by means of description, but since all descriptions must refer to universals, there must be some known by acquaintance alone (1984: 81). Russell's view of *predicates* is that they are akin to 'Platonic Ideas' and 'Scholastic universals'. But Russell, perhaps chary of the metaphysical baggage carried by Platonists and Scholastics or worried about a slippage back toward Idealism, is content to claim that they are just those features of particulars which are had in common when two particulars are similar in respect to, e.g. color. It is in the midst of this discussion that Russell returns to a discussion of inferred entities. For, on Russell's view, predicates are not properties of 'things' but of the immediate particular sense-data which form the inferential basis for our belief in the thing (1984: 94). Where the thing, as experienced, is a 'bundle of predicates' (1984: 91).

Chapter IX on 'Logical Data', is arguably a candidate for the strangest three pages of philosophy Russell ever wrote.[26] Russell recognized that what he was proposing was strange, but rested in a kind of confidence that he was describing something given. He wrote that: 'I am content to point

---

[26]There are actually almost five pages of text, but Russell concludes the section with a long summary of Part I. See Russell 1984: 97–101.

out that there certainly is such a thing as "logical experience," by which I mean that kind of immediate knowledge other than judgment' (1984: 97). Thus, logical experience, and the 'logical objects' it gives are given in a kind of acquaintance, although, Russell admits, this acquaintance is different from other varieties (later he reverts to calling it 'logical intuition'). Russell characterized the objects of logical acquaintance as akin to a *summum genus*: E.g. all dual relations have their dual relation-ness in common. This general structure is the logical form given in acquaintance. And, this form must be given over and beyond the terms and relating relation in instances of acquaintance with complexes. But, Russell cautions, the logical form of an experience is not another constituent of the complex. Rather it functions as a condition of the possibility of making judgments employing dual relations, or of recognizing the relation in a given complex. To his discredit, however, Russell defers a full account of logical form as exceeding the scope of his epistemological investigation (1984: 98).

Before moving on to a discussion of intentionality and belief, we need to consider the last two points made by Husserl, that the isolation of universals establishes an indication of transcendence within the field of pure data, and that there is a temporal structuring of experience. In reverse order, the question of temporal ordering is easily assessed. Chapter VI of *TK* Part I, 'On the Experience of Time' makes multiple references to the temporal structure of certain experiences. His discussion there focuses upon the present but Russell too writes of a fading sound that, 'we heard a few seconds ago, but are not hearing now, [and] may still be an object of acquaintance, but it is given in a different way from that in which it was given when it was a sense-datum' (1984: 72).[27] Thus it seems clear that Russell was using the distinction between a now-phase and a past-phase, even if he had not explicitly formulated it.

On the final question of the implicit transcendence of universals, I am not sure what conclusion to draw. Russell's view still seems to discourage talk in such terms as too alien to his project. But we do get hints. First the status of objects of imagination was said to differ from those of sensation due to their failure to be experienced as in time. Likewise, the ability to be acquainted with the absent tone of a fading sound suggests a kind of transcendence of the immediate bounds of consciousness. And if Husserl's arguments about universals and logical forms are sound, then they should apply *mutatis mutandis* to Russell's universals and logical forms. Thus I am satisfied that Russell has met the descriptive requirement.

---

[27]Other similar discussions are present as well. For details see Russell 1984: 64–78.

6   The Intentionality Requirement

Early on I suggested that we should distinguish between the Phenomenology of Husserl and the minimal analytic phenomenology I think we should attribute to Russell. One key factor that helps to draw a line between phenomenology and Phenomenology is the fact that Russell and Husserl seem to exhibit significant differences in the way each approaches intentionality. Thus, I shall hold Russell to a less strict standard insofar as the intentionality requirement is concerned. But let us get a general sense of Husserl's basic position in his *Idea of Phenomenology*. Following Brentano, Husserl writes:

> Cognitive mental processes (and this belongs to their essence) have an intentio, they refer to something, they are related in this way or that way to an object. This activity of relating itself to an object belongs to them even if the object itself does not. And what is objective can appear, can have a certain kind of givenness in appearance, even though it is at the same time neither genuinely (reell) within the cognitive phenomenon, nor does it exist in any other way as a cogitation (Husserl 1964: 43).

This pairing of *cogitatio* (phenomenal data) and *intentio* (object) has already been recognized in our formulation of the intentionality requirement. In our previous terms the 'target of an intention' would be the *intentio*.[28] We also noted the distinction between target and mode, which Husserl labels in *Logical Investigations* the 'matter and quality' of intentional acts. Certainly, Husserl's account of intentionality is far richer than our criterion suggests, but I think that if Russell's view can be shown to satisfy a standard which is formally demanding, but materially permissive, then we may still say in fairness that Russell's view was both an intentional view and a phenomenological view.

Russell's views on complex intentional states are formulated relationally. Each intentional state will be a mental fact expressible as a complex that a subject S stands in a certain type of relation to the relevant objects of consciousness. And this fact is expressible as a proposition. According to Russell, the basic cognitive relation to a proposition which is presumed by all other cognitive relations of the present type is called '*understanding*'. Other relations of this type would be 'belief' (which Russell assimilates to the more traditional 'judgment'), 'doubt', 'disbelief', 'and probably many others'. Thus Russell would say that a subject S stands in a relation of understanding to some proposition. The proposition will itself be analyzable into

---

[28]The relation between *cogitatio* and the 'given' *intentio* I take to be similar to the implicit inference from correlated data to inferred object.

the constituents of the complex: terms and relations, and the logical form of the relation.[29]

The interesting part of this account for our purposes comes in Russell's explanation of the 'understanding relation'. He explains that 'when I speak of "understanding a proposition," I am speaking of *a state of mind* from which both affirmation and negation are wholly absent' (Russell 1984: 108). This is significant for at least two reasons. First, in distinction to belief/judgment understanding does not involve the affirmation of what is described by the proposition, yet the content of the proposition, its meaning, is grasped. Second, he characterizes the relation as a 'state of mind' which is exactly the phrase he uses to describe Meinong's intentional contents.[30] This strongly suggests that the mind somehow functions to represent the state of affairs described by the proposition in question. And it is this state of mind which is presupposed by relations like belief.[31]

Russell distinguishes between understanding and acquaintance in a way which relates to the role of objects of acquaintance as data. Data are given. There is no question of whether they are true or false, they just are. Understanding always implicitly involves questions of truth since the proposition understood may be either true or false. Thus, what one understands may differ from what is the case. But the ability to recognize this would depend upon the object of understanding having some independence from the acquaintance or lack of acquaintance we have with its constituents. Further, belief differs from understanding in that belief affirms the proposition in question. Russell has a well-known view regarding propositions; on his theory of descriptions, they are incomplete symbols which depend upon

---

[29]If S understands that A precedes B, then this would be symbolically represented by Russell with the following complex expression: [*] U (S, A, B, precedes, xRy). Here S is the subject, A, B, and 'precedes' are constituents of the relation, and xRy is the relational form.

[30]See Russell 1984: 42. One may argue that this could be a chance similarity, the vocabulary of descriptive psychology being in perpetual need of precisification, but I think the choice of words is intended given that the context of discussion includes a long comparison between Russell's 'understanding' and Meinong's notion of 'assumption.' Others may point to the discussion of Meinong and Russell's explicit disavowal of contents in Chapter III. There, Russell's best argument against contents is that he cannot discover them in introspection. I would suggest that he has isolated evidence which supports their presence, but he does not recognize this. Further, Russell seems to want to make a distinction between the experience and the content which represents the experience. This is probably an error. Russell is objecting to an unneeded intermediary layer in consciousness, but does not consider the possibility that consciousness itself is, in some sense, the content.

[31]As before [*] expresses that S understands the complex in question. ([*] U (S, A, B, precedes, xRy)). To change the mode, replace the U relation with a B relation symbol: [**] B (S, A, B, precedes, xRy). Now [**] expresses that S believes the complex.

some context to determine their full meaning. Thus, even 'a false belief or a false statement is an entity; but it seems obvious that they owe their falsehood to something which would be real if they were true' (Russell 1984: 109). However, Russell also notes that, the fact that a subject understands or believes a proposition retains the 'same logical form whether the proposition is true or whether it is false; for if this were not so, there would be an intrinsic difference between true and false beliefs, and mere attention to the mental fact would be capable of showing whether the belief was true or whether it was false' (1984).

Let us take stock. At this point we have a clear indication that Russell thinks of propositional understanding as a state of mind related to a particular object or complex. In a sense the state of mind represents the object in question. Thus the state of mind is about or intends the object. Thus the object or complex which we understand is the intentional 'target.' Likewise in the distinction between understanding and belief, and the other possible relations, which are other possible states of mind (and arguably therefore states of the subject), we have located the 'mode'. So, to some extent, Russell formally satisfies the intentionality requirement—but to what extent? This is where things get tricky. I think I may, with some justification, claim that there is a content-object distinction in play as well. A proposition is understood regardless of whether it is true or false, and on the theory of descriptions truth or falsehood depends upon there being an entity which satisfies each term of the complex. This suggests that what a subject understands or believes is, when made fully perspicuous, about the complex organization of data of acquaintance (contents), and not inferred objects (objects). However, truth is ultimately about the transcendent object—in some sense. The belief in a hidden content-object distinction is also supported by the virtual character of logical objects, more data—logical data, with which we are in a dual relation, and which though given to us in the relation need not themselves be proper entities.[32]

7   Discussion

It now seems clear in any event that Russell does satisfy all three criteria, at least to a minimal degree, and deserves the title of analytic phenomenologist; conversely one could also contend that Husserl justly deserves a

---

[32]Russell's theory of descriptions allowed him to represent the infamous round square without being committed to its existence. By imposing this model of propositions upon the structure of belief and understanding, Russell creates a space for an intentional representation of the round square which is distinct from the transcendent object.

seat at the table usually reserved for analytic philosophers. If what Russell was doing in *POP* and *TK* was analytic philosophy and phenomenology at the same time, then perhaps doing phenomenology (at least before the transcendental turn) is enough to count as a kind of analytic philosophy? My primary aim in this paper was to make a plausible case in favor of recognizing the deep similarities in methods and results between Russell's epistemology in *Problems* and the 1913 *Theory of Knowledge* manuscript and the early phenomenology of Husserl. To the best of my knowledge there is no reason to suppose that either was more than only generally aware (directly at least) of the work of the other, and in Russell[33] I find no mention of Husserl in either *POP* or *TK*, although Meinong is mentioned. In my consideration of each of the above criteria, I have found the resemblance between the two positions eerily acute.

The reading I am suggesting is neither obvious nor widely appreciated. It seems worthwhile to reflect upon why that might be. There is a cryptic remark in Wittgenstein 1922 (5.5422): 'The correct explanation of the form of the proposition "A judges p" must show that it is impossible to judge a nonsense. (Russell's theory does not satisfy this condition)'. While it is easy for us to miss this remark, or to dismiss it, the significance of this remark should not be underestimated. In effect, it summarizes a series of criticisms made by Wittgenstein to Russell's multiple relation theory of judgment that caused Russell to set aside and never publish *as a whole* over 300 manuscript pages on epistemology.[34] We now have access to this 'lost document' as the *Theory of Knowledge*. Some sections of the text were published, e.g. Chapters I-III became 'On the Nature of Acquaintance' and were published in *Monist* in 1914.[35] Some other material was reused in other places as well, but never in a single piece. For example the introduction to the reprinted *Monist* papers in *Logic and Knowledge* emphasizes the dialectical engagement with American philosophers. The broader context I have been developing is nowhere to be seen.

From a historical point of view, more than just a theory of judgment was set aside by Wittgenstein's criticisms. There has already been scholarly work exploring the question of how Wittgenstein's criticisms changed the

---

[33]N.B. John Shosky has recently informed me that Russell has in fact cited Husserl's *Ideas*. However since the publication date of *Ideas* post dates the period prior to Russell beginning work on *Theory of Knowledge*, I suspect that Russell was unaware of the work at that time.

[34]For discussions of Russell's reaction to Wittgenstein's criticisms, see Griffin 1985: 227-45 and Eames' introduction to Russell 1984: vii-xx. The criticisms apparently date from correspondence exchanged in May 1913.

[35]These are widely available in Russell 1956: 125-74.

trajectory of Russellian philosophy. I have attempted to highlight another effect of Russell's change of heart—the loss of a potential point of contact between adherents of logical analysis and those of the emerging school of Phenomenological philosophy. Philosophy in the Twentieth Century might have been very different had Russell finished and published the work we know as *Theory of Knowledge*. Certainly it would have been too much to expect that the anti-Idealist manifestos of Moore and Russell might have been read alongside those outlining the emerging transcendental idealism of Husserl or the existentialist tomes of Heidegger and Sartre. But upon the occasion of some cooler reflection, it might have been possible to recognize the very deep affinities exhibited by these early works as they lay the foundation for two important traditions in philosophy.

References

Addis, L. 1989. *Natural Signs: A Theory of Intentionality*. Philadelphia: Temple University Press.

Brentano, F. 1995. *Psychology from an Empirical Standpoint*. London: Routledge.

Frege, G. 1960. *Translations from the Philosophical Writings of Gottlob Frege*, eds. P. Geach and M. Black. Oxford: Basil Blackwell.

Giaretta, P. 1997. Analysis and Logical Form in Russell: The 1913 Paradigm. *Dialectica* 51: 273–293.

Griffin, N. 1985. Russell's Multiple Relation Theory of Judgment. *Philosophical Studies* 47: 213–247.

Husserl, E. 1962. *Ideas: General Introduction to Pure Phenomenology*, trans. R. C. Boyce. New York: Collier Books.

Husserl, E. 1964. *The Idea of Phenomenology*, trans. W. P. Alston and G. Nakhnikian. The Hague: Martinus Nijhoff.

Husserl, E. 1970. *Logical Investigations*, 2 volumes, trans. J. N. Findlay. New Jersey: Humanities Press. (Translation of 2nd German edition of 1922. This was originally published as two separate volumes, Volume I containing the 'Prolegomena' and Investigations I and II was first published in 1900, Volume II part I containing Investigations III-V was published in 1913, and Volume II part II was published in 1921.)

Husserl, E. 1995. *Cartesian Meditations: An Introduction to Phenomenology*, trans. D. Cairns. Dordrecht: Kluwer.

Hylton, P. 2015. *Problems of Philosophy* as a Stage in the Evolution of Russell's Views on Knowledge. In this volume: 25–44.

Linsky, B. 2015. Acquaintance and Certainty in *The Problems of Philosophy*. In this volume: 65–85.

Meinong, A. 1899. Über Gegenstande hoherer Ordnung und deren Verhaltnis zur inneren Wahrnemung. *Zeitschrift fur Psychologie und Physiologie der Sinnesorgane* 31: 181–272.

Meinong, A. 1972. *On Emotional Presentation*, trans. M. S. Kalsi. Evanston: Northwestern University Press.

Messer, A. 1908. *Empfindung und Denken*. Leipzig: Quelle and Meyer.

Milkov, N. 2004a. Husserl and Russell, 1911-1913. *Papers of the 27th International Wittgenstein Symposium 8-14 August 2004. Erfahrung und Analyse - Experience and Analysis*. Eds. J. C. Marek, M. E. Reicher. Kirchberg am Wechsel: ALWS 2004. < http://wab.uib.no/ojs/agora-alws/article/view/1326/1102>

Milkov, N. 2004b. G. E. Moore and the Greifswald Objectivists on the Given, and the Beginning of Analytic Philosophy. *Axiomathes* 14: 361–379.

Moore, G. E. 1910. Review of A. Messer, Empfindung und Denken. *Mind* 19: 395–409.

Proops, I. 2015. Certainty, Error, and Acquaintance in *The Problems of Philosophy*. In this volume: 45–63.

Russell, B. 1912. *The Problems of Philosophy*. London: Williams and Norgate. Reprinted Oxford: Oxford University Press 1959. [*POP*]

Russell, B. 1913. *Theory of Knowledge: The 1913 Manuscript*, ed. E. R. Eames and K. Blackwell, London: Routledge 1984.

Russell, B. 1918. *The Philosophy of Logical Atomism*. La Salle: Open Court 1985. Also in Russell 1956: 175–281.

Russell, B. 1956. *Logic and Knowledge*, ed. R.C. Marsh. London: Routledge.

Russell, B. 1961. *The Basic Writings of Bertrand Russell 1903-59*, eds. R. E. Egner and L. E. Denonn. New York: Simon and Schuster.

Russell, B. 1973. *Essays in Analysis*, ed. D. Lackey. London: George Allen and Unwin.

Smith, B. and D. Woodruff Smith, eds. 1995. *Cambridge Companion to Husserl*. New York: Cambridge University Press.

Twardowski, K. 1977. *On the Content and Object of Presentations: A Psychological Investigation*, trans. R. Grossmann. The Hague: Martinus Nijhoff.

Whitehead, A. N. and B. Russell. 1962. *Principia Mathematica to *56*. New York: Cambridge University Press.

Wittgenstein, L. 1922. *Tractatus Logico-Philosophicus*, trans. C. K. Ogden. London: Kegan Paul.

9

The Importance of Russell's Regress Argument for Universals

Katarina Perovic

1 Russell's Regress Argument for Universals

In his 1912 classic *The Problems of Philosophy*, Russell presented his famous regress argument against the nominalist denial of universals. In this paper I will explore the origin of the argument in Russell and its relevance in contemporary metaphysical debate. I will argue that a hundred years on, the argument still presents a powerful tool for realists in their debate with nominalists and trope theorists.

Russell introduces the regress as follows:

> If we wish to avoid the universals whiteness and triangularity, we shall choose some particular patch of white or some particular triangle, and say that anything is white or a triangle if it has the right sort of resemblance to our chosen particular. But then the resemblance required will have to be a universal. Since there are many white things, the resemblance must hold between many pairs of particular white things; and this is the characteristic of a universal. It will be useless to say that there is a different resemblance for each pair, for then we shall have to say that these resemblances resemble each other, and thus at last we shall be forced to admit resemblance as a universal. The relation of resemblance, therefore, must be a true universal. And having been forced to admit this universal, we find that it is no longer worth while to invent difficult and unplausible theories to avoid the admission of such universals as whiteness and triangularity. (Russell 1912: 96–7)

Acquaintance, Knowledge, and Logic.
Donovan Wishon and Bernard Linsky (eds.).
Copyright © 2015, CSLI Publications.

Thus, if a nominalist wants to avoid postulating universals such as *whiteness* and *triangularity*, she needs to find alternative ways of accounting for properties. One way of doing this is to pick out some particular *d* – a particular patch of white or a particular triangle – and then take the properties of whiteness and triangularity to consist in the 'right sort of resemblance' of particulars to the chosen paradigm *d*. This, in contemporary literature, is known as resemblance nominalism, or more specifically, as paradigm resemblance nominalism. Now, as there are many white and triangular things, there will be many pairs of things resembling each other in the relevant way. Multiple recurrence is a characteristic of universals and if one wants to avoid admitting resemblance as a universal, a way to do this is by saying that there is a *different* resemblance for each pair (a, d), (b, d), (c, d), ... – $r(a,d)$, $r(b,d)$, $r(c,d)$ ... But if a nominalist says this, she finds herself again having to explain what makes all the resemblances $r(a,d)$, $r(b,d)$, $r(c,d)$... resemble each other. She may say that all of them resemble each other because each of them resembles some arbitrarily picked resemblance $r(x,d)$. In this way we get new pairs $(r(a,d), r(x,d))$, $(r(b,d), r(x,d))$, $(r(c,d), r(x, d))$,... of resembling resemblances. And again, if in each case we ascribe the same resemblance there arises a risk for the nominalist of admitting a universal into her system. Therefore, she has to say that each of the new pairs of resemblances are *different* particular resemblances, and so on. The conclusion that Russell draws from this is that since the resistance to admit universals leads to an infinite regress of resemblance *relations*, a nominalist might as well have accepted the resemblance relation as a universal in the first place.

2 The Context of Russell's Regress Argument

Right after his presentation of the regress argument for universals, Russell notes that Berkeley and Hume failed to appreciate the force of this argument because they thought of *qualities* rather than *relations* as exemplars of universals. For Russell in the *Problems*, as well as in his paper from the same period – 'On the Relations of Universals and Particulars' (1911) – the opposite is the case: it is *relations* that are the main candidates for universals. Qualities can be treated, as the regress argument itself suggests, in terms of resemblance of one particular to another; relations, however, are irreducible. An attempt to rid oneself of relations leads to an infinite regress of further relations of *resemblance* or *likeness*. The argument thus proves very simply for Russell that an ontology that admits only particulars is flawed – it overlooks the fact that *relations* are ineliminable, and thus that universals are too.

It is difficult to determine when exactly Russell formulated the argument he perceived to be so powerful. Russell's discussion of the relation of 'difference' in his *Principles of Mathematics* (1903) can perhaps be seen as containing a proto-version of his later regress argument. In chapter IV, on 'Proper Names, Adjectives, and Verbs', §55, he discusses the view he attributes to Moore – i.e. a view that takes the *relation* of *difference* to be a different *instance* of a general 'Platonic' relation in various propositions in which it features.[1] Russell then argues that such a conception of a relation of 'difference' would *not*: 1) help reconstitute the proposition; and 2) show what all the different pairs have in common:

> [T]he view that no two pairs of terms can have the same relation both contains difficulties of its own and fails to solve the difficulty for the sake of which it was invented. For, even if the difference of A and B be absolutely peculiar to A and B, still the three terms, A, B, difference of A from B, do not reconstitute the proposition "A differs from B", any more than A and B and difference did. And it seems plain that, even if differences did differ, they would still have to have something in common. But the most general way in which two terms can have something in common is by both having a given relation to a given term. Hence if no two pairs of terms can have the same relation, it follows that no two terms can have anything in common, and hence different differences will not be in any definable sense *instances* of difference. I conclude, then, that the relation affirmed between A and B in the proposition "A differs from B" is the general relation of difference, and is precisely and numerically the same as the relation affirmed between C and D in "C differs from D". And this doctrine must be held, for the same reasons, to be true of all other relations; relations do not have instances, but are strictly the same in all propositions in which they occur. (Russell 1903: 51–2).

It seems that for Russell in *The Principles*, if we are to properly explain what various pairs of different terms have in common, we need to do it with the help of a numerically identical *relation of difference*. Moorean various *instances* of 'difference' cannot do the job because something then has to further explain what makes those different instances instances of *difference* and not of something else. If we disregard the awkwardness of the example that Russell has chosen (with his insistence on the relation of *difference*), and add the additional steps that Moore would have had to take to explain what all the instances of difference have in common (i.e. that they would

---

[1]Russell himself argued for this Moorean approach to relations in his unpublished manuscript 'Do Differences Differ?' (1899). For a detailed discussion of Russell's arguments in that paper and of what might have prompted him to move away from particularized relations see Foster 2009–10. For a thorough discussion of arguments for universal relations employed by Russell in *The Principles*, see Griffin and Zak 1981.

have to resemble some higher order difference relation, and so on *ad infinitum*), we seem to have Russell's regress argument for relational universals in its rudimentary form.

A version of the regress argument that seems to be even closer to the regress that appears in *Problems* has been recently uncovered by Bernard Linsky (2013). He found the following notes that Russell wrote circa 1903 on Meinong's 'Abstracting and Comparing' (1900):

> Comparison-theory supposes similarity of a and b discovered by that of (a,b) and (c,d). Hence endless regress. (67)

> This regress, unlike many, is objectionable, since its beginning, not its end, goes to infinity. (68)

It looks as if Russell was here thinking that taking resemblance between *a* and *b* to hold in virtue of their resemblance to another pair (*c, d*) would lead to a regress. The missing regress-generating step is the question: in virtue of what do the pairs (*a, b*) and (*c, d*) resemble one another? It would have to be in virtue of resemblance to some other pair of resembling pairs ((*e, f*), (*g, h*)); but then the question would arise again.

It is also possible, however, that Russell was taking the pair (*c, d*) as a paradigm of resemblance. The thought in that case would be that *a* and *b* resemble in virtue of their resemblance resembling the paradigm of resemblance (*c, d*). Without further clues from Russell, it is not clear which reading of these notes is correct. The fact that he thought that the regress he was describing would arise at its beginning, rather than its end, does little to dispel the mystery.

3   Is Russell's Regress Vicious?

At the time when Russell provided his regress argument for universals, infinite regresses were widely used and discussed. Bradley's regress arguments against relations in *Appearance and Reality* (1893) had certainly drawn the attention of Russell's contemporaries, as well as of Russell himself.[2] Furthermore, Russell was clearly sensitive to the fact that not all regresses or 'endless processes' are bad, as the following passage from *The Principles* illustrates:

> ...in the present work, it will be maintained that there are no contradictions peculiar to the notion of infinity, and that an endless process is not to be objected to unless it arises in the analysis of the actual meaning of a proposition. (Russell 1903: §55, 51)

---

[2] For Russell's initial response to Bradley, see *The Principles*, chapter IX, §99.

With this in mind, it is all the more clear that Russell viewed his regress argument for relational universals as being of the objectionable kind, for it was meant to force the opponents of universals to admit at least one relational universal of *resemblance*. Was Russell right to think this way? Is his regress argument indeed as vicious and powerful as he seemed to assume?

Although charges of infinite regress are a fairly common occurrence in philosophical arguments, there are still no uniform criteria for determining which regresses should count as benign or vicious. Daniel Nolan (2001), in his article 'What's wrong with infinite regresses?', analyzes some well-known regresses and tries to individuate the intuitions involved in philosophers' decisions over whether a regress should count as vicious or not. He points out that most philosophers tend to agree that a truth regress is a perfectly benign regress: for any sentence p, if it is true, then so is 'p is true', as well as '"p is true" is true', and so on, ad infinitum. Thus, given Tarski's schema and adequate substitution instances, a harmless regress can be generated so that to every truth corresponds an infinite number of truths.

There is also a broad consensus over straightforwardly vicious regresses such as Plato's *Third Man Argument*, as reconstructed by Vlastos (1954), and the regress generated by the assumption that $\sqrt{2}$ is rational.[3] These regresses are caused by (and are *symptoms* of) inconsistencies or even outright contradictions in the premises and they often function as *reductio* arguments.

Some regresses, however, are neither straightforwardly benign, nor vicious; they are more difficult to pin down. Regresses that Nolan (2001) calls 'non-reductive' can be problematic in this way. They involve no apparent contradiction. Their main fault, as the name indicates, is that they do not succeed in explaining the phenomenon in question in terms of something more fundamental, but keep relying on the very terms that need explaining. If a theory promises a reductive explanation of a phenomenon and then falls into an infinite 'non-reductive' regress, the regress is considered *vicious* and the theory a failure. However, what happens if such a regress appears in a theory (or part of the theory) that does not aim to be reductive, or at least that does not aim to reduce the phenomenon that is at the center of the non-reductive infinite regress? The truth regress above is a case in point: it is only considered benign because it is not used to reductively explain the notion of the truth of a sentence in terms of something more fundamental. In other words, if Tarski ran into such a regress while trying to explain what the truth of p in L consists in (and ended up saying that 'p is true if and only

---

[3] See Nolan 2001 for a detailed discussion of these examples.

if "*p* is true" is true', and so on ad infinitum) then he would be in serious trouble.

Thus, it seems that the 'viciousness' of certain regresses depends largely on contextual factors. Russell's regress argument appears to be such a context-sensitive regress - it emerges in an explanatory context in which a nominalist attempts to explain away properties in terms of resemblance to some paradigm instances of those properties. In this context, the regress seems to show that no amount of particular resemblance relations will ever give the nominalist the explanation she was after.

But does a nominalist have to commit herself to such an infinite regress in the first place? Can she stop short of attempting such an explanation? And would this kind of strategy work well against Russell's challenge? The next section addresses these questions.

4 Recent Nominalist and Trope Theorists' Responses to Russell's Regress Argument

In contemporary metaphysical debate, 'nominalism' is usually taken to refer to an ontology that admits only of particulars. Properties and relations are, according to such theories, constructed out of particulars as natural classes of particulars, resemblances between particulars, etc. Nominalists not only reject the existence of universals (be it universal properties or universal relations) but also deny the ontological reality of properties and relations as anything else but constructions out of particulars.

Trope theorists, on the other hand, tend to agree with nominalists in their rejection of universals, but unlike them, they take properties and relations to be ontologically real. Some trope theorists – such as bundle trope theorists – take properties and relations to be their most fundamental entities out of which they attempt to construct ordinary particulars. Their main divergence from realists about universals lies in taking such properties and relations as *particularized* rather than universal multiply repeatable entities.

Due to their rejection of universals, both trope theorists and nominalists have been sometimes referred to as 'nominalists', with the former called 'moderate nominalists' and the latter 'extreme nominalists'. Here, however, I reserve the term 'nominalism' for theories that completely reject the ontological reality of properties and relations – that is, I will not be applying the term to trope theories.

Now, Russell's regress argument is aimed at *all* those who reject universals, which is why in the sections that follow I will examine how some contemporary nominalists *and* trope theorists have responded to Russell's argument. If their responses are found wanting, perhaps Russell's argument *against the rejection of universals* can be treated as a forceful *positive* argument *for* their acceptance.

4.1 Paradigm Resemblance Nominalism and Russell's Regress

Paradigm resemblance nominalism is the primary target of Russell's regress argument in *Problems*. This kind of nominalism avoids postulating universal properties such as *whiteness* and *triangularity* and relations such as *north of* and *two feet apart* by analyzing them away in terms of resemblance of particulars (or *pairs* of particulars) to a given paradigm particular (or *pair* of particulars). Thus, particular *a's being white* is nothing more for a paradigm resemblance nominalist than particular *a's* resemblance to some chosen paradigm of *whiteness* – say, a particular piece of white chalk. Similarly, *a's being north of b* is nothing more than the resemblance of the pair (*a*, *b*) to some chosen paradigm of *north of* relation – say, a pair of cities (*Edinburgh, London*).

In the way that the paradigm nominalist position is presented, it is usually taken for granted that the very pairing of the paradigm with the particular that resembles it is unproblematic. And yet it is not clear what grounds the particular pairings. What grounds the pairing of a white ball and a white piece of chalk as opposed to a white ball and a red ball? Taking a white ball as a paradigm does not automatically determine what it is a paradigm of – whether it is the paradigm of the property 'white' or the paradigm of the property 'round'. And since there is no ordinary particular with just one property, the paradigm resemblance nominalist seems to be making use of the notion of resemblance-with-respect-to-a-certain-property such as resemblance-with-respect-to-whiteness or resemblance-with-respect-to-roundness in the very analysis of properties such as *whiteness* and *roundness*. Thus, there is an explanatory circularity that the paradigm resemblance nominalist must address before tackling Russell's regress proper.

One way that a paradigm resemblance nominalist may choose to respond is by claiming that the pairings of paradigms and particulars do not present an *ontological* problem. The pairings are based on *our recognition* of respects of resemblance and this *recognition* – a paradigm resemblance nominalist might insist – has nothing to do with the *analysis* of properties. The trouble with this line of response, however, is that it moves away from resemblance nominalists' declared goal, which is an account of properties and relations in terms of objective mind-independent resemblances of particulars and paradigms. It cannot therefore be part of the notion of a paradigm that it be picked out by us.

Another problem for the paradigm resemblance nominalist is presented by the question of what happens if there were only one object left in the universe. Would such an object still have properties such as being white and if yes, what would be the ontological ground of its whiteness? It could not be the resemblance of the remaining object with itself, since every object resembles itself. Could it then be the resemblance of the object with its proper part, the proper part being taken as a paradigm of whiteness? And if this were possible, what would happen if there were only one atomic white particular left, without any proper parts?[4]

But crucially, how might a paradigm resemblance nominalist respond to the charge of infinite regress of resemblance relations brought about by Russell's argument? James Cargile (2003) has argued that paradigms actually help avoid Russell's regress, and that without them it could not be avoided. Paradigms, according to him, gradually reduce the number of resemblances at each level in the regress until only one resemblance is left. Thus Russell's infinite regress turns finite. Cargile suggests that this can be done by considering only the resemblances between non-paradigms and paradigms. For example, if we have three resembling particulars a, b, c, one of which, say a, is taken as a white paradigm, and the other two, b and c, resemble a, this gives us two resemblances – between a and b and between a and c. Now, one of them is the paradigm resemblance between white things, say the one between a and b. The other resemblance, the one between a and c, is resemblance in virtue of resembling the paradigm resemblance. This then results in a further resemblance, a second order resemblance, between the paradigm resemblance holding between a and b, and the resemblance between a and c. But at this point there are no other second order resemblances and the regress is stopped (Cargile 2003: 555–6).

As Rodriguez-Pereyra (2004) rightly points out, this proposal has two flaws: first, it seems to simply assume that there must be a finite number of white particulars; and second, even with a finite number of white particulars, considering just the resemblances between paradigms and non-paradigms at one level does not by itself reduce the number of resemblances at the next. In the previous example of three white particulars a, b, c what makes b and c white is their resemblance to the paradigm a. This, however,

---

[4]If a paradigm resemblance nominalist makes an appeal here to white objects in other possible worlds, then she will be embracing Lewisian inflated ontology of possibilia, discussed in more detail below. An alternative that has been suggested to me is to invoke *merely possible* white objects. However, I struggle to see how such 'merely possible' objects can solve the problem if they are not fully fledged white objects. But if they are then indeed fully fledged white objects, what makes them *merely possible*?

does not mean that b and c do not resemble each other – just not considering their resemblance does not make it fail to exist. Thus, it seems that the reduction of the number of resemblances does not go as planned. And the same seems to happen at the next level too: even if what makes the latter two resemblances first order resemblances is that they resemble the resemblance between a and b, the resemblances between a and c and between b and c resemble each other and so we have three second order resemblances rather than two, and so on. In short, it appears that the infinite regress has not been avoided.

4.2 Non-paradigm Resemblance Nominalism and Russell's Regress

Now what about non-paradigm resemblance nominalism? Does it do any better than the paradigm resemblance nominalism in countering the Russell's regress argument? Gonzalo Rodriguez-Pereyra (2002) has endorsed what he calls 'Egalitarian Resemblance Nominalism' (as opposed to 'Aristocratic' or paradigm resemblance nominalism discussed above) which accounts for a particular having a property in terms of its resemblance to *all* the other particulars having the same property; i.e., for a particular a to have a property F is for it to resemble *all* other F-particulars. So, if we have three white particulars a, b, and c, a's whiteness is due to its resemblance to b and c. But then, what makes the resemblances between a and b, a and c, and b and c, resemble one other? Each one of them resembles the other two resemblances. And what makes these new resemblances resemble one other? Russell's regress is looming again and no amount of higher order resemblances will give us what the egalitarian resemblance nominalist had promised – an explanation of what the having of the property 'white' of particulars a, b, and c consists in. This account appears to do no better than the one provided by the paradigm resemblance nominalist above.

There is, however, a strategy that may be used to block Russell's regress and it is to maintain that particulars resemble one another just in virtue of being the particulars that they are. Rodriguez-Pereyra puts this position as follows:

> What makes it true that a and b are both white is that they resemble each other but this does not mean that there is an extra entity, the resemblance between a and b. What makes a and b resemble each other? Simply a and b. So if there are resembling particulars but no resemblances there is no regress of resemblances … Resemblance Nominalism can avoid the regress by refusing to reify resemblances. (Rodriguez-Pereyra 2004: 645)

Rodriguez-Pereyra is careful to point out that he does not mean that it is the *intrinsic natures* of *a* and *b* that ground the resemblance between the two.[5] If resemblance were taken to be an internal relation that supervenes on the *particularized natures* of particulars, the regress could be avoided – but potentially at a high price. For how should particularized natures be understood? Armstrong (1989) sees them as a number of properties (taken as particulars, of course) somehow 'sealed' together into one grand property within which no differentiation can be made. The problem with this suggestion, as Rodriguez-Pereyra notes, is that it goes against the very spirit of Resemblance Nominalism.[6] Namely, a position that starts off by explaining away properties in terms of resemblance would do better to then not proceed to explain resemblance in terms of specific combinations of properties.

So what then does Rodriguez-Pereyra suggest in the passage above? Apparently, all he wishes to claim is that particulars themselves – not their intrinsic or particularized natures – are what is needed for grounding of resemblance. But if the answer can be this simple, was Russell wrong all along in believing that the resemblance nominalist has a problem where there isn't one? It doesn't seem so. Russell might have been wrong to assume that a nominalist would want to explain resemblance in terms of an *additional* entity of some sort. As we have seen in the case of Rodriguez-Pereyra's resemblance nominalism, there is no such further ontological commitment going on. There are just pairs of particulars, and nothing else. However, Russell did seem correct in his insistence that if an explication of properties was going to run in terms of resemblances, some sort of story about what resemblances *are* ought to be given. Otherwise, why promise an explanation and then at the very first step not deliver?

Thus, the resemblance nominalist is faced with an unpalatable choice between an infinite vicious regress if he tries to explain resemblance, and the inexplicability of resemblance if he doesn't. And if he chooses the latter, what grounds the groupings of particulars into the ones that have a certain property and the ones that do not? Resemblance nominalists may still call upon 'resemblance', but there is not much more that can be said about it. As Rodriguez-Pereyra puts it: 'What is the resemblance invoked by Resem-

---

[5]This proposal was made by Armstrong (1989: 44).

[6]Rodrigues Pereyra writes: 'For if that *a* and *b* resemble each other is determined by their natures, then their natures are not determined by their resembling each other, and so what is doing all the work is their natures, not their resembling each other. Indeed, if in the case of one-instance properties what grounds the attribution of the property to the instance is its nature, why appeal to resemblances in the cases of multiple-instance properties?' (Rodriguez-Pereyra 2002: 88).

blance Nominalism? It is an objective, ontological, primitive, reflexive, symmetrical, non-transitive "relation" that comes by degrees and can obtain between no more than two entities' (Rodriguez-Pereyra 2002: 62).

By saying that resemblance is *primitive* Rodriguez-Pereyra means 'that Resemblance Nominalism does not account for the facts of resemblance it invokes in terms of any other, more basic kinds of facts. If *a* and *b* resemble each other, there is no other fact to which the resemblance between *a* and *b* reduces' (2002: 64). Thus, facts of resemblance are themselves to be taken as a brute fact.

Still, Rodriguez-Pereyra's primitive resemblance is an odd primitive. It is supposed to refer to an ontological *relation* that is reflexive, symmetrical, and non-transitive; yet the relation is not to be understood with ontological seriousness, as is indicated by the quotation marks in the above quote (If it were taken seriously, we would have Russell's regress all over again.) So, it is not the resemblance *relation* that is primitive. What is primitive is the predicate 'resemblance' and its application that we should take as a given. Such a predicate refers (or applies) to facts of resemblance, which in their own right should be taken as obvious and irreducible. Hence, what Rodriguez-Pereyra seems to be suggesting is that resemblances are to be taken as brute ontologically-non-committing facts: in this way the resemblance nominalist's ontology stays economical, containing nothing but particulars. The trade-off though is that a primitive *predicate* of resemblance needs to be accepted and, as we will see in more detail below, it is a very complex one.

4.3 Class Nominalism and Russell's Regress

Russell's regress is not just aimed at resemblance nominalism but at any account of properties that avoids universals. Class nominalism is no exception. According to class nominalism, properties are constructed as classes of particulars, and having a property comes down to being a member of a class of things that all have that property. For instance, for a particular to be white is for it simply to be a member of the class of white things.

To this, Russell could respond by pointing out that *being a member* is a relation that needs explaining. If a class nominalist attempts to explain it without appealing to universals he will have to do it in terms of membership of a class of things that are members. But then we are already caught up in Russell's regress, explaining away a membership relation in terms of further higher order membership relations.

To their advantage, class nominalists can say that membership relation is a primitive of their theory which does not need any further analysis, because it is sufficiently familiar from set theory. But even if this is granted, there is a different problem that the class nominalist needs to address. Namely, very few classes of particulars make for genuine properties, i.e. for properties whose members genuinely resemble one another. David Lewis famously traced the difference between such genuine, sparse properties, and abundant ones in terms of the notion of *naturalness*. For him, natural classes are the ones that in a realist theory would be picked out by universals. But how does a class nominalist, who doesn't have universals at his disposition, pick out natural classes? Lewis explains as follows:

> Instead of employing universals it [a nominalist theory] could draw primitive distinctions among particulars. Most simply, a Nominalist could take it as a primitive fact that some classes of things are perfectly natural properties; others are less-than-perfectly natural to various degrees; and most are not at all natural. Such a Nominalist takes "natural" as a primitive predicate, and offers no analysis of what he means in predicating it of classes. (Lewis 1983: 14)

According to this, a property such as *whiteness* would be analyzed away in terms of a perfectly natural class of white things, where perfect naturalness is understood to be a primitive predicate. This is rather unsatisfactory as far as analysis goes, but what are the alternatives? Lewis suggests that natural properties could perhaps be defined in terms of 'the mutual resemblances of the members of their class and the lack of resemblance between their members and their non-members'. The trouble with this strategy is that it is not fine grained enough – that is, mutual resemblance of the members of a certain class may not be due to the sharing of any *one* property.[7]

Lewis thus suggests a predicate of resemblance that is contrastive and variably polyadic and which ought to be ta taken as understood without any further analysis: '$x_1, x_2, \ldots$ resemble one another and do not likewise resemble any of $y_1, y_2, \ldots$' (where the strings of variables can be infinite) (Lewis 1983: 14–5). Then, to get from such a primitive predicate of resemblance to perfectly natural properties Lewis suggests to define N, another variably

---

[7]Take for instance three particulars a, b, and c, each of which has only three properties – color, shape, and temperature. Now, let a be red, round, and hot, b, red, square, and cold, and c blue, square, and hot. It is easy to see that each pair a and b, b and c, and a and c resemble each other in being red, square, and hot respectively. However, although they resemble each other, it doesn't make them have any one common property. As this example illustrates well, it is not enough to have a group of properties that resemble one another to say that they all have the property F: they could resemble each other in different respects without it being the case that all share the same property. The problem is about delimiting the proper resemblance classes – letting in the particulars that resemble in such ways that make for properties and leave out those that do not.

polyadic predicate, so that it turns out that $Nx_1,x_2, \ldots$ iff $x_1,x_2, \ldots$ are all and only the members of some perfectly natural property (this, again for possibly infinitely many xs). The definition of $Nx_1,x_2, \ldots$ then runs as follows: '$\exists y_1, y_2, \ldots \forall z (z, x_1,x_2 \ldots R y_1, y_2, \ldots \equiv z= x_1 \vee z= x_2 \vee \ldots)$'. And a perfectly natural property would then be defined as a class such that, if $x_1,x_2 \ldots$ are all and only its members, then $N x_1,x_2 \ldots$. (Lewis 1983: 15).

Lewis concludes his discussion of these nominalist alternatives as follows: 'if an adequate Nominalism requires us to choose between this [a primitive, contrastive, and a variably polyadic predicate of resemblance] and a primitive predicate of classes, we might well wonder whether the game is worth the candle' (1983: 15). One might wonder the same thing not only on the basis of having to choose between excessively complex primitive predicates and primitive *naturalness*, but also on the basis of quantitative extravagance – the infinite concrete *possibilia* - that both contemporary versions of resemblance nominalism and class nominalism are committed to.

4.4 The Coextension Problem and Possibilia

Class and resemblance nominalists' rejection of universals makes them also susceptible to the *coextension problem*. The problem arises in an attempt to distinguish between coextensive properties (like 'renate' – the property of having a kidney, and 'cordate' – the property of having a heart). If all the *F* particulars are *G* and all the *G* particulars are *F*, neither class nominalist nor resemblance nominalist has the resources to distinguish between these two properties. The way Lewis's class nominalism gets around this problem is by introducing *possibilia*. The most recent version of resemblance nominalism developed by Rodriguez-Pereyra does the same. Possibilia appear to solve the coextension problem: the two types of nominalism can say that what grounds a particular's having the property *F* is that it resembles all actual and *possible F* particulars, and the same with *G* particulars; or, that what grounds a particular's having of the property *F* is that it is a member of the class of all actual and *possible F* particulars, and the same with G particulars. Then the contingently coextensive properties *F* and *G* become distinguishable, since all the *possible F*s will not be all the *possible G*s and vice versa.

This solution, however, comes at a high price: the entire possible world ontology, with all its possible inhabitants, has to be admitted. Nominalists like Lewis and Rodriguez-Pereyra have tried to minimize this boost in ontology by arguing in favor of distinctions between *qualitative* and *quantitative* ontological economy; qualitative economy is measured by the number of *kinds* of postulated entities, quantitative economy is measured by the number of *entities*, of any kind, postulated by a theory (Rodriguez-Pereyra 2002: 204–10). Lewis has argued that only qualitative economy matters – a position that allows him to claim that his ontology is more economical than the realist's. Rodriguez-Pereyra, on the other hand, argues that both sorts of economy matter but that *qualitative* economy 'takes precedence' over the quantitative one. This would make the boost in ontology caused by admitting concrete *possibilia* only a quantitative gain, and therefore a not very important one. The qualitative economy of the resemblance nominalist would still remain sparse.

It is hard not to see both Lewis's and Rodriguez-Pereyra's interpretations of ontological economy as *ad hoc*. They assume that it is obvious that the admission of *possibilia* is just a gain in the number of particulars. And yet, it is not at all clear that possible talking donkeys, flying pigs, unicorns, gods etc. are indeed just 'more of the same sort of thing', more of the same ontological category of plain old particulars. Lewis and Rodriguez-Pereyra need to offer more substantive arguments to disperse the suspicion that an addition of possible particulars is as ontologically innocuous as they seem to suggest.

4.5 Tropes and Russell's Regress

Like realists about universals, trope theorists treat properties with ontological seriousness; but unlike realists, they take them to be particulars, not universals. Thus, trope theorists can explain a particular's *being white* in terms of that particular's possession of a white property trope w_1 (a response which is not available to a nominalist). But at this point Russell could press on with his regress argument: for what makes all the white tropes w_1, w_2, w_3, ... w_n instances of white? A trope theorist cannot appeal to a universal of *whiteness* to unite the class of white tropes.

One line of response is to claim that the class of white tropes is closed under exact resemblance.[8] The trouble with this response is that a trope theorist ought to be able to explain what exact resemblance amounts to. If this is done in terms of tropes, then Russell could step in again and demand an explanation of what all the different relational resemblance tropes have in common. What makes them instances of resemblance? Do they resemble one another? If so, we are off to a regress of higher order relational tropes of resemblance, a regress which appears to be of the non-reductive vicious kind (for it never delivers an explanation of resemblance in terms of some-

---

[8]See Williams 1953: 118 and Campbell 1990: 30–2 and 43–5 for this approach.

thing more fundamental; rather, it keeps introducing higher order resemblance tropes). Alternatively, a trope theorist can insist on taking exact resemblance to be a primitive predicate of the theory. Such a predicate, however, would then have to be construed along the lines of Lewis's contrastive and variably polyadic predicate we saw in section 4.3 above; thus, it would have to be a very complex and to that extent unattractive kind of primitive.

Perhaps a more promising line of response to Russell's regress argument for the trope theorist is to take resemblance to be an internal relation that simply supervenes on the natures of tropes that resemble one another. For instance, Peter Simons argues that it is 'plausible that the resemblance (exact or not) between two tropes is an internal relation, deriving from the separate natures of the two tropes themselves' (Simons 1994: 558). In a similar vein Campbell writes: 'if … resemblance is an internal relation grounded in particular natures in the terms, then the red tropes *a*, *b*, and *c* will generate the whole edifice of supervening resemblance triples' (Campbell 1990: 37). Resemblance would thus not present an ontological addition of any kind. However, although Russell's regress is avoided in this way, it is done at the high cost of not illuminating resemblance at all: particulars have properties and stand in relations to one another in virtue of property tropes and relational tropes that they have; but what makes those property and relation tropes the tropes of whiteness, triangularity, etc. is left unexplained and the resemblance between different property and relation tropes ontologically ungrounded.

5 Russell's Regress as a Positive Argument for Universals?

Our exploration of Russell's regress argument against the rejection of universals has led us to consider a number of challenges that nominalists and trope theorists face in attempting to respond to Russell. We have seen that these challenges are not small and that the ontological economy that nominalists and trope theorists attempt to achieve with their avoidance of universals comes at a high cost. Nominalists tend to take either resemblance or naturalness as primitive predicates – both of which, as we have seen, have to be quite complex. Furthermore, to avoid universals, both resemblance and class nominalists commit themselves to infinite concrete *possibilia* which present a significant ontological addition.

Trope theories enjoy an advantage over nominalists in being able to provide an ontological ground for properties; but they fall short of explaining what unites classes of exactly resembling tropes. Recourse to a primitive predicate of resemblance or internal resemblance relations does little to illuminate the issue.

Does this show Russell to be right when he thought to have shown that 'it is no longer worth while to invent difficult and unplausible theories to avoid the admission of such universals as whiteness and triangularity' (Russell 1912: 96–7)? This conclusion is perhaps too quick. What Russell's regress argument certainly shows is that avoidance of universals comes with its own set of problems and that such problems should not be underestimated. Avoiding universals leaves nominalists and trope theorists without a satisfactory account of what having properties and relations amounts to, and it commits them to some very odd entities (*possibilia*) and primitive predicates.

One of the most prominent realists of our time – David Armstrong – made use of Russell's regress argument in his *Universals and Scientific Realism* (1978) as an argument against resemblance nominalism. However, in his later *Universals: An Opinionated Introduction* (1989) he had a change of heart and considered Russell's regress argument still a 'brilliant argument' but no longer effective against nominalists. The reasons for this change of heart are two: 1) Armstrong came to think that all solutions to the problem of universals – including the realists' – face a version of Russell's argument; and 2) he found the resemblance nominalist's treatment of resemblance relations as internal, and thus supervenient on the natures of particulars, satisfactory. I disagree with both 1) and 2). I have said enough about the criticism of 2) above, so let me say a few words about 1).

A realist about universals like Armstrong postulates universals as genuine respects of resemblance between particulars. Universals are thus the ones that provide the ontological ground for the having and the sharing of genuine properties and relations. A particular a's being white and triangular is thus due to its having the universals of *whiteness* and *triangularity*. Now, this *having* or *instantiation* has been thought of as a relation that automatically gives rise to Bradley's infinite and vicious regress of relations. I, however, disagree with such a treatment of Bradley's regress and favor a view according to which all relations – including the relation of instantiation, if such is postulated – unproblematically relate their relata.[9] I find that contemporary discussions of Bradley's regress contain a series of confusions and that as a result, the threat of this regress to realists has been overstated. Armstrong, on the other hand, by equating the two regresses, and even taking Bradley's regress to present a greater threat to realists than Russell's

---

[9]For my detailed treatment of Bradley's regress see Perovic 2014.

regress presents to nominalists and trope theorists, has contributed to the perception that Russell's regress argument is no longer relevant in contemporary ontological discussions.

In conclusion, contemporary realists should keep using Russell's regress argument and its versions in their disputes with nominalists and trope theorists to pinpoint the difficulties in their theories. For those convinced of the drawbacks of those theories, and convinced of the importance of providing a substantial ontological ground for properties and relations, the argument may even present a positive case for universals. For those who have nominalist tendencies, the argument at least needs to be addressed. Either way, the argument appears to be still extraordinarily relevant, one hundred years after its publication in Russell's *The Problems of Philosophy*.

References

Armstrong, D. M. 1978. *Nominalism and Realism: Universals and Scientific Realism, Volume I*. Cambridge: Cambridge University Press.

Armstrong, D. M. 1989. *Universals: An Opinionated Introduction*. Boulder: Westview Press.

Bradley. F. H. 1893. *Appearance and Reality*. Oxford: Clarendon Press.

Campbell, K. 1990. *Abstract Particulars*. Oxford: Basil Blackwell.

Cargile, J. 2003. On Russell's Argument against Resemblance Nominalism. *Australasian Journal of Philosophy* 81: 549–560.

Foster, T. R. 2009–10. Russell's 'Do Differences Differ?'. *Russell: The Journal of Bertrand Russell Studies* 29: 129–147.

Griffin, N. and G. Zak. 1982. Russell on Specific and Universal Relations: *The Principles of Mathematics*, §55. *History and Philosophy of Logic* 3: 55–67.

Lewis, D. 1983. New Work for a Theory of Universals. *Australasian Journal of Philosophy* 61: 343–377. In Lewis 1999.

Lewis, D. 1999. *Papers in Metaphysics and Epistemology*. Cambridge: Cambridge University Press.

Linsky, B. 2013. Russell's Notes For 'Meinong's Theory of Complexes and Assumptions'. *Russell: The Journal of Bertrand Russell Studies* 33: 143–70.

Nolan, D. 2001. What's Wrong with Infinite Regresses? *Metaphilosophy* 32: 523–38.

Perovic, K. 2014. The Import of The Original Bradley's Regress(es). *Axiomathes* DOI 10.1007/s10516-014-9229-8.

Rodriguez-Pereyra, G. 2002. *Resemblance Nominalism*. Oxford: Oxford University Press.

Rodriguez-Pereyra, G. 2004. Paradigms and Russell's Resemblance Regress. *Australasian Journal of Philosophy* 82: 644–51.

Russell, B. 1899. Do Differences Differ? In *CP* 3: 555–7.

Russell, B. 1903. *The Principles of Mathematics*. Cambridge: Cambridge University Press.

Russell, B. 1911–12. On the Relations of Universals and Particulars. *Proceedings of the Aristotelian Society* 12: 1–24. In Russell 1956: 105–24.

Russell, B. 1912. *The Problems of Philosophy*. London: Williams and Norgate. Reprinted Oxford: Oxford University Press 1959.

Russell, B. 1956. *Logic and Knowledge: Essays, 1901–1950*, ed. R. Marsh. London: Unwin Hyman.

Russell, B. 1993. *The Collected Papers of Bertrand Russell, Volume 3: Toward the 'Principles of Mathematics', 1900–02*, ed. G. H. Moore. London: Routledge. [*CP* 3]

Simons, P. 1994. Particulars in Particular Clothing: Three Trope Theories of Substance. *Philosophy and Phenomenological Research* 54: 553–75.

Vlastos, G. 1954. The Third Man Argument in the Parmenides. *Philosophical Review* 63: 313–49.

Williams, D. C. 1953. On the Elements of Being: I. *The Review of Metaphysics* 7: 3–18.

10

The Constituents of the Propositions of Logic

Kevin C. Klement

1 Introduction

Many founders of modern logic—Frege and Russell among them—
bemoaned the tendency, still found in most textbook treatments, to define
the subject matter of logic as 'the laws of thought' or 'the principles of inference'. Such descriptions fail to capture logic's objective nature; they
make it too dependent on human psychology or linguistic practices. It is one
thing to identify what logic is *not* about. It is another to say what it *is* about.
I tell my students that logic studies relationships between the truth-values of
propositions that hold in virtue of their form. But even this characterization
leaves me uneasy. I do not really know what a 'form' is, and even worse
perhaps, I do not really know what these 'propositions' are that have these
forms. If propositions are considered merely as sentences or linguistic assertions, the definition does not seem like much of an improvement over the
psychological definitions. Language is a human invention, but logic is more
than that, or so it seems.

It is perhaps forgiveable then that at certain times Russell would not
have been prepared to give a very good answer to the question 'What is
Logic?', such as when he attempted, but failed, to compose a paper with
that title in October 1912. Given that Russell had recently completed *Principia Mathematica*, a work alleging to establish the reducibility of mathematics to logic, one might think this overly generous. What does the claim
that mathematics reduces to logic come to if we cannot independently speci-

Acquaintance, Knowledge, and Logic.
Donovan Wishon and Bernard Linsky (eds.).
Copyright © 2015, CSLI Publications.

fy what logic is? But a response might be that we know what logic is when we see it, whether or not we can put its essence into words. Still it is puzzling that less than a year prior to attempting 'What Is Logic?', Russell professed to have an understanding both of the nature of logical truths and even of our knowledge of them. In *The Problems of Philosophy* (chaps. VII, X especially), written in 1911 and published in 1912, Russell argued that logical propositions are general propositions that assert relations between 'certain abstract logical universals' (Russell 1912: 109), and that our knowledge of logic and mathematics consists of intuitive or direct knowledge of truths about these universals. The same view is found in other 1911 works by Russell, including 'The Philosophical Importance of Mathematical Logic' and 'Analytic Realism'. In the former, he writes:

> Logic and mathematics force us, then, to admit a kind of realism in the scholastic sense, that is to say, to admit there is a world of universals and of truths which do not bear directly on such and such a particular existence. This world of universals must *subsist*, although it cannot *exist* in the same sense as that in which particular data exist. We have immediate knowledge of an indefinite number of propositions about universals: this is an ultimate fact, as ultimate as sensation is. Pure mathematics—which is usually called "logic" in its elementary parts—is the sum of everything that we can know, whether directly or by demonstration, about certain universals. (Russell 1992e: 39–40)

Russell comes across as brazen, taking himself to have shown more or less conclusively that not all knowledge is empirical, and not all of what is known is mind-dependent.

I am not convinced that Russell was as confident about these issues as he pretended to be at the time. He certainly *shouldn't* have been very confident. The view that logic and pure mathematics concern themselves with knowledge of certain universals fits reasonably well with the views he held early on in his logicist years, such as when composing *The Principles of Mathematics* (hereafter *PoM*), published in 1903. However, his views changed quite a lot between then and the publication of *Principia Mathematica* (hereafter *PM*), mostly as a result of his attempts to deal with the logical paradoxes. These changes in most cases brought him further away from a Pythagorean or Platonist metaphysics of special logical and mathematical entities. Even when it comes to the primitive logical constants, the changes make it much more difficult to think of them as standing for anything like universals.

A close examination, especially of Russell's manuscripts written prior to *PM*, show some awareness of some of the difficulties that arise for maintaining his original view about the particular nature of the propositions of logic and their constituents. This leaves an interpretive difficulty as to why Russell shows little hesitation in *Problems* and in other works of the period in writing as if these difficulties do not exist. Unfortunately, there is not enough in Russell's writings to provide a definitive solution to this interpretive difficulty. But there are some clues from which we can speculate. I shall argue that there is reason to think that although Russell did not have a fully worked out view of the nature of 'logical universals' in this period, he had a variety of ideas about what some of them might be. These ideas include some rather strange ones such as an understanding of negation and implication as 'multiple relations' between *constituents* of propositions, much like his view of the nature of judgment or belief during this period. However, I think he was never fully satisfied with these ideas, and soon came to abandon them. If these speculations are correct, they also shed light on certain other changes to Russell's metaphysics, especially his understanding of general facts and higher-order truths. In the end, however, he was still uncertain as to the nature of the constituents of the propositions of logic for quite some years to follow, until finally settling on a purely linguistic conception of logic later in his life.

2 The Earlier Development of Russell's Ideas

My focus in this paper is primarily Russell's views around the time of *Problems of Philosophy*. It is important, however, to contrast these views with those that came before. In the opening chapter of *PoM*, Russell characterized a proposition of logic as one containing no constants but logical constants, and a proposition of pure mathematics as a proposition of logic taking the form of a formal implication (quantified conditional). The notion of a logical constant, Russell argued, was too primitive to be defined, and so the logical constants could only be given by enumeration. In 1903, Russell's list included formal and material implication ($\supset$), the membership relation ($\square$), the 'such that' class abstraction operator ($\square$) and the notion of a relation (Rel). With at least some of these, it is fairly obvious how early Russell might have seen them as representing universals. Early Russell understood classes realistically, and hence ε could easily be taken as a relation holding between an individual and a class of which it is a member. In *PoM*, Russell similarly took material implication as a relation. The relation $\supset$ holds p and q when p and q are both propositions, and either both are true, both are false, or p false and q true (see Russell 1906: 162).

Russell's views on philosophical logic, however, changed drastically in between *PoM* and *PM*, as he struggled to devise a solution to the class-theoretic and other logical paradoxes plaguing his work on the foundations of mathematics. These changes left Russell with a much sparser metaphysics of abstracta.[1] As a result, the candidate 'relata' for possible purely logical relations begin to disappear. Firstly, and perhaps most importantly, according to Russell's 'no class' theory, apparent terms for classes must be analyzed away using higher-order quantification. Classes are not taken as genuine *things*, and hence cannot enter into basic relations. The membership sign ε is no longer taken as a primitive logical constant in *PM*, and a formula of the form

$$a \in \hat{x}(\varphi x)$$

is, according to the stipulations of *PM*'s *20, merely an abbreviation of one of the form

$$(\exists f)((x)(f!x \equiv \varphi x).f!a)$$

In the full rendering, the only logical constants left are truth-functional connectives and quantifiers, and nothing represents any relation or property of a class treated as a genuine thing. In Russell's vocabulary, a class is a 'logical fiction' and a class-term an 'incomplete symbol' having no meaning in isolation.

Russell had toyed with versions of a 'no class' theory as early as May 1903 (see Frege 1980: 158), but seems to have definitively settled on it as a response to the paradoxes in late 1905 (Russell 1973: 64). By 1906, he had come to the conclusion that something very much like a 'no classes' theory (see, e.g., Grattan-Guinness 1977: 89) must be applied to deal with talk of 'propositions' as well. Prior to this, Russell had understood propositions as objectively real complex entities similar to states of affairs, containing the entities they are about. However, taking propositions realistically led to various paradoxes of propositions (see, e.g., Russell 1931: §500, 2014d; 131–85, and *passim*; for discussion see Landini 1998, and Klement 2010b). These included contingent paradoxes such as the liar paradoxes, as well as logical antinomies stemming from violations of Cantor's powerclass theorem. By it, there must be more classes of propositions than propositions. But it seems possible to generate a distinct proposition for each class thereof, for instance, the proposition that all members of that class are true. These paradoxes, and other considerations, led Russell to become increasingly wary of his realism about propositions, but his abandonment of them proceeded in stages.

---

[1] I discuss the development of Russell's views on such matters in more detail in Klement 2004, 2014.

In the 1906 'On "Insolubilia" and their Solution by Symbolic Logic' (Russell 1973c: 207), Russell took the intermediate position of a realism about non-quantified propositions, but posited only quantified or general 'statements'. An manuscript from the same period summarizes:

> The philosophical ground for this view is that judgments only have objective counterparts when they are *particular*; the *general* is purely mental; all *facts* involve no apparent [bound] variables. Much to be said for this. E.g. "I met a man"; the *fact* is "I met Jones" (Russell 2014a: 562)

Russell's willingness to consider the idea that there is no objective counterpart to quantification may have been in part a result of his having abandoned the view of *PoM* according to which quantifier phrases such as 'everything' or 'anything' represented special entities called 'denoting concepts' in favor of the new theory of meaning of 1905's 'On Denoting' (1994b; cf. Russell 1994d: 385–6).

Through the next few years, (see e.g, Russell 1907, 2014e) Russell's views on propositions seem somewhat up in the air. By 1910, however, Russell had settled on his new 'Multiple Relation Theory of Judgment' according to which a belief is not a dyadic relation between a believer and a proposition, but a polyadic relation between a believer and the various constituents of the would-be fact potentially making it true (Russell 1992d). On this view, all propositions, quantified or elementary, are taken as mere *façons de parler*, much like classes. They too, then, could no longer be taken as entering in as relata of basic or unanalyzable relations. This is clearly incompatible with Russell's former understanding of ⊃ and other truth-functional connectives. Indeed, while the views of *PoM* are readily compatible with the view that logical constants represent certain kinds of universals, the same is not quite so clear for Russell's post-*PM* views.

3 The Beings of the World of Logic

So if when Russell claimed in *Problems* and other works of that period that logic was concerned with 'certain abstract universals' he could not have meant it in quite the same way he might have had he made the same claim in 1903, what did he mean?

The most extended discussion in *Problems* of a logical or mathematical truth which he claims asserts a relation between universals concerns 'two and two are four':

> It is fairly obvious, in view of what has been said, that this proposition states a relation between the universal 'two' and the universal 'four'. This suggests a proposition which we shall now endeavour to establish: name-

ly, *All* a *priori knowledge deals exclusively with the relations of universals.* (Russell 1912: 103)

In this example, the universals that this proposition is supposed to assert a relation between are *two* and *four*. But what are these? Clues come in the next paragraph, where Russell claims that the proposition may be rephrased as 'any two and any other two are four' or 'any collection formed of two twos is a collection of four' (104). This suggests interpreting *two* as a property certain collections have. Russell goes on to claim that the proposition must be interpreted as about the *property* rather than the collections which exhibit this property on the grounds that we are not acquainted with all couples or groups of two, and if it were about them, we could not understand it.

It is striking how simple-minded this description is in comparison to the kind of complicated analysis that would be given to '2 + 2 = 4' in his technical work. Therein, '2' and '4' would be taken as typically ambiguous representations of certain classes of classes, which would themselves require elimination by means of the contextual definition of all class-talk in terms of higher-order quantification. The fully analyzed form of this proposition is therefore *much* more complicated than the discussion in *Problems* lets on, and this disguises difficulties with the contention that what are involved here are universals. In Russell's considered view, there are no such 'things' as classes or collections, so how could there be properties thereof? Number terms are incomplete symbols and numbers are 'logical fictions'; all truths about them are supposed to reduce to truths about simpler entities. They cannot enter into the acquaintance relation in any direct fashion; in some sense they simply *aren't there* to do so.

There might be at least two broad kinds of explanations for why Russell might allow himself to write in this simplistic way in *Problems*. According to the first, Russell is simply meeting his audience half way. *Problems* was meant as a popular general introduction to philosophy with a large target audience; it is not a treatise for specialists in mathematical logic. In similar fashion, Russell sometimes temporarily ignored his view of historical proper names like 'Socrates' and 'Plato' according to which they ought to be treated as 'truncated descriptions' (Russell 1992b: 152ff and 1918: 242–3) and spoke of something like 'Socrates loves Plato' as if it were an atomic proposition, at least until he had explained enough of the basics of his philosophical logic for the reader to follow along with the complications that were developed later (Whitehead and Russell 1925–7: 45). This practice is excusable, because the claims made about 'Socrates loves Plato' will not depend on anything in particular about Socrates or Plato as individuals, and hence what is said about this case will transfer over to the true atomic propositions of the form *aRb*, whatever those turn out to be. One might suspect that Russell is similarly making use of a familiar, cognitively friendly, example with 'two and two are four', and ignoring, for the sake of presentation, that its full analysis would bring in further complications. Again, this will be excusable provided that what is said about 'two and two are four' will remain true of the more technically correct instances of the phenomena in question. But of course, this prompts us to ask: is this the case? When it comes to *fully analyzed* propositions of logic and pure mathematics, can they too be understood as asserting relations of universals?

Before taking up that question, let us consider the other sort of explanation that might be offered for why Russell allows himself to speak here in such simple terms. On some ways of interpreting Russell's metaphysics of 'logical constructions',[2] it is perhaps not quite correct to say that Russell denies whole-scale the reality of collections, or of properties, identifiable as complex universals, that would hold of collections just in case they have a certain number of members. Such things are simply non-fundamental, or derivative in some sense. Whitehead and Russell give many instances of 'primitive ideas' in *PM*, but in the modern sense, the undefined logical constants of *PM* are just disjunction ($\vee$), negation ($\sim$) and the universal and existential quantifiers for the various types. Perhaps these are the only *simple* logical notions, but one can define more complicated notions in terms of them, including, according to the logicist program, class-theoretic and mathematical notions, such as, e.g., the higher-type propositional function of type $n+1$ satisfied by all and only those (predicative) propositional functions of type n which are satisfied by exactly two things. This is more or less how numbers were described in Russell's 1911 lectures on logic at Cambridge, where Moore wrote in his notes:[3]

> Number is a property (= prop. function of) of prop. functions:
>
> E.g. (x is an even prime) (prop. function): 1 is a property of this; i.e. it is satisfied by 1 value of x & no more. (Moore forthcoming)

Could such propositional functions be the 'universals' Russell thinks is involved in 'two and two are four' as analyzed in *Problems*?

---

[2]For interpretations that might follow these lines, see, e.g., Linsky 1999: chap. 2, Levine 2013, and Levine forthcoming.

[3]It is perhaps worth noting that these notes also contain the more usual 'Frege-Russell' definition of numbers as classes of equinumerous classes, and the view taking numbers to be properties of propositional functions is even objected to on the grounds that properties are intensionally individuated. There are many distinct, but equivalent, way to formulate a higher-type propositional function that will be satisfied by just in case is itself satisfied by exactly two arguments, but there would seem to be only one number two.

Exactly how Russell understood propositional functions, and indeed, whether or not he took them to be genuine entities at all, is a matter of some controversy.[4] In at least some pre-*PM* manuscripts, Russell argues that its being nonsense to speak of a propositional function taking itself as argument is evidence that '[a] function must be an incomplete symbol' (Russell 2014: 498) and 'not a new thing over and above its values' (2014e: 363). When he first considered dropping propositions from his ontology, he warned himself 'not to let functions creep back into being' (2014c: 265), intimating that taking them realistically would be as bad as a realism about propositions. At any rate, a propositional function for him would not have been taken as a *simple* or *fundamental* entity, but instead at best as a kind of complex or constructed entity. While he does sometimes use the word 'property' interchangeably with 'propositional function', there is significant evidence that Russell did not equate single-argument propositional functions with the kinds of simple universals he called 'predicates' or 'qualities'.[5]

In the 1911 piece 'Knowledge by Acquaintance and Knowledge by Description', Russell gives a characterization of universals compatible with the existence of complex universals:

> Among universals I include all objects of which no particular is a constituent. Thus the disjunction "universal-particular" includes all objects. We might also call it the disjunction "abstract-concrete." (Russell 1992b: 150)

As near as I can tell, Russell makes the distinction this way so that *facts* about particular existents, such as the fact that a certain sense-datum is a certain color or that one sense-datum is to the left of another, will count as particulars. Facts, for Russell, are not 'logical constructions' or 'logical fictions', and can enter into relations. At this time, Russell understood perception to involve a relation between a perceiver and a fact (Russell 1992d: 122–3, Whitehead and Russell 1925–7: 43), and hence believed that perceptions were always veridical. All objects of perception would be particulars. However, those facts involving only a relation holding between relations, such as the truth maker of the proposition 'priority implies diversity' (Russell 1992a: 135) would count as a complex universal on this definition, as no particular is a constituent. To my knowledge, however, Russell never speaks of any other kind of complex universals.

---

[4] I develop my own views in Klement 2010a, 2013.

[5] I have argued this elsewhere; see Klement 2004. For what it's worth, Linsky 1999: chap. 2 too thinks Russell is committed to differentiating between propositional functions and universals.

There is something to be said for the suggestion that it is possible to understand 'two and two are four' without having a full understanding of all the logically simple entities involved in its full *PM*-style analysis. If that were required, it seems unlikely that any lay person could grasp even such a simple mathematical truth. Russell is at times open to the possibility that we might be acquainted with something complex and not be aware of its complexity. In that case, it would be a blessing to be able to read 'complex universals' into the layperson's understanding of mathematical statements, and to posit some epistemological method of gaining direct insight into the properties and relations of such complex universals that doesn't require a full understanding of their complexity. According to Russell's epistemology of mathematics (see, esp. Russell 1973e), '2 + 2 = 4' is known more directly than the more general logical axioms from which it is deduced in a system such as *PM*. Indeed, he claims that the seeming obviousness of '2 + 2 = 4' can be used as epistemological evidence in favor of a certain set of fundamental logical axioms from which it and other obvious results can be deductively derived, rather than vice versa.

During this period, Russell often speaks of a distinction between 'the world of logic' and 'the actual world'. He talks of the 'world of logic' as if it were made up of a special kind of inactual or non-existent object. Consider the following passages:

> Instead of talking about "entities", we will talk about "individuals". Then propositions, classes, relations, etc. are "Gegenstände höherer Ordnung" [objects of higher-order]. As opposed to individuals, they may be called "logical objects". They are all essentially incapable of existence. (Russell 2014d: 197)

> [Individuals are s]uch objects as constitute the real world as opposed to the world of logic. They may be defined as whatever can be subject of any proposition not containing any apparent variable. (Russell 2014b: 525)

> Here the word *individual* contrasts with class, function, proposition, etc. In other words, *an individual is a being in the actual world, as opposed to the beings in the logical world*. (Russell 1992c: 44)

Because Russell *also* describes universals as entities which 'subsist' rather than 'exist' in the sense that particulars do during this period (Russell 1912: 100, 1992e: 39, and 1992a: 135), some commentators have been led to the conclusion that Russell simply equates the particular/universal distinction with the individual/higher-order object distinction,[6] a view no doubt reinforced by the fact that he uses the words 'particular' and 'individual' interchangeably in later works (roughly those from 1918 on, e.g., Russell

---

[6]See, e.g., Levine 2013 and forthcoming.

1919a: 141 and Whitehead and Russell 1925–7, 2cnd ed.: xix. But I think this interpretation is mistaken. The distinction between individuals and 'higher-order objects' is a distinction between those genuine entities or logical atoms which make up the irreducible building blocks of facts and those *apparent* entities which seem to be involved in various truths due to an unfinished analysis of 'incomplete symbols'. This is clearer perhaps in other descriptions of the difference from the period:

> We may define an individual as something destitute of complexity. (Russell 1908: 76)

> For this purpose, we will use such letters as a, b, x, y, z, w, to denote objects which are neither propositions nor functions. Such objects we shall call *individuals*. Such objects will be constituents of propositions or functions, and will be genuine constituents, in the sense that they do not disappear on analysis, as (for example) classes do, or phrases of the form "the so-and-so." (Whitehead and Russell 1925–7: 51)

> We may explain an individual as something which exists on its own account; it is then obviously not a proposition, since propositions ... are incomplete symbols, having no meaning except in use. (Whitehead and Russell 1925–7: 162)

Russell's use of the German phrase 'Gegenstände höherer Ordnung' for non-individuals in the quotation above is almost certainly a reference to Meinong 1899. Meinong's 'objects of higher order' are objects that are completely dependent or, to use contemporary vocabulary, 'supervenient upon' or 'grounded in' simpler or more basic objects. The closest one has to this in Russell's metaphysics is the notion of a logical construction, an 'apparent' entity which is not really an entity at all but just a convenient way of talking about other things. For Russell, classes, functions and propositions are such things; statements that (as Russell puts it) 'verbally employ classes' (Russell 1992f: 357) upon analysis, turn out 'really' to be about some or all of their members, and their members' properties and relations.

I think if we want to make sense of Russell's understanding of the nature of logical truths during this period, we cannot avoid posing it eventually in terms of the nature of the 'ultimate' or 'primitive' notions of logic rather than the derivative or definable ones. Russell's claim that mathematical or logical 'intuition' provides us with knowledge about the relations of certain universals cannot *merely* mean that it provides us with knowledge 'about' derivative or higher-order 'apparent' entities that disappear on analysis, like classes and numbers. Both in *Problems* (chap. VIII) and in 'Analytic Realism' he writes as if, by providing this account of *a priori* knowledge, he is striking a blow against both those empiricists who deny any kind of knowledge of 'abstract ideas' as well as those idealists (e.g., Kant) who think that *a priori* knowledge is knowledge only of our own forms of understanding and not of any kind of mind-independent reality. Russell's argument that our knowledge of universals is knowledge of things that are independent of the mind requires that these universals be *simple* universals, which, in virtue of their simplicity, *must* be independent of the mind:

> Universals ... do not depend on us in any way. In the case of particulars, we have a causal dependence, but there could not be a causal dependence in the case of universals, since they do not exist in time. A logical dependence is equally impossible, since simple things do not logically depend on anything, and complex things logically depend only on their constituents. Therefore, universals are completely independent of the mind, as is everything else which exists, in the narrow sense. The laws of logic, for example, while they are customarily called "laws of thought", are just as objective, and depend as little on the mind as the law of gravity. Abstract truths express relations which hold between universals; the mind can recognize these relations, but it cannot create them. (Russell 1992a: 136)

If Russell's argument for the objectivity of logic has any bite, then the universals involved must be ones which subsist 'on their own account' and are 'destitute of complexity'. They *must*, in effect, be individuals and not higher-order, complex or derivative entities.

The difference between particulars and universals then is not the same as the difference between individuals and the 'beings of logic'. Aside from the kinds of complex universals (and particulars) Russell makes room for in 'Knowledge by Acquaintance and Knowledge by Description', Russell usually explains the difference between particulars and universals as the difference between those entities that can occur only as terms of a relation and those that can occur in a relational or predicating way:

> You will observe that in every complex there are two kinds of constituents: there are terms and the relation which relates them: or there might be (perhaps) a term qualified by a predicate. Note that the terms of a complex can themselves be relations, as, for example, in the statement that priority implies diversity. But there are some terms which appear only as terms and can never appear as predicates or relations. These terms are what I call *particulars*. The other terms found in a complex, those which can appear as predicates or relations, I call *universals*. Terms like diversity, causality, father, white, etc., are *universals*. (Russell 1992a: 13; cf. 1911: 170)

Notice that this is essentially the same distinction as that drawn between *things* and *concepts* in §48 of *PoM*. Notice, moreover, that Russell still maintains that universals have a 'two-fold nature', which is essential to Russell's doctrine of acquaintance, as explained by Landini (this volume).

A relation may occur in a relating way in a complex, but it may also occur as one of the 'terms' being related in the complex. Particulars lack this two-fold nature. We saw earlier that Russell defined 'individuals' as 'whatever can be subject of any proposition not containing any apparent variable [i.e., an elementary proposition]' (Russell 2014b: 529; cf. 1908: 76). Individuals include whatever *may* occur as a relatum in a complex; particulars are those individuals that can *only* occur that way. These definitions leave room for (at least some, arguably all) universals to be individuals as well.[7]

4   Logical Constants and Variables

The above clarifies what sorts of universals the propositions of logic would have to assert relations between in order for Russell's account of *a priori* logical and mathematical knowledge to work. But bearing in mind the changes to his logical views after *PoM*, we are not really any closer to an understanding of how any of the 'primitive ideas' found in Russell's technical writings could reasonably count as standing for such universals.

This brings us to 1911's 'The Philosophical Importance of Mathematical Logic' (1992e). There Russell sketches an account not only of what distinguishes a proposition of logic from others, but also of what makes something a logical constant. The account is not far from the view of *PoM*. A proposition of pure logic is one that 'does not contain any other constants than logical constants' (35), and a mathematical proposition will 'only contain variables and logical constants' (38). Similarly, he explains that pure mathematical propositions typically take the form of quantified conditionals, which can then be *applied* by finding particular instances of the variables which will affirm the antecedents. One difference is that, unlike in *PoM*, in this work he attempts to provide at least a partial definition of the notion of a logical constant:

> To obtain a proposition of pure mathematics ... we must submit a deduction of any kind to a process [of generalization] ... that is to say, when an argument remains valid if one of its terms is changed, this term must be replaced by a variable, i.e. by an indeterminate object. In this way we finally reach a proposition of pure logic, that is to say a proposition which

---

[7]Russell later changes his mind on these issues and comes to the conclusion that universals can *only* occur in complexes in a relating way and never as subject, but as he himself tells us (Russell 1918: 204–5), this is a view he adopted under the influence of Wittgenstein. Notice that in earlier writings Russell himself claims that predicates (by which he means monadic universals, not anything linguistic) are individuals, e.g., (Russell 1931: §499). Clearly, the particular/universal distinction for him is not the same as the individual/higher-order object distinction in his early writings, as I have also argued elsewhere (Klement 2004, 2005).

does not contain any other constant than logical constants. The definition of the *logical constants* is not easy, but this much may be said: A *constant* is *logical* if the propositions in which it is found still contain it when we try to replace it by a variable. More exactly, we may perhaps characterize the logical constants in the following manner: If we take any deduction and replace its terms by variables, it will happen, after a certain number of stages, that the constants which still remain in the deduction belong to a certain group, and, if we try to push generalization still farther, there will always remain constants which belong to the same group. This group is the group of logical constants. The logical constants are those which constitute pure form; a formal proposition is a proposition which does not contain any other constants than logical constants. (Russell 1992e: 35-6)

Russell illustrates with an example. One begins with a deduction such as:

> All humans are mortal.
>
> Socrates is a human.
>
> Therefore, Socrates is a mortal.

One then forms a hypothetical proposition with the premises of the deduction as 'hypotheses' (antecedents) and the conclusion as 'thesis' (consequent):

> If all humans are mortal, then if Socrates is a human, then Socrates is a mortal.

One then replaces whatever constants one can with variables provided that by doing so, the result remains 'valid' (presumably this means true for every value of the variable). In this case, this yields:

> If all α are β, then if x is-a α, then x is-a β.

Any constants remaining after this process count as logical constants. For this example, Russell writes: 'The constants here are: *is-a*, *all*, and *if-then*. These are logical constants and evidently they are purely formal concepts' (piml). What sets them apart from the non-logical constants is that the conditional would no longer be true for all values of the variable if we attempted to replace *them* with a variable. Suppose we replaced 'is-a' with 'R' to obtain:

> If all α are β, then if $xR\alpha$, then $xR\beta$.

In that case, if we gave 'R' the value 'is-not-a' instead of 'is-a', 'α' the value 'cat', 'β' the value 'animal' and 'x' the value 'Lassie', we'd have a false instance of the conditional, which shows that we cannot replace 'is-a' with a variable while preserving the validity of the argument, and hence, it is a logical constant.

I find this description unhelpful. The most natural interpretation of how we are to apply it presupposes prior knowledge of what counts as a 'valid' deduction.[8] Suppose someone thought '2 + 2 = 4. Therefore, snow is white' were a valid deduction. It could then be argued that 'snow' and 'white' are logical constants, because if we were to replace either of them with variables in 'if 2 + 2 = 4 then snow is white' we'd get something no longer true for every instance of the variable. A natural account of validity—one to which Russell himself might have been attracted—presupposes a *prior* way of distinguishing logical from non-logical constants. According to the popular Tarskian account of logical consequence, $A_1, ..., A_n, \therefore B$ is valid just in case there is no interpretation of the non-logical constants which make all of $A_1, ..., A_n$ true but B false. If we let $A^*[x_1, ..., x_m]$ be obtained by conjoining $A_1, ..., A_n$ and replacing each non-logical constant with an appropriate variable (of the appropriate type) and let $B^*[x_1, ..., x_m]$ be obtained in similar fashion from B, then the argument will be valid just in case $\ulcorner \forall x_1 ... \forall x_m (A^*[x_1, ... x_m] \rightarrow B^*[x_1, ... x_m] \urcorner$ is true in those models where the domain of quantification for the variables includes all possible interpretations for constants of the same type. But as Tarski was himself aware,[9] this conception of logical consequence presupposes a prior way of differentiating logical from non-logical constants. It is not clear to me which is prior—conceptually or epistemologically—my understanding of the special nature of logical constants or my understanding of in what cases an argument is valid *in virtue* of them alone, or rather *in virtue of its form*. Perhaps Russell would be sympathetic to a hybrid approach,[10] in which one seeks to identify both what the valid deductions are and what the logical constants are by attempting to achieve a kind of 'reflective equilibrium', balancing the demands of both; if so, however, there is no clear indication of this in Russell's 1911 paper.

At least we here have confirmation concerning the sort of thing Russell had in mind when thinking of 'purely logical concepts'—they are the sorts of things which are taken as the 'primitive ideas' or undefined symbols of the formal language of *PM*, things such as truth-functional operations (e.g., *if-then*) and quantifiers (e.g., *all*). (The inclusion of *is-a* is perhaps a bit strange, since it disappears on analysis of class-talk *à la PM* *20.02, but again, this can be chalked up to the attempt to avoid delving into complex analyses for the purposes of presentation.) Frustratingly, while he concludes the essay with the remark that logic and mathematics 'force us' to recognize truths 'about universals', he never explicitly claims that these universals are

---

[8]Proops (2007: 18) gives similar reasons for worrying about Russell's definition of a logical constant.
[9]Tarski 1983, 1986. There's a fair bit of secondary literature here that Russell's discussion prefigures, though an even earlier anticipation of these issues is found in Bolzano 1972.
[10]Thanks to an anonymous referee for this suggestion.

the 'purely formal concepts' that logical constants represent. Even more frustratingly, he does not clarify in what ways these 'formal concepts' are similar to or different from other universals. As we have seen, his usual way of formulating the universal/particular distinction make universals those constituents of complexes that can occur 'as predicates or relations'. Are *all* and *implication* then qualities or relations, and if so, what kinds of things have these qualities or stand in these relations? 'The Philosophical Importance of Mathematical Logic' does not help us answer these questions.

I shall return to the status of truth functional operations in the next section. For the moment, let us consider how Russell might have thought that quantification could make a proposition 'involve' universals. A universally quantified statement typically takes the form '$(x)(\varphi x \supset \psi x)$', which is naturally read as as 'if x has property φ, then x has property ψ, for all x'. In *Problems*, he discusses 'all men are mortal', and claims of it that it asserts that 'if x is a man, then x is mortal' so that the universals *men* and *mortal* are invoked. To understand the proposition, one must be acquainted with these universals (Russell 1912: 106). At the level of meaning, he claims that this is just like the case of 'two and two are four' analyzed as making a general claim about instances of the universals 'couple' and 'four membered collection'. We do not need acquaintance with the *values* of the variable, only the concepts or universals which the values of the variable would have to exemplify to be relevant to the truth or falsity of the quantified statement. In 'Analytic Realism', he writes:

> Pure mathematics, if I am not mistaken, is concerned exclusively with propositions which can be expressed by means of universals. Instead of having constants as terms in relations, we have *variables*, i.e. we only have the concept of an entity of a certain kind instead of a particular entity of this kind. Thus to know the universal which defines a kind is to know what is necessary for pure mathematics. It follows that pure mathematics is composed of propositions which contain no actual constituents, neither psychological as idealists believe, nor physical as empiricists believe. There are two worlds, the world of existence and the world of essence; pure mathematics belongs to the world of essence. (Russell 1992a: 137–8)

And later, in discussion, he claims that 'it is the variable which makes the transition from the universal to the particular' (144). Unfortunately, however, it is hard to see how the case of 'all men are mortal' is supposed to be like propositions that *only* contain variables and logical constants. The word 'mortal' represents 'the concept of an entity of a certain kind', but the word 'mortal' could not be used in pure mathematics. In pure mathematics or logic, we'd have to use *nothing but* variables, truth-functional operators and quantifiers. Instead of '$(x)(x \text{ is human} \supset x \text{ is mortal})$' one might have instead, e.g., '$(\varphi)(x)(\varphi! x \supset \varphi! x)$'. Are there any 'universals which define a kind' in this latter example? One might suggest that the *type* of the variable is what is involved, but treating these as universals seems to violate the core thought in their type theory that type-restrictions are *internal* restrictions on meaningfulness (Whitehead and Russell 1925-7). '$(\varphi)(x)(\varphi! x \supset \varphi! x)$' cannot be taken to mean '$(x)(\varphi)((x$ is an individual $. \varphi! \hat{x}$ is a predicative first-level propositional function$) \supset (\varphi! x \supset \varphi! x))$' without violating some of the basic ideas of type theory. Perhaps Russell can be read as already holding something like the *Tractatus* conception of a 'formal concept' which is properly expressed by the variable itself, rather than by any kind of constant (Wittgenstein 1922: §4.127), but this may be reaching. In a 1910 letter to Bradley (quoted in Slater 1992: 250), Russell claims that 'the conception of the variable is the conception of something standing midway between particular and universal; I do not pretend to have solved all the difficulties in this conception'. This does not sound like someone with a firm view in mind.

More than once in *Problems* (52, 93), and also in 'Knowledge by Acquaintance and Knowledge by Description' (1992b: 161), Russell claims that every complete sentence must contain at least one word for a universal. In context, Russell seems to be thinking of ordinary language noncompound ('atomic') sentences, so it is not entirely clear he'd extend the claim also to cover all closed quantified formulæ of a formal language. Let us consider a formula made up of nothing but quantifiers and variables, e.g.:

$$(\exists \varphi)(\exists x)\varphi! x$$

This second-order proposition is *true*[11], but which, if any, universals needed for its proper interpretation? When Russell writes in the quotation from 'Analytic Realism' above, that 'pure mathematics is composed of propositions which contain no actual constituents', I take it that he means that none of the entities of which propositions of pure mathematics are composed are actual (i.e., existent, or as he says there, physical or psychological), rather than that, actually, they have no constituents at all. Unfortunately, here we

---

[11] Indeed it is a theorem of the formal system of *PM*. It is perhaps not altogether clear that it ought to be, as it requires there to be at least one individual. Russell eventually came to regard it as a 'defect in logical purity' (Russell 1919a: 203n) that one can derive results in *PM* from any given number of individuals, even one. But this is not important for present purposes. Whether or not it's *logically necessary*, it's certainly *true*. Our interest here lies in whether or not the presence of quantifiers or variables alone suffices to make it the case that the propositions of logic involve universals. Whether or not this counts as a proposition of logic, its proper interpretation is still relevant to the question as to whether or not quantification is always to be understood as involving universals.

run up against an unfortunate turn of phrase Russell often uses, the 'constituents of a proposition'.[12] He employs this turn of phrase also when formulating his 'principle of acquaintance'—one must be acquainted with all the 'constituents of any proposition' which one understands. Of course, Russell no longer believes in propositions as mind-independent complexes with parts, so what does it mean for something to be a constituent of a proposition? Understood as a piece of language, the parts of a proposition would just be the words or symbols making it up, but clearly that is not what Russell has in mind. He tries to clarify in 'Knowledge by Acquaintance and Knowledge by Description' by invoking his multiple relations theory of judgment, writing 'the constituents of the judgment are simply the constituents of the complex which is the judgment' (Russell 1992b: 154). Presumably, then, the constituents of a proposition are the constituents of the judgment which the assertion of the proposition would indicate (cf. Russell 1992d: 117). It is natural then to frame the question regarding how universals are involved in the proper understanding of quantified formulæ of a formal logical language in terms of what sorts of things are involved in the judgment complexes that subsist when we make general judgments.

Unfortunately, prior to the *Theory of Knowledge* manuscript, the multiple relations theory of judgment was only clearly formulated for elementary judgments. If I judge that aRb where 'aRb' is an atomic formula, it is clear what Russell believed the relata to the judgment relation are supposed to be: me, a, R and b. But if I judge, say that '$(\exists\varphi)(\exists x)\varphi!x$', what are the relata to the judgment relation, and are any of them universals? All we have to go on is a brief and tortured passage from the introduction to *PM*:

> We do not mean to deny that there may be some relation of the concept *man* to the concept *mortal* which may be *equivalent* to "all men are mortal," but in any case this relation is not the same thing as what we affirm when we say that all men are mortal. Our judgment that all men are mortal collects together a number of elementary judgments. It is not, however, composed of these since (e.g.) the fact that Socrates is mortal is no part of what we assert, as may be seen by considering the fact that our assertion can be understood by a person who has never heard of Socrates. In order to understand the judgment "all men are mortal," it is not necessary to know what men there are. We must admit, therefore, as a radically new kind of judgment, such general assertions as "all men are mortal." We assert that, given that x is human, x is always mortal. That is, we assert "x is mortal" of *every* x which is human. Thus we are able to judge (whether

---

[12] I have unfortunately replicated this sad phrase in the title of my paper. Russell himself acknowledged that he had given no very exact definition to the notion of 'occurring in' a proposition (Russell 1931, 2cnd ed.: xi).

truly or falsely) that *all* the objects which have some assigned property also have some other assigned property. That is, given any propositional functions $\varphi\hat{x}$ and $\psi\hat{x}$, there is a judgment asserting ψx with every x for which we have φx. Such judgments we shall call *general judgments*. (Whitehead and Russell 1925–7: 45)

Part of what makes this passage so obscure is that there seems to be a systematic confusion of the notion of judgment with the notion of *assertion*. Can't someone make a general judgment without 'asserting' anything (save perhaps in some kind of metaphorical, inward sense)? What Russell means by 'collecting together' elementary judgments without actually making them individually is not adequately clarified. He seems only to have in mind quantified propositions of the form '$(x)(\varphi x \supset \psi x)$', and not more or less complex forms. Existential quantification is not addressed at all. Personally, I cannot glean from this any clear reason to think that *merely* in virtue of making use of variables or quantifiers, the propositions of logic ought to be understood as somehow providing access to special logical universals.

Russell's subsequent discussion of different notions of truth that apply to quantified as opposed to elementary propositions is somewhat clearer. Whatever the make-up of the judgment complexes for general judgments, Russell is explicit that 'truth makers' (in contemporary vocabulary) for general judgments are just the truth makers of their instances:

> But now take such a proposition as "all men are mortal". Here the judgment does not correspond to *one* complex, but to many, namely "Socrates is mortal," "Plato is mortal," "Aristotle is mortal," etc. (Whitehead and Russell 1925–7: 44–5)

> If φx is an elementary judgment, it is true when it *points to* a corresponding complex. But $(x).\varphi x$ does not point to a single corresponding complex: the corresponding complexes are as numerous as the possible values of x. (Whitehead and Russell 1925–7: 46)

Russell at this time uses 'complex' and 'fact' more or less interchangeably. It is natural to think that Russell's metaphysics is exhausted by what facts there are and their components. If only elementary propositions/judgments correspond to facts, this seems to suggest that there quite simply is no metaphysical phenomenon corresponding to the logical notion of quantification.[13] Elementary complexes, which involve no quantifiers, make elemen-

---

[13]In the 'On Substitution' manuscript, while Russell is exploring the view that there are no quantified propositions, only quantified statements, Russell writes:

> The case of $(x).\varphi x$ is queer. Suppose $f(a, b, c, d)$ is a proposition of which a, b, c, d are all the constituents. Then

$$(x, y, z, w).f(x, y, z, w)$$

tary propositions true. These in turn make first-order propositions true, and they in turn make second-order propositions true, and so on up the hierarchy of different senses of truth. But then if there is nothing in reality corresponding to *all* or the variable, it seems at best to be a feature of our psychology. This seems to put him back to the view of 'On "Insolubilia" ' that 'the general is purely mental'. At the same time he seems to all but define a logical proposition as a *fully* general one, so that the use of variables and quantifiers is not only unavoidable in logic and pure mathematics, the use thereof is fundamental to what sets logic apart from other areas of study. As Whitehead and Russell themselves write, '[t]he ideas and propositions of logic are all *general*' (Whitehead and Russell 1925–7: 93). If the 'general is purely mental', it would appear that logic is too. This sits *very uncomfortably* with Russell's ambition to cite our knowledge of logic to bolster a case for 'realism in a scholastic sense'.

5 A 'Multiple Relations Theory' of Truth Functions?

When it comes to quantification, I do not know how to resolve these tensions in Russell's philosophy of logic circa 1910–12. However, I think there is *more hope* that Russell may have had an understanding of truth-functional operations (disjunction, negation, implication, etc.) during the *PM* period and that immediately following which could support the claim that our knowledge of logic involves knowledge of certain abstract universals. However, I must admit from the outset that what I have to say is *highly speculative*, and derives largely from hints left behind in unpublished manuscripts, quite often not even in the context of arguing for a view but explaining his misgivings about pursuing a certain hypothesis.

---

is a proposition which has no constituents ...(Russell 2014d: 136)

It was also explicit in his 1912 lectures on logic at Cambridge that he did not believe in objective counterparts of quantification. Moore's notes contain:

Well, this being so, there is *nothing meant* by words "all" or "some" in these [quantified] props.: there is no constituent of the prop. corresponding to them. *Also* 'all men' means nothing: if there were such a thing, it is certainly not it which is asserted to be mortal.

So too in 'I met *a man*' there is no *separate* thing called '*a man*' over & above the men there are; & no *man* is a constituent of the prop. And this explains how you can say there is no such thing as a centaur.

It is possible, however, that Russell had already changed his mind at the time of these lectures from *PM*; see the beginning of sec. 6 below.

Again, the early view of ⊃ was that it was a dyadic relation that held between propositions *p* and *q* when both are true, both are false, or *p* false and *q* true. Russell was not unaware that this precise understanding of implication could not survive the abandonment of the old view of propositions countenancing 'objective falsehoods'. Indeed, in the pre-*PM* manuscripts, in his 'arguments with himself' about whether or not 'propositions are entities', he cited this as a reason, and indeed this comes to the fore just as much as the issue of explaining what is involved with erroneous beliefs. In 'The Paradox of the Liar', he notes that on the view that propositions are not entities, negation cannot represent the property of *falsehood*, and for a while explores the idea that 'there is no such thing as "not" ', only disbelief. He continues:

> We may suppose this a satisfactory answer, and proceed to other difficulties. The proposition "*p* implies *q*" will be all right when *p* and *q* are true, but will need a new interpretation when *p* is false. The proposition is then true, but the constituent *p* is a non-entity. We must substitute "not-*p* or *q*". But there is still a difficulty. If we hold to the view that negative statements express disbeliefs, not beliefs in negative propositions, "not-*p* or *q*" expresses either a belief or a disbelief. But this is plainly false. We *neither* believe *q* nor disbelieve *p* when we assert "not-p or q". Thus we shall have to admit the objectivity of true negative propositions. (Russell 2014e: 321)

Russell then tables the suggestion of dismissing propositions as non-entities temporarily.

In the published 1907 paper 'On the Nature of Truth', Russell discusses the nature of disjunctive facts where only one disjunct is true as an argument in favor of 'objective falsehood'. The sign ∨ clearly cannot stand for a relation between facts on a view according to which there are no 'false facts' or 'objective falsehoods', since disjunctions are sometimes true when one disjunct is not. In such cases there would be no 'fact' or 'complex' to occupy the other relation spot of the ∨-relation. Russell writes:

> There is, however, another argument in favor of objective falsehood, derived from the case of true propositions which contain false ones as constituent parts. Take, e.g., "Either the earth goes round the sun, or it does not." This is certainly true, and therefore, on the theory we are considering, it represents *a fact*, i.e., an objective complex, which is not constituted by our apprehension of it. But it is, at least apparently, compounded of two (unasserted) constituents, namely: "The earth goes round the sun" and "the earth does not go round the sun" of which one must be false. Thus our fact seems to be composed of two parts, of which one is a fact, while the other is an objective falsehood. (Russell 1907: 48)

Russell's tantalizingly brief sketch of a *response* to this argument immediately follows:

If this argument is to be rejected, it can only be on the ground that, given a fact, it cannot always be validly analysed into subordinate related complexes, even when such analysis *seems* possible. A valid analysis we shall have to contend, must break up any apparent subordinate complexes into their constituents, except when such complexes are facts. (Russell 1907: 48)

Russell is usually read here as talking about the analysis of belief or judgment facts,[14] but given the context, it is more likely that Russell is speaking about the analysis of what we would now call 'molecular complexes' or 'molecular facts'.

The thought would be something like this. Consider a disjunction where only one disjunct is true, e.g.:

Desdemona loves Cassio ∨ Desdemona loves Othello

Desdemona does not love Cassio so there is no such complex as Desdemona-loving-Cassio. Desdemona does love Othello so there is a complex Desdemona-loving-Othello. The disjunction above is true so it is a complex or fact as well. But what is the logical structure of this fact? Here we have the case of a complex fact where it might seem like its structure is one fact relating to another fact, i.e., something like $(d - L - c) - \vee - (d - L - o)$, where $(d - L - c)$ is one complex, $(d - L - o)$ is another, and $- \vee -$ is a relation that relates these two complexes. Obviously, that cannot be right here, as there is no such complex as $(d - L - c)$. So instead, a valid analysis has to 'break up' the 'apparent subordinate complexes into their constituents'. So in this case, $- \vee -$ is not a *dyadic* relation, but a multiple relation with even greater polyadicity. Russell's precise wording in the quotation above seems to suggest it ought to be something like $(d, L, c) - \vee - (d - L - o)$ where $- \vee -$ is then a relation with *four* relata, one of which is a complex, and the others are Desdemona, Love, and Cassio, each entering in separately. Another possible (and perhaps in some ways better[15]) view would be one that treated the disjuncts in parallel fashion, so we'd have rather $(d, L, c) - \vee - (d, L, o)$, or, if you prefer, $\vee (d, L, c, d, L, o)$, i.e., a six-place relation that forms a complex with certain relata just in case either the

---

[14]Indeed, the paper sketches instead a very different alternative theory of judgment on which a belief consists of ideas standing in relation to one another (see Russell 2014d: 185), and in some ways better prefigures Russell's views in 1919 (see Russell 1919b).

[15]This view seems better in the sense that it does not require disjunctive facts to have different logical forms depending on which disjunct is true. Often times, we have knowledge of disjunctions without knowing which disjunct is true. If the logical form of what we knew was different depending on which disjunct were true, it would seem possible to determine which disjunct were true simply by analyzing the form of the disjunction.

first three, or its last three, of those relata form a simpler complex. A similar kind of analysis could be given for conjunctions and implications. I think it would be natural to call this 'the multiple relations theory of truth functions'. Notice that it continues to think of ∨, ⊃, etc., as relations. They're just not dyadic relations between propositions, but rather multiple relations between the constituents thereof. This is completely analogous to the change his views underwent from thinking of belief as a dyadic relation between a believer and a proposition to thinking of belief as a multiple relation between a believer and the constituents of a complex (when true) instead. Like that view, it gives rise to 'direction problems' (see, e.g., Griffin 1985) but those direction problems appear to be no worse here than in the case of judgment.

Russell seems halfway to this view in the 'Fundamentals' manuscript, where he writes:

> The chief difficulty in the view that there are no false complexes is ... subordinate (false) complexes in true propositions, e.g., p in $p \supset q$ when p. It seems as though, for the sake of homogeneity, we must allow that a proposition differs from a complex, and subsists equally when true and when false, but is plural, not singular: the corresponding singular (if any) is the complex, which only subsists when the proposition is true. (Russell 2014a: 542)

What does Russell mean when, here, he suggests that a proposition is 'plural'? I think he means merely that a proposition is not one entity, but many entities. Those entities sometimes form a complex, but when we speak about 'the proposition', we are not speaking about that complex, but rather about those entities, plural. A 'property' of a proposition is not really a monadic quality of one thing but just a misleading way of describing what would now be called a 'plural property', i.e., a property of *many* things. A relation between propositions 'p' and 'q' is not a relation between two things, but a relation between several things, as many things as p and q together make up. This is rather like Russell's distinction in *PoM* between 'a class as many' and 'a class as one' and is consistent with the idea that a proposition is not 'an entity', just as Russell explained to Jourdain, 'a *class as many* is not an entity' (Grattan-Guinness 1977: 68). It is not that propositions are nothing, it is rather that they are not *individual* things; a proposition is not an 'it', but a 'they'.

In the manuscript 'Logic in Which Propositions are Not Entities', Russell writes:

> Roughly speaking, the view that propositions are not entities amounts to this, that the predicates that can be significantly asserted of propositions are different from those that can be asserted of entities. "The Law of Con-

tradiction is fond of cream cheese" is to be as inadmissible as "the number 1 is fond of cream cheese." I can't help thinking this would solve some problems as to the nature of truth, also the *Epimenides* and kindred puzzles. All significant propositions about propositions, on this view, will really be propositions about entities; just as propositions about classes are. A proposition about a proposition, if it can't be reduced to the form of a proposition about entities, is to be meaningless. (Russell 2014c: 265)

The words 'the number 1' do not name one individual thing, and thus claiming that 'it' is fond of cream cheese involves treating a monadic property as if it had a different polyadicity, and the similar claim about 'the Law of Contradiction' is nonsense for precisely the same reason.

Compare what Russell writes in *PM* (48):

> A proposition is not a single entity, but a relation of several; hence a statement in which a proposition appears as subject will be significant if it can be reduced to a statement about the terms which appear in the proposition. A proposition, like a phrase of the form "the so-and-so", where it grammatically appears as subject, must be broken up if we are to find the true subject or subjects. But in such a statement as "p is a man," where p is a proposition, this is not possible. Hence "$\{(x).\varphi x\}$ is a man" is meaningless.

A similar, but different in detail, approach along these lines is explored elsewhere in the 'Fundamentals' manuscript. Here the 'heavy lifting' seems to be done by negation rather than by the dyadic operators such as $\lor$ and $\supset$. He writes:

> We can't say "A believes φx" unless φx is true, for there is no such proposition as φx unless it is true. And then "believes" is used in a derivative sense. But A can believe that x has the property φ even when x does not have property φ. We shall have to say that $\varphi x \supset \psi x$ means an implication when φx and ψx are true, but means $\varphi x . \lor . \psi x$ when φx is false and ψx is true, and means "$\psi x . \supset . \varphi x$" when both are false, and has no independent meaning when φx is true and ψx is false. (Russell 2014a: 543)

I interpret this as follows. In the first part of the quotation, Russell is just sketching the basics of the multiple relations theory of judgment. Belief cannot be a relation between the believer A and the *complex* φx, but it can be a relation between A and φ and x. Negation $\sim$, rather than being a property of a single entity, a proposition, is now a *multiple relation* which forms a complex with its relata just in case its relata do not form a complex (in the right way) on their own. The relation $\supset$ holds between complexes, but which complexes? Take $dLc \supset dLo$. If this is a fact, then there are three possibilities. The first is that there are two complexes $d - L - c$ and $d - L - o$, and the complex $dLc \supset dLo$ is a relation holding between them having the form $(d - L - c) - \supset -(d - L - o)$. Another is that there is a complex $\sim - d - L - c$ and another one $\sim - d - L - o$ and the complex corresponding to $dLc \supset dLo$ is a complex that has those two complexes as its parts, though related in the reverse order as before. Finally, we might have the one complex $\sim -d - L - c$ and the complex $d - L - o$ and the complex corresponding to the conditional statement is the holding of a different relation between these complexes, better written as ∨, so we have $(\sim - d - L - c) - \lor -(d - L - o)$. If none of these three possibilities obtain, i.e., if there is neither a complex $\sim - d - L - c$ nor a complex $d - L - o$, then there is no complex, i.e., no fact that $dLc \supset dLo$; in that case, one may speak of 'the proposition', but when one does, one will not be naming some 'thing'.

These little tidbits from the manuscripts are not much to go on. Russell is constantly experimenting with various ideas in these manuscripts, and seldom do these ideas become his considered view or make it into his published writings. I admit it is highly speculative to suggest that anything like these views should be considered the official view of *PM* or the immediate period afterwards. In *PM*, when negation and disjunction are introduced they are called 'the Contradictory function' and 'the Disjunctive function' (6), and nowhere are they called relations (of any sort), though this appears in the first chapter of the introduction, written by Whitehead (Russell 1948: 138), who may not have seen things the same way.

In a letter to Jourdain dated 2 January 1911, Russell writes:

I no longer think it significant to deny

$$x \supset q,$$

where *x* is not a proposition. I think that, strictly, one ought not to use a single letter for a proposition, but always some such symbol as φx. But so long as this is remembered, it is not necessary always to do what strictly ought to be done. (Grattan-Guinness 1977: 136)

Landini (1998: 258) takes this to mean that *PM*'s $\supset$ and ∨ should not be read as any kind of relation symbols, but rather as statement connectives in the modern sense, flanked by formulæ to form formulæ. But this is by no means the only way of interpreting this letter. The reason one cannot write '$x \supset y$', where these are variables for individuals, is that $\supset$ is not a *dyadic* relation; '$x \supset y$' does not give it enough relata. In order to 'do what strictly ought to be done', one must make use of a *complex* symbol for a proposition so that one has an indication of *all* the relata that enter into the relation. In practice, however, Russell seems to think it safe to ignore this 'strict method' to make it, e.g., easier to state axiom schemata and rules in a uniform way, as is done in *PM* itself. This is not unlike the use of single letters as variables for classes which can be misleading with regard to the strictly correct philosophical analysis of classes, but is convenient in practice. The suggestion that propositions are *best* not represented by single letters was not a new idea. Russell claimed the same thing as early as the 'Logic in Which Propositions are Not Entities' manuscript, where immediately after writing the passage quoted above, he wrote:

> Formally, propositions must not be expressed, to begin with, by simple letters, but by φx ... (Russell 2014c: 265)

I think this is perhaps evidence that Russell's way of thinking of the matter in 1911 had not changed much since these pre-*PM* manuscripts.

Another bit of confirming evidence can be found in the fact that White-head and Russell never speak of a distinction between 'molecular' and 'atomic' in *PM*. There are elementary propositions, and then there are quantified propositions. They describe 'elementary judgments' as follows:

> We will give the name of "a *complex*" to any such object as "a in the relation R to b" or "a having the quality q", or "a and b and c standing in the relation S". Broadly speaking, a *complex* is anything which occurs in the universe and is not simple. We will call a judgment *elementary* when it merely asserts such things as "a has the relation R to b", "a has the quality q" or "a and b and c stand in the relation S". Then an elementary judgment is true when there is a corresponding complex, and false when there is no corresponding complex. (44)

The use of negation and disjunction is not enough to raise a proposition above the level of an elementary proposition, only quantifiers can do that. So why don't Whitehead and Russell mention molecular forms when introducing elementary judgments? One obvious answer is that they thought that those too could be considered as asserting relations. On the first view considered in this section, consider what an embedded disjunction would be, if true:

$$aRb \lor (cSd \lor eTf)$$

Suppose now that e bears relation T to f. Then there is a complex $e - T - f$. But *this* is not a component of the fact that $cSd \lor eTf$; that complex instead has the form $\lor (c, S, d, e, T, f)$. But *that* complex isn't a component of the fact for the whole disjunction either. It rather has the form $\lor (a, R, b, \lor, c, S, d, e, T, f)$! [16] We could, if we wish to use later terminology, claim that this complex is still 'atomic', but it would be less misleading

---

[16] The internal $\lor$ here is just like the internal J one would get if one were to analyze a judgment about judgment under the multiple relations theory of judgment. If the form of the fact that Mary judges that aRb is $J(m, a, R, b)$, then the form of my judging that Mary judges that aRb has the form $J(k, J, m, a, R, b)$.

to say that there simply is no atomic/molecular distinction: there are only elementary propositions and complexes.

At first, it might seem as if this understanding of truth functions would only be adequate to molecular propositions where quantifiers do not appear subordinate to truth functions. Especially if it is right, as I argued in the previous section, that there is no ontological correlate of quantification for Russell during this period, it might be unclear what the relata to the disjunctive relation would be in a case such as:

$$aRb \lor (x).xSd$$

Indeed, Whitehead and Russell claim that 'negation and disjunction and their derivatives have a different meaning' when applied to quantified formulæ (1925–7: 127). However, the way they proceed is to define negation and disjunctions of quantified formulæ in terms of negations and disjunctions of non-quantified formulæ, so that ultimately, all quantifiers are 'pulled out' to the front of formulæ, resulting in prenex normal forms. Thus, according to the definition *9.04 of *PM*, the above disjunction is definitionally equivalent with:

$$(x)(aRb \lor xSd)$$

There is then nothing preventing us from understanding *this* $\lor$ as a multiple relation. In this way, disjunctions and negations with subordinate quantifiers are wholly eliminated. It is plausible to suppose that the definitions of *9 are designed at least in part to preserve the understanding of truth functions as multiple relations and to explain how it might be extended to cover what appear to be other kinds of cases.

If this, again, highly speculative reading of truth functions in *PM* is correct, it has the advantage of vindicating Russell's contention that there are at least *some* logical universals with which we are acquainted and are involved in the analysis of the propositions of logic. Here, $\supset$, $\sim$, $\lor$ and friends, although not understood quite as simply as they had been in *PoM*, still count as *relations* not in any significant way different from other relations. There nothing keeping us from understanding them as mind-independent, as far as I can tell

6   'What is Logic?' and *The Theory of Knowledge*

Our efforts to make sense of the claim in *Problems* that logical knowledge consists of knowledge about certain abstract logical universals have garnered mixed results. When it comes to truth functions, Russell's understanding seems at least compatible with this conclusion. When it comes to other notions important for logic—quantification and variables—Russell seems to have inconsistent commitments. It may be that Russell was misled by simpler cases of quantification such as 'all men are mortal' into thinking that the final analysis of all quantified statements would reveal universals, or entities 'standing between' universals and particulars, to be the entities which their understanding would require. As he made clear in the letter to Bradley, he had not thought his way completely through all the issues to which the themes of quantification and variation give rise, but he was confident enough for the purposes of a popular piece to outline, in a programmatic sort of way, a basic account of *a priori* knowledge that gave pride of place to our acquaintance with universals. However, he realized the matter needed further thought, and intended to launch further investigations when he had the leisure.

In February 1912, Russell lectured on the nature of logic at Cambridge, and attending were Moore and Wittgenstein (a new figure on the scene at this time). Therein, he summarized the view of logical constants from 'The Philosophical Importance of Mathematical Logic' according to which they are those for which variables cannot be substituted without spoiling the validity of a deduction. Moore's notes continue (Moore forthcoming):

> *Logical* constants are *not* the sort of constants wh[ich] can be substituted: e.g., *or*, *not*, *true*, 0, 1, 2 etc.
>
> All of these are incomplete symbols. (I think, but am not sure).
>
> But this = all the ideas of logic & mathem. are *meaningless*.

It seems that Russell had already begun to doubt that there are any specifically logical entities, a trend that would become more pronounced over the next year. Given the professed uncertainty, it would probably be unwise to read much into this remark, though it is intriguing.

Russell began seriously to think of writing a piece entitled 'What is Logic?' in September 1912 and made an abortive attempt to do so in October. All that remains is a rather short manuscript in which Russell does little more than reveal his own confused state of mind. Apparently, whatever confidence he had in the basic view outlined in *Problems* and works of that period was gone. It shows, however, that Russell had spotted the core tension in his former position. Putting variables and variation at the centerpiece of his characterization of logic, while at the same time thinking of quantification or generality as a purely linguistic or mental phenomenon, was inconsistent with his basic realist leanings. To avoid a position on which logic would collapse back into mere 'laws of thought', it would have to be possible to state the subject matter of logic in objective terms, as involving complexes, not beliefs or judgments or 'propositions' understood in a linguistic fashion. Given his theory of truth at the time this meant that truth could not be a central concern for the logician:

> Difficulties of supposing there are objective falsehoods compels us to suppose that what *can* be *false* must be judgments or forms of words. Logic is not concerned with forms of words. Hence logic is not concerned with propositions.
>
> *True* and *False* are extra-logical. (Russell 1992g: 55)

Russell had always connected the subject matter of logic with 'forms' but the exact relationship remained to be spelled out. We saw, for example, that in 'The Philosophical Importance of Mathematical Logic', Russell had claimed that the 'logical constants are those which constitute pure form'. His prior understanding of the relationship between forms and the nature of the truths of logic seems to have been tied to the importance of generality in logic. In pure mathematics, one 'generalizes' as much as possible, replacing whatever constituents of a proposition or judgment one can with a variable, so that the result depends not on the particular subject matter or content of the proposition, but only what remains when that particular content has been abstracted way from—the form. Quantified conditionals are called 'formal implications' because they identify a group of propositions all having a common form and assert all of them; the propositions of pure mathematics are formal implications of the highest degree of generality.

But what exactly is a form, and is it an 'entity' distinguishable from those propositions (early on) or complexes (later on) that have it? This is not something Russell had discussed much in published writings, and there is no indication that he would have had a consistent answer over the years. In 1904 manuscripts, Russell spoke of 'modes of combination' in the following way:

> A complex is determined by its constituents together with their mode of combination; it is not determined by the constituents alone. E.g. "*A* is greater than *B*" and "*B* is greater than *A*" have the same constituents, but differently combined.

> The mode of combination of the constituents of a complex is not itself one of the constituents of the complex. For if it were, it would be combined with the other constituents to form the complex; hence we should need to specify the mode of combination of the constituents with their mode of combination ...

> A mode of combination, like everything else, is an entity; but it is not one of the entities occurring in a complex composed of entities combined in the mode of combination. Thus e.g., in the case of "*A* is greater than *B*", the mode of combination may be denoted by $\hat{x}\hat{R}\hat{y}$ ...(Russell 1994c: 98)

As might be evident from the circumflection notation he uses, Russell at this time thought of modes of combinations in terms of propositional functions. Propositional functions were understood as proposition-like complexes where one or more constituents is replaced by a variable, and modes of combination are those where *all* constituents are replaced by variables. Prior to 1905, Russell had a realist understanding of in variables, taking them as something similar to denoting concepts (Russell 1931: §93, 1994e: 330, 335). On this view, he could maintain that speaking about a mode of combination itself as opposed to a complex having it is much like speaking of a denoting concept or denoting complex itself rather than what it denotes (Russell 1994a: 128–9). But Russell abandoned his former view of denoting concepts in 'On Denoting' (1994b), arguing in its infamous Gray's Elegy passage that any attempt to disambiguate between a denoting complex and what it means must fail.

At any rate, by the time of 'What is Logic?' Russell no longer had a non-linguistic understanding of variables to employ in understanding the nature of forms. Thus he wrote:

> A *form* is not a mere symbol: a symbol composed entirely of variables symbolizes a form, but is not a form. (Russell 1992g: 55–6)

However, echoing his 1904 understanding of modes of combination, he claims that forms are not constituents of the complexes that have them:

> In a complex, there must be something, which we may call the *form*, which is *not* a constituent, but the way the constituents are put together. If we made this a constituent, it would have to be somehow related to the other constituents, and the way in which it was related would really be the form; hence an endless regress. Thus the form is not a constituent. Take e.g. "Antony killed Brutus". We may put *a* for Antony, etc., and get "*aRb*". (Russell 1992g: 55)

A view Russell might have considered, both early and late, is one according to which a form is just a *sui generis* entity. But I think Russell realized he needed to be careful. To reify forms would be very close to reifying propositional functions, to treat them as genuine things—individuals—rather than constructions of some sort, which might reintroduce the paradoxes. One must imagine Russell thinking to himself: 'Consider the form of any complex which is the fact that a form does not stand in itself to itself. Does it stand in itself to itself?' Given his treatment of classes, functions, propositions, etc., as logical constructions, it seems that Russell was interested in thinking of forms that way too. A cardinal number, for example, is just a roundabout way of talking about all those collections of 'like cardinality' as if that were a single thing. Perhaps a form is just a roundabout way of talking about all those complexes of 'like form'. So in 'What is Logic?', Russell considers defining not forms, but the relation sameness-of-form, and using that to define what would make a form a 'logical' one:

> Two complexes "have the same form" if one can be obtained from the other by mere substitution of new terms in other places. Df.
>
> ...
>
> A complex is *logical* if it remains a complex whatever substitutions may be effected in it. Df. (Russell 1992g: 55)

But he immediately saw objections to the approach. What could it mean for a complex to 'remain' when substitutions are effected in it? If substitution is a relation $C \frac{x}{y} ! C'$ holding when exchanging x for y in C yields C', then this relation is one that only holds between complexes, so it will not be possible for C' not to 'remain' a complex, unless the substitution relation is put in terms of symbols or propositions-as-pluralities, etc., instead. But this would make logic again a study of language or thought, which Russell wanted to avoid. Moreover, if forms are 'logical fictions' derived from speaking at once about all those complexes having the same form, it would be impossible to speak of forms that no complex has, such as $x \neq x$.

In the end, Russell abandoned work on the manuscript, despairing in a letter to Ottoline Morrell:

> I can't get on with "what is logic? ", the subject is hopelessly difficult, and for the present I am stuck. I feel very much inclined to leave it to Wittgenstein. (Quoted in Slater 1992: 54)

Try as he might, however, Russell could not completely escape the issue. Wittgenstein had developed a keen interest in the themes involved here, and one suspects it would have been a frequent subject of discussion between them whether Russell would have wanted it to be or not. Moreover, Russell had been attempting to deal with issues in epistemology, and needed to give an account both of our acquaintance with 'logical data' and of the role our understanding of logical form plays in understanding and judgment. Russell's struggles are evident throughout in the *Theory of Knowledge* manuscript (hereafter *TK*).

Part I of *TK* gives the impression of a Russell who is still deeply uncertain about the exact status of logical notions, i.e., whether or not there are any 'entities' of logic, and if so, whether or not they stand in relations to other entities of the normal sort. Russell is perfectly happy even to admit his ignorance when it comes to such issues:

> It should be said, to begin with, that "acquaintance" has, perhaps, a somewhat different meaning, where logical objects are concerned, from that which it has when particulars are concerned. Whether this is the case or

not, it is impossible to decide without more knowledge concerning the nature of logical objects than I possess. (Russell 1984: 97)

Such words as *or, not, all, some*, plainly involve logical notions; and since
we can use such words intelligently, we must be acquainted with the logical objects involved. But the difficulty of isolation here is very great, and I
do not know what the logical objects involved really are.

In the present chaotic state of our knowledge concerning the primitive
ideas of logic, it is impossible to pursue this topic further. (1984: 99)

Somewhat surprisingly, however, as the book progresses, Russell seems to
'find his feet' and adopts a more and more committal position especially
with regard to the notion of a form in Part II.[17]

One change of mind evident during this period is that Russell has
scrapped the idea that there are any 'logical universals' even when it comes
to truth-functional operators. Most likely, Russell came to appreciate that
there was a significant tension in his earlier views according to which logic
is fully general, and therefore not about any *specific things*, and the view
that there are certain specific relations or other universals of special interest
to the logician, such as ~, ∨ and ⊃. It seems likely that Wittgenstein was an
influence here as well. He wrote the following to Russell as early as June
1912:

...one thing gets more and more obvious to me: The propositions of Logic
contain ONLY *apparent* variables and whatever may turn out to be the
proper explanation of apparent variables, its consequences *must* be that
there are NO *logical* constants.

Logic must turn out to be a *totally* different kind than any other science.
(Wittgenstein 1979: 120)

Logic must be totally different in the sense that it must not be about any
specific individuals, whether universal *or* particular: in short, it must not
have its own subject matter in the sense that other sciences do. The upshot
of this point for Russell's views at the time is expressed in the *Tractatus*
this way:

At this point it becomes manifest that there are no 'logical objects' or 'logical constants' (in Frege's and Russell's sense). (§5.4)

It is self-evident that ∨, ⊃, etc. are not relations in the sense in which right
and left etc. are relations. (§5.42)

Whether it was due to Wittgenstein, or his own realization of the prior tension, in *TK*, Russell finally rejects his earlier position (assuming my inter-

---

[17]See Griffin 1980: 167–8 on the apparent change of attitude that seem to occur as the book
progresses.

pretation in the last section was correct) that truth-functional operators stand for a kind of relation. Russell now writes:

> A proposition which mentions any definite entity, whether universal or particular, is not logical: no one definite entity, of any sort or kind, is ever a constituent of any truly logical proposition. "Logical constants", which might seem to be entities occurring in logical propositions, are really concerned with pure *form*, and are not actually constituents of the propositions in the verbal expression of which their names occur. (Russell 1984: 97-8)

Landini (this volume) takes these passages in *TK* to show that there are no constituents in facts corresponding to logical particles even as early as *PM*. I think instead that they show a change in mind. Whereas, as I stressed earlier, in *PM* he spoke only of elementary complexes, now Russell begins to mark a distinction between 'atomic' and 'molecular' complexes (Russell 1984: 80) and along with this distinction, a distinction between atomic and molecular thought (176), though he abandoned the project before writing everything he initially intended about molecular thought.

Another change involves Russell's attitudes about general or quantified facts. As I argued earlier, the theory of truth for quantified formulæ of various orders in *PM* seems to leave in place the result of 'On "Insolubilia"' that 'judgments only have objective counterparts when they are particular' and that 'the general is purely mental'. Russell, however, wishes to maintain the insight of 'What is Logic?' that logic must concern itself not with forms of judgments or propositions but rather forms of things which are fully objective—complexes and facts. Although not much is said in *TK* about the precise nature of general or existential facts, Russell now believes there must be such things. This is especially important for the new 'form-centric' (rather than 'universal-centric') conception of logic Russell wishes to develop. Russell suggests that forms might be identified with certain existential facts. I.e., the form that atomic complexes have when they involve two things related by a dyadic relation, e.g., Desdemona loving Cassio, is identified with the *fact* that $(\exists x)(\exists y)(\exists R).xRy$ (Russell 1984: 114). Although the linguistic representation of this fact is complex, Russell does not conceive of this fact as complex. All the constituents of the complex made up of Desdemona, Love and Cassio have been generalized away. Forms, despite being objective facts, are simple entities.

There is still quite a bit that is obscure and problematic here. Russell does not address the problem mentioned in 'What is Logic?' with regard to *impossible forms*. There is no such fact as $(\exists x).x \neq x$. At first, one might think this is not such a problem after all. Russell is interested in forms of *complexes*, not forms of judgments or propositions. There is no such complex as 'Socrates $\neq$ Socrates' (or anything else of this *so-called* form), and so there is no objective entity which one would be tempted to think 'has' this form. Nonetheless, however, it would seem that contradictions or other impossibilities would fall under the purview of what logic studies, which is surely in part what Russell hoped to invoke forms to explain. Another puzzle he mentions is '[w]hy, if pure forms are simple, is it so obviously inappropriate to give them simple proper names such as John and Peter?' (130), but puts it aside with the excuse that his interest in that work is epistemological rather than logical.

Another worry I have is that by reintroducing objective realities corresponding to quantified formulæ, Russell is forgetting the reason he first abandoned quantified propositions in 1906. Are there as many 'objective-complexes' as there are classes thereof, or other 'paradoxes' of complexes? It scarcely seems to matter whether we phrase the problems in terms of propositions or in terms of facts, and it hardly seems to matter that there are no 'false facts'. For each class of facts *m*, for example, there will either be a fact *all members of m are subject-predicate in form* or a fact *not all members of m are subject-predicate in form*, and hence, it seems, as many facts as classes thereof. What blocks the resulting diagonal contradiction? Is there a hierarchy of facts about which the same things cannot meaningfully be said? (E.g., is it not even *meaningful* to say that a quantified fact is subject-predicate in form?) There are all sorts of responses Russell might have given to this worry, but it is hard to tell what his answer would have been from what is written in *TK*.

7   Later Views

We know that Russell abandoned the *TK* project in mid-1913, largely due to criticisms made by Wittgenstein.[18] Most of the secondary literature has focused on Wittgenstein's criticisms of Russell's theory of judgment. These are important and I would not wish to downplay them. However, I think Wittgenstein's attack was probably more broadly based, and involved also whether or not the conception of logical forms and their connection to logical constants Russell gave in *TK* was tenable.[19] In *TK*, Russell attempted to

---

[18]The evidence for this comes mainly from Russell's letters to Ottoline Morrell, summarized nicely by Eames in her introduction to *TK* (xvii–xx).

[19]These issues are of course not unrelated, especially if, in the background, is something like a 'multiple relations' theory of logical particles as I sketched in sec. 5. I think it would be not unfair to say that Wittgenstein's attack was on Russell's account of *propositions* as incomplete symbols as it played out both in his theory of judgment and in his account of the nature of logic.

make good on his understanding of logic as fully general by denying that logical constants represent definite entities which might be thought of as constituents or components of facts (or judgments). Instead, we are now told, their contribution is purely formal. But forms themselves, Russell tells us, can be identified with certain facts, and this, Russell tells us fulfills the desideratum that a form 'is not a mere incomplete symbol' (Russell 1984: 114). Facts are there all right, they are not mere *façons de parler*, and so, neither are forms. It would appear that by attempting to eliminate any kind of specifically logical objects, Russell has simply swapped out one kind of logical object for another. Forms may themselves have properties and stand in relations to one another, or to our minds (through, e.g., acquaintance or judgment). If one were to catalog all the facts there are, one would have to include in the catalog facts which are themselves *about* forms. But what then does logic study—all the facts in the catalog equally, or principally those facts which are *about* forms? Is logic a special science or not? If there are forms, and there are facts about them separate from the facts about concrete individuals, *they* would appear to be the subject matter of logic. We seem to have the following paradox: logic is the science which has no specific subject matter, and hence its subject matter is form. This appears contradictory. The subject matter of logic cannot *both* be 'nothing in particular' *and* be form, unless forms are themselves nothing.

In later works, Russell seems to be aware of the difficulty, but finds it difficult to reconcile the tension. In *Our Knowledge of the External World*, Russell still endorses what might be called a form-centric account of the subject matter of logic, but at least at some points wants to describe logical knowledge as a kind of knowledge of something. At the same time, however, it is supposed to be a very *different* kind of knowledge:

> In every proposition and in every inference, there is, besides the particular subject-matter concerned, a certain *form*, a way in which the constituents of the proposition or inference are put together. ... It is forms, in this sense, that are the proper object of philosophical logic.
>
> ...
>
> It is obvious that the knowledge of logical forms is something quite different from knowledge of existing things. ... some kind of knowledge of logical forms, though with most people it is not explicit, is involved in all understanding of discourse. It is the business of philosophical logic to extract this knowledge from its concrete ingredients, and to render it explicit and pure. (Russell 1956b: 41)

Elsewhere he specifically mentions the issue of how logic differs from other sciences.

If the theory that classes are merely symbolic is accepted, it follows that numbers are not actual entities, but that propositions in which numbers verbally occur have not really any constituents corresponding to numbers, but only a certain logical form which is not a part of propositions having this form. This is in fact the case with all the apparent objects of logic and mathematics. Such words as *or*, *not*, *if*, *there is*, *identity*, *greater*, *plus*, *nothing*, *everything*, *function*, and so on, are not names of definite objects, like "John" or "Jones," but are words which require a context in order to have meaning. All of them are *formal*, that is to say, their occurrence indicates a certain form of a proposition, not a certain constituent. "Logical constants," in short, are not entities; the words expressing them are not names, and cannot significantly be made into logical subjects except when it is the words themselves, as opposed to their meanings, that are being discussed.[*Footnote: "In the above remarks I am making use of unpublished work by my friend Ludwig Wittgenstein."] This fact has a very important bearing on all logic and philosophy, since it shows how they differ from the special sciences. But the questions raised are so large and so difficult that it is impossible to pursue them further on this occasion. (Russell 1956b: 161–2)

It seems clear that something has changed from *TK*. He claims not only that logical constants are not names of entities, which had already been his view in *TK*, but that, in some sense, it is not even *possible* to speak of their meanings in a direct fashion. This would seem to imply that not only are there no 'logical universals' which can be spoken of, there are not even any 'logical forms' which can be spoken of. This is dangerously close to the 'logical mysticism' that is sometimes read into the *Tractatus*.[20] However, the thought is not developed.

In works of the 1918–19 period, he seems more content to state the problem than attempt to solve it. E.g., in his 'Philosophy of Logical Atomism' lectures, he writes:

> It is not a very easy thing to see what are the constituents of a logical proposition ... it seems as though all the propositions of logic are entirely devoid of constituents. I do not think this can be quite true. But then the only other thing you can seem to say is that the *form* is a constituent, that propositions of a certain form are always true: that *may* be the right analysis, though I much doubt whether it is.
>
> ...
>
> I can only say, in conclusion, as regards the constituents of logical propositions, that it is a problem which is rather new. There has not been much opportunity to consider it. I do not think any literature exists at all which

---

[20]There are of course different interpretations of the *Tractatus*'s final position on this matter. I do not mean to be taking sides in such disputes here.

deals with it in any way whatever, and it is an interesting problem. (Russell 1918: 239)

Similarly, in *Introduction to Mathematical Philosophy*, he poses the subject matter of logic as a 'problem which is easier to state than solve' (198). He describes, in more or less the same way he always has, how propositions of logic are derived from generalization by substituting variables for definite terms. Again, he claims that logical constants do not represent constituents of propositions, but are purely formal. He surmises that words *for* forms can always be dispensed with (200). However, he refuses either to assert that propositions of logic have no constituents or to assert that forms are constituents of propositions of logic, intimating that this is an unsolved problem. In both works, he adds a new wrinkle, which is that he no longer thinks that a proposition being fully general and true is enough to make it a logical truth, as in the case of propositions claiming that the universe contains a certain number of individuals. He claims that there must be some additional property of being a *tautology*, which he demurs from attempting to define, and simply claims it is a concept Wittgenstein had been working on and perhaps might eventually be able to explain.

Even though Russell is not prepared in this period to admit that one simply cannot speak of forms as being 'constituents of' certain propositions, it seems that he would now reject the view of *TK* that forms are themselves facts. Russell now claims that facts are not the sorts of things one can 'name' (Russell 1918: 187), a view he also claims to have been the result of the influence of Wittgenstein. If forms were facts, then he would certainly be committed to denying that they entered into such relations as 'being constituent of', or were 'there' to name somehow. He also claims that no facts are simple, all are complex (Russell 1918: 202), which is again, clearly incompatible with the *TK* view.

Nonetheless, during this period, Russell still seems to maintain that, somehow, logic studies objective reality, that it 'is concerned with the real world just as truly as zoology, though with its more abstract and general features' (Russell 1919a: 169). However, he seems to have thought that this study could only be carried out successfully in a kind of *oblique* way. Rather than attempting to study form directly, we instead focus our attention on symbols. The necessity for this is perhaps evident already from the quotation from *Our Knowledge* above; since forms cannot be named, we can perhaps at best discuss the symbols that represent these forms. Yet he still seems to think it possible, though only 'perhaps once in six months for half a minute', at least in thought if not in language, to break through and think about the real subject-matter of logic, adding that '[t]he rest of the time you think about the symbols, because they are tangible' (Russell 1918: 185).

At some point, Russell gave up even the hope for such semiannual communions with the world of form, and concluded that mathematics and logic were purely linguistic in nature. It is difficult to pin down exactly when this might have been. Ray Monk (1996: 568–9) dates this change to Russell's meetings to discuss the (then published) *Tractatus* in December 1919. Monk draws our attention to a review Russell published soon thereafter in which he claims that the laws of logic 'are concerned with symbols' and that they involve 'different ways of saying the same thing' (Russell 1988d: 405). It seems somewhat hasty to me to conclude that Russell then thought that logic was *purely* linguistic, even if it primarily dealt with symbols. Through the 1920s, Russell believed that when two logical expressions have the same meaning that this owed to a 'relation between their forms' (Russell 1988c: 129), and he continued to think that it is 'easier to think about words than about what they stand for' (Russell 1988b: 169), suggesting that he perhaps continued to believe that investigation of symbols obliquely brought us knowledge about form. In the introduction to the *Tractatus* (Russell 1988a: 111), he suggested that ascending a hierarchy of languages might provide a 'loophole' making it possible to say things Wittgenstein claimed could not be said, which includes statements about logical form.

At least by the 1930s, however, he seems to have concluded that there is nothing at all in objective reality corresponding to logical particles. He then held that they contribute to the syntax of expressions, not their extra-linguistic meaning, writing that they 'must be treated as part of the language, not as part of what the language speaks about' (Russell 1931, 2nd ed.: xi). He adds elsewhere that the 'non-mental world' can be 'completely described' without use of the words 'or', 'not', 'all', and 'some' (Russell 1996a: 362). In the early 1950s he wrote that 'All the propositions of mathematics and logic are assertions as to the correct use of a certain small number of words. This conclusion, if valid, may be regarded as an epitaph on Pythagoras' (Russell 1973b: 306). Elsewhere, he admits that 'I have therefore ceased to hope to meet "if" and "or" and "not" in heaven' (Russell 1951: 41). The reasons he gave in these later works for these conclusions, however, are sketchy and not very convincing. It is one thing to suggest that these issues *can* be approached by discussing linguistic phenomena rather than objective phenomena. There are facts in language, and those facts have logical forms just as any other facts would. It is quite another to insist that when we do study the structure of language we must not at the same time be gaining knowledge of something extra-linguistic as well, something the structure of language has *in common* with reality as a whole. To my knowledge, Russell never fully explained why he moved away from such a position.

I think the paradox that logic seems at once to have no specific subject matter and that *this therefore is* its subject matter is one to which there is no obvious answer, and *because of this* it is one to which philosophers must continue to give serious thought.

References

Bolzano, B. 1972. *Theory of Science*, trans. R. George. Oxford: Oxford University Press. (Originally published in 1837 as *Wissenschaftslehre*, Sulzbach: J. E. von Seidel).

Frege, G. 1980. *Philosophical and Mathematical Correspondence*, ed. H. Kaal. Chicago: University of Chicago Press.

Grattan-Guinness, I., ed. 1977. *Dear Russell–Dear Jourdain*. New York: Columbia University Press.

Griffin, N. 1980. Russell on the Nature of Logic (1903–1913). *Synthese* 45: 117–88.

Griffin, N. 1985. Russell's Multiple Relation Theory of Judgment. *Philosophical Studies* 47: 213–48.

Klement, K. C. 2004. Putting Form Before Function: Logical Grammar in Frege, Russell and Wittgenstein. *Philosopher's Imprint* 4: 1–47.

Klement, K. C. 2005. The Origins of the Propositional Functions Version of Russell's Paradox. *Russell: The Journal of Bertrand Russell Studies* 24: 101–32.

Klement, K. C. 2010a. The Functions of Russell's No Class Theory. *Review of Symbolic Logic* 3: 633–664.

Klement, K. C. 2010b. Russell, His Paradoxes, and Cantor's Theorem: Part II. *Philosophy Compass* 5: 29–41.

Klement, K. C. 2013. *PM*'s Circumflex, Syntax and Philosophy of Types. *The Palgrave Centenary Companion to Principia Mathematica*, eds. N. Griffin and B. Linsky, 218–46. New York: Palgrave Macmillan.

Klement, K. C. 2014. The Paradoxes and Russell's Theory of Incomplete Symbols. *Philosophical Studies* 169: 183–207.

Landini, G. 1998. *Russell's Hidden Substitutional Theory*. Oxford: Oxford University Press.

Landini, G. 2015. Types* and Russellian Facts. In this volume: 231–73.

Levine, J. 2013. On the Interpretation of *Principia Mathematica* and the Multiple–Relation Theory of Judgment. *The Palgrave Centenary Companion to Principia Mathematica*, eds. N. Griffin and B. Linsky, 247–304. New York: Palgrave Macmillan.

Levine, J. forthcoming. Russell on Types and Universals.

Linsky, B. 1999. *Russell's Metaphysical Logic*. Stanford: CSLI Publications.

Meinong, A. 1899. Über Gegenstände höherer Ordnung und deren Verhältnis zur inneren Wahrnehmung. *Zeitschrift für Psychologie und Physiologie der Sinnesorgane* 21: 182–272.

Monk, R. 1996. *Bertrand Russell: The Spirit of Solitude 1872–1921*. New York: The Free Press.

Moore, G. E. Forthcoming. *Russell on Philosophy of Mathematics: Notes 1911–12*, ed. J. Levine.

Proops, I. 2007. Russell and the Universalist Conception of Logic. *Noûs* 41: 1–32.

Russell, B. 1906. The Theory of Implication. *American Journal of Mathematics* 28: 159–202.

Russell, B. 1907. On the Nature of Truth. *Proceedings of the Aristotelian Society* 7: 28–49.

Russell, B. 1908. Mathematical Logic as Based on the Theory of Types. In Russell 1956: 57–102.

Russell, B. 1911. On the Relations of Universals and Particulars. *Proceedings of the Aristotelian Society* 12: 1–24. In Russell 1956: 105–24.

Russell, B. 1912. *The Problems of Philosophy*. London: Williams and Norgate. Reprinted Oxford: Oxford University Press 1959.

Russell, B. 1918. The Philosophy of Logical Atomism. In Russell 1956: 175–281.

Russell, B. 1919a. *Introduction to Mathematical Philosophy*. London: George Allen and Unwin.

Russell, B. 1919b. On Propositions: What They Are and How They Mean. In Russell 1956: 283–320.

Russell, B. 1931. *The Principles of Mathematics*. Cambridge: Cambridge University Press. (First edition 1903.) [*PoM*]

Russell, B. 1948. Whitehead and *Principia Mathematica*. *Mind* 57: 137–38.

Russell, B. 1951. *Portraits from Memory*. New York: Simon and Schuster.

Russell, B. 1956a. *Logic and Knowledge: Essays, 1901–1950*, ed. R. Marsh. London: Unwin Hyman.

Russell, B. 1956b. *Our Knowledge of the External World*, 2nd ed. New York: Mentor Books. (First edition 1914.)

Russell, B. 1973a. *Essays in Analysis*, ed. D. Lackey. New York: George Braziller.

Russell, B. 1973b. Is Mathematics Purely Linguistic? In Russell 1973a: 295–306. (Written 1951–52.)

Russell, B. 1973c. On 'Insolubilia' and their Solution by Symbolic Logic. In Russell 1973a: 190–214. (First published 1906 in French as 'Les paradoxes de la logique'.)

Russell, B. 1973d. On Some Difficulties in the Theory of Transfinite Numbers and Order Types. In Russell 1973a: 135–64. (First published 1906.)

Russell, B. 1973e. The Regressive Method of Discovering the Premises of Mathematics. In Russell 1973a: 272–83. (First published 1907.)

Russell, B. 1984. *The Collected Papers of Bertrand Russell, Volume 7: Theory of Knowledge: The 1913 Manuscript*, ed. E. R. Eames with K. Blackwell. London: Routledge. [*TK*] [*CP 7*]

Russell, B. 1988a. Introduction to *Tractatus Logico-Philosophicus*, by L. Wittgenstein. In *CP* 9: 101–12. (First published 1921.)

Russell, B. 1988b. Logical Atomism. In *CP* 9: 162–79. (First published 1924.)

Russell, B. 1988c. Physics and Perception. In *CP* 9: 126–33. (First published 1922.)

Russell, B. 1988d. Wisdom of our Ancestors. In *CP* 9: 403–6. (First published 1920.)

Russell, B. 1988e. *The Collected Papers of Bertrand Russell, Volume 9: Essays on Language, Mind and Matter, 1919–26*, ed. J. Slater. London: Unwin Hyman. [*CP 9*]

Russell, B. 1992a. Analytic Realism. In *CP* 6: 132–146. (First published 1911.)

Russell, B. 1992b. Knowledge by Acquaintance and Knowledge By Description. In *CP* 6: 147–66. (First published 1911.)

Russell, B. 1992c. On the Axioms of the Infinite and of the Transfinite. In *CP* 6: 41–53. (First published 1911.)

Russell, B. 1992d. On the Nature of Truth and Falsehood. In *CP* 6: 115–24.

Russell, B. 1992e. The Philosophical Importance of Mathematical Logic. In *CP* 6: 32–42. (First published 1911.)

Russell, B. 1992f. Some Explanations in Reply to Mr. Bradley. In *CP* 6: 349–57. (First published 1910).

Russell, B. 1992g. What is Logic? In *CP* 6: 54–56. (Written 1912.)

Russell, B. 1992h. *The Collected Papers of Bertrand Russell, Volume 6: Logical and Philosophical Papers, 1909–13*, ed. J. Slater with B. Frohmann. New York: Routledge. [*CP 6*]

Russell, B. 1994a. Fundamental Notions. In *CP* 4: 111–263. (Written 1904.)

Russell, B. 1994b. On Denoting. In *CP* 4: 414–427. (First published 1905.)

Russell, B. 1994c. On Functions. In *CP* 4: 96–110. (Written 1904.)

Russell, B. 1994d. On Fundamentals. In *CP* 4: 359–413. (Written 1905.)

Russell, B. 1994e. On Meaning and Denotation. In *CP* 4: 314–358. (Written 1903.)

Russell, B. 1994f. *The Collected Papers of Bertrand Russell, Volume 4: Foundations of Logic, 1903–05*, ed. A. Urquhart with A. C. Lewis. London: Routledge. [*CP 4*]

Russell, B. 1996a. The Relevance of Psychology to Logic. In *CP* 10: 362–70. (First published 1938.)

Russell, B. 1996b. *The Collected Papers of Bertrand Russell, Volume 10: A Fresh Look at Empiricism, 1927-42*, ed. J. Slater. London: Routledge. [*CP* 10]

Russell, B. 2014a. Fundamentals. In *CP* 5: 536–70. (Likely written 1907.)

Russell, B. 2014b. Individuals. In *CP* 5: 529–35. (Likely written 1907–08.)

Russell, B. 2014c. Logic in which Propositions are not Entities. In *CP* 5: 262–7. (Likely written 1906.)

Russell, B. 2014d. On Substitution. In *CP* 5: 126–235. (Likely written 1906.)

Russell, B. 2014e. The Paradox of the Liar. In *CP* 5: 317–74. (Likely written 1906.)

Russell, B. 2014f. Types. In *CP* 5: 498–514. (Likely written 1907.)

Russell, B. 2014g. *The Collected Papers of Bertrand Russell, Volume 5: Toward 'Principia Mathematica', 1905–08*, ed. G. H. Moore. London: Routledge. [*CP* 5]

Tarski, A. 1983. The Concept of Logical Consequence. *Logic, Semantics, Metamathematics*, 409–20. Indianapolis: Hackett. (First published 1936.)

Tarksi, A. 1986. What are Logical Notions? *History and Philosophy of Logic* 7: 143–54.

Whitehead, A. N. and B. Russell. 1925–27. *Principia Mathematica*, 3 vols. Cambridge: Cambridge University Press. (First edition 1910–13.)

Wittgenstein, L. 1922. *Tractatus Logico-Philosophicus*, trans. D. Pears and B. McGuinness. London: Routledge 1961.

Wittgenstein, L. 1979. *Notebooks 1914–1916*, eds. G. H. von Wright and G. E. M. Anscombe. Chicago: University of Chicago Press.

11

Types* and Russellian Facts

GREGORY LANDINI

1 Introduction

There is an important era of Russell's philosophy that lasts roughly from 1910 through 1913. It overlaps with the appearance of the three volumes of *Principia Mathematica*. It is an era in which Russell adopted a theory of facts and with it a multiple-relation theory of judgment and a correspondence definition of 'truth' and 'falsehood'. It is an era in which Russell attempted to develop an epistemology of mathematical logic whose foundation was a doctrine of acquaintance with universals. *Principia* has no epistemology whatsoever. It sets forth only the ontology of mathematical logic, and the principles by means of which its truths may be derived. The epistemology of mathematical logic emerges in Russell's wonderful little introductory book *The Problems of Philosophy*. The full treatment of the position was to have been set forth in Russell's 1913 book *The Theory of Knowledge*. By appeal to acquaintance with universals, a sort of 'logical intuition', Russell embraced a non-Kantian solution to the impasse between Rationalism and Empiricism.

Russell held that mathematical logic is synthetic *a priori*. Nowhere is this more clearly stated than in *The Principles of Mathematics* (1903). He writes:

> The question of the nature of mathematical reasoning was obscured in Kant's day by several causes. In the first place, Kant never doubted for a moment that the propositions of logic are analytic, whereas he rightly perceived that those of mathematics are synthetic. It has since appeared that logic is just as synthetic as all other kinds of truth. (Russell 1903: 457)

Acquaintance, Knowledge, and Logic.
Donovan Wishon and Bernard Linsky (eds.).
Copyright © 2015, CSLI Publications.

Rejecting Kant's *Transcendental Aesthetic* (with its thesis that pure forms of sensory intuition of *space* and *time* are imposed by the mind on the data of sense), Russell was loath to put his position about logic quite this way in his later writings. The new logic is synthetic (informative) because it transcends the new quantification theory and embraces the existence theorems of impredicative comprehension. This gave rise to a new, non-Kantian notion of 'analytic', meaning true in virtue of ^{cp}Logic (impredicative comprehension principle logic). The new notion of 'analytic' enables one to say that ^{cp}Logic is analytic. But this lends itself to confusion unless this new notion of 'analytic' is sharply distinguished from Kant's notion.[1]

In *Problems*, Russell tells us that what makes mathematical logic epistemically accessible is not an occult Rationalist faculty of intuition connecting the mind to a Platonic realm of objects of ontological necessity (numbers, triangles, and the like). What makes is accessible is a faculty for an immediate acquaintance with *relations between universals*— an acquaintance that is attained even when nothing exemplifies the universals. The following passages are telling:

...All a priori knowledge deals exclusively with the relations of universals (Russell 1912a: 103)

...It must be taken as a fact, discovered by reflecting on our knowledge, that we have the power of sometimes perceiving such relations between universals and there of sometimes knowing general *a priori* propositions such as those of arithmetic and logic (1912a: 105)

...Thus, the difference between an *a priori* general proposition and an empirical generalization does not come in the *meaning* of the proposition; it comes in the nature of the *evidence* for it. In the empirical case, the evidence consists in the particular instances... (1912a: 106)

Among universals, there seems to be no principle by which we can decide which can be known by acquaintance, but it is clear that among those that can be so known are sensible qualities, relations of space and time, similarity, and certain abstract logical universals. Our derivative knowledge of things, which we call knowledge by *description*, always involves both acquaintance with something and knowledge of truths. Our immediate knowledge of *truths* may be called *intuitive knowledge* and the truths so known may be *called self-evident* truths. Among such truths are included those which merely state what is given in sense, and also certain abstract logical arithmetical principles, and (though with less certainty) some ethical propositions. (1912a: 109).

---

[1] Indeed, the logical positivist notion of 'analytic' as 'true in virtue of the meaning of the logical words of quantification theory', serves as well to confuse matters.

It is thus very important that the era of *acquaintance* from 1910 through 1913 overlaps exactly with Whitehead and Russell's *Principia Mathematica*. The work set out the new ^{cp}Logic with comprehension axiom schemas such as

*12.1 $(\exists f)(\varphi x \equiv_x f!x)$

*12.11 $(\exists f)(\varphi x \equiv_{xy} f!xy)$

It endeavored to show that the new revolution in logic supports the new Cantorian revolution in mathematics and the thesis that mathematics, including the new geometries (Euclidean and otherwise), are part of ^{cp}Logic-- a general synthetic *a priori* science studying relational order. The 'logical' next step was for Russell to advance an epistemology for his ^{cp}Logic.

Principia consists of three volumes, with volume 1 appearing in 1910, volume II in 1912 and volume III appearing in 1913. While the first three volumes were very much a collaboration, the fourth volume on geometry was to be Whitehead's work alone. It was delayed by Whitehead's investigation of Einstein's great philosophical and scientific discoveries on relativity and new notion of 'space-time'. Whitehead was also distracted by is efforts to develop his own theory rival of relativity— a theory which was taken seriously in physics and empirically disconfirmed. Volume IV never appeared and Evelyn Whitehead dutifully carried out her husband's strict order to destroy it.

Both Whitehead's volume IV of *Principia* and Russell's *Theory of Knowledge* are widely regarded as failed projects. They were, after all, abandoned by their authors. But history should not make too hasty an assessment. In this paper, we shall focus on certain aspects of Russell's multiple-relation theory in an effort to show that its difficulties are not insurmountable. In particular, we shall focus on the problem of defining what it is for a fact to be permutative.

2   Preliminaries[2]

Before we can hope to discuss the multiple-relation theory of judgment and the problem of permutative facts, we must first focus our attention on Russellian facts in general. It is quite important not to conflate Russellian facts embraced in the era 1910–13 with other sorts of entities that occurred before this era and that occur after it. Prior to *Principia* Russell did not embrace facts. He embraced an ontology of *obtaining* (true) propositions and

---

[2]See Landini 1998a.

of *non-obtaining* (false) propositions, all of which exist of logical necessity. (Indeed, logical necessity is the only genuine necessity for Russell.) Some propositions have the property of being logically true (necessarily obtaining). A striking feature of the era is that Russell does not embrace an *ontology* of facts. Of course, this point turns on the meaning we assign to the word 'ontology'. The word's meaning has been changed many times in the history of philosophy, most recently by Quine for whom ontological matters are just empirical matters of 'what there is'. For Quine, the existence of universals, numbers, geometric objects and the like is on a par with the question of whether there are coelacanths in the West Indian Ocean. For Russell, matters of ontology are distinctly philosophical non-empirical and concern the ground of necessity in mathematical logic and other fields. Some facts exist of necessity and some are contingent. All propositions exist of logical necessity.

The words 'fact' and 'proposition' are thus dangerous words to interpret and we must be on guard not to fall into conflations concerning these notions. There are many twists and turns to keep straight. Let me try to set out the major epochs involving Russell's notion of a *proposition*:

(1) 1903 *The Principles of Mathematics*

(2) 1905 'On Denoting'

(3) 1906 ' "On Insolubilia" and Their Solution by Symbolic Logic'

(4) 1908 'Mathematical Logic as Based on the theory of Types'

The appearance of *Principia* (1910–13) is a boundary. After that, Russell embraces a no-propositions theory and $^{1903-08}$propositions never recur in Russell's philosophy.

It is of central importance to keep the changes clear. Perhaps it is best to do it by dating as indicated above. Thus, we shall use the expression ^{1903}proposition to mean propositions as understood in *The Principles of Mathematics*, ^{1905}proposition to mean propositions as Russell understood them in 'On Denoting', and ^{1906}proposition to mean propositions as understood in 'On Insolubilia', and so on. Similarly, we use the expression ^{1910}fact to mean facts as understood in *Principia*. That Russell changed his mind about philosophical fundamentals is fairly well understood. Nonetheless, there is a persistent tendency blur distinctions. One major example occurs with those who maintain that ^{1910}facts are true ^{1905}propositions. Let us see precisely why this cannot be so.

In the *Principles of Mathematics*, Russell adopts the logical particle sign '⊃' as a relation sign for *implication* and regards '$x \supset y$' as a well-formed-formula (*wff*). It *must* be flanked by terms to form a *wff*. This is quite different from the modern horseshoe sign occurring in A $\supset$ B (and the modern arrow sign A $\rightarrow$ B) which *must* be flanked by *wffs* A and B to form a *wff*. To emphasize the difference, I shall use the sign $\supset$ and write $x \supset y$, or generally $\alpha \supset \beta$, where α and β are used for any terms of Russell's formal language of propositions. The individual variables, x, y, z, and indeed any lower case letter of the English alphabet, is a term in Russell's early language of propositions. Moreover, any *wff* A of the formal language for logic set out in *Principles* can be nominalized to form a term {A} for a [1903]proposition. Thus, for example,

$$x \supset \{y \supset x\}$$

is a *wff* and says that x implies y's implying x. For convenience, subordinate occurrences of brackets can be dropped, and dots can be used for punctuation. Thus we have $x \, . \supset . \, y \supset x$ instead of the cumbersome $x \supset \{y \supset x\}$.

The inference rule *Modus Ponens* for the logic of [1903]propositions must be set out carefully and it must not be confused with the following incoherent rule:

From p and $p \supset q$, infer q.

In Russell's language p and q are individual variables (not special letters standing in for *wffs*) and the above is just a notational variant of

From x and $x \supset y$, infer y.

The proper inference rule is this:

Modus Ponens: From A and {A} $\supset$ {B}, infer B.

This impacts derived inference rules such as *Simplification*. Once again the rule is not the incoherent

From $p \bullet q$, infer p.

That is just a notational variant of

From $x \bullet y$, infer x.

The inference rule is this:

Simplification: From {A} $\bullet \, \alpha$ infer A

Indeed, it should be noted that in 1905 Russell introduces definitions as follows:

$\alpha \bullet \beta =df \sim(\alpha \supset \sim\beta)$

$\alpha \equiv \beta =df (\alpha \supset \beta) \bullet (\beta \supset \alpha)$

$\alpha \lor \beta =df \sim\alpha \supset \beta$

$\sim\alpha =df (z)(\alpha \supset z)$

It is incoherent to read '$x \bullet y$' as saying 'x and y'. It is to be read as saying

$$(z)(x \supset (w)(y \supset w) . \supset . z).$$

In words, this it says that x's implying y's implying everything implies everything. A convenient alternative system which Russell discussed is to put

$$\sim\alpha =_{df} \alpha \supset f$$

$$f =_{df} \{(x)(y)(x \supset y)\}.$$

Either way, such definitions are impossible in the syntax of *Principia* and in modern logic, with the modern horseshoe sign $\supset$.

In Russell's view, [1903]propositions are akin to states of affairs, some of which contain physical entities such as mountains. Russell's famous example is the [1903]proposition {Mont Blanc is more than 4000 meters high} which contains Mont Blanc with all its snowfields as a constituent. But let us consider the [1903]proposition {the cat is on the mat}. It has among its constituents the cat, the mat and the relation '*on*.' The relation '*on*' occurs in this proposition in an indefinable way which Russell calls an occurrence 'as concept'. Concepts have a two-fold capacity. They may occur in a [1903]proposition *as concept*, but they may also occur in a [1903]proposition as *logical subject*. Russell gives the example of the [1903]proposition {Socrates is human} in which *Humanity* occurs as concept. In contrast, *Humanity* occurs as logical subject in the [1903]proposition {Humanity belongs to Socrates}. It is its occurring as concept that accounts for the *unity* of a [1903]proposition.

When he embraced propositions, the property of 'truth' (obtaining) and the property of 'falsehood' (non-obtaining) were primitive and indefinable properties. They are, as Russell put it, like the whiteness and redness of roses (Russell 1904: 76). Now Russell is explicit that the exemplification of the property 'truth' by a [1903]proposition does not alter it. It is the very same [1903]proposition whether it has the property 'truth' or it has the property 'falsehood'. This is important. Consider again the [1903]proposition {the cat is on the mat}. Whether it is true or false has no bearing whatsoever on whether the relation '*on*' occurs in the [1903]proposition as concept. This demonstrates without question that when the relation occurs as concept it does not relate the cat to the mat. Thus, for a relation to occur as concept in a [1903]proposition is *not* for it to occur as a *relating* relation. The [1903]proposition {the cat is on the mat} is true just when the relation '*on*' relates the cat to the mat. It is false just when the relation '*on*' does not relate the cat to the mat. But whether it is true or false, the relation '*on*' occurs as concept in the [1903]proposition. In the no-propositions theory of *Principia*, a statement is made true by [1910]facts. A relation *relating* in a [1910]fact is *not* the same notion of a relation occurring 'as concept' in a [1903]proposition (and the same goes for [1905]propositions and [1907]propositions.) Thus *obtaining* (true) propositions cannot be identified with [1910]facts. [3]

One distinctive feature of [1903]propositions is that some of them have *denoting concepts* among their constituents. Others do not. Denoting concepts, as with concepts generally, have a two-fold capacity. The denoting concept '*every man*' occurs as concept in the [1903]proposition {Every man is mortal}. It occurs as logical subject in the [1903]proposition {'Every man' is a denoting concept}. Russell's theory of denoting concepts collapsed in 1904. A new 1905 theory of propositions emerged which modified the earlier theory by the rejection of denoting concepts entirely. The purpose of Russell's theory of denoting concepts was to give an ontological account of the constituents of general [1903]propositions. [4] For example, in the [1903]proposition {Every man is mortal}, the denoting concept '*every man*' occurs together with the universal '*mortality*'. Russell also wants to accommodate *wffs* such as '$(x)(x = x)$' of the new quantification theory. This *wff* involves single letters '*x*' used as individual variables. Russell endeavors to give an account of its constituents of a [1903]proposition referred to by the nominalization of such a *wff*. In *Principles,* he offers the following sort of analysis. '$(x)(x = x)$' abbreviates

Every entity obtained by substituting any entity for a in $\{a = a\}$ is true.

Thus, the [1903]proposition {every entity obtained by substituting any entity for a in $\{a = a\}$ is true} has among its constituents the denoting concepts '*every entity*' and '*any entity*'. The theory of denoting concepts of *Principles* was supposed to form a bridge from to the new quantification theory with its use of variables bound and free.

The bridge failed in June 1905 when Russell discovered a major problem with his theory of denoting concepts. It is a violation of logical form to attempt a substitution of Socrates for the denoting concept '*every man*' in the [1903]proposition {Every man is mortal}. Socrates occurs as logical subject in {Socrates is mortal} and '*every man*' occurs as concept in {Every man is mortal}. Russell could not find a logical analysis of the logical form of [1903]propostions involving the two-fold occurrence of denoting concepts. As a result, he abandoned denoting concepts altogether and embraced a distinction between what he called the *determination* of the variable and the *substitution* of entities. [5] That is, Russell's new 1905 theory shelved the question as to the constituents of general [1905]propositions. As a result,

---

[3] This was first pointed out in Cocchiarella 1980.
[4] See Landini 1998a, 1998b.
[5] See Landini 1998b.

[1905]propositions must be distinguished from those [1903]propositions which contain denoting concepts. (This is indicated by our '1905' label.)

Using single letters as variables (and not attempting to analyze variation in terms of substitution of entities in propositions), Russell was able to form a new theory of definite descriptions as incomplete symbols. The following is a stipulative definition of a convenient notation:

$$[\iota x \varphi x][\psi(\iota x \varphi x)] =_{df} (\exists x)(\varphi y \equiv_y y = x\ .\&.\ \psi x).$$

Scope markers $[\iota x \varphi x][...\iota x \varphi x...]$ are dropped when smallest scope is intended. With this in place, Russell formed definite descriptions of [1905]propositions. This is the foundation of his new substitutional theory of [1905]propositional structure. For example he has, $(\iota q)(p\frac{x}{a}!q)$. This is a definite description: 'the q exactly like p except at most for containing x wherever a occurs in p'. For instance, the following is a logical truth:

$$(p, a)(x)(\ (\iota q)(p\frac{x}{a}!q) \supset (\iota q)(p\frac{x}{a}!q)).$$

For convenience Russell writes this as:

$$(p, a)(x)(\ p\frac{x}{a} \supset p\frac{x}{a}).$$

The analog in the language of simple type-theory is the following quite familiar logical truth:

$$(\varphi)(x)(\ \varphi!x \supset \varphi!x).$$

In Tarskian lingo, this is true in *virtue of its form* (structure).[6] But according to Russell, logical truths are *about* (kinds of) structures. Thus they include more than what is true in virtue of *its* structure. This is evident in the substitutional theory, for Russell takes it to be a logical truth of structure that

$$(p, a)(x)(\exists q)(\ p\frac{x}{a}!r \equiv_r r = q).$$

This says that for any p and a, there is a q whose structure is exactly like that of p except at most for containing x wherever a occurs in p. Observe that it is not true in virtue of its structure. It is a truth about structures (the structures of propositions).

The impredicative comprehension principles of a [cp]Logic of attributes in intension are emulated in the substitutional theory. Russell was able to use the notion of substitution of entities occurring in [1905]propositions to emulate structure without logical types of entities. Any *wff* in the primitive

---

[6]Tarski would put as being true in every admissible interpretation of its structure over domains of varying cardinality.

language of impredicative simple type theory can be emulated in the substitutional theory.

It should be noted that during the era of substitution, Russell embraces universals, not the least of which is the relation of implication itself. Russell embraces a fundamental logical difference between a universal and a particular (*thing*). But particulars, unlike universals, are not capable of occurring 'as concept'. Implication is a relation, a universal, and it has a two-fold nature. Thus, not only is '$x \supset z$' a *wff* but '$\supset \supset \supset$' is also a *wff* of the formal language of substitution. But in the language of substitution, it is ungrammatical to put a variable in the position of a predicate (property or relation sign) in a *wff*. For instance, the language embraces the *wff* '$x \supset z$' but '$x\ y\ z$' is certainly not a *wff* of the language of the logic of propositional structure. There are no types of entities embraced by Russell's substitutional theory. This is important and worth emphasizing. The logical difference between a *universal* and a *particular* (*thing*) is not represented in Russell's substitutional emulation of a hierarchy of types of attributes.

This is as it should be. Just as in *Principles*, what Russell calls *things* are distinct from *concepts* precisely because only the latter have the capacity to occur as concept. *Universals* have a *two-fold* nature and so also do denoting concepts.[7] Denoting concepts are abandoned in 1905, but Russell held and that only concepts (which includes universals) have the capacity of occurring as concept in a [1905] proposition. Nonetheless this is not represented in the language of substitution by special variables for universals. Universals are values of individual variables in the language of substitution and the language of logic embraces only one kind of variables: namely, individual variables. Russell never doubted that at least some universals exist of logical necessity. But he came to hold that it is not the business of logic to find principles that determine what universals there are (what predicates or open *wffs* of language comprehend universals).

In September of 1906 Russell published a paper in French replying to Poincaré's published diatribe against Logicism and Cantor's revolutionary reorientation of mathematics. Cantor had employed *diagonal* arguments to show that some infinite classes are larger than others. Poincaré's paper is called 'Les Paradoxes de la Logistique'. Russell's reply has the English title: 'On "Insolubilia" and their Solution by Symbolic Logic' (*InS*). In the paper, Russell dismisses the attempts by Richard, König, and Dixon to form paradoxes which undermine Cantor's result that every class can be well-ordered. Russell's substitutional theory endeavors to preserve Cantor's

---

[7]See Landini 1998b.

work and reject Poincarè's thesis that such puzzles reveal that Cantor's new conception of mathematics and the new logicism embracing it involves viciously circular definitions embracing an actual infinite. Following Peano, Russell says that the Richard, Konig, Dixon and Berry puzzles are not genuinely paradoxes at all, but depend on incoherent equivocations on words such 'naming', 'defining', and the like.[8] In stark contrast, Russell maintains that his paradoxes of sets/classes and attributes, Cantor's paradox of the greatest cardinal, and the Burali-Forti paradox are genuine paradoxes (so called 'insolubilia') that do require revisions to the first principles of logic. Russell heralds his substitutional theory as offering the needed revisions and providing the complete *solution* of these genuine paradoxes

Russell's paper was a reworked version of an earlier paper on the substitutional theory which he withdrew from publication.[9] Russell withdrew the earlier paper because in April of 1906 he had discovered a new *diagonal* argument which generates a paradox plaguing the theory of propositional substitutions allowed in the substitutional theory. I called this 'Russell's p_0/a_0 paradox'.[10] It is a diagonal paradox that violates Cantor's power-theorem. It has nothing to do with the propositional liar paradox which, of course, is *not* a diagonal paradox at all.[11] Russell's task was to preserve Cantor's diagonal arguments and at the same time avoid the use of a diagonal argument that generated the p_0/a_0 paradox. This, he thought, was achieved in his paper *InS*. In an effort to avoid the p_0/a_0 paradox Russell abandons *general propositions* and thus is born Russell's [1906]propositions. On this theory, one can nominalize a well-formed formula A to make a term {A} if and only if the formula A is quantifier-free. This impacts quantification theory when couched in a theory of [1906]propositions. The expression

---

[8]Berry's paradox of 'the least number not nameable in fewer than nineteen syllables' is a simple example. The notion of '… is nameable' is meaningless unless it is to mean nameable using the grammatical rules $R_1,..,R_m$ the and symbols $s_1,...s_n$. Now the listed symbols listed might well allow one to form the predicate '…is nameable using the grammatical rules $R_1,..,R_m$ the and symbols $s_1,...s_n$' but nothing assures that 'R_i' in this predicate must refer to the rule R_i, or that 's_i' refer to the symbols s_i.

[9]See Russell 1906a.

[10]See Landni 1998a.

[11]The propositional liar requires that there be some *wff* φ of the language such that $(q)(\varphi q \equiv q = \{(p)(\varphi p \supset p)\})$ is a theorem. There is no such *wff* φ and no such theorem in the substitutional theory. Of course, if a belief predicate 's believes q' were added then we might assume *contingently* that there is a person s such that

$(q)(\ s\ believes\ q\ .\equiv.\ q = \{(p)(\ s\ believes\ p \supset p)\})$.

But this not a diagonal construction and does not violate Cantor's power-theorem and, most importantly, it has no role to play in Russell's substitutional theory.

$$\{(x)(x = x)\} \supset \{y = y\}$$

becomes ill-formed. Russell solves this problem by reforming quantification theory defining the above as the following:

$$(\exists x)(\ \{x = x\} \supset \{y = y\}).$$

This theory of quantification would eventually find its way into section *9 of *Principia* though its role there is quite different.[12]

Unfortunately, Russell's solution in *InS* to the p_o/a_o makes the development of mathematics in the theory impossible. To revive mathematics, Russell required the addition of mitigating axioms which, he came to discover, enable the resurrection of a new version of the p_o/a_o paradox. This led Russell to abandon *InS* in favor of a new theory of propositions— and we now have [1907] propositions. In 1907 Russell revived his ontology of general propositions but now imagined them to be regimented into a hierarchy of *orders*. Though the new version of the substitutional theory embraces *orders* of propositions, it remains free of all ontological commitments to logical *types* of entities. The orders block the p_o/a_o paradox. Unfortunately, it waited for a year in the queue at the *American Journal of Mathematics* and appeared in 1908 as 'Mathematical Logic as Based on the Theory of Types'. The new theory enables Russell to introduce an axiom of Reducibility concerning propositions. In a simple case, the Reducibility axiom is this:

$$(q_n, b_o)(\exists p_1, a_o)(x_o)(p_1 \frac{x_o}{a_o} \equiv q_n \frac{x_o}{b_o}\ ).$$

The axiom of Reducibility of propositions, unlike the mitigating axioms of *InS* do not resurrect the p_o/a_o paradox. In this way, the theory emulates comprehension in the simple (impredicative) type theory of attributes. It emulates a *ramified* [cp]Logic of logical types of attributes with Reducibility.

Our historical summary has been unfortunately dogmatic. If we are to advance to our discussion of the multiple-relation theory and the problem of permutative [1910]facts, we do not have the space to set out all the evidence for the positions so far advanced.[13] And we shall have to continue a bit further in our dogmatic style for the same reason. *Principia* embraces the language of a *simple* type theory of attributes. Its language adopts predicate variables $\varphi!$, $\psi!$, $\chi!$, $f!$ $g!$ and so on, with simple type indices (dropped for convenience). The letters φ, ψ, χ, f, g in *Principia* without the exclamation (shriek) are schematic letters for *wffs* and as such they do not have type indices.

---

[12]It was this theory that gave Wittgenstein the idea that quantification theory consists of generalized tautologies. See Landini 2007.

[13]For details see Landini 1998.

This has been a subject of ongoing controversy. But there can be little doubt that that is the formal grammar of *Principia*. It is stated most explicitly when, e.g., *Principia* asserts that φ, ψ, χ, *f*, *g* are not bindable and that no loss of generality occurs from this (1910: 165).

Admittedly, many follow Church (1976) in ignoring (or 'improving') the historical *Principia* in favor of a grammar of predicate variables adorned with *r*-type (*ramified* type) indices. An *r*-type index introduces an order designation coded into the syntax. The order can be any number greater than or equal to the order of its simple type. Church designed his ramified type theory of attributes in parallel with the theory of 'Mathematical Logic'. And not surprisingly, Church's theory is fully emulated by Russell's ramified substitutional theory of propositions—a theory Russell once entertained for an appendix to *Principia*. But *Principia* does not espouse the substitutional theory and does not parallel 'Mathematical Logic'. This was first pointed out by Nino Cocchiarella.[14] *Principia* is explicit in describing itself as a theory which does not embrace an ontology of propositions. This means that the logical particles ∨, ∼ of *Principia* are not as they were in Russell's earlier logic. In the syntax of the substitutional theories, they are flanked by terms to form *wffs*. In *Principia*, they are clearly flanked by *wffs* to form *wffs*, there being no propositions.

With its syntax of predicate variables φ! , ψ!, χ!, *f*! *g*! and so on, and their type indices (though they are suppressed), one might readily get the impression that Whitehead and Russell intend a realist (objectual) semantics for the formal theory of *Principia* that embraces an ontology of *logical* types of entities as values of its predicate variables. Nothing could be further from Whitehead's and Russell's intent. The semantics Whitehead and Russell intended is substitutional (in the modern sense). It is a nominalistic semantics. They intended a semantics for *Principia* which makes no ontological commitment to logical types (or orders) of entities. Whatever is, be it universal or particular, abstract or concrete, is a value of *Principia's* genuine variables –its individual variables (of type 0). The predicate variables of *Principia* are, in accordance with their nominalistic semantic interpretation, not genuine. Their intended range is *internally limited* by their significance conditions.

Universals are not entities which are split into logical types (in the sense of *Principia Mathematica*). Russell does respect the *logical* difference between a universal and a particular. Particulars necessarily do not have a predicable nature. Universals necessarily have both a predicable and an in-

---

[14]See Cocchiarella 1980.

dividual nature. The predicable nature of a universal is what grounds the unity of a fact. Nonetheless, universals are values of the individual variables of *Principia*, not its predicate variables. The logical distinction between an individual and a universal is no more coded into *Principia's* formal syntax than it was coded into the syntax of the language of the substitutional theory.

3 ^{1910}Facts

The theory of the nature of facts that occurs in *Principia* extends through *Problems*. We have been calling them ^{1910}facts. This is the primary notion of a fact. Extended notions of facts do not appear until *Theory of Knowledge* and after. Thus, we needn't always use the label ^{1910}fact unless there is a need to contrast it with the later notions.

In the *Problems*, Russell took himself to be *acquainted* directly with many universals (properties and relations). Echoing his stand in *Principia* (and in during the era of substitution), we saw that he acknowledges that 'among universals there seems to be no principle by which we can decide which can be known by acquaintance' (Russell 1912a: 109). Russell accepts that there is an acquaintance with universals and with some particulars (among which are certain facts themselves). He maintains that *a priori* knowledge lies in the power of sometimes perceiving (being acquainted with) relations between universals.

The theory of acquaintance requires that universals have an individual as well as a predicable nature. The relation of '*acquaintance*' is a dyadic relation and thus there are acquaintance-facts such as

Russell's being acquainted with *wisdom*.

Indeed, it is absolutely essential to the multiple-relation theory that universals have both individual nature as well as a predicable nature. Their predicational nature accounts for the unity of a fact. Their individual nature allows them to be among the relata. In the fact

Russell's being wise

the universal *wisdom* occurs predicationally and generates the unity. In contrast, the unity of

Russell's being acquainted with *wisdom*

lies in the occurrence in it of the relation of '*acquaintance*' relating Russell to '*wisdom.*' Indeed, the very same relation '*acquaintance*' may occur *relating* the constituents of the fact and as one of the relata. We have the fact:

Russell's being acquainted with *acquaintance.*

Universals (properties and relations) must be wholly type-free and have both a predicable and an individual nature for this to be intelligible. [15]

There is a persistent confusion concerning Russellian facts that conflates the question of what accounts for the *unity* of a given fact with the distinct question of why the given fact exists at all. We noted that the unity of a fact lies in the occurrence in the fact of a universal (property or relation) occurring in the fact in a special way: if it is a property, it occurs in a *predicational* way; if it is a relation, it occurs *relating* the constituents of the fact. Now Russell holds that the relation R and the entities x and y may each severally exist without there being any fact composed of them. Why, then, are there any [1910]facts? This is related to the vexing question of why there is something rather than nothing. Russell's thesis about unity does not address, and was never intended to address, the question of why there is something (some fact) rather than not. [16] The relation 'loves' exists and so do Desdemona, Cassio and Othello (or so we are assuming for the sake of Russell's examples). But there is no fact of Desdemona's loving Cassio, and there is a fact of Desdemona's loving Othello. This is surely compatible with Russell's thesis that the unity of a fact lies in the occurrence in it of its relating relation R. The unity of the fact of Desdemona's loving Othello is due to the occurrence of 'loves' in it relating Desdemona to Othello. But quite obviously, it is Desdemona's mind that brings about the *existence* of this fact, not the relation 'loves.'

In *Principia*, Russell assumes that one can name certain [1910]facts and he suggests hyphenated names such as 'the redness of this', or '*a*-in-the-relation-R-to-*b*' ('*a*-R-*b*' for short). These expressions are terms, not *wffs*. When we know the relation in question, the hyphens are unnecessary because we can nominalize the *wff* to make a term. Thus, for example, the *wff* '*a* loves *b*' is nominalized to form the term '*a*'s loving *b*'. The term names something. The *wff* asserts and does not name anything. In order to quantify over facts, we would presumably need to accept a property of being a fact. We may then employ the following:

$$(f)Af =df (z)(\text{fact}(z) \supset Az)$$

$$(\exists f)Af =df (\exists z)(\text{fact}(z) \ \& \ Az).$$

The predicate '... is a fact' is a genuine predicate of the theory of facts. But the theory of facts is not part of pure logic even if some facts exist neces-

---

[15]As we shall see, in *Theory of Knowledge*, Russell began to worry about whether it is the same relation of 'acquaintance' in all these cases.

[16]I owe this point to Katarina Perovic. See Perovic 2014.

sarily. The predicate '... is a fact' is certainly not part of the language of *Principia*. Indeed, it is important to realize that *Principia's* recursive definition of 'truth' and 'falsehood' is not part of its pure logic. It is a part of the informal semantics Whitehead and Russell intended for the work. In *Problems* and in *Theory of Knowledge*, it is part of a philosophical theory of what the mind must be like for it to know the synthetic *a priori* propositions of ^{cp}logic.

The multiple-relation theory forms the base case (*and only the base case*) of *Principia's* recursive definition of 'truth' and 'falsehood' as applied to the *wffs* of *Principia*. The plan is to define 'truth' as applied to an atomic *wff* in terms of the existence of a would-be fact that corresponds to a discursive judgment (or belief) fact entertained by the mind *m* judging or believing. 'Falsehood' is then defined as the absence of any corresponding fact. Recursion handles the rest. *Principia* offers the following:

> That the words "true" and "false" have different meanings, according to the kind of proposition to which they are applied, is not difficult to see. ...Let us call the sort of truth which is applicable to φa "*first truth.*" ... Consider now the proposition $(x). \varphi x$. If this has truth of the sort appropriate to it, that will mean that every value of φx has "first truth." Thus if we call the sort of truth that is appropriate to $(x). \varphi x$ "*second* truth," we may define "$\{(x). \varphi x\}$ has second truth" as meaning "every value for $\varphi \hat{x}$ has first truth," i.e., "$(x). (\varphi x$ has first truth)." (Russell 1903)

This is unquestionably a recursion. Extrapolating, we arrive at the following:

[$\sim p$] is true $=df$ p is not true

[$p \vee q$] is true $=df$ Either p is true or q is true

$[(\forall x_1)(\forall x_2)...(\forall x_n)\varphi^{1. \ a;e.1}(x_1, x_2, ..., x_n)]$ is $true_{1.n+a;e.1}$

$=df$ For all x_1, $[(\forall x_2)...(\forall x_n)) \varphi^{1. \ a;e.1}((x_1, x_2, ..., x_n)]$ is $true_{1.n+a-1;e.1}$

In cases where subordinate occurrences of quantifiers occur, *Principia* intends the following:

$[(x)\varphi x \vee p]$ is $true_n$ $=df$ $(x)(\varphi x \vee p)$ is $true_n$.

This is made possible by definitions such as

$(x)\varphi x \vee p =df (x)(\varphi x \vee p)$.

These definitions are set out in *Principia's* section *9.

Unfortunately, *Principia* only gave a sketch of its intended the recursive definition and does not explicitly apply it *wffs* with bound predicate variables. Whitehead and Russell simply write:

We use the symbol "$(x) . \varphi x$" to express the general judgment which asserts all judgments of the form "φx."

... And generally, in any judgment $(x) . \varphi x$ the sense in which this judgment is or may be true is not the same as that in which φx is or may be true. If φx is an elementary judgment, it is true when it points to a corresponding complex. But $(x) . \varphi x$ does not point to a single corresponding complex; the corresponding complexes are as numerous as the possible values of x. (1910: 46)

But we can readily imagine what the recursion would look like when applied to predicate variables. In a simple case we have:

$$[(\forall \varphi!^{1.a;e.1})(\forall x_1)(\forall x_2)...(\forall x_n)\varphi!^{1.a;\ e.1}(x_1, x_2, ..., x_n)] \text{ is}$$
$$true_{2.1;\ 1.n+a;\ e.1} = df$$

For all *wffs*, A capable of being $true_{1.a;e.1}$,

$$[(\forall x_1)(\forall x_2)...(\forall x_n) \text{ A}(x_1, x_2, ..., x_n)] \text{ is } true_{2.1-1;\ 1.n+a;\ e.1}$$

It should be clear that Whitehead and Russell intend the recursive theory to apply only to *wffs* of *Principia*. When they speak of the truth conditions for a 'general judgment', they intend a *wff* such as $(x)\varphi x$. They do not mean a statement such as 'Othello believes that $(x)\varphi x$'.

The multiple-relation theory employs Russell's theory of definite descriptions. This is clear from two passages. The first is in *Principia* itself (Whitehead and Russell 1910: 44):

> Owing to the plurality of the objects of a single judgment, it follows that what we call a "proposition" (in the sense in which this is distinguished from the phrase expressing it) is not a single entity at all. That is to say, the phrase which expresses a proposition is what we call an "incomplete" symbol*; it does not have meaning in itself, but requires some supplementation in order to acquire a complete meaning. (Whitehead and Russell 1910: 44)

The asterisk * marks a footnote to *Principia*'s Chapter III devoted to the theory of definite descriptions. The second passage is in Russell's early paper 'On the Nature of Truth', where we find the following:

> This is an extension of the principle applied in my article "On Denoting" (Mind, October, 1905), where it is pointed out that such propositions as "the King of France is bald" contain no constituent corresponding to the phrase "the King of France." (Russell 1907: 49*fn*)

Admittedly, *Principia* is not explicit about exactly how the theory of descriptions is to be used. But it seems clear enough that the plan is to form a definite description of a fact that would, if the statement is true, correspond to a given judgment fact made by the mind of a person making a discursive judgment. On this interpretation, when an atomic *wff*, say '*a* R *b*' is flanked by 'is true' it is a disguised definite description of the form

$$(\imath f)(m\text{-judging-}\begin{pmatrix} a \\ R \\ b \end{pmatrix} \text{ corresponds to } f).$$

Here we have

$$m\text{-judging-}\begin{pmatrix} a \\ R \\ b \end{pmatrix}$$

as the judgment-fact of the mind of the person making the discursive judgment. In this way, 'truth' and 'falsehood' for atomic *wff*s are defined thus:

$$[a \text{ R } b] \text{ is } true^m =df \text{ E! } (\imath f)(m\text{-judging-}\begin{pmatrix} a \\ R \\ b \end{pmatrix} \text{ corresponds to } f)$$

$$[a \text{ R } b] \text{ is } false^m =df \text{ ~E! } (\imath f)(m\text{-judging-}\begin{pmatrix} a \\ R \\ b \end{pmatrix} \text{ corresponds to } f).$$

In our example, we see that the definition of 'truth' is a direct application of Russell's theory of definite descriptions. Notice that the expression '*m*-judging-$\begin{pmatrix} a \\ R \\ b \end{pmatrix}$' is a term, not a *wff*. The definite description describes the would-be corresponding fact *f*. According to the simple version of the theory set out in *Principia*, if there exists such a [1910]fact *f*, then it is true that *a* bears R to *b*. If there is no such [1910]fact *f*, then it is false that *a* bears R to *b*. Of course, it is assumed that to say that a discursive judgment complex *m*-judging-$\begin{pmatrix} a \\ R \\ b \end{pmatrix}$ corresponds to a [1910]fact *f* is to say that there is a fact *f*, namely, '*a*-R-*b*,' consisting of *a* , *b* and R in a proper order.

The multiple-relation theory serves only as the *base* case of *Principia's* recursive definition of the truth-conditions for its atomic *wff*s. Critics of *Principia's* recursion object that Russell's multiple-relation theory should have given us the judgment facts that are operative as a *truth-bearers* in cases where it is true that ~(*a* R *b*) and when it is true that (*x*)(*x* R *b*) and so forth. Critics demand that the multiple-relation theory is committed to doing this, for it is committed to the position that truth is to be defined in terms of correspondence between a judgment (or belief) and one (or more) facts. So far as *Principia* is concerned, however, we only get the judgment fact that is the truth-bearer when a mind *m* makes a discursive judgment of an atomic *wff*.

In order to reply to this objection, we need to find the judgment-facts that are truth bearers in the complicated cases. Finding the *truth-bearers* in such cases is tantamount to discerning how Russell may have imagined his multiple-relation theory to apply to find the facts that are the *truth-makers* for ascriptions of propositional attitudes such as the following:

Othello judges that ~(*aRb*)

Othello judges that $aRb \lor dSe$

Othello judges that $(x)(xRb)$.

What judgment fact is the truth-maker that exists when it is true that Othello judges that that $\sim(aRb)$? The truth-maker for the propositional attitude ascription is just the sort of judgment-fact that is the truth-bearer we need for a definition of $\sim(aRb)$ $true^m$. What judgment fact is the truth-maker that exists when it is true that Othello judges that $aRb \lor dSe$? The truth-maker for this ascription is what we seek as the truth-bearer in defining $[aRb \lor dSe]$ $true^m$. Similarly, what judgment-fact is the truth-maker that exists when it is true that Othello judges that $(x)(xRb)$? The truth-maker for the propositional attitude is just the sort of truth-bearer we need to define $[(x)(xRb)]$ is $true^m$.

But answering questions in the philosophy of mind was certainly not the purpose of *Principia*. When Othello judges that $(x)(xRb)$ there exists judgment-fact of some sort— it is of a sort that remains (to this day) a mystery for every theory of mind. Russell was not unaware, however, that he requires an epistemology of logic. There is no epistemology of ^{cp}logic to be found in *Principia*. But Russell began to develop an epistemology of logic in the *Problems of Philosophy* and in his 1913 unfinished manuscript *Theory of Knowledge*. It is here that we shall find ample hints that reveal the trajectory Russell was heading when it comes to truth-bearers.

4 Thou Shalt *Not* Undermine *Principia's* Recursive Definition

Russell's conception of ^{1910}facts persists throughout *Problems*. The discussion of facts always involves the quest to provide a theory of the truth-makers for statements that do *not* involve ascriptions of propositional attitudes. Moreover, all the ^{1910}facts that are truth-makers are logically independent. This logical independence of the ^{1910}facts that are truth-makers follows immediately from *Principia's* recursive definition of 'truth' and 'falsehood'. This leaves open, however, whether there may be other sorts of logically interdependent facts—facts that are not truth-makers.

Russell never explicitly took up the problem of providing truth-conditions for statements ascribing propositional attitudes. But in *Theory of Knowledge* there are ample hints. The hints arise because Russell takes up the question of what *logical objects* of acquaintance are involved when we understand logic. Russell was concerned to provide a theory which explains our understanding of the logical notions of *predication, fact, dual fact (complex), universal, particular, all, some, or, and, not*, etc. If our understanding of these notions is to be explained in terms of our acquaintance with something, then Russell felt that there must be something in his ontology which provides for such objects of logical acquaintance. Russell provisionally identifies them with what he calls 'abstract fully general facts' and this warrants our use of the expression [1913]facts. One thing is absolutely clear and very important. No [1910–13]fact contains an ontological analog of the logical particles 'or', 'and', 'not', 'all', 'some', etc. Russell writes that '… a molecular form is not even the form of any actual particular' no particular, however complex, has the form 'this or that' or the form 'not-this' (Russell 1913: 132). This is central to Russell's thinking, and it is quite natural that it should be central.

Abstract general facts are not themselves truth-makers for general statements. If they were, they would undermine *Principia*'s recursive definition of 'truth' and 'falsehood'. Abstract fully general facts are introduced as logical objects to account for our acquaintance involved when we understand notions such as *universal, dual complex, relation*, and the logical particles. Moreover, it is also clear from *Theory of Knowledge* that abstract fully general facts have *no* constituents. Russell wrote:

> …the logical nature of this fact is very peculiar. For 'something has the relation *R* to something' contains no constituents except *R*; and 'something has some relation to something' contains no constituents at all. In a sense, it is simple, since it cannot be analyzed. At first sight, it seems to have a structure, and therefore not to be simple, but it is more correct to say that it *is* a structure. (1913: 114)

It is perhaps easy to lampoon Russell's experimental endorsement of abstract *fully* general facts with no constituents in his effort to say that by acquaintance with such facts we are assured of an *understanding* of logical notions. How, after all, can a complex have no constituents? But it is quite another matter to imagine a theory that accounts for our understanding of logic (and mathematics). Even today there is yet no viable theory of how to render such an account—behaviorist and functionalist philosophies of mind (as well as Russell's own quasi-behaviorist neutral monist account of the 1920's) have been dismal failures when it comes to such matters.

Russell's experiment with general facts was extended liberally in his *Logical Atomism* lectures. He now entertains not only abstract fully general [1913]facts, but also general [1917]facts (that **do** have constituents). Moreover, he entertains negative [1917]facts. All the while, Russell adamantly cautions his readers that no [1913–17]facts contain ontological counterparts of logical particles. Russell is explicit in the following passage of his lectures:

> ...the components of the fact which makes a proposition true or false, as the case may be, are the meanings of the symbols which we must understand in order to understand the proposition. That is not absolutely correct, but it will enable you to understand my meaning. One reason it fails of correctness is that it does not apply to words which, like "or" and "not," are parts of propositions without corresponding to any part of the corresponding facts. (Russell 1917: 196)

A very unfortunate consequence of Russell's experiments was that, since few readers were aware of *Principia's* recursive definitions of 'truth' and 'falsehood', many readers imagined general facts and negative facts to themselves be truth-makers containing analogs of the logical particles. Indeed, negative facts do not contain an ontological analog of 'not'. We must keep it squarely in mind that Russell intended for his experiments in *Theory of Knowledge* and in the *Logical Atomism* lectures to be consistent with *Principia's* recursive definitions.

5 Permutation and Type* Distinctions

A serious problem vexed the multiple-relation theory in its role in *Principia*. The problem, named the 'narrow direction problem' by Griffin (1980), is the problem of determining what makes a given judgment-fact point to a specific sort of would-be fact when different such facts *can* exist consisting of the very same constituents in a different order. In order to grasp the problem and the nature of Russell's proposed solution, we must understand that Russell is *not* attempting to give an ontological account of the structure (order) of facts. He has assumed from the onset that [1910]facts, whether they be judgment-facts (or belief-facts) or otherwise, are structured entities and that the structure is due to a property or relation occurring predicatively (as it were) in the [1910]fact. There is no deeper account of order than this anywhere in Russell's philosophy.

Now consider the following informal example of an attempt to apply the multiple-relation theory to render the truth-conditions for the atomic *wff* '*a* loves *b*'. We have:

$$[a \text{ loves } b] \text{ is } true^m \ =df$$

$$E!(\imath f)(\ m\text{-judging-}\begin{pmatrix} a \\ R \\ b \end{pmatrix} \text{ corresponds to } f)$$

In cases where the minds *a* and *b* feel the same about each other, there are two [1910]facts whose constituents are composed of *a* and *b* and '*loves*'. There are both of the following:

a's loving *b*

b's loving a.

This leads to a difficult problem. In virtue of what does the judgment fact m-judging-$\left(\begin{smallmatrix} a \\ R \\ b \end{smallmatrix}\right)$ point to specifically to 'a's loving b' as the fact that corresponds to it? This is the narrow direction problem. And indeed, it is a very difficult problem, for a judgment fact must point to a specific *would-be* [1910]fact even if there is no fact at all to which it points.

In the *Problems of Philosophy* Russell endeavored to solve this problem by appeal to order isomorphism between the constituents of a part of a judgment (or belief or understanding) fact and order of the constituents of the would-be corresponding fact. Russell explains this thesis by giving the truth-conditions for the false statement 'Desdemona loves Cassio'. In his example, Russell employs a belief-fact and this belief-fact is one made by Othello. Russell writes:

> Thus, e.g., if Othello believes *truly* that Desdemona loves Cassio, then there is a complex unity, 'Desdemonia's love for Cassio', which is composed exclusively of the *objects* of the belief, in the same order as they had in the belief, with the relation which was one of the objects occurring now as the cement that binds together the other objects of the belief. On the other hand, when a belief is *false*, there is no such complex unity composed only of the object of the belief. If Othello believes *falsely* that Desdemona loves Cassio, then there is no such complex unity as 'Desdemona's love for Cassio'. (1912a: 128)

This order isomorphism to part of the belief-fact is easy to depict by drawing structural *maps* of the [1910]facts involved. We have:

$$o\text{-}B \overset{\displaystyle d}{\underset{\displaystyle c}{\longrightarrow}} loves \qquad \overset{\displaystyle d}{\underset{\displaystyle c}{\Longleftarrow}} loves$$

It is important to understand that the [1910]fact d's loving c is *not* a constituent of the belief-fact of o's believing with respect to d and *loves* and c. If it were its constituent, then there would exist such a fact as d's loving c simply in virtue of the existence of the belief. In the map (above) there is a partial isomorphism of the structural ordering of the constituents. For instance d is on the short leg and c is on the longer leg. It is in virtue of this that d's loving c is the would-be corresponding [1910]fact. Compare the situation with o's believing with respect to c and *loves* and d. We have:

$$o\text{-}B \overset{\displaystyle c}{\underset{\displaystyle d}{\longrightarrow}} loves \qquad \overset{\displaystyle c}{\underset{\displaystyle d}{\Longleftarrow}} loves$$

In this case, the ordering of the constituents is different. As we can see in the map (above) it is c that is on the shorter leg and d that is on the longer. In virtue of this ordering the would-be corresponding fact is c's loving d.

In *Theory of Knowledge*, Russell reveals that he is dissatisfied with the solution to the problem he had advanced in *Problems*. Such maps employ features that do not have ontological analogs: a short leg versus a long leg, or a *hook* at one end of the relation and an *eye* at another, or ontological analogs of the linguistic ordering of the expressions 'd' and 'c' in the name of the judgment-fact.[17] In *Theory of Knowledge*, Russell is searching for some way to render a definite description of the would-be corresponding fact which captures the specific ordering of its constituents.

Russell assumes that when a relation such as 'loves' occurs in a ^{1910}fact in a way that it relates the constituent of the ^{1910}fact, it generates position relations that the other constituents have to the ^{1910}fact. Thus for example, in the ^{1910}fact

a's loving b

the relation *loves* generates a position that a has in the fact and a different position that b has in the ^{1910}fact. If we call these position relations C_1^{loves} and C_2^{loves}, we can say that a bears C_1^{loves} to a's loving b. And similarly, b bears C_2^{loves} to a's loving b. By appealing to the position relations C_1^{loves} and C_2^{loves}, Russell endeavors to find a definite description of the fact a's loving b which captures the ordering that the constituents a, *loves*, and b have in the ^{1910}fact.

In *TK*, Russell is searching for some way to render a definite description of the would-be corresponding fact which captures the specific ordering of its constituents. Russell explains:

> We may now generalize this solution, without any essential change. Let γ be a complex whose constituents are x_1, x_2, ..., x_n and a relating relation R. Then each of these constituents has a certain relation to the complex. We may omit the consideration of R, which obviously has a peculiar position. The relations of x_1, x_2, ..., x_n to γ are their "positions" in the complex; let use call them C_1, C_2, ..., C_n. As soon as R is given, but not before, the n relations C_1, C_2, ..., C_n are determinate, though unless R is non-permutative, it will not be determinate which of the constituents has which of the relations....
>
> ... It is to be observed that the relations C_1, C_2, ..., C_n are not determined by the general form, but only by the relation R...

---

[17]See Russell 1913: 86.

$C_1, C_2, \ldots, C_n$ are a system of relations, determinate when R is given, but requiring to be simply recognized in each case, and not describable in general terms. When $C_1, C_2, \ldots, C_n$ are given, conversely, R is determinate. Thus our complex γ can be described, unambiguously without mentioning R, as simply "the complex γ in which $x_1 C_1 \gamma, x_2 C_2 \gamma, \ldots,$ and $x_n C_n \gamma$." (1913: 146)

Russell goes on to offer the symbolic expression as well, namely:

$$(\iota\gamma)(x_1 C_1 \gamma \,\&\, x_2 C_2 \gamma, \ldots, \& \, x_n C_n \gamma).$$

According to *Theory of Knowledge*, we have the following:

$$a \text{ loves } b \supset E!(\iota f)(\, a \; C_1^{loveso} f \,\& \, b \; C_2^{loveso} f).$$

This is Russell's solution of narrow direction problem.

One might naturally ask, however, whether a regress will occur when it comes to giving truth conditions for '$a \; C_1^{loveso} f$' and for '$b \; C_2^{loveso} f$'. There is no reason to fear that a regress will occur. There is no reason to fear a regress because Russell thinks that in such a case the simple version of the multiple-relation theory will suffice. That is, we can put:

$$[a \; C_1^{loveso} f] \; true^m =_{df} E!(\iota g)(\; m\text{-believing-}\!\left(c_1^{\genfrac{}{}{0pt}{}{a}{loves}}_{f}\right) \text{ corresponds to } g)$$

One might insist. Why is it that Russell thinks that we don't have the very same narrow direction problem arising here? Russell's answer is that the [1910]fact g described above, namely

$$a\text{-in-the-relation-}C_1^{loveso}\text{-to-}a\text{'s loving } b$$

is not *permutative*. It is not possible for a fact such as a's loving b to occupy a position in a (if it is not a complex). The regress is stopped by a distinction in type* between *permutative* and *non-permutative* [1910]facts. Thus, we see that the viability of Russell's account stands or falls on whether he can give a philosophical ground for his distinction between permutative and non-permutative facts.

We shall take up the problem of defining *permutation* in our next sections. For the present, however, let us note that we are now in a position to extrapolate from what Russell says in *Theory of Knowledge* to find a theory of the *truth-makers* for ascriptions of propositional attitudes. Moreover, we saw that in *Principia*, the multiple relation theory applies only to the base case (the atomic case) of a recursive definition of 'truth' as applied to the *wffs* of the work. Critics wanted to know the judgment or belief-fact that is the *truth-bearer* in the complicated cases. We can now readily find them. Consider the following:

m believes that $a\ R\ b \supset$

$$E!(\iota f)(\ m\ C_1^{belief}\ f\ \&\ Rel^2\ C_2^{belief}\ f\ \&\ a\ C_3^{belief}\ f\ \&\ R\ C_4^{belief}\ f\ \&\ b\ C_5^{belief}\ f\ ).$$

The truth-maker is the belief-fact f, which, if it were it to exist, can be named with this:

$$m\text{-believing-}\begin{pmatrix} Re\ 2 \\ a \\ R \\ b \end{pmatrix}.$$

Russell's account, suggested in *Theory of Knowledge*, introduces the entity Rel^2 (though he doesn't use this notation) which is the logical form of a dyadic complex—the form of the would-be dyadic fact a-R-b. This raises the difficult issue of what sort of entity Rel^2 is. Russell decides that, for the time being, it can be provisionally identified as the following abstract fully general fact

Something's being related to something.[18]

Of course, if m believes *truly* then it is true that $a\ R\ b$. Thus, we also have:

m believes that $b\ R\ a \supset$

$$E!(\iota f)(\ m\ C_1^{belief}f\ \&\ Rel^2\ C_2^{belief}f\ \&\ b\ C_3^{belief}f\ \&\ R\ C_4^{belief}f\ \&\ aC_5^{belief}f)$$

The belief-fact f, were it to exist, is this:

$$m\text{-believing-}\begin{pmatrix} Re\ 2 \\ b \\ R \\ a \end{pmatrix}.$$

These are different facts because they are different structures. So far so good.

But the cases become ever more seriously complicated. Perhaps one of Russell's most famous principles is his thesis concerning acquaintance. In the days in which Russell embraced an ontology of [1905]propositions, Russell wrote:

> ...in every proposition what we can apprehend (i.e., not only in those whose truth or falsehood we can judge of, but in all that we can think about), all the constituents are really entities with which we have immediate acquaintance. (1905: 56)

And in *Problems* he writes:

---

[18]See Russell 1913: 114.

Every proposition which we understand must be composed wholly of constituents with which we are acquainted. (1912a: 58)

Of course, from *Principia* on, there are no [1903, 1905, 1907] propositions. So clearly Russell meant to speak of the statements which we understand. In any case, what then are the constituents with which we are acquainted in believing that $\sim(a\ R\ b)$ or in believing that aRb or dSe, or in believing $(z)(z\ R\ b)$, and so on?

Consider the problem of giving truth conditions for 'M believes that $\sim(a\ R\ b)$.' Perhaps Russell wants the following:

m believes that $\sim(a\ R\ b)\ \supset$

$$E!(\imath f)(\ m\ C_1^{belief}f\ \&\ Rel^2\ C_2^{belief}f\ \&\ \text{NOT}\ C_3^{belief}f\ \&\ a\ C_4^{belief}f\ \&$$
$$R\ C_4^{belief}f\ \&\ b\ C_5^{belief}f)$$

If there is such a fact f, it is this:

$$m\text{-believing-}\begin{pmatrix}Rel^2\\ NOT\\ a\\ R\\ b\end{pmatrix}.$$

A constituent of this fact is the logical form NOT. Presumably, Russell would identify the logical object NOT with an abstract fully general fact, though it is far from clear what such a fact could be. It is acquaintance with this logical object that enables a mind to understand logical *negation* of this sort.

With this in place, we can finally reply to those critics of *Principia's* recursive definition of 'truth' who wanted the multiple-relation theory to offer truth conditions in such a way that there is always a belief-fact presented as a *truth-bearer* which is to correspond, or fail to correspond, to one or more facts. We have:

$$[\sim(a\ R\ b)]\ true^m =_{df}$$
$$(\imath f)(\ m\ C_1^{belief}f\ \&\ Rel^2\ C_2^{belief}f\ \&\ \text{NOT}\ C_3^{belief}f\ \&\ a\ C_4^{belief}f\ \&$$
$$R\ C_4^{belief}f\ \&\ b\ C_5^{belief}f)\ \text{is true.}$$

Of course, f is the belief-fact

$$m\text{-believing-}\begin{pmatrix}Rel^2\\ NOT\\ a\\ R\\ b\end{pmatrix}.$$

This belief-fact is our truth-bearer. We have the following:

$$(\imath f)(\ m\ C_1^{belief}f\ \&\ Rel^2\ C_2^{belief}f\ \&\ \text{NOT}\ C_3^{belief}f\ \&$$

$$a\ C_4^{belief}f\ \&\ R\ C_4^{belief}f\ \&\ b\ C_5^{belief}f)\ \text{is true} =_{df}$$

$$E!(\imath f)(\ m\ C_1^{belief}f\ \&\ Rel^2\ C_2^{belief}f\ \&\ \text{NOT}\ C_3^{belief}f\ \&\ a\ C_4^{belief}f\ \&$$
$$R\ C_4^{belief}f\ \&\ b\ C_5^{belief}f)\ \&\ \sim E!(\imath g)(a\ C_1^R\ g\ \&\ b\ C_2^R\ g).$$

In short, the truth-bearer is m-believing-$\begin{pmatrix} Re\ 2 \\ NO \\ a \\ R \\ b \end{pmatrix}$, and what makes it true is

the absence of there being any fact g such that $a\ C_1^R\ g\ \&\ b\ C_2^R\ g$. Nothing here requires the existence of an obscure entity that is a fact with negation as relating relation. *Principia's* recursion is intact.

Similar issues arise for the other logical connectives. To find truth-bearers, we need first to be able to understand how the multiple-relation theory applies to an ascription of a propositional attitude such as '*M* believes that aRb or dSe'. Obviously, it will not be viable to say that '*M* believes that aRb or dSe' is true *iff* either *M* believes that aRb or *M* believes that dSe. *Principia's* recursive definitions of 'truth' and 'falsehood' cannot apply in such cases.[19] *M* is clearly entertaining *disjunction* as a part of the content of his belief. But there are no disjunctive facts as truth-makers. Once again we can easily extrapolate from what Russell says in *Theory of Knowledge* to arrive at the account that he likely imagined. Consider the following:

m believes that aRb v dSe $\supset$

$$E!(\imath f)(\ m\ C_1^{belief}f\ \&\ Or\ C_2^{belief}f\ \&\ Rel^2\ a\ C_3^{belief}f\ \&\ R\ C_4^{belief}f\ \&\ b$$
$$C_5^{belief}f\ \&\ Rel^2\ C_6^{belief}f\ \&\ d\ C_7^{belief}f\ \&\ S\ C_8^{belief}f\ \&\ e\ C_9^{belief}f).$$

The [1910] fact described and said to exist as the truth-maker for the propositional attitude ascription is this:

$$m\text{-believing-}\begin{pmatrix} Or \\ Re\ 2 \\ a \\ R \\ b \\ Rel^2 \\ d \\ S \\ e \end{pmatrix}$$

This, in turn, is the truth-bearer we need for the following:

$[aRb$ v $dSe]\ true^m =_{df}$

---

[19] See Griffin 1980.

$(\imath f)(\ m\ C_1^{belief}f\ \&\ Or\ C_2^{belief}f\ \&\ Rel^2\ a\ C_3^{belief}f\ \&\ R\ C_4^{belief}f\ \&\ b\ C_5^{belief}f\ \&\ Rel^2\ C_6^{belief}f\ \&\ d\ C_7^{belief}f\ \&\ S\ C_8^{belief}f\ \&\ e\ C_9^{belief}f)$ is true.

And we have:

$(\imath f)(\ m\ C_1^{belief}f\ \&\ Or\ C_2^{belief}f\ \&\ Rel^2\ a\ C_3^{belief}f\ \&\ R\ C_4^{belief}f\ \&\ b\ C_5^{belief}f\ \&\ Rel^2\ C_6^{belief}f\ \&\ d\ C_7^{belief}f\ \&\ S\ C_8^{belief}f\ \&\ e\ C_9^{belief}f)$ is true $=df$

$E!(\imath f)(\ m\ C_1^{belief}f\ \&\ Or\ C_2^{belief}f\ \&\ Rel^2\ a\ C_3^{belief}f\ \&\ R\ C_4^{belief}f\ \&\ b\ C_5^{belief}f\ \&\ Rel^2\ C_6^{belief}f\ \&\ d\ C_7^{belief}f\ \&\ S\ C_8^{belief}f\ \&\ e\ C_9^{belief}f)\ .\&.\ E!(\imath g)(a\ C_1^{R}\ g\ \&\ b\ C_2^{R}\ g)\ \vee\ E!(\imath g)(d\ C_1^{S}\ g\ \&\ e\ C_2^{S}\ g).$

M believes truly just when it is true that aRb or dSe. *Principia's* recursive theory comes into play. The recursion tells us that it is true that $aRb \vee dSe$ *iff* either it is true that aRb or it is true that dSe. No fact contains Or⁻ as a relating relation. There are no disjunctive facts as truth-makers. Thus, we have finally found our truth-bearer.

We saw that Russell is quite explicit in *Theory of Knowledge* that no fact contains an ontological counterpart of *any* logical particle. M's belief-fact does contain Or⁻ as a constituent. But that is quite a different matter. The logical form Or⁻ is a logical object, acquaintance with which grounds M's understanding of the concept of logical *disjunction*. In *Theory of Knowledge*, Russell would identify the logical object Or⁻ with an abstract *fully* general [1913] fact. As with all abstract fully general facts, the fact Or has no constituents.

We are beginning to see, however, that a new and very serious problem that arises concerning logical forms. But this problem is *not* the narrow direction problem. The problem is that a proliferation of logical forms seem to be needed to accommodate every new case. When a mind believes that $aRb \vee \sim dSe$ as opposed to believing that $\sim aRb \vee dSe$ a new logical form for Or⁻ seems to be required. We have Or⁻ᵒᵗ as well as ⁿᵒᵗ⁻ Or⁻. Semantic compositionality is lost in such an account.

The problem of semantic compositionality becomes far worse when we consider the truth-conditions for a statement such as 'M believes that $(x)(x\ R\ b)$'. There has to be some way to find a cognitive analogue of the syntax of variable binding. We might try the following:

m believes that $(x)(x\ R\ b) \supset$

$E!(\imath f)(\ m\ C_1^{belief}f\ \&\ All\text{-}x\text{-}Rel^2\ C_2^{belief}f\ \&\ R\ C_3^{belief}f\ \&\ b\ C_4^{belief}f\ ).$

Here we have the logical object *All-x-Rel²* identified as a fully general abstract fact. This would then be distinct from

   m believes that $(x)(b\ R\ x) \supset$

$$E!(\mathit{f})(\ M\ C_1^{belief}f\ \&\ \textit{All-Rel}^2\ \text{-}x\ C_2^{belief}f\ \&\ b\ C_3^{belief}f\ \&\ R\ C_4^{belief}f\ ).$$

Here we have *All-Rel²* –x which is to be identified with a different fully general fact. Notice that the issue of permutation does not arise here. The order in the belief-facts of the constituents is different.

   The narrow direction problem is not of issue. The direction problem is adequately resolved by the position relations.[20] There is, however, a serious problem. It is the problem that Russell's account has abandoned semantic compositionality and without this feature it is very difficult to imagine how to recover the syntactic feature of variable binding especially in cases such as $(x)(d\ R\ x\ \&\ c\ S\ x)$ where multiple bound variables occur in different positions. When the multiple-relation theory is applied to ascriptions of propositional attitudes, a horrific proliferation of logical forms emerges. Semantic compositional demands that these logical forms be interdependent. But if they are identified with fully general abstract facts with no constituents, this seems hopeless.

   The case of quantification is particularly important to solve. Indeed, in our quest for *truth-bearers*, we find that solving the quantificational case is relevant to the original direction problem that arose when Russell endeavored to provide the truth-conditions for permutative cases such as '*d* loves *c*'. Recall that the solution in *Theory of Knowledge* was this:

$$d\ \text{loves}\ c \supset E!(\mathit{f})(\ d\ C_1^{lovesof}\ \&\ c\ C_2^{lovesof}) .$$

This tells us the truth-maker assuring that *d* loves *c*. To find the truth-*bearer,* however, we need to investigate the truth conditions for the ascription of a propositional attitude such as 'Othello believes that *d* loves *c*'. According to Russell's account, the belief-fact that is the truth-maker involves a cognition of quantification. Othello, in believing that Desdemona loves Cassio, is believing that there is a (unique) fact *f* such that $d\ C_1^{lovesof}$ & $c\ C_2^{lovesof}$. Othello's belief is, therefore, a quantificational belief.[21] On Russell's theory, the following are apparently interchangeable:

   Othello believes that *d* loves *c*

---

[20]For a discussion of the so called 'wide-direction' problem and Wittgenstein's criticisms, see Landini 2007.

[21]Note that for convenience of exposition we are omitting the complication that 'Desdemona' and 'Cassio' must be replace by definite descriptions and thus involve further quantificational thinking.

Othello believes $E!(\imath f)(\, d\ C_1^{loves\,o} f\ \&\ c\ C_2^{loves\,o} f)$.

Othello believes $(\exists f)(d\ C_1^{loves\,o} g\ \&\ c\ C_2^{loves}\ g\ .\equiv_g.\ g = f)$.

Thus, the treatment of the quantification case becomes of utmost importance to finding the truth-bearer involved when endeavoring to provide a definition for [d loves c] is $true^m$.

Russell was not unaware of the difficulty. In *Theory of Knowledge* he wrote:

> Where permutative complexes are concerned, our process of obtaining associated non-permutative complexes was rather elaborate, and no doubt open to objection... This seems to demand a mode of analyzing molecular propositions which requires the admission that they may contain false atomic propositions as constituents, therefore to demand the admission of false propositions in an objective sense. This is a real difficulty, but as it belongs to the theory of molecular propositions we will not consider it further at present. (1913: 154)

Russell's statement of the problem is rather infelicitous in its use of the word 'proposition'. But what seems clear enough is that he recognizes that his solution to the narrow direction problem ultimately requires him to solve the formidable difficulties of finding the judgment or belief-facts that are the truth-makers for ascriptions of molecular and quantificational propositional attitudes.

Thought seems to defy analysis. We must appreciate the difficulty of the task which confronted Russell. The richness of the content of a mental life knows no poetic bounds and even dallies with contradiction:

> Othello: By the world, I think my wife be honest, and I think she is not; I think thou are just and I think thou are not. I'll have some proof.
>
> Iago: In sleep I heard him say: "Sweet Desdemona let us be wary, let us hide our loves" ... 'Tis a shrewd doubt though it be but a dream: and this may serve to thicken other proofs that do demonstrate thinly.

What is reason that its contents may include thinking *d loves c* and thinking *d* does not love *c*. How can thought engage 'objects' such as round-squares, existent golden mountains, and non-existent loves? We shouldn't be too very hard on Russell's efforts.

Nevertheless, the loss of semantic compositionality is serious. It has to be recovered if Russell's multiple-relation theory is to be viable. To recover semantic compositionality, it would seem that the Russellian objects of acquaintance (logical forms) involved in the understanding of a complex (quantificational) statement would have to *fit together* in a way that tracks the syntactic rules governing the composition of statements. On the theory of logical forms of *Theory of Knowledge*, a theory which identifies them (albeit only provisionally) as abstract general facts with no constituents, this *fitting together* is quite impossible. Logical forms (understood as entities with no constituents) cannot 'fit together'. One needn't despair, however. It is quite possible to repair this aspect of *Theory of Knowledge* by abandoning Russell's experimental identification of logical forms with abstract fully general facts with no constituents. Russell was never wedded to this identification, and surely there are no such facts. Semantic compositionality would be recovered by the elimination of variables— the sort of elimination found in Quine's 'Variables Explained Away'.[22] We shall leave this for further development in another paper.[23] The main lesson here is that we must not conflate the narrow direction problem with the quite distinct problem of recovering semantic compositionality.

6   Permutation and Types*

Types* are not types. There is no tension whatsoever between *Principia*'s type free ontology and Russell's use of type* distinctions to ground distinction between permutative and non-permutative facts in *Theory of Knowledge*. Types* have nothing to do with *Principia*'s simple-type regimented language. [24] And types* are certainly not types of attributes (or universals or so called 'propositional functions'). The narrow direction problem was fully addressed (in principle) in *Theory of Knowledge* without any conflict with *Principia*.

It worth observing that Russell embraced a logical type* distinction as early as *Principles*. He accepted a logical difference between a universal and a 'thing'. Universals have a two-fold nature. In occurring 'as concept' they account for the unity of a [1903-07]proposition, and they are also *individuals* that can occur in a [1903-07]proposition as logical subject. Similarly, when Russell embraced [1910]facts, universals account for the unity of the [1910]fact by occurring in them predicationally, and they are also individuals which can occur in [1910]facts as such. But the type* difference between a universal and a particular (thing), though it is a *logical* difference, is *not* a feature represented in the type-regimented grammar of logic *Principia*. Restoring simple-type indices, atomic two-place *wffs* of *Principia* of lowest type would look like this

$$\varphi^{(o,o)}(x^{o}, y^{o})$$

---

[22]See Quine 1960.
[23]See Landini 2014, forthcoming.
[24]Important concerns with Russell's introduction of type* distinctions are found in Pierdaniele Giaretta 1997.

The predicate variable $\varphi^{(0,\ 0)}$ does *not* represent the position of a universal in a dual [1913]fact. The formal logic of *Principia* treats universals and particulars alike as logical subjects (values of the individual variables of type 0). The notion of types* introduced in *Theory of Knowledge*, however, goes beyond just the distinction between universal and particular. This notion of type* is caught up more fully in the notion of what is *possible*.

Type* distinctions force Russell to speak of possibilities. He must speak of *possibilities* in defining what it is for a [1910]fact to be permutative. Let's suppose that there exists the [1910]fact of Desdemona's loving Othello. Now this fact is permutative because it is *possible* for there to be a fact (even if there is no such fact) composed of the very same constituents, namely Desdemona, *loves* and Othello, but in a different order (with Othello loving Desdemona). We are inclined to speak as if this is the [1910]fact of Othello's possibly loving Desdemona. But obviously, no non-existent entities have the property of being possible. Russell's task is to offer an account of what it is for a would-be [1910]fact to be possible without being ontologically committed to the [1910]fact in question. Moreover, we must ask whether the possibilities involved in type* distinctions are always logical possibilities or may they sometimes be contingent features of physics, biology, psychology, and the like.

Russell maintains that the notion of *possibility*, like the notion of *existence*, is often badly misunderstood. Russell articulated his position, restricted to first-order statements in his lectures on Logical Atomism (1917). But the view first appeared in a 1905 manuscript entitled 'Necessity and Possibility'.[25] It also occurs in Russell's paper 'On the Notion of Cause' (1911). So there is no doubt that he held the same view at the time of writing *Theory of Knowledge*. According to Russell, possibility comes in degrees, with the *summum genius* the notion of logical possibility. Let us take some examples. Consider the statement '*d* loves *c*'. Russell has the following:

Possible (d loves c) with respect to d and c $=df$ $(\exists x, y)(x \text{ loves } y)$

Russell acknowledges that this is a very weak notion of 'possibility'. A stronger notion is this:

Logically Possible (d loves c) $=df$ $(\exists R)(\exists x, y)(x\ R\ y)$.

In the above, we have assumed (without justification) that 'loves' is a relation that is not further analyzable. Moreover, it must be understood that Russell's analysis of possibility applies only to first-order *wffs* and applies only *after* the elimination of names definite descriptions, classes and all

---

[25]This paper was read to the Oxford Philosophical Society on 22 October 1905.

incomplete symbols has been performed. Consider, the statement 'Desdemona loves Cassio'. For Russell the ordinary proper names 'Desdemona' and 'Cassio' are to be replaced definite descriptions, say '$\iota x\mathrm{D}!x$' and '$\iota x\mathrm{C}!x$' respectively. Thus we have:

Possible ($\iota x\mathrm{D}!x$ loves $\iota x\mathrm{C}!x$) *wrt* $\iota x\mathrm{D}!x$ and $\iota x\mathrm{C}!x$ $=df$

$(\exists\varphi)(\exists\psi)(\ \iota x\varphi!x$ loves $\iota z\psi!z)$

i.e., $(\exists\varphi)(\exists\psi)(\exists x)(\ \varphi!z \equiv_z z = x$.&. $(\exists y)(\ \psi!z \equiv_z z = y$.&. x loves $y))$.

This is not yet the notion of *logical possibility*. To get to that notion, Russell maintains that we must have *full* generality in the language of logic where a complete analysis has been attained. That is much more difficult, especially because we may not yet know the truth-conditions of the concepts involved. (What, after all, is love?) But for the sake of the present discussion, let us suppose that 'loves' is a simple unanalyzable relation. We then have:

Logically Possible (Desdemona loves Cassio) $=df$

$(\exists R)(\exists\varphi)(\exists\psi)(\exists x)(\ \varphi!z \equiv_z z = x$.&. $(\exists y)(\ \psi!z \equiv_z z = y$.&. $x\,R\,y))$.

Logical possibility is a purely formal matter of truth and full generality, but it can only be assessed after a complete analysis. Once the analysis is complete, it is a notion that (for first order statements) parallels Tarski's formal semantic notion of truth in every interpretation.

Can this be of help in explaining what it means to say that the fact of Desdemona's loving Othello is permutative? For the sake of convenience, let us avoid the complications arising from definite descriptions and speak of d (Desdemona) and c (Cassio) and o (Othello) themselves. Observe that it would *not* be viable to put:

Permutative (d-loving-o) $=df$ Possible (o loves d) *wrt* o and d.

Some entities are facts, and there is a property of being *permutative* that holds, or fails to hold, of a fact. On Russell's analysis, there is no property of being 'possible' that an entity has. On Russell's analysis of possibility (and necessity) the expression '… is possible' attaches to *wffs*, not names. What we seek is a relationship between the property of being permutative and the Russellian analysis of the notion of possibility.

It may seem intuitive to speak of a dyadic relation R being permutative when the possibility of its exemplification yields two possible facts, namely a-R-b and b-R-a. But as good Russellians with a robust sense of reality, our account cannot invoke an ontology of possible, non-actual, facts. It does, however, seem intuitive to hold that acquaintance with a given (say) dyadic relation R may itself be sufficient to yield an understanding of whether the relation could be exemplified by entities x and y in such a way that [$x\,R\,y$ &

y Rx] is possible with respect to x and y. A logically asymmetric relation R one might say, can be known by acquaintance to be such that if x R y then $\sim(y$ R $x)$. Care must be taken however, since Russell is very much inclined to think that, when analysis is complete, the existence of any one fact is *logically* independent of the existence of any other. (This at least holds for facts that are truth-makers of *Principia's* recursive definition.) Since there are no negative [1910–1913] facts, we may safely express the logical asymmetry of a relation R with the logical truth of,

$$(x,y)(E!(\iota f)(x \ C_1^R f \& y \ C_2^R f) \supset \sim E!(\iota f)(y \ C_1^R f \& x \ C_2^R f)).$$

Acquaintance with the logically asymmetric relation R might yield such knowledge *a priori*. But caution is in order. In *Theory of Knowledge*, Russell observes that we cannot determine the positions a relation secures in a fact by the grammatical form of an expression expressing it. The expression 'x is similar to y' is two-placed, but Russell tells us that the relation 'similarity' is such that it generates only one position relation (Russell 1913: 122). If a is similar to b then both a and b occupy the *same* position in the fact a-S-b. The definite description of this fact is

$$(\iota f)(a \ C_1^S f \& b \ C_1^S f).$$

There cannot be two facts, namely, a-S-b and b-S-a, such that it is a logical truth that the existence of the one entails the existence of the other. Facts are logically independent. Now

$$E!(\iota f)(a \ C_1^S f \& b \ C_1^S f) \supset E!(\iota f)(b \ C_1^S f \& a \ C_1^S f)$$

is a logical truth due to the commutativity of logical addition. But such a statement does not conflict with the logical independence of facts as truth-makers. The same point applies to a relation of 'identity.'

In our effort to define permutation, we shall not begin with the notion of a *relation* being permutative. We shall define the notion of a fact being R permutative. The notion of a relation R being permutative can then be derivatively defined in terms of the possibility of there being a fact z such that z is R permutative.

Let us begin by defining the notion 'z is R^2 permutative'. Our definition is given for a dyadic relation R^2 but clearly can be extended to n-adic relations. We have:

$$z \text{ is } R^2 \text{ permutative } =_{df} \text{ fact } (z) \ \& \ (\exists x,y)(x \ C_1^{R^2} z \& y \ C_2^{R^2} z \ .\&.$$
$$E!(\iota g)(y \ C_1^{R^2} g \& x \ C_2^{R^2} g)).$$

It is easy to see that we have:

$(\exists x,y)(x\ R^2\ y\ \&\ y\ R^2\ x)$ iff $(\exists x,y)(\ x\ C_1{}^{R^2}\ x\text{-}R^2\text{-}y\ \&\ y\ C_2{}^{R^2}\ x\text{-}R^2\text{-}y\ .\&.$ $E!(\iota g)(\ y\ C_1{}^{R^2}\ g\ \&\ x\ C_2{}^{R^2}\ g)).$

Putting these two together, we have:

$(a\text{-}R^2\text{-}b)$ is R^2 permutative $.iff.$

fact$(a\text{-}R^2\text{-}b)$ $\&$ $(\exists x,y)(x\ R^2\ y\ \&\ y\ R^2\ x).$

Thus, for example,

d-loves-o is loves permutative.

Since some two people do love one another, we have

fact $(d$-loves-$o)$ $\&$ $(\exists x,y)(x$ loves $y\ \&\ y$ loves $x).$

Now recall that Russell has:

$[a\ R^2\ b\ \&\ b\ R^2\ a]$ is possible with respect to a and b $=df\ (\exists x,y)(x\ R^2\ y$
$\&\ y\ R^2\ x).$

Hence, our analysis yields

$(a\text{-}R^2\text{-}b)$ is R^2 permutative $.iff.$ fact $(a\text{-}R^2\text{-}b\ )\ \&\ [a\ R^2\ b\ \&\ b\ R^2\ a]$
is possible with respect to a and b.

In this way, we can allow a property of being permutative that applies to facts and yet link it to Russell's analysis of possibility.

It is important to note that permutativeness entails possibility, but it does not consist in bare possibilities. The well-formedness of both the expression '$x\ R^2\ y$' and the expression '$y\ R^2x$' is certainly not sufficient to establish the existence of any fact and certainly not sufficient to establish permutativeness. As we have defined it, permutativeness is a property of a fact. In the case of Desdemona and Cassio there is, according to Shakespeare, no fact of Desdemona's loving Cassio and hence it will follow that,

$\sim(\exists g)(\ d\ C_1{}^{loves o}g\ \&\ c\ C_2{}^{loves o}g\ .\&.\ g$ is loves permutative).

Moreover, there is no fact of Cassio's loving Desdemona. Hence, we have:

$\sim(\exists g)(\ c\ C_1{}^{loves o}g\ \&\ d\ C_2{}^{loves o}g\ .\&.\ g$ is loves permutative).

It remains, nonetheless, that it is possible that Desdemona loves Cassio (and possible as well that Cassio loves Desdemona).

Some facts are permutative and some facts are not permutative. Russell's solution to the narrow direction problem stands or falls on making good on this. The fact of Desdemona's loving Othello is loves permutative. Let d be Desdemona and o be Othello, we have:

$(d$-loving-$o)$ is loves permutative $.iff.$

fact$(d$-loving-$o)$ $\&$ $(\exists x,y)(x$ loves $y\ \&\ y$ loves $x).$

i.e., fact(d-loving-o) & $[d\ R^2\ o\ \&\ o\ R^2\ d]$ is possible with respect to a and b.

On our definition, we see clearly that the fact of Desdemona's loving Othello is loves permutative. But some facts are not permutative and, in particular, facts involving the position relation C_1^{Loveo} are not permutative. Consider the following fact:

$d\text{-}C_1^{Love}\text{-}(d\text{-}loving\text{-}o)$.

This fact is *not* C_1^{Loveo} permutative. We have:

$(d\text{-}C_1^{loves}\text{-}(d\text{-}loving\text{-}o))$ is C_1^{Loveo} permutative *.iff*.

    fact $(d\text{-}C_1^{Love}\text{-}d\text{-}loving\text{-}o)$ & $(\exists x,z)(\ x\ C_1^{Loveo}z\ \&\ z\ C_1^{Loveo}x)$.

If we investigate the clause,

$(\exists x,z)(\ x\ C_1^{Loveo}z\ \&\ z\ C_1^{Loveo}x)$,

we see that it is false. We have

fact$(\ d\text{-}C_1^{Love}\text{-}d\text{-}loving\text{-}o\ )$ & $d\ C_1^{Loveo}d\text{-}loving\text{-}o$.

But we certainly do not have

$d\text{-}loving\text{-}o\ C_1^{Loveo}d$.

Indeed, it seems unintelligible that there could be such a [1910] fact. Only a person can love something, and no person is a [1910] fact.

But is it really *unintelligible* or is it just false? Are these truths governing *love* and *personhood* logical truths? Is it a logical truth that only a person can love something? Is it a logical truth that no person is a [1913] fact? If our analyses of 'loves' and 'person' are complete, then these are not logical truths. Is the *non-permutativeness* of the fact of Desdemona's bearing C_1^{loveo} to *Desdemona's loving Cassio* is a contingent truth? The matter may be difficult to decide. This suggests that, at least in some cases, the distinction in type* between *permutative* and *non-permutative* [1910] facts may simply be a contingent matter. Russell might well accept that. When we are considering certain facts, some of the needed type* distinctions may find their ground in contingent features of the world. Accepting this certainly poses no serious challenge to Russell's positions.

In certain cases, what makes a given fact non-permutative is simply not a matter of logic. Admittedly, we might be unsure about whether, in a given case, the type* difference involved is grounded in a contingent difference or in a logical difference. Is it unintelligible for a fact to love something or is it just contingently false? It certainly may *seem* unintelligible and not merely a contingent feature of the world. But this 'unintelligibility' may be a rather soft notion (like a moving earth must have seemed to a Pope) and not the notion of logical impossibility. Indeed, if we try to express what is at issue in the present case, we find ourselves writing the following:

$(x)(y)(\ x$ loves $y \supset$ Person$(x))$

$(x)(\$ Person $(x) \supset \sim(\exists z)(\ ^{1910}$fact $(z)\ \&\ z = x)$.

These expressions certainly do not capture the unintelligibility of a fact loving something. Quite to the contrary, the above expressions assume the intelligibility of the following statements:

(y)(*the cat's being on the mat loves y* $\supset$ Person(*the cat's being on the mat*)

Person *(the cat's being on the mat)* $\supset \sim(\exists z)(\ ^{1910}$fact $(z)\ \&\ z =$ *the cat's being on the mat*).

What is a *person*? What is the relation of *love*? Perhaps a complete analysis of the truth-conditions would make the above grammatically ill-formed. It might eliminate the predicates 'Person(x)' and 'x loves y'. It is difficult to say. The lesson here is that applying Russell's program of analysis is difficult and may involve a great deal of *a posteriori* scientific knowledge to implement.

Russell's own analyses of *self* and *person* always remained incomplete. In his neutral monism, these notions receive quite a different analysis than we find in *Problems* and *Theory of Knowledge* where Russell suggests that we may be acquainted with 'self.' Russell's neutral monism relied heavily the behaviorist psychology that was in vogue the 1920's. A *person*, Russell's neutral monism tells us, is a series of neural events (together with other events) of a special sort; and though Russell never addressed it, *love*, the account might go, is a series of oxytocin enriched neural events which constitutes part of a person. On such an analysis, it may turn out to be a purely logical matter that if any series R involves events of love, then the series R is a person. Admittedly, any such account will be met with doubt. But even if Russell's neutral monism fails, one can remain confident that some program of analysis would succeed. Whatever is the proper analysis of *person, knowledge, love, motion, matter, time, space, temperature* and the like, once it is complete, all the purely logical components will have been separated from the physical components. We cannot pretend to know in advance the outcome of such analyses. Knowledge of whether something is logically possible is not the sort of knowledge that can be discerned from the surface grammar of natural language.[26]

It may take a good deal of *a posteriori* physics, chemistry, biology, and psychology to perform the separation of logical/mathematical and physical components involved in the truth-conditions for many of our most ordinary statements. We have yet to achieve the compete reduction of psychology to biology to chemistry and physics. Some still remain, to this day, committed to the existence of unique metaphysical necessities and laws in some or another of these fields. Such non-logical necessities are anathema to Russell's research program in philosophy—a program that maintains that the only necessity is logical necessity. Nonetheless, it is only after the analysis is complete that we are in a position to decide what logical forms are involved. Once it is complete, Russell's thesis is that all the logical components are expressible as logical truths in the language of *Principia* and all other components are brute— contingent truths of physics.

7 The *Problems* of 'Exemplification' and 'Acquaintance'

Our exploration of the relationship between type* distinctions and Russell's official account of possibility has proven to have been fruitful. Nothing so far suggests that the logical forms of *Principia* are inadequate. We cannot know the nature of *love* and *person* until after our analysis is complete, and we are very far away from that. The non-permutative nature of some [1910] facts may, in some cases, be a contingent matter of physics, or chemistry or biology and not a logical matter. But difficulties remain.

The sentence 'Colorless green ideas sleep furiously' was given by Chomsky as an example of a sentence that is grammatically correct but semantically nonsensical (Chomsky 1957). There are, as we can see, some expressions are not syntactically meaningless in English but are meaningless in the sense that their truth conditions *cannot* be met. It may be difficult to gauge the force of this notion of 'cannot', and it may be difficult to decide which expressions are of this sort, but there are cases where the 'cannot' is quite unlike cases of facts involving *knowing, loving*, and the like, where clearly the logical analysis remains woefully incomplete. *Principia's* logical analyses should be complete with respect to its catalogue of *kinds* of logical forms. A concern arises, however, because certain passages of *Theory of Knowledge*, suggest that there may be important type* distinctions

---

[26]In fact, according to *Principia's* analysis of natural number (and analysis that owes its origins to Cantor and Frege), it may (epistemically) be logically possible that for some natural number n, $n = n+1$.

are *logical* distinctions not representable in the logical forms given by *Principia.*

Consider for example, the expression 'Socrates exemplifies Plato'. If we were to try to write truth-conditions for this expression using the multiple-relation theory as formulated in *Theory of Knowledge*, we would have

Socrates exemplifies Plato $\supset$

$$E!(\imath f)(\text{ Socrates } C_1^{\text{exemplifies}} f \& \text{ Plato } C_2^{\text{exemplifies}} f \ )$$

Of course, there is no such fact and indeed such a fact is impossible *wrt* Socrates. Replacing 'Socrates' and 'Plato' with the definite descriptions '$\imath x S x$' and '$\imath y P y$' respectively, we have:

Possible [$\imath x S x$ exemplifies $\imath x P x$] *wrt* $\imath x S x$ =df

$(\exists \varphi)(\exists \psi)(\exists x)(\quad \varphi!z \equiv_z z = x \ .\&. \ (\exists y)(\ Pz \equiv_z z = y \ .\&. \ x$ bears $C_1^{\text{exemplifies}}$ to y).

This analysis yields the result that it is impossible *wrt* Socrates that Socrates exemplifies Plato.

But this is because it is unintelligible for something which is not a universal to be exemplified. That Plato is not a universal might be captured as follows:

$(x)(\text{ Universal}(x) \supset \sim(\exists y)(\ Pz \equiv_z z = y \ .\&. \ y = x))$

But notice that as we saw in the case of *loves*, we get into trouble if we try to express the unintelligibility of the notion of exemplifying something that is not a universal. We might try:

(Exemplification)

$(x)(y)(\ x$ exemplifies $y \supset \text{Universal}(y))$.

But this allows the following instance as well-formed,

$(x)(x$ exemplifies Plato $\supset \text{Universal}(\text{Plato}))$.

The *logical impossibility* of Plato being exemplified is not properly captured by this grammar. Quite the contrary, it assumes that 'x exemplifies Plato' is well-formed.

Now, as before, one might be inclined to say on behalf of Russell that the trouble lies in the incompleteness of the philosophical analysis of the philosophical notions of *exemplification* and *universal*. In Russell's paper 'On the Relations of Universals and Particulars' (1911), we find a concerted attempt to discover whether ontology must embrace both universals and particulars— whether particulars form an indispensable ontological category. The paper ends without a final judgment; the analysis is incomplete. The incompleteness is important because it remains open for Russell to simply maintain that (Exemplification) does *not* properly represent the logical form involved in the nature of *exemplification*— a relation whose existence Russell thinks may be doubted, but which is such that if it exists, it 'involves a fundamental logical difference between its terms' and assures that ontology must respect the category of particulars.[27] It is certainly within Russell's prerogative to adhere to the catalogue of logical forms of *Principia* (which *excludes* forms such as *xRF* and *xRf*) and maintain that *exemplification* is not a genuine relation. Russell was painfully aware that the logical analysis of the ontology of universals versus particulars was very far from being complete. But it is very important to emphasize that it is *only* when logical analysis is complete that we are in a position to proclaim that something is missing from *Principia*, and that we have found a new logical form not contained in *Principia's* catalogue.

In *Theory of Knowledge*, Russell tentatively accepts *logical* type* distinctions which require analyses that he readily admits he does not know. Russell worries that there may well be different relations of *acquaintance* involved when a person S is acquainted with objects of different logical character. He writes:

> We then considered different kinds of acquaintance. The first classification is according to the logical character of the object, namely according as it is (a) particular, (b) universal, (c) formal, i.e., purely logical. Relations to objects differing in logical character must themselves differ in logical character; hence there is a certain looseness in using the one word "acquaintance" for immediate experience of these three kinds of objects. But from the point of view of epistemology, as opposed to logic, this looseness is somewhat immaterial, since all three kinds of acquaintance fulfill the same function of providing the data for judgment and inference. (1913: 100)

It should be noted that Russell uses the word 'object' as a technical term to mean any entity with which a mind can be acquainted. In 'On the Nature of Acquaintance', he writes:

> We will define "subject" as any entity which is acquainted with something, i.e., 'subjects' are the domain of the relation 'acquaintance'. Conversely, any entity with which something is acquainted will be called an 'object', i.e., objects are the converse domain of the relation 'acquaintance'. An entity with which nothing is acquainted will not be called an object. (1914: 152)[28]

---

[27]See Russell 1911: 123.
[28]Cf. Russell 1913: 35.

It should also be noted as well that Russell's comments about logical objects are tentative. He explicitly admonishes readers to understand and forgive him on this matter. He writes:

> It should be said, to begin with, that "acquaintance" has, perhaps, a somewhat different meaning, where logical objects are concerned, from that which it has when particulars are concerned. Whether this is the case or not, it is impossible to decide without more knowledge concerning the nature of logical objects than I possess. It would seem, that logical objects cannot be regarded as "entities", and that, therefore, what we shall call "acquaintance" with them cannot really be a dual relation. The difficulties which result are formidable, but their solution must be sought in logic. For the present, I am content to point out that there certainly is such a thing as "logical experience", by which I mean that kind of immediate knowledge, other than judgment, which is what enables us to understand logical terms. (1913: 97)

Russell suggests with trepidation that the relation of 'acquaintance' involved when a subject S is acquainted with a particular is a different relation from when a subject is acquainted with a logical object such as an abstract fully general fact. Russell is also worried that different relations of *acquaintance* may be involved when its object is a sense-datum as opposed to a universal. If Russell adopts the view that one and the same relation of 'acquaintance' occurs, then all facts of *acquaintance* have the logical form xRy (the form of a dual complex).

As we see in *Theory of Knowledge*, Russell entertains the notion that this may well not be so—that there are different relations of *acquaintance* with different forms when universals, particulars, and logical objects are the 'objects' of acquaintance. But we must not conclude from this that Russell imagines a radical departure from the theory of logical form given in *Principia*. Once again, his comments reflect his admission that his analyses are incomplete. He does not know the needed analyses in question. It would be misguided to conclude from Russell's admission of ignorance that he did know that the analyses involved, whatever they are, require new logical forms such as xRF, xRf, and perhaps even others— forms that are a radical departure from the theory espoused in *Principia*.

In the logical atomism lectures, Russell's conception of universals began to change. Russell repeats his worries over the nature of *acquaintance*, and he boldly proclaims that understanding a predicate (acquaintance with a universal) is different from understanding a particular (acquaintance with a particular) (1917: 205). In the lectures, Russell entertains the notion that universals have only a predicable nature. 'A predicate', writes Russell, 'can never occur except as a predicate' (1917: 205). This is a radical departure from his view of universals from *Principles of Mathematics* (1903) through *Principia Mathematica* (1910-13) and through *Problems* (1911/12) and *Theory of Knowledge* (1913). As we mentioned before, Russell maintained that logic cannot find any axioms to determine what universals there are (what *wffs* of the formal language of logic comprehend universals). The job of assuring the existence of universals falls outside of pure logic and wholly on the side of acquaintance. But Russell never before doubted that at least some universals exist of logical necessity. And Russell felt himself well acquainted with many universals whose existence is logically necessary. In the *Problems*, our faculty of acquaintance with logical universals is the very foundation of our *a priori* knowledge of Logic (and Mathematics).

The landscape is changing dramatically in Russell's Logical Atomism Lectures (1917) and after. Some of Russell's views in those lectures were tentative and experimental, and represents his being in the process of transition to neutral monism and a radically new theory of the nature of universals and particulars, mind and matter, space and time. Russell suggests that the existence of universals is *always* an empirical contingent matter. Russell had never before doubted that universals have both a predicable and an individual nature. Their having an individual nature is essential to the viability of the multiple-relation theory. But now he is on the verge of adopting neutral monism and a four-dimensionalism where minds (as continuants enduring in time and obeying, roughly, behavioristic laws) and matter (as physical continuants enduring in time and obeying the laws of the new relativistic physics) are series of transient physical particulars. In neutral monism, the multiple-relation theory is abandoned, and with it the relation of *acquaintance* is itself abandoned and replaced by 'noticing'. We now find Russell arguing that 'knowing' (even in the case of knowing arithmetic) is to be operationally defined in terms of advantageous behavioral responses to environmental stimuli. In short, after 1918 we have the end of an era—an era whose apex is in *The Problems of Philosophy*.

References

Church, A. 1976. Comparison of Russell's Resolution of the Semantical Antinomies with that of Tarski. *Journal of Symbolic Logic* 41: 747–60. In R. L. Martin 1984: 289–306.

Cocchiarella, N. B. 1980. The Development of the Theory of Logical Types and the Notion of a Logical Subject in Russell's Early Philosophy, *Synthese* 45: 71–115. In N. B. Cocchiarella 1987: 19–63.

Cocchiarella, N. B. 1987. *Logical Studies in Early Analytic Philosophy*. Columbus: Ohio State University Press.

Giaretta, P. 1997. Analysis and Logical form in Russell: The 1913 Paradigm. *Dialectica* 51: 273–93.

Griffin, N. 1980. Russell on the Nature of Logic (1903-1913). *Synthese* 45: 117–88.

Landini, G. 1991. A New Interpretation of Russell's Multiple-Relation Theory of Judgment. *History and Philosophy of Logic* 12: 37–69.

Landini, G. 1998a. *Russell's Hidden Substitutional Theory*. Oxford: Oxford University Press.

Landini, G. 1998b. On Denoting Against Denoting. *Russell: The Journal of Bertrand Russell Studies* 18: 43–80.

Landini, G. 2007. *Wittgenstein's Apprenticeship With Russell*. Cambridge: Cambridge University Press.

Landini, G. 2014. Repairing Russell's 1913 Theory of Knowledge. Forthcoming.

Martin, R. L., ed. 1984. *Recent Essays on Truth and the Liar Paradox*. Oxford: Clarendon Press.

Perovic, K. 2014. The Import of The Original Bradley's Regress(es). *Axiomathes* DOI 10.1007/s10516-014-9229-8.

Quine, W. V. O. 1960. Variables Explained Away. *Proceedings of the American Philosophical Society* 104: 343–7.

Russell, B. 1903. *The Principles of Mathematics*. London: George Allen and Unwin 1956.

Russell, B. 1904. Meinong's Theory of Complexes and Assumptions. In Russell 1973: 21–76.

Russell, B. 1905. Necessity and Possibility. In *CP* 4: 507–20.

Russell, B. 1906a. On the Substitutional Theory of Classes and Relations. In Russell 1973: 165–89.

Russell, B. 1906b. On 'Insolubilia' and Their Solution by Symbolic Logic. In Russell 1973: 190–214.

Russell, B. 1911. On the Relations of Universals and Particulars. *Proceedings of the Aristotelian Society* 12: 1–24. In Russell 1956: 105–24.

Russell, B. 1912a. *The Problems of Philosophy*. London: Williams and Norgate. Reprinted Oxford: Oxford University Press 1959.

Russell, B. 1912b. On the Nature of Cause. *Proceedings of the Aristotelian Society* 13: 1–26. In Russell 1918: 132–51.

Russell, B. 1913. *The Theory of Knowledge: The 1913 Manuscript*. ed. E. R. Eames with K. Blackwell. In *CP* 7.

Russell, B. 1917. The Philosophy of Logical Atomism. In Russell 1956: 175–281.

Russell, B. 1918. *Mysticism and Logic*. London: Longmans, Green, and Co.

Russell, B. 1956. *Logic and Knowledge: Essays, 1901–1950*, ed. R. Marsh. London: Unwin Hyman.

Russell, B. 1973. *Essays in Analysis*, ed. D. Lackey. London: George Allen and Unwin.

Russell, B. 1984. *The Collected Papers of Bertrand Russell, Volume 7: Theory of Knowledge: The 1913 Manuscript*, ed. E. R. Eames with K. Blackwell. London: George Allen and Unwin. [*CP* 7]

Whitehead A. N. and Russell, B. 1910. *Principia Mathematica*. Cambridge: Cambridge University Press, 2cnd ed., 1957.

Index